MW00979017

# FUNDAMENTALS OF
# SVG PROGRAMMING

THE CD-ROM WHICH ACCOMPANIES THE BOOK MAY BE USED ON A SINGLE PC ONLY. THE LICENSE DOES NOT PERMIT THE USE ON A NETWORK (OF ANY KIND). YOU FURTHER AGREE THAT THIS LICENSE GRANTS PERMISSION TO USE THE PRODUCTS CONTAINED HEREIN, BUT DOES NOT GIVE YOU RIGHT OF OWNERSHIP TO ANY OF THE CONTENT OR PRODUCT CONTAINED ON THIS CD-ROM. USE OF THIRD PARTY SOFTWARE CONTAINED ON THIS CD-ROM IS LIMITED TO AND SUBJECT TO LICENSING TERMS FOR THE RESPECTIVE PRODUCTS.

CHARLES RIVER MEDIA, INC. ("CRM") AND/OR ANYONE WHO HAS BEEN INVOLVED IN THE WRITING, CREATION, OR PRODUCTION OF THE ACCOMPANYING CODE ("THE SOFTWARE") OR THE THIRD PARTY PRODUCTS CONTAINED ON THE CD-ROM OR TEXTUAL MATERIAL IN THE BOOK, CANNOT AND DO NOT WARRANT THE PERFORMANCE OR RESULTS THAT MAY BE OBTAINED BY USING THE SOFTWARE OR CONTENTS OF THE BOOK. THE AUTHOR AND PUBLISHER HAVE USED THEIR BEST EFFORTS TO ENSURE THE ACCURACY AND FUNCTIONALITY OF THE TEXTUAL MATERIAL AND PROGRAMS CONTAINED HEREIN; WE, HOWEVER, MAKE NO WARRANTY OF ANY KIND, EXPRESS OR IMPLIED, REGARDING THE PERFORMANCE OF THESE PROGRAMS OR CONTENTS. THE SOFTWARE IS SOLD "AS IS" WITHOUT WARRANTY (EXCEPT FOR DEFECTIVE MATERIALS USED IN MANUFACTURING THE DISC OR DUE TO FAULTY WORKMANSHIP).

THE AUTHOR, THE PUBLISHER, DEVELOPERS OF THIRD PARTY SOFTWARE, AND ANYONE INVOLVED IN THE PRODUCTION AND MANUFACTURING OF THIS WORK SHALL NOT BE LIABLE FOR DAMAGES OF ANY KIND ARISING OUT OF THE USE OF (OR THE INABILITY TO USE) THE PROGRAMS, SOURCE CODE, OR TEXTUAL MATERIAL CONTAINED IN THIS PUBLICATION. THIS INCLUDES, BUT IS NOT LIMITED TO, LOSS OF REVENUE OR PROFIT, OR OTHER INCIDENTAL OR CONSEQUENTIAL DAMAGES ARISING OUT OF THE USE OF THE PRODUCT.

THE SOLE REMEDY IN THE EVENT OF A CLAIM OF ANY KIND IS EXPRESSLY LIMITED TO REPLACEMENT OF THE BOOK AND/OR CD-ROM, AND ONLY AT THE DISCRETION OF CRM.

THE USE OF "IMPLIED WARRANTY" AND CERTAIN "EXCLUSIONS" VARY FROM STATE TO STATE, AND MAY NOT APPLY TO THE PURCHASER OF THIS PRODUCT.

# Fundamentals of SVG Programming

## Oswald Campesato

**CHARLES RIVER MEDIA, INC.**
Hingham, Massachusetts

Copyright 2004 by CHARLES RIVER MEDIA, INC.
All rights reserved.

No part of this publication may be reproduced in any way, stored in a retrieval system of any type, or transmitted by any means or media, electronic or mechanical, including, but not limited to, photocopy, recording, or scanning, without *prior permission in writing* from the publisher.

Acquisitions Editor: James Walsh
Production: Data Page
Cover Design: The Printed Image


CHARLES RIVER MEDIA, INC.
10 Downer Avenue
Hingham, Massachusetts 02043
781-740-0400
781-740-8816 (FAX)
info@charlesriver.com
www.charlesriver.com

This book is printed on acid-free paper.

Oswald Campesato. *Fundamentals of SVG Programming: Concepts to Source Code.*
ISBN: 1-58450-298-3

All brand names and product names mentioned in this book are trademarks or service marks of their respective companies. Any omission or misuse (of any kind) of service marks or trademarks should not be regarded as intent to infringe on the property of others. The publisher recognizes and respects all marks used by companies, manufacturers, and developers as a means to distinguish their products.

Library of Congress Cataloging-in-Publication Data
Campesato, Oswald.
    Fundamentals of SVG programming : concepts to source code / Oswald
Campesato.— 1st ed.
        p.   cm.
    Includes bibliographical references and index.
    ISBN 1-58450-298-3
    1. Computer graphics.   2. SVG (Document markup language)   3. Web
sites—Design.   I. Title.
    T385.C356 2003
    006.6'6—dc22
                           2003015353
Printed in the United States of America
03  7  6  5  4  3  2  First Edition

CHARLES RIVER MEDIA titles are available for site license or bulk purchase by institutions, user groups, corporations, etc. For additional information, please contact the Special Sales Department at 781-740-0400.

Requests for replacement of a defective CD-ROM must be accompanied by the original disc, your mailing address, telephone number, date of purchase and purchase price. Please state the nature of the problem, and send the information to CHARLES RIVER MEDIA, INC., 10 Downer Avenue, Hingham, Massachusetts 02043. CRM's sole obligation to the purchaser is to replace the disc, based on defective materials or faulty workmanship, but not on the operation or functionality of the product.

# Contents

Introduction     xvii

**1   SVG Coordinate System, Simple Shapes, and Colors     1**

    Overview     1
    SVG and Web Development     2
    Downloading and Installing an SVG Viewer     3
    A Minimal SVG Document     3
    The SVG Coordinate System     7
    Using `rect` to Render Rectangles     8
    Using `style`     9
    Using `polygon` to Render Rectangles     10
    Using `path` to Render Rectangles     12
    Using `line` to Render Rectangles     14
    Rendering Rectangles with Opacity     14
    Rendering Rectangles with a Shadow Effect     16
    Rendering Triangular Wedges with Shading     17
    SVG viewports     18
    Colors and Their Components     20
    Standard Colors     20
    Key Constructs     21
    CD-ROM Library     21
    Summary     22

**2   Color Gradients and Style     23**

    Overview     23
    Linear Color Gradients     24
    Using the SVG `defs` Element     24
    Rendering Rectangles with Linear Gradients     25

Radial Color Gradients     27
Rendering Rectangles with Radial Gradients     27
Parallelograms as SVG Polygons     29
Using the SVG marker Element     31
Dotted and Dashed Line Segments     32
Using SVG Embedded Stylesheets     34
Embedded Stylesheets and CDATA     36
Using External Stylesheets     37
Using External Stylesheets and Classes     38
Inheriting an SVG style Attribute     40
Inheriting Attributes in Multiple SVG g Elements     41
Key Constructs     43
CD-ROM Library     44
Summary     45

**3   Circles, Ellipses, and path Elements     47**
Overview     47
Using an SVG circle Element to Render Circles     48
Using an SVG ellipse Element to Render Ellipses     49
Linear Gradient Ellipses     50
Radial Gradient Ellipses     52
Multi-Stop Radial Gradients     54
Lumination-Like Effects with Multi-Stop Radial Gradients     56
Circular and Elliptic Arcs     58
Specifying Circular and Elliptic Arcs     61
Coloring Elliptic Arcs     61
Arc-Based Petal Patterns     62
Arc-Based Diamond Patterns     64
Asymmetric Arc-Based Patterns     65
Creating 3D Effects with Circles     67
Creating Cones with Gradient Shading     68
Creating Cylinders with Gradient Shading     70
Key Constructs     71
CD-ROM Library     71
Summary     72

**4  SVG `pattern`, Grid Patterns, and `clipPath`**                          **73**

Overview                                                                      73

Defining an SVG `pattern` Element                                             74

Using an SVG `pattern` Element                                                75

Generating a Checkerboard Grid                                                76

Generating a 3D Checkerboard Grid                                             78

Generating a Gradient Checkerboard                                            80

Generating a Multi-Gradient Checkerboard                                      82

Using the SVG `clipPath` Element                                              84

Using SVG `clipPath` Elements with Grid Patterns                              85

`clipPath` and `rect` Elements with Gradient Grid Patterns                    87

Generating Slanted Venetian Gradient Patterns                                 89

Key Constructs                                                                91

CD-ROM Library                                                                92

Summary                                                                       92

**5  Quadratic and Cubic Bezier Curves**                                      **93**

Overview                                                                      93

What Are Bezier Curves?                                                       94

Rendering a Quadratic Bezier Curve                                            94

Gradient Checkerboards and Multi-Quadratic Bezier Clip Paths                  96

Venetian Checkerboards and Quadratic Bezier Clip Paths                        98

Rendering Cubic Bezier Curves                                                 101

Linear Gradient Shading and Cubic Bezier Curves                              102

Double Cubic Bezier Curves                                                    104

Double Reflected Cubic Bezier Curves                                          106

Cubic Quadratic Bezier Curves                                                 108

Key Constructs                                                                109

CD-ROM Library                                                                110

Summary                                                                       111

**6  SVG Transformations**                                                   **113**

Overview                                                                      113

Using the SVG `translate` Function                                           114

Using the SVG `rotate` Function with Checkerboards                           116

Using the SVG `scale` Function with Checkerboards        118
Using Multiple SVG `scale` Elements                      120
Zipper Effects and Scaled Cubic Bezier Curves            124
Using the SVG `skew` Function                            126
Using the SVG `matrix` Function                          128
Combining Multiple SVG Functions                         129
Cylinders and the SVG `scale` Function                   130
Hourglasses with the SVG `scale` and `skew` Functions    132
Key Constructs                                           134
CD-ROM Library                                           136
Summary                                                  136

7    **SVG Filters**                                     **137**
Overview                                                 137
Using an `feGaussianBlur` Filter Primitive               138
Shadows and the `feGaussianBlur` Filter Primitive        140
Creating an `feGaussianBlur` Filter Pattern              142
Using an `feFlood` Filter Primitive                      144
Using an `feImage` Filter Primitive                      147
Using an `feMerge` Filter Primitive                      149
Using an `feTurbulence` Filter Primitive                 151
`feTurbulence` Filter Primitives and `pattern` Elements  153
Quadratic Bezier Curves and `feTurbulence` Filter Primitives  155
`feGaussianBlur` Filter Triangles and Quadratic Bezier Curves  157
`feGaussianBlur` Filter Triangles and Checkerboards      159
List of SVG Filter Primitives                            161
Key Constructs                                           161
CD-ROM Library                                           163
Summary                                                  163

8    **Displaying Text**                                 **165**
Overview                                                 165
Rendering a Text String                                  166
Rendering a Text String with Colored Borders             167
Using Text Decoration with Text Strings                  168

Using the SVG `tspan` Element with Text Strings          169
Rendering Shadowed Text                                  171
Rendering Shadowed `blur` Text                           172
Rotating a Text String Counterclockwise                  174
Displaying Text with Linear Gradients                    175
Displaying Text with Opacity                             176
Displaying Text with `blur` Filters                      178
Text Following a Specified Path                          179
Key Constructs                                           180
CD-ROM Library                                           182
Summary                                                  182

**9    Simple SVG Animation                              185**
Overview                                                 185
Animating Transformations                                186
Rotating a Line Segment                                  186
Rotating Rectangles                                      188
Counter Rotating Ellipses                                191
Rectangles and Multiple Animation Effects                193
Chained Animation Effects                                196
Continuous Rotation of a Text String                     199
Multiple Animation Effects                               201
Key Constructs                                           203
CD-ROM Library                                           205
Summary                                                  205

**10   SVG for Bar Charts and Line Graphs                207**
Overview                                                 207
Drawing Homogeneous Bar Sets                             208
Drawing Variable Bar Sets                                209
Drawing Labeled Rectangular Grids                        211
Drawing Bar Charts                                       214
Drawing Bar Charts with 3D Effects                       218
Drawing Simple Line Graphs                               221
Drawing Multiple Line Graphs                             222

Key Constructs                                                    224

CD-ROM Library                                                    225

Summary                                                           226

**11    HTML, ECMAScript, and SVG DOM                            227**

Overview                                                          227

Protecting SVG Code                                               228

Embedding SVG in HTML Pages                                       228

HTML Pages with Images Embedded in SVG                            230

URL-Enabled Ellipses                                              232

Handling Mouse-Over Events                                        234

Hiding Rectangles                                                 235

Mouse Clicks and Gradient Colors                                  237

Determining Attribute Values of SVG Elements                      238

Mouse Clicks and Resizing Circles                                 242

Mouse Clicks and Scaled Ellipses                                  244

Key Constructs                                                    247

CD-ROM Library                                                    248

Summary                                                           249

**12    Interactive SVG and ECMAScript                          251**

Overview                                                          251

SVG Code Template for This Chapter                                252

Updating Attributes of SVG `path` Elements                        254

Updating Attributes of SVG `circle` Elements                      257

Dynamically Removing an SVG Element                               260

Adding an SVG Element via ECMAScript                              262

Updating an SVG Element via ECMAScript                            265

Interactively Adding SVG Elements                                 269

Dynamically Adding Multiple SVG `rect` Elements                   273

Key Constructs                                                    278

CD-ROM Library                                                    280

Summary                                                           280

**13    ECMAScript and SVG Animation    283**
    Overview    283
    SVG Performance    284
    Error Checking in SVG Documents    285
    SVG Code Template for This Chapter    285
    Global versus Local Variables    286
    ECMAScript and Simple SVG path Animation    287
    Animation and Dynamic Creation of SVG Elements    292
    Animation and Modifying Quadratic Bezier Curves    297
    Key Constructs    306
    CD-ROM Library    306
    Summary    307

**14    ECMAScript and Polar Equations    309**
    Overview    309
    Mathematical Terminology    310
    SVG Code Template for This Chapter    310
    Generating Sine-Based Petals    313
    Generating a Sine-Based Wire Frame Effect    317
    Multi-Fixed Point Mesh Pattern and Archimedean Spirals    324
    CD-ROM Library    331
    Summary    332

**15    SVG and Pie Charts    333**
    Overview    333
    Drawing Circular Pie Charts    334
    Converting Data for Circular Pie Charts    340
    Drawing Elliptic Pie Charts    341
    Rotating Circular Pie Charts    346
    Mouse-Controlled Rotating Circular Pie Charts    352
    Key Constructs    357
    CD-ROM Library    358
    Summary    358

16   **ECMAScript, Recursion, and SVG**                       359
         Overview                                              359
         High-Level Template for Code Examples                 360
         Rendering Nested Triangles via Recursion              361
         Rendering Sierpinski Curves                           364
         Rendering Ellipses with Recursion                     369
         Key Constructs                                        372
         CD-ROM Library                                        373
         Summary                                               373

17   **Generating SVG Documents**                             375
         Overview                                              375
         Generating XML Documents from Text Files              376
         Generating a Simple SVG Document with Perl            376
         Generating a Simple SVG Document with Perl Functions  377
         Generating Bar Sets with Perl                         379
         Generating Bar Sets with Unix Scripts                 382
         Converting Proprietary Files to SVG with Perl         386
         Generating SVG with XSLT                              388
         Generating Bar Charts with XSLT                       393
         Key Constructs                                        396
         CD-ROM Library                                        396
         Summary                                               397

18   **Supplemental Patterns**                                399
         Overview                                              399
         How to View the Files                                 400
         Making Enhancements                                   401
         The barbedRectPattern Folder                          403
         The bezierCBPattern Folder                            404
         The bezierDoubleSpinePattern Folder                   404
         The bezierSpineBlurPattern Folder                     405
         The c3DEffectCoilPattern Folder                       406
         The circleFrostedEffect Folder                        406
         The circleFrostedEffectShadow Folder                  407

The circularArcCoilPattern Folder                408

The circularSpinArcCoilPattern Folder            408

The coilLinks Folder                             409

The diamondBoxPattern Folder                     409

The dottedEllipsesAndArcs Folder                 410

The dottedTwistingPolygonPattern Folder          411

The halfEllipseLayersPattern Folder              412

The halfEllipseLayers2Pattern Folder             412

The halfEllipseTwistedLayersPattern Folder       413

The lunePattern Folder                           414

The partialPolygonPattern Folder                 414

The partialPolygonRotatedPattern Folder          415

The rotatedTriangles Folder                      416

The sineWave1Pattern Folder                      416

The tetraPattern Folder                          417

The trapezoidPattern Folder                      418

The triangleLayersPattern Folder                 419


**Appendix A   XSL Basics**                        **421**

Overview                                         421

What Is XSL?                                      421

What Software Is Required for XSL?               421

What Are XSL Stylesheets?                        422

The XSL Mindset                                  423

XSL Nodes                                         423

Traversing Trees                                 424

What Is XPath?                                    424

What Is a Location Path?                          424

XPath Axes                                        425

XPath Functions                                   425

A Simple Stylesheet                               426

The XML File book.xml                             427

The Path to an Element                            429

Finding Element Contents                          429

A Leading Slash ("/") Is Significant              430

Counting Qualified Elements     431
Index Values of Elements in a List     432
Document Order     432
XSL Variables     432
XSL Conditional Logic     432
Generating HTML Documents     433
Finding the Maximum Value of A Set of Numbers     434
Generating a Basic Bar Chart in SVG     436
Key Points     438
Summary     439

**Appendix B   Introduction to XML**     **441**
The Basics     441
XML vs. HTML     441
DTDs     444
DTD Components     445
Document Type Declaration     447
A Complete XML Document     447
Authoring XML Documents     448
XML and Java     449
XML and HTML     449
Where to Use XML     449
EDI     450
XML and OAG     451
Online XML     459
Other Opportunities     459

**Appendix C   Perl Basics**     **461**
What Is Perl?     461
What Are Perl's Strengths?     461
Updating the path Variable     462
Launching Perl from the Command Line     462
Perl Built-In Variables     464
Perl Scalar Variables     464
Perl while Loops     465

Perl for Loops                                          466
Perl Arrays                                             466
Perl Hashes                                             467
Perl Multi-Dimensional Arrays                           468
Opening and Closing Files in Perl                       470
Reading Files in Perl                                   470
Reading File Contents into Perl Arrays                  471
Writing to Files in Perl                                472
Skipping Comment Lines in Text Files                    474
Removing White Space in Text Strings                    475
Extracting Sub-Strings from Text Strings                476
Switching Word Order in Text Strings                    477
The Perl split Function and Text Strings                477
Combining split with Other Functions                    479
The Perl join Function                                  480
Creating Custom Perl Functions                          481
Passing Arrays to Perl Functions                        482
Finding Exact Matches in Text Strings                   483
Verifying Date Formats in Perl                          484
Reading File Contents into an Array                      485
Print File Contents in Reverse Order                    486
Summary                                                 487

**Appendix D   About the CD-ROM                         489**
CD Folders                                              489
Overall System Requirements                             490
License Agreements                                      490

**Index                                                 501**

# Introduction

## WHAT IS THE GOAL OF THIS BOOK?

ON THE CD

The goal is simple: to provide you with an abundance of SVG examples that will give you a thorough understanding of the major aspects of SVG. In addition, the SVG examples included on the CD-ROM will serve as a broad foundation that you can enhance and customize to suit your own needs. Whether you're looking for code to enhance your Web pages at work or simply trying to learn graphics for fun, this book has plenty of code with lots of sizzle!

## WHAT IS SVG?

Scalable Vector Graphics (a. k. a. SVG) rests on an XML-based representation of two-dimensional geometric objects that can be rendered and manipulated by means of SVG-based functions. The SVG specification is under the aegis of the World Wide Web Consortium (W3C), which can be found at *http://www.w3.org*. There, you'll find the SVG-related information by scrolling down on that page and then clicking on the SVG hyperlink. Alternatively, you can go directly to the URL *http://www.w3.org/Graphics/SVG/Overview.htm8*, where you will find a cornucopia of information regarding products, conferences, companies that use SVG, future research, and market trends.

## WHO CREATED SVG?

The SVG specification is the result of a collaborative effort on the part of several major companies, including Adobe®, Hewlett-Packard, IBM®, Microsoft®, Netscape™, SUN Microsystems, and Microsoft Visio®. The SVG specification is vast and comprehensive; it provides functionality for using JavaScript/ECMAScript, producing animation effects, and creating very complex visual patterns. This book contains thousands of SVG samples that illustrate how to use many of the features that are available in the W3C Recommendation of September 04, 2001. If you're interested, you can find the specification at *http://www.w3.org/TR/2001/REC-SVG-20010904*. Currently, there is also an SVG 1.1 specification, which is available as the "W3C Proposed Recommendation (November 15, 2002)." For more information about the SVG 1.1 specification visit *http://www.w3.org/TR/2002/PR-SVG11-20021115*. Finally, there is a so-called working draft of SVG 1.2, which is available as the "W3C Working Draft 15 November 2002." Note that this is a public working draft of the SVG 1.2 specification, and hence is subject to change. You can find the SVG 1.2 specification at the following URL: *http://www.w3.org/TR/2002/WD-SVG12-20021115*.

## WHY SVG?

SVG has many powerful features that are also simple to use, even for people with very little programming background. After you've finished reading this book, you'll appreciate the fact that some of the features in SVG would be very difficult to reproduce in other programming languages, even by experienced programmers. Furthermore, SVG has the following advantages:

- compact and portable source code
- scaled images have sharper resolution than "gif" files
- no resolution loss on zooming
- complex images can be created involving transformations such as scaling and rotations
- well suited for business charts
- easily generated on the Web
- can be generated by Java Servlets and JSPs

If necessary, you can transform text files into SVG documents in a variety of ways, including XSLT, scripting languages (e.g., Perl, Python, Ruby), or Unix shell scripts.

The hierarchical nature of SVG allows you to define "templates" of graphical components that produce very compact code. Moreover, you can also refer to external text files containing stylesheet information that can be "included" in your SVG documents. As such, SVG makes it easy to develop a library of files and documents that can be combined easily in order to enhance your library of graphics images.

## WHY SO MUCH CODE?

There are important reasons. First, most people learn best by example. Second, the depth and breadth of the sample code will save you many hours of work. Third, the many code variations will vividly illustrate the tremendous range of possibilities that are available in SVG. Fourth, relatively simple changes in the code can sometimes produce unexpected (even startling) visual effects. Indeed, the companion CD-ROM contains over 20,000 SVG documents that illustrate the sort of graphics that are possible with SVG! Similar examples have been intentionally included for your convenience so that you can choose the ones that have the visual nuances that are best suited to your needs.

ON THE CD

As you peruse the code samples on the CD-ROM, you might find it helpful to create your own sub-directory where you can store copies of the SVG documents you want to revisit at a later time. The graphics images are divided into folders that correspond to a theme or type. This logical division of the code will help you select the types of graphics images that are most appealing to you.

You might be surprised to know that the samples on the CD-ROM represent a small fraction of what you can create in SVG. The CD-ROM provides a rich set of examples, and the ideas contained therein can serve as a catalyst for sparking your own creativity. Don't be afraid to experiment with the code because that is a good way for you to strengthen your knowledge and increase your level of confidence. With practice and due diligence, you will acquire a sense of how to combine various geometric objects in order to create the effects that you're looking for.

## IS THIS BOOK FOR ME?

This book will take you on a journey that explores many aspects of SVG by revealing the powerful synergy of combining mathematics and SVG. You'll acquire a knowledge of SVG and also an appreciation of the wonderful possibilities that exist in the SVG world. The material in this book is of interest to computer enthusiasts, programmers, and anyone who enjoys working with graphics. If you're a Web developer, you'll find lots of ideas for enhancing your Web pages with aesthetically appealing graphics images. If you're a software developer, you'll appreciate the power of SVG and what it can offer you.

## WHAT SOFTWARE IS REQUIRED?

You need two things: a browser (Internet Explorer or Netscape will do fine) and an SVG viewer, such as the one from Adobe. Chapter 1 gives you the details for downloading an SVG viewer from Adobe's Web site *http://www.adobe.com.*

## WHAT ARE THE PREREQUISITES?

The mathematics in this book consists of some geometry and trigonometry. Basic knowledge of the structure of XML is important because every SVG document is an XML document. Several chapters contain SVG documents that use JavaScript functions and HTML tags in order to create animation effects. The book contains an appendix for each of these topics that provide a learning guide so that you will be able to understand the content and purpose of the SVG documents in this book.

## WHY SWITCH TO SVG?

Since SVG is a dialect of XML, it's easy to "internationalize" your SVG code and SVG-based products. There are also ways to hide your SVG code from "View Source," thereby enabling you to protect your intellectual property (which is often a concern for content developers). If you already know JavaScript, you can immediately leverage this knowledge *in toto* within the SVG framework without having to learn another scripting language such as Action Script by Macromedia Flash™, and you can leverage your existing JavaScript code base while making your transition to SVG. Incidentally, if you're interested in Java-based graphics, you can take a look at the author's Java graphics book, *Java Graphics Programming Library: Concepts to Source Code* (ISBN I-58450-092-1).

## DO I NEED TO BE A PROGRAMMER?

Not at all. Unlike traditional programming languages, there's no compilation required (such as C), nor do you need to generate intermediate byte-code (such as Java "class" files). You need only learn how to use the XML-based features of the SVG specification, most of which are fairly intuitive and straightforward. You'll be able to create SVG documents on-the-fly after a modicum of practice.

## IS SVG RELEVANT TO ARTISTS?

Indeed it is! You're probably aware of the fact that the vast majority of people are more visually oriented than text oriented. Most of us respond on a visceral level to graphics images, and in this respect, graphics transcends all language barriers. If you're an artist who works and communicates primarily via a graphics-based medium, you appreciate the value of having a keen eye and an acutely developed sense of how to combine color, texture, and shading in order to achieve meaningful effects. SVG is an invaluable tool that will enable you to explore new facets of self-ex-pression, thereby expanding your artistry.

## CONVENTIONS IN THIS BOOK

ON THE CD

Some of the SVG documents are based on some well-known polar equations. The graphics images that are rendered are variations of those equations combined with other geometric objects. For example, there are numerous graphics images on the CD-ROM that are based on polar equations that represent curves such as the Spiral of Archimedes, Cardioids, and Conchoids. The interesting part happens when the polar equations are combined with ellipses, polygons, and various types of gradient shading. You'll probably notice that the equations have been "tweaked" in a variety of ways; this was done for the purpose of generating pleasing graphics images. I hope you have as much fun learning SVG as I did while writing this book!

# 1 SVG Coordinate System, Simple Shapes, and Colors

## OVERVIEW

This chapter serves as your gentle introduction to SVG. If you are an experienced SVG developer, you need only skim through this chapter. If you are relatively new to SVG and/or programming, you will learn some of the fundamental concepts that underlie the SVG code in this book. Please glance through the appendices; at a minimum, you will become aware of their contents, thereby enabling you to locate quickly the relevant information in case you need to review it.

The first part of this chapter delves into the role of SVG on the Web, and also the rationale behind using SVG instead of other alternatives.

The second part of this chapter provides the necessary information for downloading an SVG viewer from the Adobe® home page. The introduction to this book contains a useful link, *http://www.w3.org*, that (in turn) summarizes many available SVG viewers and information about where you can download them.

The third part of this chapter provides an introductory view of SVG documents and the SVG coordinate system that will assist you in visualizing the SVG code for rendering objects such as lines, rectangles, and polygons. As you start learning about SVG documents, you can also refer to Appendix B, which can help you with basic XML. If you are already familiar with these topics, then you can quickly skim through this section.

The fourth part of this chapter introduces you to the SVG `style` element, which enables you to specify attributes such as fill colors, fonts, and borders ("stroke"). Various combinations of these attributes are used when creating rectangles by means of various SVG elements such as `rect`, `path`, and `polygon`. You will learn how to use the `opacity` attribute in order to control the color "density" of rendered graphics images.

The fifth part of the chapter contains an introduction to colors and shows four ways of representing colors in SVG. The use of color is of paramount importance for displaying graphics images, and so you need to know how to use standard colors and their many subtle shades. Later, in Chapter 2, you'll learn how to specify so-called linear and radial gradients that imbue graphics images with an aesthetically rich appearance. As you'll see, the set of possible colors exceeds sixteen million, which ought to satisfy most color requirements for graphics images.

*ON THE CD*   Finally, the code for all of the chapters in this book can be found on the companion CD-ROM under the folder that corresponds to the chapter number.

## SVG AND WEB DEVELOPMENT

If you've worked with a combination of HTML, JavaScript, and bit-mapped files, you know how tedious that code can become in terms of maintenance and enhancements of the code. Although you can dynamically generate images "on-demand," most HTML pages contain static images. What do you get when you migrate to an SVG-based environment? First, SVG allows you to embed bit-mapped files (e.g., GIF files) and perform SVG transformations on them (such as scaling) and as well as applying SVG filters. Second, you benefit from the advantages of the scalable nature of SVG, which means that SVG does not suffer from the image degradation that occurs when you magnify bit-mapped images. Third, if you work extensively with JavaScript, you're in luck: SVG supports ECMAScript, which means that you can migrate your existing code base over to SVG. This also means that you don't have to learn any new languages, such as ActionScript for Macromedia Flash. Fourth, SVG is derived from XML, which in turn is based on Unicode; consequently, you can use SVG in order to display any characters that are supported by the underlying viewer, including languages such as Arabic, Hebrew, and Japanese. For example, you can do something like this,

```
<text x="10" y="10">&#x3b1;&#x3b2;</text>
```

which renders the first two letters "alpha" and "beta" of the Greek alphabet.

Finally, online resources are available if you are interested in developing SVG-based content, such as the Yahoo group `svg-developers`, where you'll find a free exchange of ideas, SVG code, and lively discussions about all sorts of issues and events that may have an impact on SVG.

## DOWNLOADING AND INSTALLING AN SVG VIEWER

Currently there are numerous SVG viewers available in the marketplace. Some are free, and others will give you a trial evaluation. You can find the official W3C list of implementations of SVG at the following URL: *http://www.w3.org/Graphics/SVG/SVG-Implementations.htm8.* For those of you who are interested, the Adobe SVG viewer is listed on this URL, along with release notes for Windows® and for Macintosh®. In terms of functionality and best overall implementation of the SVG specification, the Adobe SVG viewer is recommended, especially if you have a Macintosh. Note that the SVG documents with code containing ECMAScript use Adobe-specific extensions, which means that you need the Adobe SVG viewer for those SVG documents. Regardless of the SVG viewer that you use, please make sure that you read the associated release notes for that viewer to familiarize yourself with any platform-specific issues.

Here's a list of the steps you need to follow in order to download and install the Adobe SVG viewer:

*Step 1:* Launch your browser and go to *http://www.adobe.com/svg/viewer/install*

*Step 2:* Select the platform that applies to you (Windows, Mac, or Solaris) in your language

*Step 3:* click on the hyperlink and save the viewer on your hard disk

*Step 4:* run the file that you saved in Step 3

For example, if you selected the combination of "English" and the link "Win 98–XP" under the heading "Operating System," the downloaded file is called *SVGView.exe.* You can run this file by typing its name on the command line or by double-clicking on the file in Internet Explorer. Select the default values for the prompts and within a minute or so you'll be done. Congratulations—you're now ready to start exploring the world of SVG!

## A MINIMAL SVG DOCUMENT

Every SVG document requires the SVG <svg> element as its outermost element. All other SVG elements are included inside this element. A minimal SVG document contains the following two lines:

```
<svg>
</svg>
```

The preceding SVG document is valid and well defined, but is trivial because it does absolutely nothing of interest. Now look at Listing 1.1, which contains an example of an SVG document that specifies a red rectangle whose width is 150 pixels and whose height is 50 pixels. Don't worry if you don't understand everything in the document, especially the first two lines (they do look daunting, don't they?). These details will be explained later in the chapter.

**Listing 1.1**   rect1.svg

```
<?xml version="1.0" encoding="iso-8859-1"?>
<!DOCTYPE svg PUBLIC "-//W3C//DTD SVG 20001102//EN"
 "http://www.w3.org/TR/2000/CR-SVG-20001102/DTD/svg-20001102.dtd">

<svg width="100%" height="100%">

<!-- draw rectangle -->
<g transform="translate(50,50)">
<rect
   x="0" y="0" width="150" height="50"
   style="fill:red;"/>
</g>

</svg>
```

Let's examine the contents of Listing 1.1 line-by-line in a more detailed fashion. The first line is an optional line that specifies the version of xml and the character-encoding of the document:

```
<?xml version="1.0" encoding="iso-8859-1"?>
```

The second line is also an optional line:

```
<!DOCTYPE svg PUBLIC "-//W3C//DTD SVG 20001102//EN"
 "http://www.w3.org/TR/2000/CR-SVG-20001102/DTD/svg-
20001102.dtd">
```

The first two lines appear in all the SVG documents in this book, even though they are optional. The DOCTYPE refers to an URL that specifies the location of a file that describes the "legal" format of a document. At this juncture, you won't need to delve any further into the reasons for doing so; suffice it to say that the inclusion of these two lines is a good programming practice and will save you the trouble of having to add them at a later point in time.

The third line specifies the SVG `svg` element:

```
<svg width="100%" height="100%">
```

The SVG `svg` element contains two *attributes* that specify the width and the height of the background canvas that will be used for rendering components. The attributes `width` and `height` have values that are specified as a percentage, which means that the background rectangle will resize accordingly whenever you resize your browser display. If you want to specify a rectangle with absolute dimensions that do not change when you resize your browser, you can use something like the following:

```
<svg width="800" height="500">
```

You can specify the values of the `width` and `height` attributes using units such as `cm`, `mm`, and `in`, which represent centimeters, millimeters, and inches, respectively. The SVG fragment specifying the values of the `width` and `height` attributes in terms of centimeters is as follows:

```
<svg width="800cm" height="500cm">
```

The SVG fragment specifying the values of the `width` and `height` attributes in terms of millimeters is as follows:

```
<svg width="800mm" height="500mm">
```

The SVG fragment specifying the values of the `width` and `height` attributes in terms of inches is as follows:

```
<svg width="800in" height="500in">
```

In case you're wondering, the complete set of allowable units in SVG consists of `em`, `ex`, `px`, `pt`, `pc`, `cm`, `mm`, `in`, and percentage values. The default unit of measure is `px`. The fourth line contains a comment:

```
<!-- draw rectangle -->
```

You can also include multi-line comments like the one below:

```
<!--
this comment
spans multiple
lines of text
-->
```

Develop a style for adding comments that provides useful information about the purpose of the code without interrupting the flow of the code. Comments are obviously useful, especially in SVG documents that contain many SVG elements. A set of well-placed succinct comments can simplify the maintenance and enhancement of SVG documents.

The fifth line contains the SVG g element:

```
<g transform="translate(50,50)">
```

The SVG `translate` function will be discussed in more detail in Chapter 6, which is devoted to SVG functions. In this example, the `translate` part of the SVG g element specifies the coordinates of the origin as (50,50) instead of the default point (0,0). This functionality is extremely useful because it allows you to move a complex graphics image anywhere you want simply by altering the coordinates of the origin. You can use the SVG g element to enclose a "group" of components that are logically related and need to be treated as a single "unit." The advantage of specifying such a grouping this way will become apparent later in the book when you need to apply additional transformations to all the components within a specific SVG g element.

The sixth line contains the SVG `rect` element, split over three lines:

```
<rect
  x="0" y="0" width="150" height="50"
  style="fill:red;"/>
```

White space is not significant, which means that you could also write the preceding SVG `rect` element using tabs, a mixture of indentation styles, or as a single line. The format is a matter of personal preference; however, the format should be as clear and consistent as possible.

The `style` attribute specifies the value of the `fill` attribute as red. In general, the `style` attribute can contain multiple attributes that are "strung together" using a semi-colon as a delimiter. Each "sub-attribute" consists of a name/value pair that is separated by a colon. More examples of the `style` attribute will be given later in this chapter.

The seventh and eighth lines contain two closing tags: the first is for the SVG g element, and the second is for the SVG `svg` element:

```
</g>
</svg>
```

Note that the nested order of these closing tags is required in order to make the SVG document well formed.

# THE SVG COORDINATE SYSTEM

Perhaps you remember the Cartesian coordinate system from one of your high school mathematics classes. The Cartesian coordinate system (also called the Euclidean coordinate system) allows you to specify any point in the Euclidean plane by means of a pair of numbers. The first number represents the horizontal value and the second number represents the vertical value. Often you'll see a pair of perpendicular line segments that represent the Cartesian coordinate system. The horizontal axis is labeled the x-axis, and positive values on the x-axis are to the right of the vertical axis (i.e., toward the right). The vertical axis is labeled the y-axis, and positive values on the y-axis are above the horizontal axis. The origin is the intersection point of the x-axis and the y-axis.

The situation is almost the same in the SVG coordinate system. The x-axis is horizontal and the positive direction is toward the right. The y-axis is vertical, but the positive direction is *downward* (i.e., south). As you can see, the positive y-axis points in the opposite direction of most graphs in a typical mathematics textbook. When we draw our graphics images, we'll have to consider this fact. This detail is easy to forget, and *often it's the underlying cause of incorrect images.*

Two more details about the SVG coordinate system: the origin is the upper-left corner of the screen, and the unit of measurement is the pixel, so the largest visible display is usually 1024x728.

Consider Figure 1.1, it displays the SVG coordinate system with four rendered points. Note that the coordinate system has been shifted downward and to the right in order to render the horizontal and vertical axes more clearly.

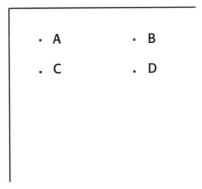

**FIGURE 1.1**   The SVG coordinate system.

Based on the definition of the SVG coordinate system, we now know that:

■ point A(50, 50) is 50 units to the right and 50 units downward
■ point B(200, 50) is 200 units to the right and 50 units downward

- point C(50, 100) is 50 units to the right and 100 units downward
- point D(200, 100) is 200 units to the right and 100 units downward

## USING rect TO RENDER RECTANGLES

Consider the rectangle in Figure 1.2 whose vertices are the four points A(50,50), B(200, 50), D(200, 100), and C(50, 100).

**FIGURE 1.2**   A red rectangle.

The following quantities are required in order to specify a rectangle:

1. the upper-left vertex (x,y)of the rectangle
2. the width width
3. the height height

Observe that the situation in which width = height results in a square, which means that the SVG rect element can be used for squares as well as rectangles.

The SVG rect element defines a rectangle by specifying values for the attributes width, height, x, and y. The SVG style element (discussed below) allows you to specify the color of the rectangle and the color and thickness of its perimeter.

The SVG document *rect1.svg* in Listing 1.2 demonstrates how to draw a red rectangle by means of the SVG rect element.

**Listing 1.2**   rect1.svg

```
<?xml version="1.0" encoding="iso-8859-1"?>
<!DOCTYPE svg PUBLIC "-//W3C//DTD SVG 20001102//EN"
"http://www.w3.org/TR/2000/CR-SVG-20001102/DTD/svg-20001102.dtd">

<svg width="100%" height="100%">

<!-- draw rectangle -->
<g transform="translate(50,50)">
<rect
   x="0" y="0" width="150" height="50"
   style="fill:red;"/>
```

```
</g>

</svg>
```

## Remarks

You can also render the rectangle in Listing 1.2 without the SVG g element as follows:

```
<rect
   x="50" y="50" width="150" height="50"
   style="fill:red;"/>
```

However, the preceding line is tantamount to specifying a "hard-coded" rectangle. If you later decide that you want to render the same rectangle elsewhere on the screen, you would need to create a new component with its own hard-coded values.

The SVG transform attribute in an SVG g element can be combined with other transformations that render sophisticated effects with surprising ease. Suffice it to say that it's a good idea to develop the habit of "wrapping" your components inside an SVG g element.

The SVT rect element also allows you to render rounded rectangles by specifying the value of two optional attributes rx and ry, which represent the x-radius and y-radius, respectively, of the ellipse that "rounds" the four vertices of the rectangle. If rx and ry are equal to half the value of the attributes width and height, respectively, then the rounded rectangle looks precisely like an ellipse!

In addition to the SVG rect element, rectangles can also be rendered by means of the SVG elements line, polyLine, path, or polygon. In addition to specifying rectangles, these SVG elements can define a broad set of geometric objects, and you'll see more examples of them later in the book.

## USING style

Notice how the color of the rectangle in Listing 1.2 is specified by means of the style attribute. If you have not worked with cascading stylesheets, here is an example of how to specify a red rectangle with a blue border of width 4 using style:

```
style="fill:red;stroke-width:4;stroke:blue"
```

Alternatively, you could specify each attribute individually as follows:

```
fill="red" stroke-width="4" stroke="blue"
```

Since white space is not significant, you could also split the preceding line into multiple lines:

```
fill="red"
stroke-width="4"
stroke="blue"
```

The point to observe regarding the SVG `style` element is that it's a quoted list of colon-delimited name/value pairs that are concatenated by means of a semi-colon; if you wish to specify an attribute and its value outside the quoted list, you need to replace the colon with an equals sign and quote the value of the attribute. Below is a simple example:

```
style="fill:red"
```

This could be replaced with:

```
fill="red"
```

The SVG `style` element allows you to specify attributes that are useful for rendering text. Here is an example of how to specify a particular combination of font family, font size, and font style:

```
style="font-family:serif;font-size:24;style:italic;"
```

The preceding attributes can also be specified as follows:

```
font-family="serif"
font-size="24"
style="italic"
```

Sometimes you need to specify the same attribute/value pair for many graphics elements in an SVG document; this can produce SVG documents that have a lot of repeated code. If you need to change a particular attribute value, you need to do so in many places, which can be tedious and error-prone. Fortunately, there is a way to define a "core" set of attribute/value pairs that are applied to all the graphics elements in an SVG document. This approach makes for smaller files and more legible SVG code in which core attribute values can be changed in one place. This technique (and the associated precedence rules) will be described in more detail in Chapter 2.

## USING polygon TO RENDER RECTANGLES

You already know that the SVG `rect` element defines a rectangle. The SVG `polygon` element can accomplish the same result. Defining a rectangle by means of this SVG element is useful in situations where you need to modify the rectangle. For example, a rectangle that is defined with an SVG polygon element allows you to modify the vertices of that rectangle during animation in order to render a quadrilateral.

The SVG document *rect2.svg* in Listing 1.3 uses the SVG polygon element in order to render a red rectangle.

### Listing 1.3    rect2.svg

```
<?xml version="1.0" encoding="iso-8859-1"?>
<!DOCTYPE svg PUBLIC "-//W3C//DTD SVG 20001102//EN"
 "http://www.w3.org/TR/2000/CR-SVG-20001102/DTD/svg-20001102.dtd">

<svg width="100%" height="100%">

<!-- draw rectangle -->
<g transform="translate(50,50)">
<polygon
 points="0,0 150,0 150,50 0,50"
 style="fill:red;"/>
</g>

</svg>
```

## Remarks

Notice the following transform attribute that qualifies the SVG g element:

```
<g transform="translate(50,50)">
```

The value of the transform attribute is the function translate(50,50), which shifts the origin of the contained graphics image (a rectangle in this case) from the SVG point (0,0) to the SVG point (50,50). The key point to notice is that the transform attribute shifts only the components that are defined inside the enclosing SVG g element. Multiple SVG g elements can be shifted independently of each other, which means that you can render the same component in multiple locations in the SVG plane without having to redefine the values of any of the attributes of the component in question. For example, you could render four non-overlapping rectangles with the following SVG code fragment:

```
<g transform="translate(100,100)">
  <rect x="0" y="0" width="50" height="50"
        style="fill:red;"/>
</g>

<g transform="translate(300,100)">
  <rect x="0" y="0" width="50" height="50"
        style="fill:red;"/>
```

```
    </g>

    <g transform="translate(100,300)">
      <rect x="0" y="0" width="50" height="50"
            style="fill:red;"/>
    </g>

    <g transform="translate(300,300)">
      <rect x="0" y="0" width="50" height="50"
            style="fill:red;"/>
    </g>
```

A more succinct technique involving xlink:href that accomplishes the same result with less code will be discussed in Chapter 3. This technique is extremely useful
when you generate bar charts and graphs, such as the examples in Chapter 10.

As you've probably surmised, an SVG polygon element contains a list of vertices
(where each vertex specifies a point in the SVG coordinate system) that represents a
polygon in the Euclidean plane. Since there is no restriction on the number of vertices, the SVG polygon element is extremely versatile. Keep in mind, though, that
while you can use this element for defining a rectangle, the purpose of your code is
clearer if you use the SVG rect element for rendering a rectangle.

You can think of a polygon as a closed path; that is, the coordinates of the first
vertex coincides with those of the final vertex in a path. You can also use the SVG
polyline element in order to render a polygon; just remember that the last vertex in
the list must be the same as the first vertex in the list, otherwise the rendered component will not look like a polygon.

## USING path TO RENDER RECTANGLES

The SVG path element is extremely powerful and it can be used for rendering many
geometric objects, including rectangles. This element is useful for defining complex
graphics images that contain curvilinear components. Defining a rectangle by means
of this element is useful in situations (e.g., animation) where you need to modify the
vertices of the rectangle in order to render a quadrilateral or a parallelogram, or perhaps collapse the rectangle into a line segment.

The SVG document *rect3.svg* in Listing 1.4 uses the SVG path element in order
to render a rectangle.

### Listing 1.4   rect3.svg

```
<?xml version="1.0" encoding="iso-8859-1"?>
<!DOCTYPE svg PUBLIC "-//W3C//DTD SVG 20001102//EN"
 "http://www.w3.org/TR/2000/CR-SVG-20001102/DTD/svg-20001102.dtd">
```

```
<svg width="100%" height="100%">

<!-- draw rectangle -->
<g transform="translate(50,50)">
<path
 d="M0,0 150,0 150,50 0,50"
 style="fill:red;"/>
</g>

</svg>
```

## Remarks

The SVG path element is more general than the SVG polygon because it can be used to specify curved components in addition to line segments, which makes the SVG path element incredibly flexible and versatile.

Notice the syntax of the points in a path:

```
d="M0,0 150,0 150,50 0,50"
```

The preceding path definition can be translated as follows: "move to the point (0,0); draw a line segment from the point (0,0) to the point (150,0); draw a line segment from the point (150,0) to the point (150,50); draw a line segment from the point (150,50) to the point (0,50)."

Note that if you inadvertently specified the following line,

```
d="0,0 150,0 150,50 0,50"
```

you will see this error message in the lower corner of your browser:

```
path data missing a moveto
```

The uppercase M refers to an absolute point. You can use a lowercase m if you need to specify a point in the plane that is relative to the preceding point (i.e., the point that is to the immediate left of the current point).

The same logic applies to uppercase L and lowercase l when rendering line segments. For example, the following snippet,

```
d="M100,0 L150,0 150,50 0,50"
```

starts with a line segment from (100,0) to (150,50), whereas the snippet,

```
d="M100,0 l150,0 150,50 0,50"
```

starts with a line segment from (100,0) to (250,0).

The reason for the difference is because L150,0 specifies an absolute point, regardless of the value of the preceding point. On the other hand, l150,0 is relative to the absolute preceding point M100,0. Adding the two x-coordinates and the two y-coordinates of M100,0 and l150,0 yields the point (250,0).

## USING line TO RENDER RECTANGLES

The SVG line element can be used for each of the four sides of a rectangle in order to define the rectangle itself. A line segment is determined by two points in the SVG plane, each of which has an x-coordinate and a y-coordinate.

The SVG document *rect4.svg* in Listing 1.5 uses the SVG line element in order to render a rectangle.

### Listing 1.5    rect4.svg

```
<?xml version="1.0" encoding="iso-8859-1"?>
<!DOCTYPE svg PUBLIC "-//W3C//DTD SVG 20001102//EN"
 "http://www.w3.org/TR/2000/CR-SVG-20001102/DTD/svg-20001102.dtd">

<svg width="100%" height="100%">

<!-- draw rectangle -->
<g transform="translate(50,50)">
<line x1="0"   y1="0"  x2="200" y2="0"  stroke="red"/>
<line x1="200" y1="0"  x2="200" y2="0"  stroke="red"/>
<line x1="0"   y1="50" x2="150" y2="50" stroke="red"/>
<line x1="0"   y1="0"  x2="0"   y2="50" stroke="red"/>
</g>

</svg>
```

### Remarks

The SVG line element defines a line segment whose end points are given by the points with coordinates (x1,y1) and (x2,y2). You can define a rectangle by means of four SVG line elements that specify the coordinates of its four vertices. Since more code is required to specify a rectangle in terms of SVG line elements and your code becomes less intuitive, it's probably better to use the SVG rect element for rendering rectangles and use the SVG line element for rendering non-rectangular components.

## RENDERING RECTANGLES WITH OPACITY

Consider the rectangles in Figure 1.3.

**FIGURE 1.3**  Rectangles
with different opacity.

The SVG rect element allows you to specify the opacity of an object, where the opacity is a decimal number between 0 and 1.

The SVG document *opacityRect1.svg* in Listing 1.6 uses the SVG rect element in order to render a set of rectangles with different opacity values.

**Listing 1.6**   opacityRect1.svg

```
<?xml version="1.0" encoding="iso-8859-1"?>
<!DOCTYPE svg PUBLIC "-//W3C//DTD SVG 20001102//EN"
  "http://www.w3.org/TR/2000/CR-SVG-20001102/DTD/svg-20001102.dtd">

<svg width="100%" height="100%">

<!-- draw rectangle -->
<g transform="translate(50,50)">
<rect
   x="0" y="0" width="150" height="50"
   style="fill:red;"
   opacity="1"/>
</g>

<g transform="translate(50,150)">
<rect
   x="0" y="0" width="150" height="50"
   style="fill:red;"
   opacity=".6"/>
</g>

<g transform="translate(50,250)">
<rect
   x="0" y="0" width="150" height="50"
```

```
        style="fill:red;"
        opacity=".2"/>
  </g>

  </svg>
```

## Remarks

Consider the case where you have a red rectangle that overlaps with a blue rectangle, and the blue rectangle is rendered after the red rectangle. When the value of the opacity attribute is 1 (which is the default value), the overlapping region will be a solid blue color. However, when the value of the opacity attribute is less than 1, you will see a composite color effect in the overlapping region. This composite color depends on the value of the opacity attribute for each of the two rectangles.

## RENDERING RECTANGLES WITH A SHADOW EFFECT

Consider the rectangle with a shadow effect in Figure 1.4.

**FIGURE 1.4**   A rectangle with a shadow effect.

The SVG document *rectShadowEffect1.svg* in Listing 1.7 uses the SVG rect element in order to render a rectangle with a shadow effect.

### Listing 1.7    rectShadowEffect1.svg

```
<?xml version="1.0" encoding="iso-8859-1"?>
<!DOCTYPE svg PUBLIC "-//W3C//DTD SVG 20001102//EN"
  "http://www.w3.org/TR/2000/CR-SVG-20001102/DTD/svg-20001102.dtd">

<svg width="100%" height="100%">
```

```
<g transform="translate(50,50)">
  <rect
      x="20" y="20" width="250" height="150"
      style="fill:black;"/>

  <rect
      x="0" y="0" width="250" height="150"
      style="fill:red;"/>
</g>
</svg>
```

## Remarks

The SVG code in Listing 1.7 demonstrates how easy it is to create a shadow effect by rendering two rectangles: the background rectangle is black and the foreground rectangle is red. The background rectangle has a (+,+) location relative to the foreground rectangle; that is, it is shifted downward and to the right. The other three possibilities for the background rectangle location are (+,-), (-,+), and (-,-) with respect to the foreground rectangle. These other locations provide different shadow effects that create the impression of different "view positions."

## RENDERING TRIANGULAR WEDGES WITH SHADING

Consider the triangular wedge in Figure 1.5.

**FIGURE 1.5**  A triangular wedge.

The SVG document *triangularWedge1.svg* in Listing 1.8 uses the SVG polygon element in order to render a triangular wedge.

**Listing 1.8**    triangularWedge1.svg

```
<?xml version="1.0" encoding="iso-8859-1"?>
<!DOCTYPE svg PUBLIC "-//W3C//DTD SVG 20001102//EN"
 "http://www.w3.org/TR/2000/CR-SVG-20001102/DTD/svg-20001102.dtd">

<svg width="100%" height="100%">

<g transform="translate(100,100)">
  <!-- render triangle -->
  <polygon
    points="200,0 300,150 100,150"
    style="fill:red;stroke:blue;"/>

  <!-- render parallelogram (clockwise) -->
  <polygon
    points="200,0 100,150 50,120 150,-30"
    style="fill:black;stroke:blue;"/>
</g>
</svg>
```

## Remarks

The SVG code in Listing 1.8 contains two SVG polygon elements: the first one renders a red triangle, and the second one renders a black parallellogram on the left side of the red triangle. The parallelogram and triangle share a common side; the other pair of parallel sides of the parallelogram are tilted upward slightly, thereby creating a three-dimensional shading effect. Usually an angle of 20° or so produces the best shading effect, but feel free to experiment with different angles of elevation until you find one that suits your preferences.

## SVG viewports

SVG allows you to shift the origin of a display and scale it vertically or horizontally with the SVG viewBox attribute. This attribute consists of four numbers (separated by commas and/or white space) that specify the upper-left vertex and the lower-right vertex of the new viewing rectangle, after taking into account any scaling effects. A value of 0 for any of these four numbers indicates that the corresponding coordinate remains unchanged. For example, consider the following code fragment:

```
<svg width="800" height="400" viewBox="0 0 800 400">
<g>
  <rect style="fill:red;"
    x="0" y="0" width="100" height="50"/>
</g>
```

The preceding fragment renders a red rectangle of width 100 and height 50 whose upper-left vertex is the origin (0, 0) because the first two numbers specified in the `viewBox` attribute are "0 0", which means the origin is still (0,0), and the last two numbers specified in the `viewBox` attribute are "800 400", which means that the lower-right vertex of the new viewport corresponds to the same point as the default. The complete SVG code is given in Listing 1.9.

**FIGURE 1.6**   A rectangle
with the first `viewBox`.

**Listing 1.9**   viewBoxRect1.svg

```
<?xml version="1.0" encoding="iso-8859-1"?>
<!DOCTYPE svg PUBLIC "-//W3C//DTD SVG 20001102//EN"
 "http://www.w3.org/TR/2000/CR-SVG-20001102/DTD/svg-20001102.dtd">

<svg width="800" height="400" viewBox="0 0 800 400">
 <g>
  <rect style="fill:red;"
    x="0" y="0" width="100" height="50"/>

  <line x1="0" y1="24" x2="100" y2="24"
        style="stroke:white;stroke-width:2"/>

  <line x1="49" y1="0" x2="49" y2="50"
        style="stroke:white;stroke-width:2"/>
 </g>
</svg>
```

## Remarks

**ON THE CD**

The CD-ROM for this chapter contains the SVG documents *viewBoxRect2.svg*, *viewBoxRect3.svg*, and *viewBoxRect4.svg* that illustrate what happens when you specify the following values for the `viewBox` attribute:

```
viewBox="50 25 800 400"
viewBox="0 0 200 100"
viewBox="50 25 200 100"
```

## COLORS AND THEIR COMPONENTS

Color is the *sine qua non* ("without that which") of graphics. Imagine if you can what graphics or art would be like without any color. Apart from watching *film noir*, could anyone look forward to such an impoverished state of affairs?

In the SVG world, a color can be defined in four ways. One way is an (R,G,B) triplet of (base ten) integers, which specify values for its red component, green component, and blue component, respectively. For example, the color red is represented as (255,0,0). The values for R, G, and B are independent of each other, and each one is a decimal integer between 0 and 255. Consequently, there are 256x256x256 = 16,777,216 possible colors combinations. The human eye cannot distinguish between every pair of possible colors, which means that interesting shading effects can be achieved. Note that the color white has all colors present, while the color black is actually the absence of all color. Several examples are given below:

```
White: (R, G, B) = (255, 255, 255)
Black: (R, G, B) = (0,  0,   0)
Red:   (R, G, B) = (255, 0,  0)
Green: (R, G, B) = (0,  255, 0)
Blue:  (R, G, B) = (0,  0,   255)
```

As the values of (R, G, B) decrease from a maximum of 255 to a minimum of 0, the associated color will darken. This behavior is consistent with the fact that white is (255, 255, 255) and black is (0, 0, 0).

A second way to specify SVG colors involves listing the relative weights of the (R, G, B) components as a percentage between 0 and 100. For example, the color red is represented as rgb(100%,0%,0%).

A third way to specify SVG colors involves a string of six hexadecimal digits. Most of the SVG code in this book uses this technique. For example, the string "#FF0000" represents the color red. Notice that the first pair of hexadecimal digits is the hexadecimal representation of the number 255. The other two pairs of hexadecimal digits correspond to the G component and the B component, respectively. For example, the SVG color with (R, G, B) values of (128, 96, 48) corresponds to the SVG color "#806030." The fourth way of specifying SVG colors is the subject of the next topic.

## STANDARD COLORS

Well-known colors can be defined in terms of their (R, G, B) components. A short list of the more common colors is provided below.

```
Blue    =   0,    0, 255
Green   =   0,  255,   0
Magenta = 255,    0, 255
```

```
Orange    = 255, 200,   0
Pink      = 255, 175, 175
Red       = 255,   0,   0
Yellow    = 255, 255,   0
LightGray = 192, 192, 192
DarkGray  =  64,  64,  64
Gray      = 128, 128, 128
Black     =   0,   0,   0
White     = 255,  255, 255
```

Your code will be more intuitive if you use the well-known name for a color instead of its corresponding hexadecimal value. However, the vast majority of colors do not have a well-known name, which means that you have no choice but to use the non-intuitive representation of the color in question. Regardless of the method you use for specifying colors, SVG enables you to easily create rich visual images with subtle shading effects.

In order to illustrate the techniques for specifying color, the following four SVG code fragments demonstrate four different ways of rendering a blue rectangle with the SVG rect element:

```
<rect width="200" height="100" fill="rgb(0,0,255)"/>
<rect width="200" height="100" fill="rgb(0%,0%,100%)"/>
<rect width="200" height="100" fill="blue"/>
<rect width="200" height="100" fill="blue"/>
```

## KEY CONSTRUCTS

A rectangle can be rendered using any of the following SVG snippets:

```
<path    d="0,0 150,0 150,50 0,50 z"/>
<polygon points="0,0 150,0 150,50 0,50"/>
<polyLine points="0,0 150,0 150,50 0,50 z"/>
<rect    x="0" y="0" width="150" height="50"/>
```

## CD-ROM LIBRARY

ON THE CD
The CD-ROM for this book contains the following SVG documents that are required for rendering the graphics images in this chapter:

*coordinateSystem1.svg*

*rect1.svg*

*opacityRect1.svg*

*rectShadowEffect1.svg*

*triangularWedge1.svg*

*viewBoxRect1.svg*

*viewBoxRect2.svg*

*viewBoxRect3.svg*

*viewBoxRect4.svg*

*nestedViewPortRect1.svg*

## SUMMARY

This chapter covered the following topics that form the basis for SVG graphics images in subsequent chapters:

- the SVG coordinate system
- the SVG `style` element for specifying fill colors
- the SVG `rect` element for drawing rectangles
- the SVG `path` element for drawing rectangles
- the SVG `rect` element combined with opacity
- the SVG `rect` element for creating 3D shadow effects
- the SVG `path` element for drawing triangular wedges
- the SVG `viewport` element
- colors and color gradients

# 2 Color Gradients and Style

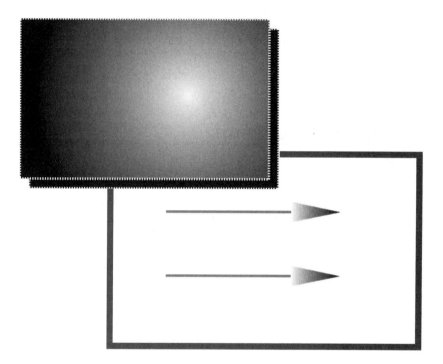

## OVERVIEW

This chapter introduces the SVG defs element that allows you to define your own graphics elements. The main use of the SVG defs element in this chapter is for defining SVG linear color gradients and radial color gradients that can be used when rendering graphics images. You'll learn how to combine linear gradients and radial gradients, defined in an SVG defs element, with simple geometric objects. In later chapters, you'll see how to combine color gradients with more sophisticated geometric objects. One advantage of defining these gradients in an SVG defs element is that you can use these definitions as "templates" which can be applied to your graphics components. The definition-based nature of the SVG defs element reduces complexity and redundancy, and hence will simplify maintenance and enhancements to your existing code.

The second part of this chapter shows you how to use embedded and external stylesheets. If you have already worked with cascading stylesheets, this material will be familiar to you, so feel free to skim through it quickly. The advantages of using stylesheets become most evident when you need to maintain several hundred SVG documents, but stylesheets can be useful even when you have a smaller number of SVG documents. One of the most important advantages of stylesheets is that they can simplify code maintenance by providing code structure, which entails performing some code analysis in order to determine their common features. All code and images for this chapter can be found on the companion CD-ROM in the Chapter 2 folder.

ON THE CD

## LINEAR COLOR GRADIENTS

SVG provides two types of color gradients: linear and radial. These two types of color gradients are defined in a defs section of an SVG document and then referenced as the color pattern for subsequent graphics images that you define. This facility is extremely powerful because it allows you to create color effects that would be very difficult to achieve in any other language.

A linear gradient is defined in terms of a "start" color and an "end" color. For example, if you define a linear gradient with a start color of "#FF0000" (which is red) and an end color of "#000000" (which is black), then the resultant color gradient will range—in a linear fashion—from red to black. A linear gradient can contain multiple start/stop color combinations; this feature allows you to create vivid color combinations.

The next topic involves the SVG defs element, and it's the mechanism by which you can provide definitions of many sorts of things. Keep in mind that "linear gradient" and "linear color gradient" are used interchangeably in this book, as are "radial gradient" and "radial color gradient."

## USING THE SVG defs ELEMENT

Listing 2.1 demonstrates how to use the SVG defs element in order to define a linear color gradient that ranges from yellow to black.

**Listing 2.1**   linearDef1.svg

```
<svg>
<defs>
```

```
<linearGradient id="gradientDefinition"
   gradientUnits="userSpaceOnUse">
   <stop stop-color="yellow" offset="0%"/>
   <stop stop-color="black"  offset="100%"/>
</linearGradient>
</defs>
</svg>
```

### Remarks

The SVG `defs` element in Listing 2.1 contains a linear gradient identified as `gradientDefinition` via the `id` attribute. The gradient ranges in a linear fashion from yellow to black. Multiple `stop` values can be specified, using standard colors, hexadecimal notation, or the (R, G, B) components of a color.

You can use the `id` value in order to specify this color definition when rendering other SVG components. Note that if you double-click on this file, you will not see anything in your browser; it is simply the definition of a linear gradient element. The next example shows you how to specify this color definition as the color of a rectangle in an SVG document.

## RENDERING RECTANGLES WITH LINEAR GRADIENTS

The rectangle displayed in Figure 2.1 is rendered with linear gradient shading.

In this example, the SVG `rect` element defines a rectangle of width `width` and height `height` whose upper-left vertex has coordinates (`x,y`).

**FIGURE 2.1**    A linear gradient rectangle.

The SVG document *rectLinearGradient1.svg* in Listing 2.2 demonstrates how to draw a rectangle with linear gradient by means of the SVG elements `rect` and `linearGradient`.

**Listing 2.2**   rectLinearGradient1.svg

```
<?xml version="1.0" encoding="iso-8859-1"?>
<!DOCTYPE svg PUBLIC "-//W3C//DTD SVG 20001102//EN"
 "http://www.w3.org/TR/2000/CR-SVG-20001102/DTD/svg-20001102.dtd">

<svg width="100%" height="100%">
  <defs>
  <linearGradient id="gradientDefinition"
      gradientUnits="userSpaceOnUse">
      <stop stop-color="yellow" offset="0%"/>
      <stop stop-color="black"  offset="100%"/>
  </linearGradient>
  </defs>

  <rect
      x="60" y="60" width="400" height="200"
      stroke-width="4"
      stroke="red"
      stroke-dasharray="2 2 2 2"
      fill="black"/>

  <rect
      x="50" y="50" width="400" height="200"
      stroke-width="4"
      stroke="red"
      stroke-dasharray="2 2 2 2"
      fill="url(#gradientDefinition)"/>
</svg>
```

## Remarks

Listing 2.2 contains two SVG rect elements, both of which have a width of 400 pixels and height of 200 pixels; the first rectangle is black and is shifted to the right and downward by 10 pixels in order to create a shadow effect. The upper-left vertex of the second rectangle has coordinates (50,50).

The color of the second rectangle references the id element (defined in the SVG defs element) whose value is gradientDefinition, which is a linear color gradient that ranges from yellow to black from left to right. The combination of the value for the stroke-dasharray attribute and the stroke attribute create a red perforated effect for the second rectangle.

You can also specify the stop-opacity attribute inside a stop attribute. The default value for stop-opacity is 1, and its allowable set of values are the numbers between 0 and 1. An example is given below:

```
<stop stop-color="yellow" stop-opacity=".2" offset="100%"/>
```

## RADIAL COLOR GRADIENTS

This is the second type of built-in color gradient that is available in SVG. A *radial* color gradient can be compared to the ripple effect that's created when you drop a stone in a pond, where each "ripple" has a color that changes in a gradient fashion. Instead of specifying the color of every ripple, you need only specify a "start" color and an "end" color. For example, if you define a radial gradient with a start color of "#FF0000" (which is red) and an end color of "#000000" (which is black), then the resultant color gradient will range—in a radial fashion—from red to black. Radial gradients can also contain multiple start/stop color combinations. The point to keep in mind is that radial gradients change colors in a *linear* fashion, but the rendered colors are drawn in an expanding *radial* fashion.

Listing 2.3 demonstrates how to use the SVG `defs` element in order to define a radial color gradient that ranges from yellow to black.

### Listing 2.3    radialDef1.svg

```
<defs>
<radialGradient id="gradientDefinition"
   gradientUnits="userSpaceOnUse">
   <stop stop-color="yellow" offset="0%"/>
   <stop stop-color="black"  offset="100%"/>
</radialGradient>
</defs>
```

### Remarks

The SVG `defs` element in Listing 2.3 contains a radial gradient identified as `gradientDefinition` via the `id` attribute. The gradient ranges in a radial fashion from yellow to black. Multiple `stop` values can be specified, using standard colors, hexadecimal notation, or the (R, G, B) components of a color.

You can use the value of the `id` attribute in order to specify this color definition when rendering other SVG components. The next example shows you how to specify this color definition while rendering a rectangle.

## RENDERING RECTANGLES WITH RADIAL GRADIENTS

Consider the rectangle with radial gradient shading in Figure 2.2.

**FIGURE 2.2**   A radial gradient rectangle.

In this example, the SVG rect element defines a rectangle of width width and height height whose upper-left vertex has coordinates (x,y).

The SVG document *rectRadialGradient1.svg* in Listing 2.4 demonstrates how to draw an SVG rectangle with radial gradient shading by means of the SVG radialGradient element.

**Listing 2.4**   rectRadialGradient1.svg

```
<?xml version="1.0" encoding="iso-8859-1"?>
<!DOCTYPE svg PUBLIC "-//W3C//DTD SVG 20001102//EN"
 "http://www.w3.org/TR/2000/CR-SVG-20001102/DTD/svg-20001102.dtd">

<svg width="100%" height="100%">
  <defs>
  <radialGradient id="gradientDefinition"
    gradientUnits="userSpaceOnUse">
    <stop stop-color="yellow" offset="0%"/>
    <stop stop-color="black"  offset="100%"/>
  </radialGradient>
  </defs>

  <rect
    x="65" y="65" width="400" height="250"
    stroke-width="4"
    stroke="yellow"
    stroke-dasharray="2 2 2 2"
    fill="black"/>

  <rect
    x="50" y="50" width="400" height="250"
```

```
        stroke-width="4"
        stroke="yellow"
        stroke-dasharray="2 2 2 2"
        style="fill:url(#gradientDefinition)"/>
    </svg>
```

## Remarks

Listing 2.4 contains two SVG `rect` elements, similar to Listing 2.3. In this example, though, the second rectangle references a radial color gradient that ranges from yellow to black in a radial fashion. The combination of the value for the `stroke-dasharray` attribute and the `stroke` attribute create a red perforated effect for the second rectangle.

# PARALLELOGRAMS AS SVG POLYGONS

Let's take a look at parallelograms, which are a generalization of rectangles (i.e., every rectangle is also a parallelogram). Unlike rectangles, which have four right angles, the internal angles of a parallelogram are not necessarily right angles (i.e., 90°). Consider the parallelogram rendered in Figure 2.3.

**FIGURE 2.3**    A parallelogram.

The SVG document *radialGradientPoly1.svg* in Listing 2.5 uses the SVG elements `polygon` and `radialGradient` in order to render the parallelogram in Figure 2.3.

**Listing 2.5**   radialGradientPoly1.svg

```
<?xml version="1.0" encoding="iso-8859-1"?>
<!DOCTYPE svg PUBLIC "-//W3C//DTD SVG 20001102//EN"
 "http://www.w3.org/TR/2000/CR-SVG-20001102/DTD/svg-20001102.dtd">

<svg width="100%" height="100%">
  <defs>
    <radialGradient id="radialGradient"
       gradientUnits="userSpaceOnUse">
       <stop stop-color="red"   offset="0%"/>
       <stop stop-color="black" offset="100%"/>
    </radialGradient>

    <linearGradient id="linearGradient"
       gradientUnits="userSpaceOnUse">
       <stop stop-color="red" offset="0%"/>
       <stop stop-color="black"  offset="100%"/>
    </linearGradient>
  </defs>

  <g transform="translate(50,20)">
    <polygon
       stroke="yellow"
       stroke-width="4"
       stroke-dasharray="8 8 8 8"
       points="50,0 450,0 400,150 0,150"
       fill="url(#linearGradient)"/>
  </g>

  <g transform="translate(50,200)">
    <polygon
       points="50,0 450,0 400,150 0,150"
       stroke="yellow"
       stroke-width="4"
       stroke-dasharray="2 2 2 2"
       fill="url(#radialGradient)"/>
  </g>
</svg>
```

## Remarks

Listing 2.5 contains two parallelograms with gradient shading attributes that are defined in the SVG defs element; the first uses a linear gradient and the second parallelogram uses a radial gradient. The following line defines the points attribute that defines the four vertices of the second parallelogram:

```
points="50,0 450,0 400,150 0,150"
```

This list of four vertices starts from the upper-left vertex and then specifies the coordinates of the other three vertices in a clockwise fashion. Note that you have the freedom to start from any vertex and list the remaining vertices of the polygon, either clockwise or in a counterclockwise fashion. Choose a style that you prefer and be as consistent as possible; you'll be surprised how much debugging time you will save by doing so.

## USING THE SVG marker ELEMENT

Consider the image in Figure 2.4.

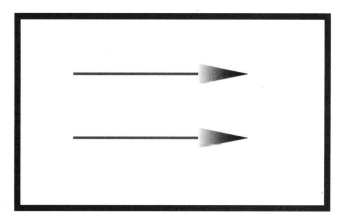

**FIGURE 2.4**  A gradient arrow.

The SVG document *linearGradientArrow1.svg* in Listing 2.6 uses the SVG elements marker and linearGradient in order to render the gradient arrow in Figure 2.4.

**Listing 2.6**  linearGradientArrow1.svg

```
<?xml version="1.0" encoding="iso-8859-1"?>
<!DOCTYPE svg PUBLIC "-//W3C//DTD SVG 20010904//EN"
  "http://www.w3.org/TR/2001/REC-SVG-20010904/DTD/svg10.dtd">

<svg width="100%" height="100%"
    xmlns="http://www.w3.org/2000/svg">

<defs>
```

```
<linearGradient id="gradientDefinition"
  x1="0" y1="0" x2="20" y2="0"
  gradientUnits="userSpaceOnUse">
  <stop offset="0%"   stop-color="#FFFF00"/>
  <stop offset="100%" stop-color="#000000"/>
</linearGradient>

<marker id="triangularMarker1"
  refX="0" refY="4"
  markerUnits="strokeWidth"
  markerWidth="20" markerHeight="8"
  fill="url(#gradientDefinition)"
  orient="auto">
  <path d="M0,0 l20,4 l-20,4 z"/>
</marker>
</defs>

<rect x="10" y="10" width="800" height="500"
      fill="none"
      stroke="blue" stroke-width="10"/>
<desc>Placing an arrowhead at the end of a path.</desc>

<path d="M 100,100 L 300,100"
      stroke="red" stroke-width="4"
      marker-end="url(#triangularMarker1)"/>

<path d="M 100,200 L 300,200"
      stroke="red" stroke-width="4"
      marker-end="url(#triangularMarker1)"/>

</svg>
```

## Remarks

Listing 2.6 contains the SVG marker element, which enables you to define more complex "templates" that consist of other SVG elements. This example contains an SVG marker element in the SVG defs element that defines a triangle. The fill attribute of the specified triangle references a linear gradient that is also defined in the SVG defs element. Experiment with refX and refY attributes in the SVG marker element to see how changes in their values affect the rendered graphics image.

## DOTTED AND DASHED LINE SEGMENTS

Consider the set of dotted and dashed line segments in Figure 2.5.

**FIGURE 2.5**  Dotted and
dashed lines.

The SVG document *dottedDashedLines1.svg* in Listing 2.7 renders a set of parallel horizontal line segments with dotted and dashed patterns.

**Listing 2.7**    dottedDashedLines1.svg

```
<?xml version="1.0" encoding="iso-8859-1"?>
<!DOCTYPE svg PUBLIC "-//W3C//DTD SVG 20001102//EN"
 "http://www.w3.org/TR/2000/CR-SVG-20001102/DTD/svg-20001102.dtd">

<svg width="100%" height="100%">
  <defs>
    <line id="lineDefinition1"
          x1="0"    y1="0"
          x2="200"  y2="0"/>
  </defs>

  <use xlink:href="#lineDefinition1"
       x="50" y="50"
       stroke="red"
       stroke-width="1"
       stroke-dasharray="4 4"/>

  <use xlink:href="#lineDefinition1"
       x="50" y="100"
       stroke="green"
       stroke-width="4"
       stroke-dasharray="8 4"/>

  <use xlink:href="#lineDefinition1"
       x="50" y="150"
       stroke="blue"
       stroke-width="8"
       stroke-dasharray="8 4 2 4"/>
```

```
<use xlink:href="#lineDefinition1"
     x="50" y="200"
     stroke="red"
     stroke-width="16"
     stroke-dasharray="8 4 20 4"/>
</svg>
```

## Remarks

Listing 2.7 contains an SVG defs element that specifies the two end points of a line segment. Notice the four SVG use elements, each of which references the same line segment by the value of its id attribute (which is lineDefinition1) in order to render four parallel line segments. The start point for each of the four line segments is specified by the value of the x attribute and the y attribute that is listed inside each SVG use element. This technique is convenient when there are multiple objects with the same dimensions. The code is compact because you specify the definition of the object once; moreover, it's much easier to update the defined object instead of making the same change in multiple locations (imagine updating the width of several thousand rectangles!).

By the way, if nothing is rendered in your browser, make sure that you did not inadvertently forget the "#" symbol (that can easily happen when you're in a hurry). Each line segment contains a different left end point that is determined by the value of the x attribute and the y attribute. The attribute stroke-dasharray determines the dot and dash pattern. Usually this attribute consists of one or more pairs of numbers, where each pair specifies the length of a line segment followed by the length of white space. (Can you guess what will happen with an odd number of numbers? Try it and see if you were right!)

You can also specify values for the stroke, stroke-width, and stroke-dasharray attributes when using SVG elements such as rect and ellipse. The judicious choice of values for these attributes can add vividness to histograms, line graphs, and pie charts.

## USING SVG EMBEDDED STYLESHEETS

Consider the pair of nested rectangles in Figure 2.6.

The SVG document *style1.svg* in Listing 2.8 uses a stylesheet in order to render a nested pair of rectangles.

### Listing 2.8   style1.svg

```
<?xml version="1.0" encoding="iso-8859-1"?>
<!DOCTYPE svg PUBLIC "-//W3C//DTD SVG 20001102//EN"
```

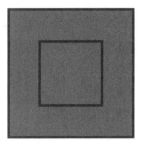

**FIGURE 2.6**  A pair of
nested rectangles.

```
"http://www.w3.org/TR/2000/CR-SVG-20001102/DTD/svg-20001102.dtd">

<svg width="800" height="500">

<style type="text/css">
rect {
  stroke-width:4;
  stroke:blue;
  fill:red;
}
</style>

  <rect x="50"  y="50"  width="200" height="200"/>
  <rect x="100" y="100" width="100" height="100"/>

</svg>
```

## Remarks

The stylesheet in Listing 2.8 specifies a set of name/value pairs that are applied to every occurrence of the SVG rect element. As a result, the SVG rect elements do not need to specify the attributes defined in the stylesheet. Moreover, the process of adding, removing, or modifying attribute values becomes very straightforward; simply make the necessary change in the stylesheet and those modifications will be applied to the corresponding elements. The stylesheet in Listing 2.8 can easily be extended to other SVG elements. For example, you could add the following snippet that would affect all the SVG ellipse elements:

```
ellipse {
  stroke-width:8;
  stroke:green;
  fill:yellow;
}
```

## EMBEDDED STYLESHEETS AND CDATA

The SVG document *style2.svg* in Listing 2.9 uses an internal stylesheet in order to define the colors of a pair of nested rectangles as illustrated in Figure 2.6.

**Listing 2.9**   style2.svg

```
<?xml version="1.0" encoding="iso-8859-1"?>
<!DOCTYPE svg PUBLIC "-//W3C//DTD SVG 20001102//EN"
 "http://www.w3.org/TR/2000/CR-SVG-20001102/DTD/svg-20001102.dtd">

<svg width="800" height="500">

<style type="text/css">
<![CDATA[
rect {
  stroke-width:4;
  stroke:blue;
  fill:red;
}
]]>
</style>

  <rect x="50"  y="50"  width="200" height="200"/>
  <rect x="100" y="100" width="100" height="100"/>

</svg>
```

### Remarks

The stylesheet definition in Listing 2.9 is embedded in a CDATA section, which starts with the following lines:

```
<style type="text/css">
<![CDATA[
```

The first line declares that the style is of type text/css, which means that what will follow consists of CSS (Cascading Style Sheet) rules. The second line contains the string CDATA, which refers to "character data," and it prevents the SVG viewer from interpreting the characters inside the CDATA section as XML. If you've worked with Unix shell scripts or Perl scripts, this might remind you of a "here" document. By the way, you'll see CDATA sections used for SVG documents that contain JavaScript/ECMAScript. Notice that the matching pair of lines is in the correctly nested order as shown below:

```
]]>
</style>
```

Now let's look at the contents of the stylesheet given in the following fragment:

```
rect {
  stroke-width:4;
  stroke:blue;
  fill:red;
}
```

The attributes above are simply name/value pairs that can be interpreted as "for any rectangle, use a width of four pixels when rendering its perimeter with the color blue; the fill color for inside a rectangle is red." These attributes are applied to every occurrence of the SVG `rect` element in the SVG document, which means that the SVG `rect` elements do not need to specify the attributes that are defined in the stylesheet. Moreover, the process of adding, removing, or modifying attribute values becomes very straightforward; simply make the necessary change in the stylesheet and those modifications will be applied to the corresponding elements. The stylesheet in Listing 2.9 can easily be extended to other SVG elements.

## USING EXTERNAL STYLESHEETS

The SVG document *style3.svg* in Listing 2.10 uses an external stylesheet in order to render a pair of nested rectangles as listed in Figure 2.6.

### Listing 2.10    style3.svg

```
<?xml version="1.0" encoding="iso-8859-1"?>
<!DOCTYPE svg PUBLIC "-//W3C//DTD SVG 20001102//EN"
 "http://www.w3.org/TR/2000/CR-SVG-20001102/DTD/svg-20001102.dtd">

<?xml-stylesheet type="text/css" href="externalStyle1.css" ?>

<svg width="800" height="500">
  <rect x="50"  y="50"  width="200" height="200"/>
  <rect x="100" y="100" width="100" height="100"/>
</svg>
```

Listing 2.11 contains three SVG style-related attributes that are applied to SVG `rect` elements.

### Listing 2.11    externalStyle1.svg

```
rect {
  stroke-width:4;
```

```
    stroke:blue;
    fill:red;
}
```

## Remarks

The external stylesheet in Listing 2.11 contains the same information as the internal stylesheet in Listing 2.9. You can specify attribute name/value pairs in an external stylesheet and then include the external stylesheet in your SVG documents. This feature allows you to centralize definitions in an external file and then include the external file in multiple SVG documents. You can edit the external file and the new contents will be automatically applied to all the SVG documents that include the external file. Since you do not need to modify the SVG documents themselves, this approach can simplify your maintenance chores.

## USING EXTERNAL STYLESHEETS AND CLASSES

Consider the nested rectangles in Figure 2.7.

**FIGURE 2.7** Rendering nested rectangles with an external stylesheet.

The SVG document *style4.svg* in Listing 2.12 uses an external stylesheet in order to render a pair of nested rectangles.

### Listing 2.12    style4.svg

```
<?xml version="1.0" encoding="iso-8859-1"?>
<!DOCTYPE svg PUBLIC "-//W3C//DTD SVG 20001102//EN"
  "http://www.w3.org/TR/2000/CR-SVG-20001102/DTD/svg-20001102.dtd">
<?xml-stylesheet type="text/css" href="externalStyle2.css" ?>
```

```
<svg width="800" height="500">
  <rect class="Larger"  x="50"  y="50"
                        width="200" height="200"/>
  <rect class="Smaller" x="100" y="100"
                        width="100" height="100"/>
</svg>
```

Listing 2.13 defines two classes and the style-related attributes in those two classes.

## Listing 2.13    externalStyle2.svg

```
.Larger
{
 stroke-width:4;
  stroke:blue;
  fill:red;
}

.Smaller
{
  stroke-width:8;
  stroke:yellow;
  fill:green;
}
```

## Remarks

The use of classes in a stylesheet gives you finer granularity in terms of how you want to apply a set of attributes to an SVG element. For example, you can specify the class `Larger` for one SVG `rect` element and then specify the class `Smaller` for a second SVG `rect` element. Compare this functionality with that of the following stylesheet:

```
rect {
 stroke-width:4;
  stroke:blue;
  fill:red;
}
```

The stylesheet definition in Listing 2.12 is applied to *all* SVG `rect` elements in your SVG document. If this definition is sufficient for your needs, then feel free to use it. On the other hand, if it's likely that you'll need a finer degree of granularity for your stylesheet, then it might be advisable to start with class definitions rather than retrofitting them at a later stage.

## INHERITING AN SVG style ATTRIBUTE

Consider the pair of rectangles in Figure 2.8.

**FIGURE 2.8** Inheriting style attributes.

The SVG document *inheritStyle1.svg* in Listing 2.14 specifies the SVG style attribute in an SVG g element that is "inherited" by the enclosed rectangles.

**Listing 2.14** inheritStyle1.svg

```
<?xml version="1.0" encoding="iso-8859-1"?>
<!DOCTYPE svg PUBLIC "-//W3C//DTD SVG 20010904//EN"
  "http://www.w3.org/TR/2001/REC-SVG-20010904/DTD/svg10.dtd">

<svg width="100%" height="100%"
    xmlns="http://www.w3.org/2000/svg">

 <g>
   <g style="fill:red;stroke:blue;stroke-width:4;">
     <rect x="100" y="50"
           width="200" height="100"/>

     <rect x="350" y="50"
           stroke-dasharray="4 4 4 4"
           width="200" height="100"/>
   </g>
 </g>
</svg>
```

### Remarks

Listing 2.14 demonstrates a useful technique for specifying an SVG style attribute that is applied to all the graphics images enclosed in a particular SVG g element. You can set different SVG style attributes for different SVG g elements, thereby specifying the display attributes for "blocks" of graphics images. Notice that the second rectangle specifies a stroke-dasharray attribute that renders the second rectangle with a dotted perimeter.

# INHERITING ATTRIBUTES IN MULTIPLE SVG g ELEMENTS

Consider the set of rectangles in Figure 2.9.

**FIGURE 2.9** Inheriting attributes in multiple SVG g elements.

The SVG document *inheritStyle2.svg* in Listing 2.15 specifies two SVG g elements, each of which uses a different style attribute in order to control the display attributes of the enclosed rectangles.

## Listing 2.15   inheritStyle2.svg

```
<?xml version="1.0" encoding="iso-8859-1"?>
<!DOCTYPE svg PUBLIC "-//W3C//DTD SVG 20010904//EN"
  "http://www.w3.org/TR/2001/REC-SVG-20010904/DTD/svg10.dtd">

<svg width="100%" height="100%"
     xmlns="http://www.w3.org/2000/svg">
   <defs>
     <linearGradient id="linearGradientDefinition1"
                     gradientUnits="objectBoundingBox">
       <stop offset="0%"   stop-color="#FF0000"/>
       <stop offset="100%" stop-color="#000000"/>
     </linearGradient>

     <linearGradient id="linearGradientDefinition2"
                     gradientUnits="objectBoundingBox">
       <stop offset="0%"   stop-color="#FFFF00"/>
       <stop offset="100%" stop-color="#000000"/>
     </linearGradient>
```

```
    </defs>

  <g>
    <g fill="url(#linearGradientDefinition1)">
      <rect x="100" y="50"
            stroke="red"
            stroke-width="3"
            stroke-dasharray="4 4 4 4"
            width="200" height="100"/>

      <rect x="400" y="50"
            stroke="green"
            stroke-width="3"
            stroke-dasharray="4 4 4 4"
            width="200" height="100"/>
    </g>

    <g fill="url(#linearGradientDefinition2)">
      <rect x="100" y="250"
            stroke="blue"
            stroke-width="3"
            stroke-dasharray="4 4 4 4"
            width="200" height="100"/>

      <rect x="400" y="250"
            stroke="yellow"
            stroke-width="3"
            stroke-dasharray="4 4 4 4"
            width="200" height="100"/>
    </g>
  </g>
</svg>
```

## Remarks

Listing 2.15 demonstrates how to specify different SVG `fill` attributes for different SVG g elements. Each SVG `fill` attribute is applied to all the graphics images contained within a given SVG g element. In Listing 2.15, there are two linear gradient definitions `linearGradientDefinition1` and `linearGradientDefinition2`, each of which is applied a pair of rectangles. You can easily create variations of Listing 2.15 that contain a combination of linear and radial gradient definitions that are applied to a variety of geometric objects, such as ellipses, polygons, and highly customized objects of your own design.

# KEY CONSTRUCTS

A *linear color gradient* can be defined with the following SVG snippet:

```
<defs>
<linearGradient id="gradientDefinition"
   gradientUnits="userSpaceOnUse">
   <stop stop-color="yellow" offset="0%"/>
   <stop stop-color="black"  offset="100%"/>
</linearGradient>
</defs>
```

A *radial color gradient* can be defined with the following SVG snippet:

```
<defs>
<radialGradient id="gradientDefinition"
   gradientUnits="userSpaceOnUse">
   <stop stop-color="yellow" offset="0%"/>
   <stop stop-color="black"  offset="100%"/>
</radialGradient>
</defs>
```

A *marker* can be defined with the following SVG snippet:

```
<defs>
 <marker id="triangularMarker1"
   refX="0" refY="4"
   markerUnits="strokeWidth"
   markerWidth="20" markerHeight="8"
   fill="url(#gradientDefinition)"
   orient="auto">
   <path d="M0,0 l20,4 l-20,4 z"/>
 </marker>
<?defs>
```

A *dotted line* can be defined with the following SVG snippet:

```
<svg width="100%" height="100%">
  <defs>
    <line id="lineDefinition1"
          x1="0"   y1="0"
          x2="200" y2="0"
          stroke="blue" stroke-width="4"/>
  </defs>

<g>
  <use xlink:href="#lineDefinition1"
```

```
        x="50" y="50"
        stroke-dasharray="4 4"/>
</g>
```

An *internal stylesheet* can be defined with the following SVG snippet:

```
<style type="text/css">
<![CDATA[
rect {
  stroke-width:4;
  stroke:blue;
  fill:red;
}
]]>
</style>
```

An *external stylesheet* can be specified with the following SVG snippet:

```
<?xml-stylesheet type="text/css" href="externalStyle2.css" ?>
```

## CD-ROM LIBRARY

ON THE CD

The folder for this chapter on the companion CD-ROM contains the following SVG documents that are required for rendering the graphics images in this chapter:

*linearDef1.svg*

*rectLinearGradient1.svg*

*radialDef1.svg*

*rectRadialGradient1.svg*

*radialGradientPoly1.svg*

*linearGradientArrow1.svg*

*dottedDashedLines1.svg*

*style1.svg*

*style4.svg*

*inheritStyle1.svg*

*inheritStyle2.svg*

## SUMMARY

This chapter described how to define linear color gradients and radial color gradients, and how to combine these gradients with rectangles. You also saw how to specify CSS attributes for SVG elements, as well as the use of inheritance for propagating attribute values. The examples in this chapter showed you how to use the following SVG elements:

- the SVG `defs` element for defining color gradients
- the SVG `linearGradient` element for linear color gradients
- the SVG `radialGradient` element for radial color gradients
- the SVG `polygon` element for drawing rectangles
- the SVG `polyLine` element for drawing rectangles
- the SVG `path` element for drawing rectangles
- the SVG `polygon` element for drawing parallelograms
- internal and external stylesheets
- inheriting style attributes

# 3 Circles, Ellipses, and path Elements

## OVERVIEW

This chapter demonstrates how to use the SVG elements circle, ellipse, and path in order to render circles, ellipses and elliptic arcs, respectively. Unlike other languages such as Java, SVG provides a separate SVG circle element for specifying a circle, even though circles are actually a special case of ellipses, which means that you could use the SVG ellipse element to specify a circle. You'll see how these SVG elements can be combined with linear color gradients and radial color gradients to create richer graphics images.

Unfortunately, rendering elliptic arcs in SVG is not nearly as straightforward or intuitive as in other languages such as Java. You may already know that Java uses intuitive drawArc and fillArc methods for rendering elliptic arcs, whereas SVG uses a path element in order to render elliptic arcs. On the other hand, the SVG path element is an *extremely* powerful construct that can be used for rendering Bezier curves in addition to elliptic arcs. This chapter contains examples that will give you a feel for the versatility of the SVG path element.

We will also explore techniques for defining radial color gradients that can be used for creating three-dimensional effects. These techniques are based on the manner in which you specify the stop-color/offset combinations. In particular, you'll see radial color gradients combined with circles in order to create pseudo spheres. All code and images for this chapter can be found on the companion CD-ROM in the Chapter 3 folder.

ON THE CD

## USING AN SVG circle ELEMENT TO RENDER CIRCLES

Consider the circle rendered in Figure 3.1.

**FIGURE 3.1**   A circle.

You can uniquely identify a circle by specifying its center point and its radius, as demonstrated in this example.

The SVG document *circle1.svg* in Listing 3.1 uses the SVG circle element in order to render a circle with radius 50.

**Listing 3.1**   circle1.svg

```
<?xml version="1.0" encoding="iso-8859-1"?>
<!DOCTYPE svg PUBLIC "-//W3C//DTD SVG 20010904//EN"
  "http://www.w3.org/TR/2001/REC-SVG-20010904/DTD/svg10.dtd">

<svg width="100%" height="100%">

<g transform="translate(200,100)">
  <circle cx="100" cy="100" r="50"
          fill="red" stroke="blue" stroke-width="10"/>
</g>

</svg>
```

## Remarks

The SVG code in Listing 3.1 first translates the origin from the point (0,0) to the point (200,100). As a result, the center of the circle is shifted from (100,100), which is the point specified by (cx,cy) in the definition of the circle, to the point (300,200). The circle that is drawn has a radius of 50 pixels, which is the value assigned to the r attribute. The circle is filled with the color red, and the blue circumference has a thickness of 10 pixels.

Since circles are a special case of ellipses (or conversely, ellipses are a generalization of circles), you can use the SVG ellipse element to render circles. The SVG ellipse element is illustrated in the next example.

## USING AN SVG ellipse ELEMENT TO RENDER ELLIPSES

Consider the ellipse rendered in Figure 3.2.

**FIGURE 3.2**    An ellipse.

You can uniquely identify a circle by specifying its center point (cx,cy), its major axis rx, and its minor axis ry.

The SVG document *simpleEllipse1.svg* in Listing 3.2 uses the SVG ellipse element in order to render an ellipse with center (100,100), a (horizontal) major axis of length 80 pixels, and a (vertical) minor axis of 50 pixels.

### Listing 3.2    simpleEllipse1.svg

```
<?xml version="1.0" encoding="iso-8859-1"?>
<!DOCTYPE svg PUBLIC "-//W3C//DTD SVG 20001102//EN"
  "http://www.w3.org/TR/2000/CR-SVG-20001102/DTD/svg-20001102.dtd">

<svg width="100%" height="100%">
    <ellipse cx="120" cy="80"
```

```
                rx="80" ry="30"
                style="fill:rgb(255,0,0)"/>

        <ellipse cx="130" cy="170"
                rx="80" ry="30"
                style="fill:black"/>

        <ellipse cx="120" cy="160"
                rx="80" ry="30"
                stroke="blue"
                stroke-width="8"
                stroke-dasharray="1 1 1 1"
                style="fill:rgb(255,0,0)"/>
    </svg>
```

## Remarks

The SVG code in Listing 3.2 contains three ellipses. The top ellipse is an unadorned red ellipse, and the second ellipse serves as a black background for the third ellipse in order to create a shadow effect.

The first ellipse has a center point of (120,80), a horizontal major axis of length 80 pixels, and a vertical minor axis of length 50 pixels. Notice that the fill attribute is specified in terms of the (R, G, B) triple of (255,0,0), which is the color red. You can also specify the same fill color (in this case, red) by using a string of six hexadecimal digits or by using the standard color name for red as given below:

```
style="fill:red"/>
style="fill:#FF0000"/>
```

Notice that if we had specified rx = ry = 80, then the rendered ellipse would actually be a circle.

The second ellipse is black and is rendered by a horizontal and vertical offset of 10 pixels in order to create a black background for the third ellipse; the latter is red and has a blue dotted circumference, as shown below:

```
stroke="blue"
stroke-width="8"
stroke-dasharray="1 1 1 1"
style="fill:rgb(255,0,0)"/>
```

## LINEAR GRADIENT ELLIPSES

Figure 3.3 depicts an ellipse with linear gradient shading.

**FIGURE 3.3**  An ellipse with a linear gradient.

The SVG document *ellipseLinearGradient1.svg* in Listing 3.3 defines a linear gradient that is used as the color of an ellipse with center (250,150) and axes of length 200 pixels and 100 pixels.

**Listing 3.3**   ellipseLinearGradient1.svg

```
<?xml version="1.0" encoding="iso-8859-1"?>
<!DOCTYPE svg PUBLIC "-//W3C//DTD SVG 20001102//EN"
 "http://www.w3.org/TR/2000/CR-SVG-20001102/DTD/svg 20001102.dtd">

<svg width="100%" height="100%">
 <defs>
  <linearGradient id="gradientDefinition"
    gradientUnits="userSpaceOnUse">
    <stop stop-color="yellow" offset="0%"/>
    <stop stop-color="black"  offset="100%"/>
  </linearGradient>
 </defs>

 <ellipse
    cx="265" cy="165" rx="200" ry="100"
    stroke-dasharray="8 8 8 8"
    stroke="black"
    stroke-width="4"
    fill="black"/>

 <ellipse
    cx="250" cy="150" rx="200" ry="100"
    stroke-dasharray="8 8 8 8"
    stroke="red"
    stroke-width="4"
    fill="url(#gradientDefinition)"/>
</svg>
```

## Remarks

The SVG code in Listing 3.3 renders two ellipses; the first ellipse is black and rendered at an offset that is relative to the second ellipse in order to create a shadow effect.

The second ellipse has center point (250,150), a horizontal major axis of length 200 pixels, and a vertical minor axis of 100 pixels. The fill color for the ellipse refers to a linear color gradient that is defined in the SVG defs element. The linear gradient has an id value of gradientDefinition, and it is referenced in the fill color by means of the following syntax:

```
style="fill:url(#gradientDefinition)"
```

The linear gradient has an initial color of yellow that is specified by the first stop-color and a final color of black that is specified in the second stop-color. The intermediate colors vary from yellow to black, and their (R, G, B) values are calculated by means of a linear gradient in order to achieve the effect that you see in the associated figure.

## RADIAL GRADIENT ELLIPSES

Figure 3.4 depicts an ellipse with radial gradient shading.

**FIGURE 3.4**   An ellipse with a radial gradient.

The SVG document *ellipseRadialGradient1.svg* in Listing 3.4 defines a radial gradient that is used as the color of an ellipse with center (250,150) and axes of length 200 pixels and 100 pixels.

## Listing 3.4    ellipseRadialGradient1.svg

```
<?xml version="1.0" encoding="iso-8859-1"?>
<!DOCTYPE svg PUBLIC "-//W3C//DTD SVG 20001102//EN"
```

```
       "http://www.w3.org/TR/2000/CR-SVG-20001102/DTD/svg-20001102.dtd">

   <svg width="100%" height="100%">

     <defs>
     <radialGradient id="gradientDefinition"
         gradientUnits="userSpaceOnUse">
         <stop stop-color="yellow" offset="0%"/>
         <stop stop-color="black"  offset="100%"/>
     </radialGradient>
     </defs>

     <ellipse
         cx="265" cy="165" rx="200" ry="100"
         stroke-dasharray="1 1 1 1"
         stroke="white"
         stroke-width="4"
         fill="black"/>

     <ellipse
         cx="250" cy="150" rx="200" ry="100"
         stroke="white"
         stroke-width="1"
         stroke-dasharray="1 1 1 1"
         style="fill:url(#gradientDefinition)"/>
   </svg>
```

## Remarks

The SVG code in Listing 3.4 renders two ellipses in order to create a shadow effect (similar to Listing 3.3). The fill color for the second ellipse refers to a radial color gradient that is defined in the SVG defs element. The radial gradient has an id value of gradientDefinition, and it is referenced in the fill color by means of the following syntax:

```
style="fill:url(#gradientDefinition)"
```

The radial gradient has an initial color of yellow and a final color of black. Unlike linear gradients, the intermediate colors are calculated by means of a radial gradient in order to achieve the effect that you see in the associated figure. In order to understand how the intermediate colors are determined, imagine the effect of dropping a stone into a pond and "capturing" the set of concentric circles. The colors of these circles are based on the set of colors that you obtain by a color gradient that starts from yellow (#FFFF00) and ends with black (#000000). Here's an interesting point about radial color gradients: if you drew a line segment with one end point coinciding with the center of all the concentric circles, that line segment would be colored with a *linear* gradient.

One more point about the second ellipse in this example: notice how the values for the stroke-dasharray attribute and the stroke attribute create a slightly "polished" effect on the circumference of the ellipse.

## MULTI-STOP RADIAL GRADIENTS

Consider the ellipse and rectangle in Figure 3.5 that are rendered with radial gradient shading.

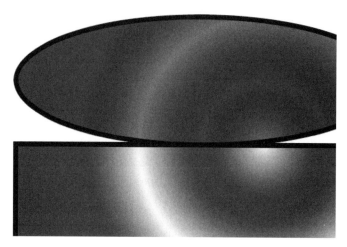

**FIGURE 3.5**    An ellipse and a rectangle with radial gradient shading.

The SVG document *ripple4RadialGradient2.svg* in Listing 3.5 renders an SVG ellipse element and an SVG rect element with radial gradient shading that creates a wave-like effect.

**Listing 3.5**    ripple4RadialGradient2.svg

```
<?xml version="1.0" encoding="iso-8859-1"?>
<!DOCTYPE svg PUBLIC "-//W3C//DTD SVG 20010904//EN"
  "http://www.w3.org/TR/2001/REC-SVG-20010904/DTD/svg10.dtd">

<svg width="100%" height="100%"
    xmlns="http://www.w3.org/2000/svg">

  <defs>
    <radialGradient id="radialGradient1"
```

```
                    gradientUnits="userSpaceOnUse"
                    cx="400" cy="200" r="300"
                    fx="400" fy="200">
        <stop offset="0%"    stop-color="red"/>
        <stop offset="33%"   stop-color="blue"/>
        <stop offset="67%"   stop-color="red"/>
        <stop offset="100%" stop-color="blue"/>
      </radialGradient>

      <radialGradient id="radialGradient2"
                    gradientUnits="userSpaceOnUse"
                    cx="400" cy="200" r="300"
                    fx="400" fy="200">
        <stop offset="0%"    stop-color="yellow"/>
        <stop offset="33%"   stop-color="blue"/>
        <stop offset="67%"   stop-color="yellow"/>
        <stop offset="100%" stop-color="blue"/>
      </radialGradient>
    </defs>

  <g transform="translate(50,20)">
    <ellipse fill="url(#radialGradient1)"
            stroke="black" stroke-width="8"
            cx="300" cy="100" rx="300" ry="100"/>

    <rect    fill="url(#radialGradient2)"
            stroke="black" stroke-width="8"
            x="0" y="200" width="600" height="300"/>
  </g>
</svg>
```

## Remarks

The SVG code in Listing 3.5 renders an ellipse and a rectangle, each of which has a fill attribute that references a radial gradient. Let's examine the code in a bit more detail.

The ellipse has a "relative" center point of (300,100) and horizontal major axis of length 300 and a vertical minor axis of 100 pixels. Since the SVG g element specifies an SVG translate function that specifies a horizontal shift of 50 pixels and a vertical shift of 20 pixels, the "absolute" center of the ellipse is (350,120).

The fill color for the ellipse refers to a radial color gradient that is defined in the SVG defs element. The radial gradient has an id value of radialGradient1 and is referenced in the fill color by means of the following syntax:

```
style="fill:url(#radialGradient1)"
```

The upper-left vertex of the rectangle is the "relative" point (0,200), it has a width of 600 pixels and its height is 200 pixels. Since the SVG g element specifies an SVG `translate` function that specifies a horizontal shift of 50 pixels and a vertical shift of 20 pixels, the "absolute" coordinates of the upper-left vertex of the rectangle are those of the point (50,220).

The `fill` color for the rectangle refers to a radial color gradient that is defined in the SVG `defs` element. The radial gradient has an `id` value of `radialGradient2`, and it is referenced in the fill color by means of the following syntax:

```
style="fill:url(#radialGradient2)"
```

The graphics image rendered by the SVG code in Listing 3.5 is probably much different from what you expected. This SVG code gives you an example of how you can create vivid and striking visual patterns by means of compact SVG code.

## LUMINATION-LIKE EFFECTS WITH MULTI-STOP RADIAL GRADIENTS

Consider the ellipse and rectangle in Figure 3.6 that are rendered with radial gradient shading.

**FIGURE 3.6**   Lumination effects with radial gradient shading.

The SVG document *ripple4RadialGradient6.svg* in Listing 3.6 renders an SVG `ellipse` element and an SVG `rect` element that creates a lumination-like effect with radial gradient shading.

**Listing 3.6**  ripple4RadialGradient6.svg

```
<?xml version="1.0" encoding="iso-8859-1"?>
<!DOCTYPE svg PUBLIC "-//W3C//DTD SVG 20010904//EN"
  "http://www.w3.org/TR/2001/REC-SVG-20010904/DTD/svg10.dtd">

<svg width="100%" height="100%"
     xmlns="http://www.w3.org/2000/svg">

  <defs>
    <radialGradient id="radialGradient1"
                    gradientUnits="userSpaceOnUse"
                    cx="400" cy="200" r="300"
                    fx="400" fy="200">
      <stop offset="0"    stop-color="white"/>
      <stop offset=".149" stop-color="red"/>
      <stop offset=".15"  stop-color="blue"/>
      <stop offset="1"    stop-color="black"/>
    </radialGradient>

    <radialGradient id="radialGradient2"
                    gradientUnits="userSpaceOnUse"
                    cx="400" cy="200" r="300"
                    fx="400" fy="200">
      <stop offset="0"    stop-color="yellow"/>
      <stop offset=".149" stop-color="red"/>
      <stop offset=".15"  stop-color="white"/>
      <stop offset="1"    stop-color="black"/>
    </radialGradient>
  </defs>

  <g transform="translate(50,20)">
    <ellipse fill="url(#radialGradient1)"
             stroke="black" stroke-width="8"
             cx="300" cy="100" rx="300" ry="100"/>

    <rect    fill="url(#radialGradient2)"
             stroke="black" stroke-width="8"
             x="0" y="200" width="600" height="300"/>
  </g>
</svg>
```

## Remarks

Since the code in Listing 3.6 is very similar to that of Listing 3.5, why is there such a different visual effect? The answer lies in the manner in which the radial gradients are specified. In Listing 3.5, the radial gradient is defined as follows:

```
<stop offset="0%"   stop-color="yellow"/>
<stop offset="33%"  stop-color="blue"/>
<stop offset="67%"  stop-color="yellow"/>
<stop offset="100%" stop-color="blue"/>
```

The `offset` values specified above are more or less uniformly distributed between 0% and 100%. Now look at the radial gradient defined in Listing 3.6 that's given below:

```
<stop offset="0"    stop-color="yellow"/>
<stop offset=".149" stop-color="red"/>
<stop offset=".15"  stop-color="white"/>
<stop offset="1"    stop-color="black"/>
```

As you can see, the `offset` values are *not* uniformly distributed between 0% and 100%. This type of gradient might be called (informally) an "extreme" gradient because the close proximity of consecutive `offset` values causes very sudden gradient changes.

The SVG code in Listing 3.6 shows you how to create unexpected visual effects when the values of consecutive `stop offset` terms are very close together. The impression created is of a light shining on an ellipse and a rectangle such that the radial color effect seems to emanate from the a point that is between the rectangle and the ellipse. The interesting aspect of this image is that the radial color effect is from white to black for the rectangle, whereas the radial color effect is from blue to black for the ellipse.

## CIRCULAR AND ELLIPTIC ARCS

Consider the set of circular arcs in Figure 3.7.

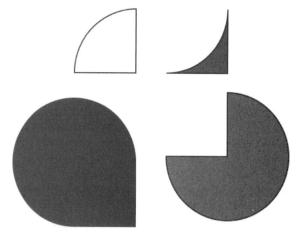

**FIGURE 3.7**   A set of circular arcs.

In a language such as Java, you define a circular or an elliptic arc in terms of its width, the height, the start angle, the end angle, and the coordinates of the upper-left vertex of the smallest rectangle that bounds the circle or the ellipse. On the other hand, SVG requires that you specify a start point and an end point and then whether you want to render a major or a minor arc, either clockwise or counterclockwise.

The SVG document *circularArcs1.svg* in Listing 3.7 defines a set of circular arcs.

**Listing 3.7**    circularArcs1.svg

```
<?xml version="1.0" encoding="iso-8859-1"?>
<!DOCTYPE svg PUBLIC "-//W3C//DTD SVG 20010904//EN"
  "http://www.w3.org/TR/2001/REC-SVG-20010904/DTD/svg10.dtd">

<svg width="100%" height="100%"
    xmlns="http://www.w3.org/2000/svg">

<g transform="translate(50,20)">
  <path d="M200,100 v-100 a100,100 0 0,0 -100,100 z"
        fill="white" stroke="blue" stroke-width="2" />
</g>

<g transform="translate(300,20)">
  <path d="M200,100 v-100 a100,100 0 0,1 -100,100 z"
        fill="green" stroke="blue" stroke-width="2" />
</g>

<g transform="translate(50,350)">
  <path d="M200,100 v-100 a100,100 0 1,0 -100,100 z"
        fill="blue" stroke="blue" stroke-width="2" />
</g>

<g transform="translate(300,220)">
  <path d="M200,100 v-100 a100,100 0 1,1 -100,100 z"
        fill="red" stroke="blue" stroke-width="2" />
</g>

</svg>
```

## Remarks

The SVG code in Listing 3.7 demonstrates how to use the SVG path element in order to draw circular arcs. The fill color of these elliptic arcs is white, green, blue, and red. All four circular arcs have a blue circumference with a thickness of two pixels. Before we examine the contents of the SVG path elements, notice that each circular arc is wrapped inside an SVG g element that specifies a transform attribute with a translate function. This is done for two reasons: first, you can move each elliptic arc independently of the others simply by changing the coordinates of the point in the `translate` function, and second, the SVG `path` elements for the circular arcs are virtually identically to each other.

The first portion of the first SVG `path` element consists of the following,

```
<path d="M200,100
```

which specifies an absolute start point of (200,100) for the circular arc that will be rendered. The second portion of the four arcs consists of the following,

```
v-100
```

which specifies a vertical line segment with relative coordinates of (0,-100). Specifying this relative point has two consequences. First, a line segment of length 100 is drawn in the positive vertical (i.e., upward) direction. Second, this point represents the coordinates of the new "start" point. The third portion of the four arcs consists of the following,

```
a100,100
```

which specifies that an elliptic arc is to be rendered. Both the major axis and the minor axis of this circular arc have length 100. Let's skip ahead to the last part of this line:

```
-100,100 z
```

This is a relative "terminal" point of the elliptic arc that is to be rendered. Since the start point is the point with coordinates (100,100) as discussed above, the actual "terminal" point is computed relative to the point (100,100). You can determine the coordinates of the terminal point simply by adding the x-coordinates and the y-coordinates together as follows: (100,100) + (-100,100) = (0,200). Note that the final "z" in the SVG path element specifies that the final point must be connected to the initial point (in this case, the initial point is M200,100) with a line segment.

The intermediate portion of the SVG `path` element consists of three numbers—for example, 0 0,0. The first integer represents a rotation value, and since it is equal to zero in all four cases, there is no rotation.

At this point, all that remains is to understand the purpose of the comma-separated pair of integers. This pair of integers specifies a combination of an "arc type" (i.e., major arc versus minor arc) and rotation (i.e., clockwise versus counterclockwise). A value of zero for the first integer specifies a minor arc, and a value of 1 specifies a major arc. A value of zero for the second integer specifies counterclockwise, and a value of 1 for the second integer specifies clockwise. Confusing? The next section summarizes the preceding information so that you can use it as a handy reference.

## SPECIFYING CIRCULAR AND ELLIPTIC ARCS

The four possible combinations (minor/major combined with clockwise/counter-clockwise) are given below for specifying circular and elliptic arcs in an SVG path element, along with their meaning:

```
0,0: minor arc + counterclockwise
0,1: minor arc + clockwise
1,0: major arc + counterclockwise
1,1: major arc + clockwise
```

## COLORING ELLIPTIC ARCS

Figure 3.8 portrays a set of colored elliptic arcs that form an ellipse.

**FIGURE 3.8**   Colored elliptic arcs.

The SVG document *ellipticArcSegments2.svg* in Listing 3.8 defines four colored elliptic arcs that form an ellipse.

**Listing 3.8**   ellipticArcSegments2.svg

```
<?xml version="1.0" encoding="iso-8859-1"?>
<!DOCTYPE svg PUBLIC "-//W3C//DTD SVG 20010904//EN"
  "http://www.w3.org/TR/2001/REC-SVG-20010904/DTD/svg10.dtd">

<svg width="100%" height="100%"
    xmlns="http://www.w3.org/2000/svg">

<g transform="translate(20,20)">
  <!-- upper-left quadrant -->
  <path d="M100,100 A150,50 0 0,1 250,50"
        fill="black" stroke="red" stroke-width="8"/>

  <!-- upper-right quadrant -->
```

```
<path d="M250,50 A150,50 0 0,1 400,100"
      fill="black" stroke="green" stroke-width="8"/>

<!-- lower-right quadrant -->
<path d="M400,100 A150,50 0 0,1 250,150"
      fill="black" stroke="blue" stroke-width="8"/>

<!-- lower-right quadrant -->
<path d="M250,150 A150,50 0 0,1 100,100"
      fill="black" stroke="yellow" stroke-width="8"/>
</g>

</svg>
```

## Remarks

The SVG code in Listing 3.8 demonstrates how to use the SVG path element in order to draw a set of elliptic arcs. Consider the points in the first SVG path element:

```
<path d="M100,100 A150,50 0 0,1 250,50"
```

The letter M specifies an absolute start point of (100,100) with an elliptic arc having a horizontal axis of length 150 and vertical axis of length 50. The final point has coordinates (250,50). A "minor" elliptic arc is drawn clockwise from the start point to the final point. In a similar fashion, the other three SVG path elements define elliptic "quarter" arcs (as indicated by the comment lines) which, together with the first elliptic arc, comprise an ellipse. Notice how the elliptic arcs represent minor arcs that are rendered in a clockwise fashion; hence, all four SVG path elements have the element 0,1 immediately prior to the end point of the path, which is consistent with the information you saw in a previous section regarding minor/major sectors.

## ARC-BASED PETAL PATTERNS

Figure 3.9 depicts a set of elliptic arcs that create a petal-like pattern.
The SVG document *ellipticPetals1.svg* in Listing 3.9 defines a set of elliptic arcs.

**Listing 3.9** ellipticPetals1.svg

```
<?xml version="1.0" encoding="iso-8859-1"?>
<!DOCTYPE svg PUBLIC "-//W3C//DTD SVG 20010904//EN"
  "http://www.w3.org/TR/2001/REC-SVG-20010904/DTD/svg10.dtd">
```

```
<svg width="100%" height="100%"
     xmlns="http://www.w3.org/2000/svg">

<g transform="translate(0,0)">
  <path d="M150,150 a100,100 0 0,0 100,100 z"
        fill="red" stroke="black" stroke-width="4"/>

  <path d="M150,150 a100,100 0 0,0 -100,100 z"
        fill="green" stroke="black" stroke-width="4"/>

  <path d="M150,150 a100,100 0 0,0 -100,-100 z"
        fill="blue" stroke="black" stroke-width="4"/>

  <path d="M150,150 a100,100 0 0,0 100,-100 z"
        fill="yellow" stroke="black" stroke-width="4"/>
</g>
</svg>
```

**FIGURE 3.9**    Elliptic petals.

## Remarks

The SVG code in Listing 3.9 demonstrates how to use the SVG path element in order to draw a set of elliptic arcs. Consider the points in the first SVG path element:

```
<path d="M150,150 a100,100 0 0,0 100,100 z"
```

The letter M specifies an absolute start point of (150,100) with an elliptic arc having a horizontal axis of length 100 and vertical axis of length 100. The final point is computed by adding the absolute start point with the relative terminal point as follows: (150,150) + (100,100) = (250,250). A "minor" elliptic arc is drawn counterclockwise from the start point (150,150) to the final point (250,250). The remaining three SVG path elements define the other three elliptic "petals" that form the graphics image.

## ARC-BASED DIAMOND PATTERNS

Consider the image in Figure 3.10 that is based on a set of four elliptic arcs.

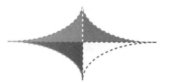

**FIGURE 3.10** An elliptic diamond.

The SVG document *ellipticDiamond1.svg* in Listing 3.10 defines an elliptic diamond.

**Listing 3.10** ellipticDiamond1.svg

```
<?xml version="1.0" encoding="iso-8859-1"?>
<!DOCTYPE svg PUBLIC "-//W3C//DTD SVG 20010904//EN"
 "http://www.w3.org/TR/2001/REC-SVG-20010904/DTD/svg10.dtd">

<svg width="100%" height="100%"
     xmlns="http://www.w3.org/2000/svg">

  <!-- upper quadrants -->
  <g transform="translate(50,50)">
    <path d="M200,100 v-60 a120,60 0 0,1 -120,60 z"
          stroke-dasharray="4 4 4 4"
          fill="red" stroke="green" stroke-width="2"/>
  </g>

  <g transform="translate(50,50)">
    <path d="M200,100 v-60 a120,60 0 0,0 120,60 z"
          stroke-dasharray="4 4 4 4"
          fill="green" stroke="yellow" stroke-width="2"/>
  </g>

  <!-- lower quadrants -->
  <g transform="translate(50,50)">
    <path d="M200,100 v60 a120,60 0 0,0 -120,-60 z"
          stroke-dasharray="4 4 4 4"
          fill="blue" stroke="red" stroke-width="2"/>
  </g>

  <g transform="translate(50,50)">
```

```
    <path d="M200,100 v60 a120,60 0 0,1 120,-60 z"
          stroke-dasharray="4 4 4 4"
          fill="yellow" stroke="blue" stroke-width="2"/>
  </g>
</svg>
```

## Remarks

The SVG code in Listing 3.10 demonstrates how to use the SVG path element in order to draw a set of elliptic arcs, all of which have a stroke-dasharray attribute that creates a dotted effect.

Consider the elements in the d attribute of the second SVG path element:

```
<path d="M200,100 v-60 a120,60 0 0,0 120,60 z"
```

The letter M specifies an absolute start point of (200,100), followed by a vertical shift to the point (200,40) by the component v-60.

The term a120,160 specifies an elliptic arc having a horizontal axis of length 120 and a vertical axis of length 60 that is rendered from the final point to the start point in a relative fashion. You can compute the coordinates of the final point by adding the absolute start point with the relative terminal point as follows: (120,40) + (120,60) = (240,100). A "minor" elliptic arc is drawn counter clockwise from the start point (200,40) to the final point (240,100). Notice that two of the elliptic arcs are rendered clockwise and the other two elliptic arcs are rendered counterclockwise. Consequently, two of the elliptic arcs have "0,1" in their definition and the other two elliptic arcs have "0,0" in their definition.

## ASYMMETRIC ARC-BASED PATTERNS

Consider the image in Figure 3.11, which is based on a set of four elliptic arcs.

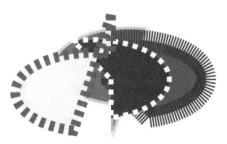

**FIGURE 3.11**  A set of asymmetric elliptic arcs.

The document *ellipticAsymmetricSegments3.svg* in Listing 3.11 defines an asymmetric set of elliptic arcs.

**Listing 3.11**    ellipticAsymmetricSegments3.svg

```
<?xml version="1.0" encoding="iso-8859-1"?>
<!DOCTYPE svg PUBLIC "-//W3C//DTD SVG 20010904//EN"
  "http://www.w3.org/TR/2001/REC-SVG-20010904/DTD/svg10.dtd">

<svg width="100%" height="100%"
    xmlns="http://www.w3.org/2000/svg">

<!-- upper quadrants -->
<g transform="translate(50,150)">
  <path d="M200,100 v-60 a120,60 0 1,1 60,-120 z"
    stroke-dasharray="1 1 1 1"
    fill="red" stroke="yellow" stroke-width="8"/></g>

<g transform="translate(50,50)">
  <path d="M200,100 v-60 a120,60 0 1,1 60,120 z"
    stroke-dasharray="2 2 2 2"
    fill="green" stroke="blue" stroke-width="32"/></g>

<!-- lower quadrants -->
<g transform="translate(50,50)">
  <path d="M200,100 v60 a120,60 0 1,0 -60,-120 z"
    stroke-dasharray="8 8 8 8"
    fill="blue" stroke="white" stroke-width="8"/></g>

<g transform="translate(50,-50)">
  <path d="M200,100 v60 a120,60 0 1,0 -60,120 z"
    stroke-dasharray="8 8 8 8"
    fill="yellow" stroke="green" stroke-width="16"/></g>
</svg>
```

## Remarks

The SVG code in Listing 3.11 demonstrates how to use the SVG path element in order to draw a set of elliptic arcs. Consider the points in the first SVG path element:

```
<path d="M200,100 v-60 a120,60 0 1,1 60,-120 z"
```

The letter M specifies an absolute start point of (200,100) that is shifted to the point (200,40) by the component v-60. An elliptic arc having a horizontal axis of length 120 and a vertical axis of length 60 is rendered from the final point to the start point. Therefore, the coordinates of the final point are computed by adding the absolute start point with the relative terminal point as follows: (120,40) + (120,60) =

(240,100). A "minor" elliptic arc is drawn counterclockwise from the start point (200,40) to the final point (240,100).

If you've managed to reach this point after having read all the details of the preceding examples pertaining to elliptic arcs, consider it a job well done! Knowing how to specify elliptic arcs in SVG can definitely be a challenge, so don't feel discouraged if you've had to struggle through the code. The remaining examples in this chapter pertain to graphics images that are based on entire circles and ellipses rather than arcs, which means that you'll progress through the code much more quickly.

## CREATING 3D EFFECTS WITH CIRCLES

Consider the image in Figure 3.12 that is based on a circle with gradient shading.

**FIGURE 3.12** A circle with a 3D effect.

The SVG document *blue3DCircle1.svg* in Listing 3.12 renders a circle with gradient shading in order to create a three-dimensional effect.

**Listing 3.12**   blue3DCircle1.svg

```
<?xml version="1.0" encoding="iso-8859-1"?>
<!DOCTYPE svg PUBLIC "-//W3C//DTD SVG 1.0//EN"
 "http://www.w3.org/TR/2001/REC-SVG-20010904/DTD/svg10.dtd">

<svg xmlns="http://www.w3.org/2000/svg"
    xmlns:xlink="http://www.w3.org/1999/xlink"
    width="100%" height="100%">

  <defs>
    <radialGradient id="blueCircle"
                    gradientUnits="objectBoundingBox"
                    fx="30%" fy="30%">
```

```
            <stop offset="0%"   style="stop-color:#FFFFFF"/>
            <stop offset="40%"  style="stop-color:#0000AA"/>
            <stop offset="100%" style="stop-color:#000066"/>
        </radialGradient>

        <circle id="3DBlueCircle" cx="0" cy="0" r="80"
                style="fill:url(#blueCircle)"/>
    </defs>

<g width="100%" height="100%">
  <use xlink:href="#3DBlueCircle" x="100" y="100"/>
</g>

</svg>
```

### Remarks

The SVG code in Listing 3.12 demonstrates how to render a circle with a radial gradient in order to create a three-dimensional effect. The key idea behind this technique involves the use of three `stop` colors in the definition of the radial gradient. In this example, the initial stop color is white, which is specified by the hexadecimal string `FFFFFF`. The second stop color is the hexadecimal string `0000AA`, which is a darkened blue color. The final stop color is the hexadecimal string `000066`, which is an even darker shade of blue. This technique can be adapted in order to create three-dimensional effects based on the colors red, green, or yellow.

## CREATING CONES WITH GRADIENT SHADING

Consider the gradient cone rendered in Figure 3.13.

**FIGURE 3.13**   A cone with linear gradient shading.

The SVG document *vGradientCone1.svg* in Listing 3.13 renders a cone with linear gradient shading.

**Listing 3.13** vGradientCone1.svg

```
<?xml version="1.0" encoding="iso-8859-1"?>
<!DOCTYPE svg PUBLIC "-//W3C//DTD SVG 20001102//EN"
 "http://www.w3.org/TR/2000/CR-SVG-20001102/DTD/svg-
20001102.dtd">

<svg width="100%" height="100%">

<defs>
   <linearGradient id="gradientDefinition1"
      x1="0" y1="0" x2="200" y2="0"
      gradientUnits="userSpaceOnUse">
      <stop offset="0%"   style="stop-color:#FF0000"/>
      <stop offset="100%" style="stop-color:#000000"/>
   </linearGradient>
</defs>

<g transform="translate(50,50)">
   <polygon points="0,50 200,50 100,300"
         style="fill:url(#gradientDefinition1);"/>

   <ellipse cx="100" cy="50"
            rx="100" ry="20"
            style="fill:blue;"/>
</g>

</svg>
```

## Remarks

A cone in the Euclidean plane can be rendered with a triangle and an ellipse, as demonstrated in the SVG code in Listing 3.13. The triangle is rendered by means of the SVG polygon element whose fill attribute references a linear gradient (defined in the SVG defs element) that creates a more realistic visual effect. You can experiment with radial shading or add gradient shading for the ellipse that represents the top of the cone. Incidentally, you can replace the triangle with a set of colored line segments, and then use JavaScript/ECMAScript in order to update the color of the line segments to create the impression of a rotating cone. This is similar to controlling the manner in which the lights in a circular neon are switched on and off so that one light appears to be rotating in a circular fashion.

## CREATING CYLINDERS WITH GRADIENT SHADING

Consider the gradient cylinder rendered in Figure 3.14.

**FIGURE 3.14**   A cylinder with linear
gradient shading.

The SVG document *hGradientCylinder1.svg* in Listing 3.14 renders a cylinder
with linear gradient shading.

**Listing 3.14**   hGradientCylinder1.svg

```
<?xml version="1.0" encoding="iso-8859-1"?>
<!DOCTYPE svg PUBLIC "-//W3C//DTD SVG 20001102//EN"
 "http://www.w3.org/TR/2000/CR-SVG-20001102/DTD/svg-20001102.dtd">

<svg width="100%" height="100%">

<defs>
  <linearGradient id="gradientDefinition1"
    x1="0" y1="0" x2="200" y2="0"
    gradientUnits="userSpaceOnUse">
    <stop offset="0%"   style="stop-color:#FF0000"/>
    <stop offset="100%" style="stop-color:#440000"/>
  </linearGradient>
</defs>

<g transform="translate(100,100)">
  <ellipse cx="0"  cy="50"
           rx="20" ry="50"
           stroke="blue" stroke-width="4"
           style="fill:url(#gradientDefinition1)"/>

  <rect x="0" y="0" width="300" height="100"
        style="fill:url(#gradientDefinition1)"/>

  <ellipse cx="300" cy="50"
           rx="20"  ry="50"
           stroke="blue" stroke-width="4"
           style="fill:yellow;"/>
```

```
</g>

</svg>
```

## Remarks

A cylinder in the Euclidean plane can be rendered with an ellipse at both ends and a rectangle in the middle, as demonstrated in the SVG code in Listing 3.14. The left-most ellipse and the rectangle are rendered with linear gradient shading, which creates a more realistic visual effect, whereas the right-most ellipse is rendered in yellow. You can also use a combination of radial shading and gradient shading for the rectangle and the ellipse to create many variations of this example. Another variant is to add the dash-strokearray attribute for creating a dashed-line effect. Just as you can create the impression of a spinning cone, you can also create the impression of a spinning cylinder; that is, replace the rectangle with a set of parallel line segments that are rendered by means of weighted shading, and then use JavaScript to update the color of the line segments in order to create a spinning effect.

## KEY CONSTRUCTS

An ellipse can be rendered using the following SVG snippet:

```
<ellipse cx="100" cy="100" rx="80" ry="50"/>
```

A circle can be rendered using the following SVG snippet:

```
<circle cx="100" cy="100" r="50"/>
```

An elliptic arc can be rendered using the following SVG snippet:

```
<g transform="translate(50,50)">
  <path d="M200,100 v-60 a120,60 0 0,1 -120,60 z"
        fill="red" stroke="blue" stroke-width="2" />
</g>
```

## CD-ROM LIBRARY

ON THE CD
The folder for this chapter on the CD-ROM contains the following SVG documents that are required for rendering the graphics images in this chapter:

*circle1.svg*

*simpleEllipse1.svg*

*ellipseLinearGradient1.svg*

*ellipseRadialGradient1.svg*

*ripple4RadialGradient2.svg*

*ripple4RadialGradient6.svg*

*circularArcs1.svg*

*ellipticArcSegments2.svg*

*ellipticPetals1.svg*

*ellipticDiamond1.svg*

*ellipticAsymmetricSegments3.svg*

*blue3DCircle1.svg*

*vGradientCone1.svg*

*hGradientCylinder1.svg*

## SUMMARY

This chapter presented techniques for rendering circles, ellipses, cones, and cylinders in conjunction with linear gradient shading and radial gradient shading. The examples demonstrated how to use the following SVG elements:

- the SVG `circle` element for drawing circles
- the SVG `ellipse` element for drawing ellipses
- the SVG `path` element for drawing elliptic arcs
- creating wave-like color effects with radial gradients
- rendering sphere-like images with radial gradients
- rendering cones with linear gradients
- rendering cylinders with linear gradients
- creating lumination-like effects with radial gradients

# 4

## SVG pattern, Grid Patterns, and clipPath

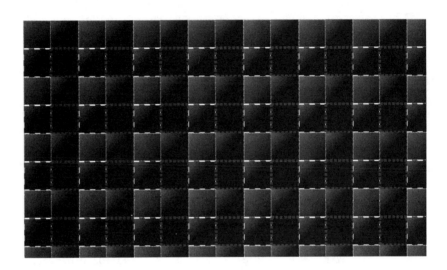

## OVERVIEW

This chapter demonstrates how to use the SVG elements pattern, clipPath, and path in conjunction with rectangles and ellipses in order to generate repeating patterns of graphics images. An SVG pattern element is akin to a "template" definition in the sense that it specifies a graphics image by means of one or more SVG elements. An SVG pattern element is defined inside an SVG defs element and then referenced inside an SVG g element (by means of the value of the id attribute of the pattern) and the specified pattern is replicated in a rectangular, grid-like fashion. The actual replication of the pattern is based on the dimensions of the SVG rect element that is specified in the SVG g element.

Another powerful mechanism in SVG is the SVG clipPath element, which allows you to specify a "window" for viewing geometric objects. Since your computer screen is limited in size, you are always looking at information through some type of window. For example, you can think of a rectangle as a "clip path" that is used in spreadsheet programs and word processing software. The SVG clipPath element is extremely powerful and goes far beyond a simple rectangle: you can easily specify polygons and complex curves as the clip path for a geometric object.

The static images in this chapter give you a foundation for pattern-based images. In Chapter 6 you'll learn how to combine SVG functions with the SVG elements in this chapter in order to create complex animation effects. All code and images for this chapter can be found on the companion CD-ROM in the Chapter 4 folder.

ON THE CD

## DEFINING AN SVG pattern ELEMENT

The SVG document *patternDef1.svg* in Listing 4.1 demonstrates how to use the SVG pattern element in order to define a 2x2 grid of rectangles whose color alternates between red and blue. When this pattern is referenced in the fill attribute of an SVG element, the graphics element defined therein is repeated in a grid-like pattern.

**Listing 4.1**   patternDef1.svg

```
<?xml version="1.0" encoding="iso-8859-1"?>
<!DOCTYPE svg PUBLIC "-//W3C//DTD SVG 20001102//EN"
 "http://www.w3.org/TR/2000/CR-SVG-20001102/DTD/svg-20001102.dtd">

<svg width="800" height="500">
  <defs>
  <pattern id="checkerPattern"
           width="80" height="80"
           patternUnits="userSpaceOnUse">

     <rect fill="red"
           x="0"  y="0"  width="40" height="40"/>

     <rect fill="blue"
           x="40" y="0"  width="40" height="40"/>

     <rect fill="blue"
           x="0"  y="40" width="40" height="40"/>

     <rect fill="red"
           x="40" y="40" width="40" height="40"/>
  </pattern>
```

```
    </defs>
  </svg>
```

## Remarks

The SVG `defs` element in Listing 4.1 contains an SVG `pattern` element that has an `id` attribute with the value `checkerPattern`. This pattern consists of an outer square whose length is 80 pixels. The inside of the pattern consists of a 2x2 grid of squares (each with side length of 40 pixels) whose colors form a checkerboard pattern.

You use the id value in order to reference this pattern definition when rendering other SVG components. Note that if you double-click on this file, you will not see anything in your browser; it is simply the definition of a pattern. The next example shows you how to specify this pattern definition and reference it while rendering a set of rectangles.

## USING AN SVG `pattern` ELEMENT

Consider the grid pattern rendered in Figure 4.1.

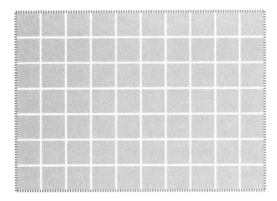

**FIGURE 4.1**  A rectangular grid pattern.

The SVG document *rectangularGrid1.svg* in Listing 4.2 demonstrates how to define and then reference an SVG `pattern` element in order to render a grid pattern.

## Listing 4.2  rectangularGrid1.svg

```
<?xml version="1.0" encoding="iso-8859-1"?>
<!DOCTYPE svg PUBLIC "-//W3C//DTD SVG 20001102//EN"
```

```
    "http://www.w3.org/TR/2000/CR-SVG-20001102/DTD/svg-20001102.dtd">
<svg width="100%" height="100%">
  <defs>
  <pattern id="gridPattern"
           width="40" height="40"
           patternUnits="userSpaceOnUse">

    <rect x="0" y="0"
          width="40" height="40"
          fill="#CCCCCC"
          style="stroke:white;stroke-width:3;"/>
  </pattern>
  </defs>

<g transform="translate(20,20)">
  <rect
    fill="url(#gridPattern)"
    stroke="red" stroke-width="4"
    stroke-dasharray="2 2 2 2"
    x="0" y="0" width="400" height="280"/>
</g>
</svg>
```

## Remarks

The SVG `defs` element in Listing 4.2 contains an SVG `pattern` element that has an `id` attribute with the value `checkerPattern`. This pattern is very simple: it consists of one square whose length is 40 with a `fill` color of white and a blue perimeter.

The SVG g element defines a rectangle with width 600 pixels and a height of 400 pixels that has a red perimeter. The `fill` attribute of this rectangle refers to the pattern `gridPattern` defined in the SVG `defs` element by using the following syntax:

```
fill="url(#gridPattern)"
```

If you double-click on this file, you will see a rectangular grid of blue rectangles enclosed in a red outer border.

## GENERATING A CHECKERBOARD GRID

Consider the checkerboard pattern rendered in Figure 4.2.

The SVG document *checkerBoard1.svg* in Listing 4.3 demonstrates how to define and then reference an SVG `pattern` element in order to render a checkerboard pattern. Note that the bulk of the code is mainly for defining the 2x2 checkerboard pattern in the SVG `defs` element.

**FIGURE 4.2**    A checkerboard pattern.

**Listing 4.3**    checkerBoard1.svg

```
<?xml version="1.0" encoding="iso-8859-1"?>
<!DOCTYPE svg PUBLIC "-//W3C//DTD SVG 20001102//EN"
 "http://www.w3.org/TR/2000/CR-SVG-20001102/DTD/svg-20001102.dtd">

<svg width="800" height="500">
  <defs>
   <pattern id="checkerPattern"
           width="80" height="80"
           patternUnits="userSpaceOnUse">

      <rect fill="red"
           x="0"  y="0"  width="40" height="40"/>

      <rect fill="blue"
           x="40" y="0"  width="40" height="40"/>

      <rect fill="blue"
           x="0"  y="40" width="40" height="40"/>

      <rect fill="red"
           x="40" y="40" width="40" height="40"/>
   </pattern>
   </defs>

 <g transform="translate(50,50)">
   <rect
```

```
              fill="url(#checkerPattern)"
              style="stroke:white"
              x="0" y="0" width="400" height="400"/>
    </g>
    </svg>
```

## Remarks

The SVG `defs` element in Listing 4.3 contains an SVG `pattern` element that has an `id` attribute with the value `checkerPattern`. This pattern consists of an outer square whose length is 80 pixels, whose "interior" consists of a 2x2 grid of squares with alternating red and blue colors that form a 2x2 checkerboard pattern.

The SVG `g` element defines a rectangle with width 400 and a height of 400. This rectangle has a `fill` attribute that refers to the pattern `checkerPattern` defined in the SVG `defs` element by using the following syntax:

```
    fill="url(#checkerPattern)"
```

If you double-click on this file, you will see a checkerboard pattern.

## GENERATING A 3D CHECKERBOARD GRID

Consider the three-dimensional checkerboard pattern rendered in Figure 4.3.

**FIGURE 4.3** A 3D checkerboard pattern.

The SVG document *checkerBoard3D1.svg* in Listing 4.4 demonstrates how to use the SVG pattern element in order to generate a three-dimensional checkerboard pattern.

**Listing 4.4**    checkerBoard3D1.svg

```
<?xml version="1.0" encoding="iso-8859-1"?>
<!DOCTYPE svg PUBLIC "-//W3C//DTD SVG 20001102//EN"
 "http://www.w3.org/TR/2000/CR-SVG-20001102/DTD/svg-20001102.dtd">
<svg width="800" height="500">
  <defs>
  <pattern id="checkerPattern"
           width="80" height="80"
           patternUnits="userSpaceOnUse">

     <rect fill="red"
           x="0"  y="0"  width="40" height="40"/>

     <rect fill="blue"
           x="40" y="0"  width="40" height="40"/>

     <rect fill="blue"
           x="0"  y="40" width="40" height="40"/>

     <rect fill="red"
           x="40" y="40" width="40" height="40"/>
  </pattern>
  </defs>

<g transform="translate(50,50)">
  <rect
     fill="url(#checkerPattern)"
     style="stroke:white"
     x="0" y="0" width="400" height="400"/>
</g>

<!-- top horizontal strip -->
<g transform="translate(50,50)">
  <path
    d="M 0 0 L 400 0 L 430 -20 L 30 -20 z"
    style="fill:black;stroke:none"/>
</g>

<!-- right vertical strip -->
<g transform="translate(450,50)">
  <path
```

```
        d="M 0 0 L 30 -20 L 30 380 L 0 400 z"
        style="fill:black;stroke:none"/>
</g>
</svg>
```

## Remarks

The SVG `defs` element in Listing 4.4 contains an SVG `pattern` element that has an `id` attribute with the value `checkerPattern`. This pattern consists of an outer square whose length is 80. The inside of the pattern consists of a 2x2 grid of squares whose colors form a checkerboard pattern.

The SVG `g` element defines a rectangle with a width of 400 and a height of 400. This rectangle has a `fill` attribute that refers to the pattern `checkerPattern` defined in the SVG `defs` element by using the following syntax:

```
fill="url(#checkerPattern)"
```

The next two SVG `path` elements define parallelograms that are used for shading the checkerboard pattern: one parallelogram provides the upper shading, and the other provides the shading on the right side of the checkerboard. If you double-click on this file, you will see a rectangular grid of blue rectangles with a black horizontal strip at the top and a black vertical strip on the right of the checkerboard that create a three-dimensional effect.

## GENERATING A GRADIENT CHECKERBOARD

Consider the gradient checkerboard pattern rendered in Figure 4.4.

**FIGURE 4.4**   A gradient checkerboard pattern.

The SVG document *checkerBoardGradient1.svg* in Listing 4.5 demonstrates how to define and reference an SVG `pattern` element in order to generate a gradient checkerboard pattern.

**Listing 4.5**    checkerBoardGradient1.svg

```
<?xml version="1.0" encoding="iso-8859-1"?>
<!DOCTYPE svg PUBLIC "-//W3C//DTD SVG 20001102//EN"
 "http://www.w3.org/TR/2000/CR-SVG-20001102/DTD/svg-20001102.dtd">

<svg width="800" height="400">
  <defs>
  <linearGradient id="gradientDefinition"
      x1="0" y1="0" x2="40" y2="40"
      gradientUnits="userSpaceOnUse">
      <stop offset="0%"   style="stop-color:#FF0000"/>
      <stop offset="100%" style="stop-color:#000000"/>
  </linearGradient>

  <pattern id="checkerPattern"
           width="40" height="40"
           patternUnits="userSpaceOnUse">

      <rect fill="url(#gradientDefinition)"
            stroke="yellow" stroke-dasharray="4 4 4 4"
            x="0" y="0" width="40" height="40"/>
  </pattern>
  </defs>

  <rect
      fill="url(#checkerPattern)"
      style="stroke:red"
      x="0" y="0" width="800" height="400"/>
</svg>
```

## Remarks

The SVG `defs` element in Listing 4.5 contains an SVG `pattern` element that has an `id` attribute with the value `checkerPattern`. This pattern consists of one square whose length is 40 with a `fill` color that refers to a linear gradient whose `id` value is `gradientDefinition`.

The diagonal gradient effect is achieved by means of the following line:

```
x1="0" y1="0" x2="40" y2="40"
```

The preceding line specifies a (relative) start point of (0,0) and an end point of (40,40), which renders a linear gradient by means of a set of contiguous diagonal line segments. This is a subtle yet important point when you're trying to achieve color effects whose nuances are not obvious.

The SVG g element defines a rectangle with a width of 800 and a height of 400. This rectangle has a fill attribute that refers to the pattern checkerPattern defined in the SVG defs element by using the following syntax:

```
fill="url(#checkerPattern)"
```

If you double-click on this file, you will see a rectangular grid of rectangles, each of which is rendered with a linear gradient that varies from red to black.

## GENERATING A MULTI-GRADIENT CHECKERBOARD

Consider the multi-gradient checkerboard pattern rendered in Figure 4.5.

**FIGURE 4.5** A multi-gradient checkerboard pattern.

The SVG document *checkerBoardMultiGradient1.svg* in Listing 4.6 demonstrates how to use the SVG pattern element in order to generate a multi-gradient checkerboard pattern.

**Listing 4.6** checkerBoardMultiGradient1.svg

```
<?xml version="1.0" encoding="iso-8859-1"?>
<!DOCTYPE svg PUBLIC "-//W3C//DTD SVG 20001102//EN"
 "http://www.w3.org/TR/2000/CR-SVG-20001102/DTD/svg-20001102.dtd">
```

```
<svg width="800" height="400">
  <defs>
  <linearGradient id="gradientDefinition1"
     x1="0" y1="0" x2="40" y2="40"
     gradientUnits="userSpaceOnUse">
     <stop offset="0%"    style="stop-color:#FF0000"/>
     <stop offset="100%" style="stop-color:#000000"/>
  </linearGradient>

  <linearGradient id="gradientDefinition2"
     x1="0" y1="0" x2="40" y2="40"
     gradientUnits="userSpaceOnUse">
     <stop offset="0%"    style="stop-color:#FFFF00"/>
     <stop offset="100%" style="stop-color:#000000"/>
  </linearGradient>

  <pattern id="checkerPattern"
           width="80" height="80"
           stroke-width="1"
           patternUnits="userSpaceOnUse">

     <rect fill="url(#gradientDefinition1)"
           stroke="white" stroke-dasharray="1 1 1 1"
           stroke-width="2"
           x="0" y="0" width="40" height="40"/>

     <rect fill="url(#gradientDefinition2)"
           stroke="green" stroke-dasharray="4 4 4 4"
           x="40" y="0" width="40" height="40"/>

     <rect fill="url(#gradientDefinition2)"
           stroke-width="2"
           stroke="white" stroke-dasharray="8 8 8 8"
           x="0" y="40" width="40" height="40"/>

     <rect fill="url(#gradientDefinition1)"
           stroke="#880088" stroke-dasharray="4 2 4 2"
           stroke-width="4"
           x="40" y="40" width="40" height="40"/>

  </pattern>
  </defs>

  <rect
     fill="url(#checkerPattern)"
     style="stroke:red"
     x="0" y="0" width="800" height="400"/>
</svg>
```

## Remarks

The SVG defs element in Listing 4.6 contains an SVG pattern element that has an id attribute with the value checkerPattern. This pattern consists of a 2x2 grid of squares with a color pattern that references two linear gradients with id values of gradientDefinition1 and gradientDefinition2, both of which define diagonal linear color gradients in order to create a quasi checkerboard pattern. The key point to observe is that both of these linear color gradients contain the following line:

```
x1="0" y1="0" x2="40" y2="40"
```

Because of the preceding line, both linear gradients start from the point (0,0) and end at the point (40,40), thereby creating the diagonal linear gradient effect.

The SVG g element defines a rectangle with a width of 800 and a height of 400. This rectangle has a fill attribute that refers to the pattern checkerPattern defined in the SVG defs element by using the following syntax:

```
fill="url(#checkerPattern)"
```

If you double-click on this file, you will see a quasi-checkerboard pattern that is the result of using two linear gradients.

## USING THE SVG clipPath ELEMENT

The SVG document *clipPathDef1.svg* in Listing 4.7 demonstrates how to use the SVG clipPath element in order to define a "clip path" that specifies the dimensions and border of a region. When this clip path is specified in an SVG component, only the portion of the component that lies inside the clip path will be rendered.

**Listing 4.7**    clipPathDef1.svg

```
<?xml version="1.0" encoding="iso-8859-1"?>
<!DOCTYPE svg PUBLIC "-//W3C//DTD SVG 20001102//EN"
 "http://www.w3.org/TR/2000/CR-SVG-20001102/DTD/svg-20001102.dtd">

<svg>
<defs>
  <clipPath id="clipPathDefinition"
            clipPathUnits="userSpaceOnUse">
    <path d="m0,200 l100,-100 100,100 -100,100z"/>
  </clipPath>
</defs>
</svg>
```

### Remarks

You can think of a clip path as a "window" that restricts the view of a graphics image to only the portion that is contained inside the "window." The SVG `defs` element in Listing 4.7 contains a clip path identified via an `id` attribute with the value of `clip-PathDefinition`. This clip path defines a diamond pattern (a rhombus, to be precise) starting from the left-most vertex and then specifying the other three vertices by moving in a clockwise fashion. You use the `id` value in order to specify this clip path definition when rendering other SVG components. Note that if you double-click on this file, you will not see anything in your browser; it is simply the definition of a clip path. The next example shows you how to specify this clip path definition and reference it while rendering a set of rectangles.

## USING SVG `clipPath` ELEMENTS WITH GRID PATTERNS

Consider the clipped checkerboard pattern rendered in Figure 4.6.

**FIGURE 4.6**   A clipped checkerboard pattern.

The SVG document *checkerBoardCP1.svg* in Listing 4.8 uses the SVG `clipPath` element and the SVG `rect` element in order to render a checkerboard inside a diamond-like pattern.

**Listing 4.8**   checkerBoardCP1.svg

```
<?xml version="1.0" encoding="iso-8859-1"?>
<!DOCTYPE svg PUBLIC "-//W3C//DTD SVG 20001102//EN"
 "http://www.w3.org/TR/2000/CR-SVG-20001102/DTD/svg-20001102.dtd">

<svg width="800" height="500">
  <defs>
```

```
                <pattern id="checkerPattern"
                        width="80" height="80"
                        patternUnits="userSpaceOnUse">

           <rect fill="red"
                   stroke="white" stroke-dasharray="4 4 4 4"
                   stroke-width="8"
                   x="0"  y="0"  width="40" height="40"/>

           <rect fill="blue"
                   stroke="green" stroke-dasharray="2 2 2 2"
                   stroke-width="2"
                   x="40" y="0"  width="40" height="40"/>

           <rect fill="blue"
                   stroke="yellow" stroke-dasharray="1 1 1 1"
                   stroke-width="6"
                   x="0"  y="40" width="40" height="40"/>

           <rect fill="red"
                   stroke="blue" stroke-dasharray="4 4 4 4"
                   stroke-width="4"
                   x="40" y="40" width="40" height="40"/>
         </pattern>
         <clipPath id="clipPathDefinition"
                   clipPathUnits="userSpaceOnUse">
           <path d="m0,200 l100,-100 100,100 -100,100z"/>
         </clipPath>

         </defs>

    <g transform="translate(50,10)"
       clip-path="url(#clipPathDefinition)"
                   stroke="black" fill="none">

       <rect
          fill="url(#checkerPattern)"
          style="stroke:white"
          x="0" y="0" width="400" height="400"/>
    </g>
    </svg>
```

## Remarks

The SVG defs element in Listing 4.8 contains an SVG pattern element that has an id attribute with the value checkerPattern. This pattern consists of a 2x2 grid of squares whose alternating red/blue colors form a checkerboard pattern.

The SVG g element defines a rectangle with width 400 and a height of 400. Notice how this SVG element is further qualified with a clip-path attribute that references a clip path definition in the SVG defs element. The rectangle defined inside the SVG g element has a fill attribute that refers to the pattern checkerPattern defined in the SVG defs element by using the following syntax:

```
fill="url(#checkerPattern)"
```

If you double-click on this file, you will see a portion of a rectangular grid of blue rectangles with a red outer border that is restricted to the inside of the diamond pattern defined in the clip path.

## clipPath AND rect ELEMENTS WITH GRADIENT GRID PATTERNS

Consider the clipped gradient checkerboard pattern rendered in Figure 4.7.

**FIGURE 4.7** A clipped gradient checkerboard pattern.

The SVG document *checkerBoardGradientCP1.svg* in Listing 4.9 uses the SVG elements clipPath, rect, and linearGradient in order to render a gradient-shaded checkerboard inside a diamond-like pattern.

**Listing 4.9** checkerBoardGradientCP1.svg

```
<?xml version="1.0" encoding="iso-8859-1"?>
<!DOCTYPE svg PUBLIC "-//W3C//DTD SVG 20001102//EN"
 "http://www.w3.org/TR/2000/CR-SVG-20001102/DTD/svg-20001102.dtd">
<svg width="800" height="400">
```

```
<defs>
<linearGradient id="gradientDefinition"
    x1="0" y1="0" x2="40" y2="40"
    gradientUnits="userSpaceOnUse">
    <stop offset="0%"   style="stop-color:#FF0000"/>
    <stop offset="100%" style="stop-color:#000000"/>
</linearGradient>

<pattern id="checkerPattern"
        width="40" height="40"
        patternUnits="userSpaceOnUse">

    <rect fill="url(#gradientDefinition)"
        stroke="yellow" stroke-dasharray="4 4 4 4"
        stroke-width="8"
        x="0" y="0" width="40" height="40"/>

    <rect fill="white"
        stroke="black" stroke-dasharray="4 4 4 4"
        stroke-width="1"
        x="15" y="15" width="10" height="10"/>
</pattern>

<clipPath id="clipPathDefinition"
        clipPathUnits="userSpaceOnUse">
  <path d="m0,200 l100,-100 100,100 -100,100z"/>
</clipPath>

</defs>

<g transform="translate(50,0)"
  clip-path="url(#clipPathDefinition)"
        stroke="black" fill="none">
  <rect
    fill="url(#checkerPattern)"
    style="stroke:red"
    x="0" y="0" width="800" height="400"/>
</g>
</svg>
```

## Remarks

The SVG defs element in Listing 4.9 contains an SVG pattern element that has
a fill attribute that references an SVG pattern element whose id has the
value checkerPattern. This pattern consists of one square whose length is 40 with
a fill color that references a linear gradient whose id attribute value is
gradientDefinition.

The SVG g element defines a rectangle with a width of 800 and a height of 400. This rectangle contains a `fill` attribute that refers to the pattern `checkerPattern` defined in the SVG `defs` element by using the following syntax:

```
fill="url(#checkerPattern)"
```

If you double-click on this file, you will see a portion of a rectangular grid of rectangles (each of which is rendered with a diagonal linear gradient), where the visible portion is restricted to a diamond-shaped clip path.

## GENERATING SLANTED VENETIAN GRADIENT PATTERNS

Consider the slanted Venetian gradient checkerboard pattern rendered in Figure 4.8.

The SVG document *sVenetianMultiRect1.svg* in Listing 4.10 uses the SVG elements `linearGradient` and `rect` in order to render a slanted Venetian gradient rectangular pattern.

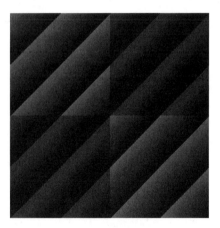

**FIGURE 4.8**  A slanted Venetian gradient pattern.

**Listing 4.10**   sVenetianMultiRect1.svg

```
<?xml version="1.0" encoding="iso-8859-1"?>
<!DOCTYPE svg PUBLIC "-//W3C//DTD SVG 20001102//EN"
 "http://www.w3.org/TR/2000/CR-SVG-20001102/DTD/svg-20001102.dtd">

<svg width="100%" height="100%">

  <defs>
```

```
<linearGradient id="redGradientDefinition"
    x1="0" y1="0" x2="40" y2="40"
    gradientUnits="userSpaceOnUse"
    spreadMethod="repeat">
    <stop offset="0%" style="stop-color:#FF0000"/>
    <stop offset="100%" style="stop-color:#000000"/>
</linearGradient>

<linearGradient id="blueGradientDefinition"
    x1="0" y1="0" x2="40" y2="40"
    gradientUnits="userSpaceOnUse"
    spreadMethod="repeat">
    <stop offset="20%" style="stop-color:#0000FF"/>
    <stop offset="80%" style="stop-color:#000000"/>
</linearGradient>
</defs>
<rect
    x="0" y="0" width="160" height="160"
 style="fill:url(#redGradientDefinition);stroke:none"/>

<rect
    x="160" y="0" width="160" height="160"
style="fill:url(#blueGradientDefinition);stroke:none"/>

<rect
    x="0" y="160" width="160" height="160"
 style="fill:url(#blueGradientDefinition);stroke:none"/>

<rect
    x="160" y="160" width="160" height="160"
style="fill:url(#redGradientDefinition);stroke:none"/>
</svg>
```

## Remarks

The SVG defs element in Listing 4.10 contains two linear gradients with id values of redGradientDefinition and blueGradientDefinition. One linear gradient defines a color gradient from red to black and the other defines a color gradient from blue to black. Both of these color gradients are diagonal because of the following line in their definition:

```
x1="0" y1="0" x2="40" y2="40"
```

The path for this gradient specifies a set of diagonal lines that move from the upper-left vertex (0,0) to the lower-right vertex (40,40), thereby creating a diagonal shading effect.

The four SVG `rect` elements define a 2x2 rectangular grid pattern consisting of four rectangles that have a side length of 160, whose color alternates between the two linear gradients by specifying,

```
style="fill:url(#blueGradientDefinition);stroke:none"/>
```

for the blue gradient rectangles and by specifying,

```
style="fill:url(#redGradientDefinition);stroke:none"/>
```

for the red gradient rectangles.

If you double-click on this file, you will see a rectangular grid of rectangles that are rendered with slanted linear gradients.


## KEY CONSTRUCTS

An SVG `pattern` can be defined with the following SVG snippet:

```
<defs>
 <pattern id="checkerPattern"
          width-"80" height-"80"
          patternUnits="userSpaceOnUse">

    <!-- specify element definitions -->

 </pattern>
</defs>
```

An SVG `clipPath` element can be defined with the following SVG snippet:

```
<defs>
 <clipPath id="clipPathDefinition"
           clipPathUnits="userSpaceOnUse">
   <path d="m0,200 l100,-100 100,100 -100,100z"/>
 </clipPath>
</defs>

<!-- other code fragments -->
<g transform="translate(50,50)"
   clip-path="url(#clipPathDefinition)"
             stroke="black" fill="none">

   <!-- specify element definitions -->
</g>
```

## CD-ROM LIBRARY

*ON THE CD*    The folder for this chapter on the CD-ROM contains the following SVG documents that are required for rendering the graphics images in this chapter:

> *rectangularGrid1.svg*
>
> *patternDef1.svg*
>
> *checkerBoard1.svg*
>
> *checkerBoard3D1.svg*
>
> *checkerBoardGradient1.svg*
>
> *checkerBoardMultiGradient1.svg*
>
> *clipPathDef1.svg*
>
> *checkerBoardCP1.svg*
>
> *checkerBoardGradientCP1.svg*
>
> *sVenetianMultiRect1.svg*

## SUMMARY

This chapter introduced a more hierarchical type of structure in SVG documents (which will be developed extensively in Chapter 6) by means of the SVG `pattern` elements and the SVG `clipPath` element in order to generate the following types of graphics images:

- checkerboard patterns
- gradient checkerboard patterns
- multi-gradient checkerboard patterns
- Venetian gradient patterns

# 5 Quadratic and Cubic Bezier Curves

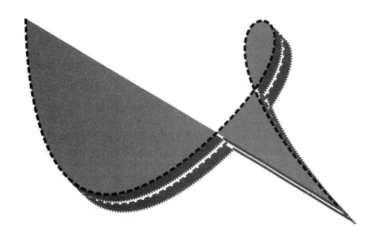

## OVERVIEW

This chapter demonstrates how to use the SVG path element in order to specify quadratic Bezier curves and cubic Bezier curves. This SVG element provides an extremely powerful mechanism for defining Bezier curves, which can be easily exploited to produce some very exotic graphics images. This chapter will show you how to generate some interesting combinations of Bezier curves, checkerboard patterns, and various types of gradient shading; it will provide ideas and techniques that you can use as a starting point for your own experimentation.

As a rule, it's better to avoid hard-coded values whenever possible in SVG documents because such values tend to make it more difficult to create other SVG documents leverage and generalize those features. While you certainly create beautiful SVG-based graphics with thousands of hard-coded values, imagine yourself trying to enhance this type of code after a six-month hiatus. (Just trying to remember what the code *does* will probably be a task unto itself.) The exception to this rule is when you are experimenting with new geometric objects; use as many different combinations of hard-coded values as you can in order to understand how those objects react to subtle (as well as not-so-subtle) changes in attribute values. In Chapters 13 and 14 you will learn how to use ECMAScript in order to programmatically change the values of attributes using a variety of techniques. As was the case in previous chapters, all the code and images for this chapter can be found on the companion CD-ROM in the Chapter 5 folder.

ON THE CD

## WHAT ARE BEZIER CURVES?

Bezier curves are named after Pierre Bézier (recently deceased), who invented them during the 1970s. Since Bezier curves can represent many non-linear shapes, they can be found in interesting applications, including PostScript for the representation of fonts. Search the Web for Bezier and you will find many Web pages with interesting demonstrations (some of which also require additional plug-ins). You'll also find computer programs written in C and Java, some of which are interactive, that demonstrate Bezier curves.

Cubic Bezier curves have two end points and two control points, whereas quadratic Bezier curves have two end points and a single control point. The x-coordinate and y-coordinate of a cubic Bezier curve can be represented as a parameterized cubic equation whose coefficients are derived from the control points and the end points. The beauty of SVG is that it allows you to define both quadratic and cubic Bezier curves via the SVG path element without having to delve into the mathematical underpinnings of Bezier curves. If you're interested in learning the specific details, you can browse the Web, where you'll find books and plenty of articles that cover this topic.

## RENDERING A QUADRATIC BEZIER CURVE

Consider the quadratic Bezier curve rendered in Figure 5.1.

The SVG document *quadraticBezier1.svg* in Listing 5.1 demonstrates how to use the SVG path element in order to render a quadratic Bezier curve.

**FIGURE 5.1**  A quadratic Bezier curve.

**Listing 5.1**   quadraticBezier1.svg

```
<?xml version="1.0" encoding="iso-8859-1"?>
<!DOCTYPE svg PUBLIC "-//W3C//DTD SVG 20001102//EN"
 "http://www.w3.org/TR/2000/CR-SVG-20001102/DTD/svg-20001102.dtd">

<svg width="800" height="400">

<g transform="translate(50,50)">
    <path d="m20,20 Q100,0 200,200 T340,240 z"
     fill="black"
     stroke-dasharray="2 2 2 2"
     style="stroke:blue;stroke-width:4;"/>

    <path d="m0,0 Q100,0 200,200 T300,200 z"
     fill="red"
     stroke-dasharray="2 2 2 2"
     style="stroke:blue;stroke-width:4;"/>
</g>
</svg>
```

### Remarks

The SVG code in Listing 5.1 contains an SVG g element that translates the origin from the point (0,0) to the point (50,50). Next, the SVG path element specifies a red quadratic Bezier curve whose blue outline has a width of four. The presence of a term such as "Q100,0 " or "q100,0" lets you know that you're dealing with a quadratic Bezier curve. Let's take a look at the code that specifies the Bezier curve:

```
<path d="m0,0 Q100,0 200,200 T300,200 z"
```

The starting point of the second Bezier curve is the origin because of the term m0,0. Next, the fragment Q100,0 200,200 specifies the control point at the point (100,0), and it draws a quadratic Bezier curve from the current point—which is the origin—to the point (200,200) using the point (100,0) as the control point. Next, the term T300,200 draws a quadratic Bezier curve from the point (200,200) to the point (300,200). Note that the control point for the T term is the reflection of the previous control point (100,0) relative to the point (200,200), which is the point (400,300). Finally, the term z connects the point (300,200) to the initial point (0,0) with a line segment.

Note that the uppercase letters M, Q, and T in a quadratic Bezier curve refer to absolute points whereas the lowercase letters m, q, and t refer to relative points.

The first Bezier curve shows how you can create interesting "asymmetric" shadow effects by manipulating the control points as demonstrated in the code.

## GRADIENT CHECKERBOARDS AND MULTI-QUADRATIC BEZIER CLIP PATHS

Consider the gradient checkerboard pattern rendered in Figure 5.2.

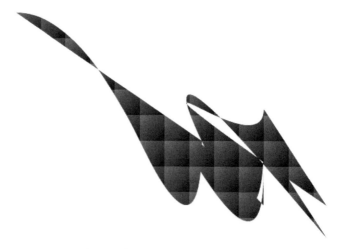

**FIGURE 5.2**  A multi-quadratic Bezier-bound gradient checkerboard pattern.

The SVG document *checkerBoardGradientMQBCP1.svg* in Listing 5.2 demonstrates how to use the SVG path element in order to generate a gradient checkerboard pattern bound by a multi-quadratic Bezier curve.

**Listing 5.2**    checkerBoardGradientMQBCP1.svg

```
<?xml version="1.0" encoding="iso-8859-1"?>
<!DOCTYPE svg PUBLIC "-//W3C//DTD SVG 20001102//EN"
 "http://www.w3.org/TR/2000/CR-SVG-20001102/DTD/svg-20001102.dtd">
<svg width="800" height="400">
  <defs>
  <linearGradient id="gradientDefinition"
     x1="0" y1="0" x2="40" y2="40"
     gradientUnits="userSpaceOnUse">
     <stop offset="0%"   style="stop-color:#FF0000"/>
     <stop offset="100%" style="stop-color:#000000"/>
  </linearGradient>

  <pattern id="checkerPattern"
           width="40" height="40"
           patternUnits="userSpaceOnUse">

     <rect fill="url(#gradientDefinition)"
           style="stroke:white;stroke-width:4;"
           stroke-dasharray="6 6 6 6"
           x="0" y="0" width="36" height="36"/>
  </pattern>

  <clipPath id="clipPathDefinition"
            clipPathUnits="userSpaceOnUse">
    <path d="m0,0     Q100,0    200,200 T300,200
             m100,100 Q200,100 300,250 T400,250
             m100,100 Q200,0   300,200 T400,200
             m100,100 Q200,100 300,150 T400,150"
          style="fill:red;stroke:white;stroke-width:4;"/>
  </clipPath>
  </defs>

  <g transform="translate(50,50)"
     clip-path="url(#clipPathDefinition)"
        stroke="black" fill="none">
   <rect
       fill="url(#checkerPattern)"
       x="0" y="0" width="800" height="400"/>
  </g>
</svg>
```

## Remarks

The SVG code in Listing 5.2 contains an SVG defs element that defines a checker-board pattern using diagonal linear grading shading that ranges from red to black.

The SVG `defs` element also defines a clip path that consists of four connected quadratic Bezier curves as given below:

```
<path d="m0,0     Q100,0   200,200 T300,200
          m100,100 Q200,100 300,250 T400,250
          m100,100 Q200,0   300,200 T400,200
          m100,100 Q200,100 300,150 T400,150"
```

The first quadratic Bezier curve is the same as the quadratic Bezier curve defined in Listing 5.1, and the other three Bezier curves are essentially variations of the first Bezier curve. The resultant graphics image is reminiscent of a dragon.

The actual rendering takes place in the SVG `g` element, which first translates the origin from the point (0,0) to the point (50,50). Notice how the SVG `g` element also contains the following line that specifies the clip path that is defined in the SVG `defs` element:

```
clip-path="url(#clipPathDefinition)"
          stroke="black" fill="none">
```

The SVG code contains an SVG `rect` element that creates a "wiggly" effect because the `width` and `height` attributes are slightly smaller than the corresponding attributes specified in the pattern element in conjunction with the `stroke-dasharray` attribute, as shown below:

```
<rect fill="url(#gradientDefinition)"
      style="stroke:white;stroke-width:4;"
      stroke-dasharray="6 6 6 6"
      x="0" y="0" width="36" height="36"/>
```

## VENETIAN CHECKERBOARDS AND QUADRATIC BEZIER CLIP PATHS

Consider the gradient checkerboard pattern rendered in Figure 5.3.

The SVG document *vVenetianGradientPatternQBCP1.svg* in Listing 5.3 demonstrates how to use the SVG `path` element in order to generate a Venetian gradient checkerboard pattern bound by a quadratic Bezier curve.

**FIGURE 5.3**  A Venetian quadratic Bezier-bound gradient checkerboard pattern.

**Listing 5.3**  vVenetianGradientPatternQBCP1.svg

```
<?xml version="1.0" encoding="iso-8859-1"?>
<!DOCTYPE svg PUBLIC "-//W3C//DTD SVG 20001102//EN"
 "http://www.w3.org/TR/2000/CR-SVG-20001102/DTD/svg-20001102.dtd">

 <svg width="100%" height="100%">
 <defs>
  <pattern id="multiPattern"
         width="50" height="50"
         patternUnits="userSpaceOnUse">

   <linearGradient id="repeatedGradientDefinition"
     x1="0" y1="0" x2="50" y2="0"
       gradientUnits="userSpaceOnUse"
       spreadMethod="repeat">
     <stop offset="0%"   style="stop-color:#FF0000"/>
     <stop offset="100%" style="stop-color:#000000"/>
   </linearGradient>

   <rect
     style="fill:url(#repeatedGradientDefinition)"
     x="0" y="0" width="50" height="50"/>
   </pattern>

   <clipPath id="clipPathDefinition"
         clipPathUnits="userSpaceOnUse">
```

```
<path d="m0,0 Q100,0 200,200 T300,200"
      style="fill:red;stroke:blue;stroke-width:4;"/>

<path d="m0,0 150,50 150,-50"/>

<rect   x="30"      y="50"
        width="40" height="80"/>

<circle cx="100" cy="50"  r="10"/>
<circle cx="150" cy="90"  r="40"/>
<circle cx="200" cy="125" r="10"/>
<ellipse cx="250" cy="150" rx="40" ry="20"/>
 </clipPath>
</defs>

<g transform="translate(50,50)"
 clip-path="url(#clipPathDefinition)"
 stroke="black" fill="none">

<rect
    style="fill:url(#multiPattern)"
    x="0" y="0" width="400" height="400"/>
</g>
</svg>
```

## Remarks

The SVG code in Listing 5.3 contains the same quadratic Bezier curve as Listing 5.1, and it uses this Bezier curve as a clip path while rendering a gradient checkerboard pattern consisting of rectangles. These rectangles are rendered with vertical linear gradient shading that varies linearly from red to black in order to create a "Venetian shading" effect. Now look at the SVG defs element, which starts with the definition of a checkerboard pattern whose id attribute has the value checkerPattern, followed by an SVG clipPath element whose id attribute equals clipPathDefinition.

The actual rendering takes place in the SVG g element, which first translates the origin from the point (0,0) to the point (50,50). Notice how the SVG g element also contains the following line that specifies the clip path that is defined in the SVG defs element:

```
clip-path="url(#clipPathDefinition)"
          stroke="black" fill="none">
```

Now that the "core" definition and code is in place, you can add various SVG elements as you see fit; in this example, we have an SVG rect element, three SVG circle elements, and one SVG ellipse element, all of which have the same fill attribute applied to them.

# RENDERING CUBIC BEZIER CURVES

Consider the cubic Bezier curves rendered in Figure 5.4.

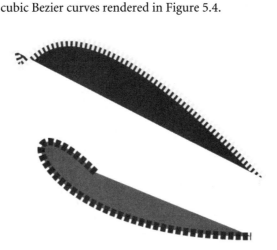

**FIGURE 5.4**    A pair of cubic Bezier curves.

The SVG document *cBezier1.svg* in Listing 5.4 demonstrates how to use the SVG path element in order to render a pair of cubic Bezier curves.

## Listing 5.4    cBezier1.svg

```
<?xml version="1.0" encoding="iso-8859-1"?>
<!DOCTYPE svg PUBLIC "-//W3C//DTD SVG 20001102//EN"
 "http://www.w3.org/TR/2000/CR-SVG-20001102/DTD/svg-
20001102.dtd">

<svg width="100%" height="100%">
  <g transform="translate(20,40)">
  <path
    d="M0,0 C20,100 20,-200 400,200"
    fill="#880088"
    stroke-dasharray="4 4 4 4"
    style="stroke:yellow;stroke-width:16;"/>
  </g>

  <g transform="translate(0,80)">
  <path
    d="M150,150 C0,0 20,250 400,250"
```

```
        stroke-dasharray="8 4 8 4"
        fill="red"
        style="stroke:blue;stroke-width:12;"/>
   </g>
</svg>
```

## Remarks

The two SVG `path` element contain the terms `C20,100` and `C0,0`, respectively, which signals the presence of cubic Bezier curves. Let's take a look at the code that specifies the first cubic Bezier curve:

```
d="M0,0 C20,100 20,-200 400,200"
```

The start point of the Bezier curve is the point (0,0) because of the term `M0,0`, and the terminal point of the Bezier curve is the point (400,200) which is listed at the end of the code fragment. The fragment `C20,100  20,250` specifies two control points (20,100) and (20,250) that are used for drawing the start and end of the Bezier curve, respectively. Remember the rule in SVG: uppercase letters refer to absolute points whereas lowercase letters refer to relative points.

The SVG attributes `fill`, `stroke-dasharray`, `stroke`, and `stroke-width`—experiment with these attributes to create your own visual effects. Remember that SVG allows you to use hexadecimal-based values for the `fill` attribute (in this example, `fill` is #880088); consequently, you have a tremendous number of subtle color shades at your disposal.

## LINEAR GRADIENT SHADING AND CUBIC BEZIER CURVES

Consider the cubic Bezier curves rendered in Figure 5.5.

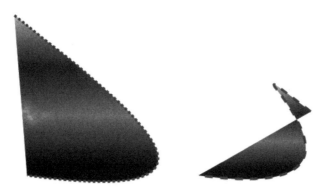

**FIGURE 5.5**  Linear gradient shading and cubic Bezier curves.

The SVG document *cBezier2LG4Pipe1.svg* in Listing 5.5 demonstrates how to use the SVG path element in order to combine linear gradient shading with a pair of cubic Bezier curves.

### Listing 5.5   cBezier2LG4Pipe1.svg

```
<?xml version="1.0" encoding="iso-8859-1"?>
<!DOCTYPE svg PUBLIC "-//W3C//DTD SVG 20001102//EN"
 "http://www.w3.org/TR/2000/CR-SVG-20001102/DTD/svg-
20001102.dtd">

<svg width="100%" height="100%">

<defs>
   <linearGradient id="gradientDefinition1"
                   gradientTransform="rotate(90)">
      <stop offset="0%"    stop-color="#C0C040"/>
      <stop offset="30%"   stop-color="#303000"/>
      <stop offset="60%"   stop-color="#FF0F0F"/>
      <stop offset="90%"   stop-color="#101000"/>
   </linearGradient>
</defs>

<g transform="translate(20,20)">
<path
   d="M0,0 C200,150 400,300 20,250"

   stroke-dasharray="4 4 4 4"
   fill="url(#gradientDefinition1)"
   style="stroke:blue;stroke-width:4;"/>
</g>

<g transform="translate(20,200)">
<path
   d="M200,150 C0,0 400,300 20,250"
   stroke-dasharray="12 12 12 12"
   fill="url(#gradientDefinition1)"
   style="stroke:blue;stroke-width:4;"/>
</g>

</svg>
```

### Remarks

The SVG code in Listing 5.5 contains the two cubic Bezier curves given below:

```
d="M0,0 C200,150 400,300 20,250"
d="M200,150 C0,0 400,300 20,250"
```

By now you understand the purpose of each component of a cubic Bezier curve. The visual effect in this example is achieved by setting the fill attribute to the value gradientDefinition1, which is a linear gradient that is defined in the SVG defs element. Notice how different values for the stroke-dasharray can affect the appearance of an SVG element: the first Bezier curve has a dimpled effect whereas the second Bezier curve has a more "standard" dotted border. You can create a Venetian shading effect by means of the following specification in the SVG defs element:

```
<defs>
 <linearGradient id="gradientDefinition"
      x1="10" y1="10" x2="100" y2="10"
      gradientUnits="userSpaceOnUse"
      spreadMethod="repeat">
      <stop offset="20%" style="stop-color:#FF0000"/>
      <stop offset="80%" style="stop-color:#000000"/>
  </linearGradient>
</defs>
```

Notice that the spreadMethod attribute has the value repeat; this results in a repetition of the linear gradient, which in turn creates a Venetian shading effect. Try removing this attribute and see how the modified code creates a much different effect. In Chapter 14 you'll learn techniques that will enable you to create much more sophisticated patterns.

## DOUBLE CUBIC BEZIER CURVES

Consider the double cubic Bezier curves rendered in Figure 5.6.

**FIGURE 5.6** A double cubic Bezier curve.

The SVG document *doubleCubicBezier1.svg* in Listing 5.6 demonstrates how to render a double cubic Bezier curve.

**Listing 5.6**    doubleCubicBezier1.svg

```
<?xml version="1.0" encoding="iso-8859-1"?>
<!DOCTYPE svg PUBLIC "-//W3C//DTD SVG 20001102//EN"
"http://www.w3.org/TR/2000/CR-SVG-20001102/DTD/svg-20001102.dtd">

<svg width="100%" height="100%">

<g transform="translate(60,-10)">
  <path
    d="M50,50    C20,100 20,250 400,250
       M100,150 C80,-80 80,150 300,100"
    stroke-dasharray="8 1 8 4"
    fill="blue"
    style="stroke:#880000;stroke-width:8;"/>
  </g>

<g transform="translate(20,-20)">
  <path
    d="M50,50    C20,100 20,250 400,200
       M100,150 C80,-80 80,150 300,150"
    stroke-dasharray="8 1 8 4"
    fill="444444"
    style="stroke:#000044;stroke-width:4;"/>
</g>

<g transform="translate(0,0)">
  <path
    d="M50,50    C20,100 20,250 400,300
       M100,150 C80,-80 80,150 300,350"
    stroke-dasharray="8 1 8 4"
    fill="#880088"
    style="stroke:red;stroke-width:8;"/>
  </g>
</svg>
```

## Remarks

The code in Listing 5.6 contains three SVG path  elements, each of which specifies two cubic Bezier curves, as illustrated below:

```
d="m50,50   C20,100 20,250 400,300
  M100,150 C80,-80 80,150 400,400"
```

Although you've already seen examples that combine multiple Bezier curves, the interesting feature of this particular example is the color pattern of the graphics image. You probably expected to see two overlapping cubic Bezier curves; instead, the overlapping portion of the Bezier curves is white! This counter-intuitive color pattern creates the impression of two quasi orthogonal cubic Bezier curves.

## DOUBLE REFLECTED CUBIC BEZIER CURVES

Consider the double reflected cubic Bezier curves rendered in Figure 5.7.

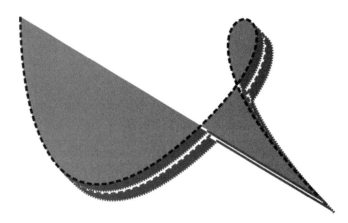

**FIGURE 5.7**   A double cubic Bezier curve.

The SVG document *doubleReflectedCubicBezier1.svg* in Listing 5.7 demonstrates how to render a double reflected cubic Bezier curve.

**Listing 5.7**   doubleReflectedCubicBezier1.svg

```
<?xml version="1.0" encoding="iso-8859-1"?>
<!DOCTYPE svg PUBLIC "-//W3C//DTD SVG 20001102//EN"
 "http://www.w3.org/TR/2000/CR-SVG-20001102/DTD/svg-20001102.dtd">

<svg width="100%" height="100%">
<g transform="translate(45,45)">
<path
  d="m20,20 C20,50 20,450 300,200 s-150,-250 200,100"
  fill="blue"
```

```
      stroke-dasharray="2 2 2 2"
      style="stroke:#880088;stroke-width:4;"/>
  </g>

  <g transform="translate(35,35)">
  <path
      d="m20,20 C20,50 20,450 300,200 s-150,-250 200,100"
      fill="white"
      stroke-dasharray="8 4 8 4"
      style="stroke:#880088;stroke-width:4;"/>
  </g>

  <g transform="translate(30,30)">
  <path
      d="m20,20 C20,50 20,450 300,200 s-150,-250 200,100"
      fill="blue"
      stroke-dasharray="2 2 2 2"
      style="stroke:#880088;stroke-width:4;"/>
  </g>

  <g transform="translate(20,20)">
  <path
      d="m20,20 C20,50 20,450 300,200 s-150,-250 200,100"
      fill="red"
      stroke-dasharray="8 4 8 4"
      style="stroke:black;stroke-width:4;"/>
  </g>
  </svg>
```

## Remarks

The code in Listing 5.7 contains four cubic Bezier curves that create a reflection based on the s command such as the one listed below:

```
s-150,-350 200,200"
```

The s command has two control points. The first control point is (-150,-350), and the second control point is determined as follows:

1. determine the current point, which is (400,200)
2. determine the second control point of the "C" command: (20,450)
3. reflect the point (20,450) through the point (400,200)

As you can see, the reflected cubic Bezier curve in this example produces an interesting graphics image; however, understanding how to specify such a curve does requires more effort than the previous examples of Bezier curves.

## CUBIC QUADRATIC BEZIER CURVES

Consider the cubic quadratic Bezier curves rendered in Figure 5.8.

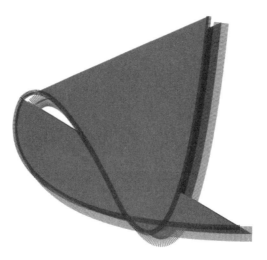

**FIGURE 5.8**   A cubic quadratic Bezier curve.

The SVG document *cubicQuadraticBezier1.svg* in Listing 5.8 demonstrates how to render a cubic quadratic Bezier curve.

### Listing 5.8   cubicQuadraticBezier1.svg

```
<?xml version="1.0" encoding="iso-8859-1"?>
<!DOCTYPE svg PUBLIC "-//W3C//DTD SVG 20001102//EN"
 "http://www.w3.org/TR/2000/CR-SVG-20001102/DTD/svg-
20001102.dtd">

<svg width="100%" height="100%">
<g transform="translate(20,110)">
<path
  d="m50,50 C20,100 20,250 400,250
     M50,50 Q100,0 200,200 T350,-80"
  fill="blue"
  stroke-dasharray="1 1 1 1"
  style="stroke:red;stroke-width:24;"/>
</g>

<g transform="translate(0,100)">
```

```
<path
  d="m50,50 C20,100 20,250 400,250
     M50,50 Q100,0 200,200 T350,-80"
  fill="red"
  stroke-dasharray="1 1 1 1"
  style="stroke:blue;stroke-width:8;"/>
</g>
</svg>
```

## Remarks

The code in Listing 5.8 defines two cubic Bezier curves, each of which is immediately followed by a quadratic Bezier curve by means of the following type of code:

```
d="m50,50 C20,100 20,250 400,250
   M50,50 Q100,0 200,200 T350,-80"
```

You've already seen examples of both of the Bezier curves in the preceding code fragment; this example demonstrates how to combine a cubic Bezier curve and a quadratic Bezier curve in order to create a sail-like image. Notice the "buzzed" effect that is produced by the following attribute values:

```
stroke-dasharray="1 1 1 1"
style="stroke:red;stroke-width:24;"/>
```

The key idea involves a large value for the `stroke-width` attribute combined with small integer values in the `stroke-dasharray` attribute. The juxtaposition of finely-grained line segments contrasts nicely with the curvilinear nature of Bezier curves.

## KEY CONSTRUCTS

An SVG *quadratic Bezier curve* can be defined with the following SVG snippet:

```
<g transform="translate(50,50)">
  <path d="m0,0 Q100,0 200,200 T300,200 z"
    fill="red"
    style="stroke:blue;stroke-width:4;"/>
</g>
```

An SVG *cubic Bezier curve* can be defined with the following SVG snippet:

```
<g transform="translate(20,20)">
<path
```

```
        d="M0,0 C20,100 20,250 400,300"
        fill="red"
        style="stroke:blue;stroke-width:4;"/>
</g>
```

An SVG *Bezier clip path* can be defined with the following SVG snippet:

```
<defs>
 <clipPath id="clipPathDefinition"
           clipPathUnits="userSpaceOnUse">
   <path d="m0,0 Q100,0 200,200 T300,200"
         style="fill:red;stroke:blue;stroke-width:4;"/>
 </clipPath>
</defs>

<g transform="translate(50,50)"
   clip-path="url(#clipPathDefinition)"
   stroke="black" fill="none">

   <!-- specify geometric elements here -->
</g>
```

# CD-ROM LIBRARY

ON THE CD The folder for this chapter on the CD-ROM contains the following SVG documents that are required for rendering the graphics images in this chapter:

*quadraticBezier1.svg*

*checkerBoardGradientQBCP1.svg*

*vVenetianGradientPatternQBCP1.svg*

*cBezier1.svg*

*cBezier2LG4Pipe1.svg*

*doubleCubicBezier1.svg*

*doubleReflectedCubicBezier1.svg*

*cubicQuadraticBezier1.svg*

*cBezierVenetianGradient2.svg*

*checkerBoardGradientMQBCP1.svg*

*checkerBoardQBCP1.svg*

## SUMMARY

This chapter focused on how you can create very pleasing curvilinear graphics images that are based on quadratic Bezier curves and cubic Bezier curves. In particular, you saw examples of the following:

- the SVG `path` element for generating quadratic Bezier curves
- the SVG `path` element for generating cubic Bezier curves
- the SVG `path` element for generating multiple Bezier curves

# 6 ∷ SVG Transformations

## OVERVIEW

This chapter demonstrates how to use the SVG functions `translate`, `scale`, `rotate`, and `skew` that can be specified as part of the SVG `transform` element. Although you have already seen the SVG `translate` function, this chapter presents a consolidated location and description of these functions; you'll see how to use them in conjunction with rectangles and ellipses in order to perform manipulations on a variety of graphics images.

These SVG functions provide sophisticated geometric manipulations that can greatly enhance the visual appeal of your graphics images. For instance, you can easily shift the contents of an SVG g element anywhere in the plane by means of the `translate` function. This functionality makes for cleaner SVG code because you can avoid hard-coded values in SVG elements. For example, you can define a rectangle whose upper-left vertex is the origin (0,0), and then use the `translate` function in order to render multiple copies of that rectangle on the screen. This functionality is extremely useful when you need to render business charts that can be decomposed into many logical components.

The SVG `scale` function makes it trivial to resize the graphics image rendered inside an SVG g element. While this functionality is much more difficult to achieve in other programming languages, SVG makes it available by means of a very simple code fragment. You can also combine the SVG `translate` and `scale` functions, which enable you to render many scaled copies of a graphics image. Keep in mind that there is no practical limit to the complexity of the graphics image defined in an SVG g element; consequently, you can easily create a visually rich collage based on a single graphics image. The SVG `rotate` function allows you to rotate a graphics image that is defined in an SVG g element by means of a very simple code fragment.

There are two SVG skew functions, `skewX` and `skewY` that allow you to "tilt" the contents of an SVG g element. They can be specified by a very simple code fragment.

The SVG `matrix` function is probably the most sophisticated of the SVG functions. This function allows you to perform a linear transformation on the contents of an SVG g element, and it can be specified by a very simple code fragment. Unless you happen to have a solid understanding of the mathematics of linear transformations, it's probably easier to find an equivalent set of transformations based on the other SVG functions.

When you've finished this chapter, you'll have a glimpse into the tremendous number of ways to combine SVG functions. They can also be easily combined with other SVG elements, such as patterns and color gradients, in order to create graphics images that are impossible to achieve with a comparable amount of effort in traditional programming languages. All code and images for this chapter can be found on the companion CD-ROM in the Chapter 6 folder.

ON THE CD

## USING THE SVG `translate` FUNCTION

Consider the rectangles rendered in Figure 6.1.

**FIGURE 6.1**    Drawing rectangles with the SVG `translate` function.

The SVG document *translateRect1.svg* in Listing 6.1 demonstrates how to use the SVG `translate` function in order to shift a set of rectangles in the plane.

### Listing 6.1    translateRect1.svg

```
<?xml version="1.0" encoding="iso-8859-1"?>
<!DOCTYPE svg PUBLIC "-//W3C//DTD SVG 20001102//EN"
 "http://www.w3.org/TR/2000/CR-SVG-20001102/DTD/svg-20001102.dtd">

<svg width="100%" height="100%">

<g transform="translate(0,0)">
<rect
    x="0" y="0" width="50" height="50"
    style="fill:red;stroke:yellow"/>
</g>

<g transform="translate(50,50)">
<rect
    x="0" y="0" width="50" height="50"
    style="fill:green;stroke:red"/>
</g>

<g transform="translate(100,100)">
<rect
    x="0" y="0" width="50" height="50"
    style="fill:blue;stroke:green"/>
</g>
</svg>
```

### Remarks

The SVG code in Listing 6.1 renders three rectangles (which also happen to be squares) with a `fill` color of red, green, and blue whose perimeter is yellow, red, and green, respectively. The upper-left vertex, width, and height values for all three rectangles are specified in the following line:

```
x="0" y="0" width="50" height="50"
```

The rectangles do not overlap because they are shifted downward and to the right by means of the following three SVG g elements:

```
<g transform="translate(0,0)">
<g transform="translate(50,50)">
<g transform="translate(100,100)">
```

Before rendering each rectangle, the enclosing SVG g element performs a simple shift of the origin. Specifically, the first SVG transform attribute does not perform any translation of the origin because the specified "target" point is the same as the origin itself. The second SVG transform attribute translates the origin from the point (0,0) to the point (50,50), while the third SVG transform attribute translates the origin from the point (0,0) to the point (100,100).

Although the SVG transform attribute is very simple, it can be very useful for shifting graphics images of arbitrary complexity from the default origin (0,0) to any other point. This feature is extremely useful when rendering business charts that can be rendered by "components" that consist of logically related graphics images. For example, the "tic" marks and labels and line segment for the horizontal axis can be grouped together in one component that is enclosed in an SVG g element that has its own translation of the origin, while the corresponding component for the vertical axis can be contained in a separate SVG g element with a different translation of the origin.

## USING THE SVG rotate FUNCTION WITH CHECKERBOARDS

Consider the checkerboard pattern rendered in Figure 6.2.

**FIGURE 6.2** Rotated checkerboard with the SVG rotate function.

The SVG document *rotatedCheckerBoard1.svg* in Listing 6.2 demonstrates how to use the SVG rotate function in order to rotate a checkerboard pattern.

**Listing 6.2** rotatedCheckerBoard1.svg

```
<?xml version="1.0" encoding="iso-8859-1"?>
<!DOCTYPE svg PUBLIC "-//W3C//DTD SVG 20001102//EN"
 "http://www.w3.org/TR/2000/CR-SVG-20001102/DTD/svg-20001102.dtd">

<svg width="800" height="500">
  <defs>
  <pattern id="checkerPattern"
           width="80" height="80"
           patternUnits="userSpaceOnUse">

    <rect fill="red"
          x="0"  y="0"  width="40" height="40"/>

    <rect fill="blue"
          x="40" y="0"  width="40" height="40"/>

    <rect fill="blue"
          x="0"  y="40" width="40" height="40"/>

    <rect fill="red"
          x="40" y="40" width="40" height="40"/>
  </pattern>
  </defs>

<g transform="translate(300,50)">
  <g transform="rotate(30)">
    <rect
       fill="url(#checkerPattern)"
       style="stroke:white"
       x="0" y="0" width="320" height="320"/>
  </g>
</g>
</svg>
```

## Remarks

The SVG defs element in Listing 6.2 contains an SVG pattern element that has an id attribute with the value checkerPattern. This pattern consists of an outer square whose length is 80. The inside of the pattern consists of a 2x2 grid of squares whose colors form a checkerboard pattern.

The SVG g element defines a rectangle with width 400 and height 400. This rectangle refers to the pattern checkerPattern defined in the SVG defs element by using the following syntax:

```
fill="url(#checkerPattern)"
```

The rotation of the checkerboard pattern is specified in the following SVG fragment:

```
<g transform="translate(300,50)">
 <g transform="rotate(30)">
   <rect
       fill="url(#checkerPattern)"
       style="stroke:white"
       x="0" y="0" width="320" height="320"/>
 </g>
</g>
```

Notice the pair of nested SVG g elements: the outer SVG g element performs a translation of the origin from the point (0,0) to the point (300,50). The inner SVG g element performs a clockwise (*not* counterclockwise) rotation of 30° of the following rectangle:

```
<rect
    fill="url(#checkerPattern)"
    style="stroke:white"
    x="0" y="0" width="320" height="320"/>
```

The rectangle has a fill value that references an SVG pattern element defined in the SVG defs element in Listing 6.2. As you can see, a lot is happening in a very small amount of code!

## USING THE SVG scale FUNCTION WITH CHECKERBOARDS

Consider the scaled checkerboard pattern rendered in Figure 6.3.

**FIGURE 6.3**   A scaled checkerboard
with the SVG scale function.

The SVG document *scaledCheckerBoard1.svg* in Listing 6.3 demonstrates how to use the SVG scale function in order to scale a checkerboard pattern.

**Listing 6.3**   scaledCheckerBoard1.svg

```
<?xml version="1.0" encoding="iso-8859-1"?>
<!DOCTYPE svg PUBLIC "-//W3C//DTD SVG 20001102//EN"
 "http://www.w3.org/TR/2000/CR-SVG-20001102/DTD/svg-20001102.dtd">

<svg width="800" height="500">
  <defs>
  <pattern id="checkerPattern"
           width="80" height="80"
           patternUnits="userSpaceOnUse">

     <rect fill="red"
           x="0"  y="0"  width="40" height="40"/>
     <rect fill="blue"
           x="40" y="0"  width="40" height="40"/>

     <rect fill="blue"
           x="0"  y="40" width="40" height="40"/>

     <rect fill="red"
           x="40" y="40" width="40" height="40"/>
  </pattern>
  </defs>

<g transform="translate(50,50)">
  <g transform="scale(.5)">
    <rect
       fill="url(#checkerPattern)"
       style="stroke:white"
       x="0" y="0" width="320" height="320"/>
  </g>
</g>
</svg>
```

## Remarks

The SVG defs element in Listing 6.3 contains an SVG pattern element that has an id attribute with the value checkerPattern. This pattern consists of an outer square whose length is 80. The inside of the pattern consists of a 2x2 grid of squares whose colors form a checkerboard pattern.

The SVG g element defines a rectangle with a width of 400 and a height of 400. This rectangle refers to the pattern checkerPattern defined in the SVG defs element by using the following syntax:

```
fill="url(#checkerPattern)"
```

The scaling performed on the checkerboard pattern is specified in the following SVG fragment:

```
<g transform="translate(50,50)">
  <g transform="scale(.5)">
    <rect
        fill="url(#checkerPattern)"
        style="stroke:white"
        x="0" y="0" width="320" height="320"/>
  </g>
</g>
```

Notice the pair of nested SVG g elements: the outer SVG g element performs a translation of the origin from the point (0,0) to the point (50,50). The inner SVG g element performs a clockwise (*not* counterclockwise) rotation of 30° of the following rectangle:

```
<rect
    fill="url(#checkerPattern)"
    style="stroke:white"
    x="0" y="0" width="320" height="320"/>
```

The rectangle has a `fill` value that references an SVG `pattern` element defined in the SVG `defs` element in Listing 6.3.

Incidentally, you can specify two numbers in the SVG `scale` function: the first number is used for scaling in the horizontal direction and the second number is used for scaling in the vertical direction. For example, the following snippet scales by a factor of 2 in the horizontal direction and by a factor of .5 in the vertical direction:

```
<g transform="scale(2,.5)">
```

If you specify only the first number, then the second number defaults to the value of the first number. For example, the following snippet,

```
<g transform="scale(3)">
```

is equivalent to:

```
<g transform="scale(3,3)">
```

## USING MULTIPLE SVG scale ELEMENTS

Consider the checkerboard pattern rendered in Figure 6.4.

**FIGURE 6.4**   Rendering multiple scaled checkerboards.

The SVG document *multiScaledCheckerBoard1.svg* in Listing 6.4 demonstrates multiple invocations of the SVG scale function in order to scale a checkerboard pattern.

**Listing 6.4**   multiScaledCheckerBoard1.svg

```
<?xml version="1.0" encoding="iso-8859-1"?>
<!DOCTYPE svg PUBLIC "-//W3C//DTD SVG 20001102//EN"
 "http://www.w3.org/TR/2000/CR-SVG-20001102/DTD/svg-20001102.dtd">
<svg width="800" height="500">
  <defs>
  <pattern id="checkerPattern"
           width="80" height="80"
           patternUnits="userSpaceOnUse">

     <rect fill="red"
           x="0"  y="0"  width="40" height="40"/>

     <rect fill="blue"
           x="40" y="0"  width="40" height="40"/>

     <rect fill="blue"
           x="0"  y="40" width="40" height="40"/>

     <rect fill="red"
           x="40" y="40" width="40" height="40"/>
  </pattern>
  </defs>
```

```
<g transform="translate(50,50)">
  <g transform="scale(1)">
    <rect
       fill="url(#checkerPattern)"
       style="stroke:white"
       x="0" y="0" width="320" height="320">
    </rect>
  </g>
</g>

<g transform="translate(50,50)">
  <g transform="scale(.6)">
    <rect
       fill="url(#checkerPattern)"
       style="stroke:white"
       x="0" y="0" width="320" height="320">
    </rect>
  </g>
</g>

<g transform="translate(50,50)">
  <g transform="scale(.2)">
    <rect
       fill="url(#checkerPattern)"
       style="stroke:white"
       x="0" y="0" width="320" height="320">
    </rect>
  </g>
</g>
</svg>
```

## Remarks

The SVG defs element in Listing 6.4 contains an SVG pattern element that has an id attribute with the value checkerPattern. This pattern consists of an outer square whose length is 80. The inside of the pattern consists of a 2x2 grid of squares whose colors form a checkerboard pattern.

The first SVG g element is given below:

```
<g transform="translate(50,50)">
  <g transform="scale(1)">
    <rect
       fill="url(#checkerPattern)"
       style="stroke:white"
       x="0" y="0" width="320" height="320">
```

```
      </rect>
    </g>
  </g>
```

As you can see, the preceding SVG g element defines a rectangle with width 320 and a height of 320 that refers to the pattern checkerPattern defined in the SVG defs element. As a result, this SVG g element renders a checkerboard pattern.

Since a scale value of 1 means that no scaling takes place, the following pair of SVG lines:

```
<g transform="translate(50,50)">
  <g transform="scale(1)">
```

is functionally equivalent to the following:

```
<g transform="translate(50,50)">
```

The second SVG g element is reproduced below:

```
<g transform="translate(50,50)">
  <g transform="scale(.6)">
    <rect
       fill="url(#checkerPattern)"
       style="stroke:white"
       x="0" y="0" width="320" height="320">
    </rect>
  </g>
</g>
```

The second SVG g element differs from the first SVG g element only in terms of the scale factor; the former specifies 1 whereas the latter specifies .6. The second SVG g element also defines a rectangle with width 320 and a height of 320 that refers to the pattern checkerPattern defined in the SVG defs element. Thus, this SVG g element renders an image that is a 0.6 scaled version of the first checkerboard pattern.

The third and final SVG g element is given below:

```
<g transform="translate(50,50)">
 <g transform="scale(.2)">
    <rect
       fill="url(#checkerPattern)"
       style="stroke:white"
       x="0" y="0" width="320" height="320">
    </rect>
  </g>
</g>
```

The third SVG g element differs from the first SVG g element only in terms of the scale factor; the former specifies 1 whereas the latter specifies .2. The third SVG g element also defines a rectangle with width 320 and a height of 320 that refers to the pattern checkerPattern defined in the SVG defs element. Thus, this SVG g element renders an image that is a 0.2 scaled version of the first checkerboard pattern.

## ZIPPER EFFECTS AND SCALED CUBIC BEZIER CURVES

Consider the set of scaled cubic Bezier curves rendered in Figure 6.5.

**FIGURE 6.5**  A set of scaled cubic Bezier curves.

The SVG document *multiScaledCBezier3.svg* in Listing 6.5 demonstrates how to render a set of scaled cubic Bezier curves with a zipper effect.

### Listing 6.5   multiScaledCBezier3.svg

```
<?xml version="1.0" encoding="iso-8859-1"?>
<!DOCTYPE svg PUBLIC "-//W3C//DTD SVG 20001102//EN"
 "http://www.w3.org/TR/2000/CR-SVG-20001102/DTD/svg-20001102.dtd">

<svg width="100%" height="100%">
  <defs>
  <linearGradient id="gradientDefinition1"
    x1="0" y1="0" x2="40" y2="40"
```

```
            gradientUnits="userSpaceOnUse">
        <stop offset="0%"   style="stop-color:#FFFFFF"/>
        <stop offset="80%"  style="stop-color:#FFFF00"/>
        <stop offset="100%" style="stop-color:#0000AA"/>
    </linearGradient>

    </defs>

<g transform="translate(20,20) scale(2)">
    <path id="bezierPattern"
        d="M0,0 C75,150 150,10 10,80"
        fill="url(#gradientDefinition1)"
        stroke-dasharray="4 4"
        style="stroke:red;stroke-width:4;"/>
</g>
<g transform="translate(40,80) scale(2.5)">
    <path id="bezierPattern"
        d="M0,0 C75,150 150,10 10,80"
        fill="url(#gradientDefinition1)"
        stroke-dasharray="4 4"
        style="stroke:green;stroke-width:2;"/>
</g>

<g transform="translate(80,140) scale(3)">
    <path id="bezierPattern"
        d="M0,0 C75,150 150,10 10,80"
        fill="url(#gradientDefinition1)"
        stroke-dasharray="4 4"
        style="stroke:blue;stroke-width:3;"/>
</g>

<g transform="translate(120,200) scale(3.5)">
    <path id="bezierPattern"
        d="M0,0 C75,150 150,10 10,80"
        fill="url(#gradientDefinition1)"
        stroke-dasharray="4 4"
        style="stroke:black;stroke-width:8;"/>
</g>
</svg>
```

## Remarks

The code in Listing 6.5 contains four SVG g elements, each of which contains the SVG translate function and the SVG scale element, as well as a fill attribute with a value of gradientDefinition1 that references a linear color gradient that is defined in the SVG defs element.

Since all four SVG g elements render a scaled version of the same cubic Bezier function, we'll only examine the first one in detail. The first SVG g element specifies a red cubic Bezier curve whose blue "dotted" outline has a width of four because of the following code fragment:

```
stroke-dasharray="4 4"
style="stroke:red;stroke-width:4;"/>
```

The cubic Bezier curve itself is specified by the following line of code:

```
d="M0,0 C75,150 150,10 10,80"
```

The starting point of the Bezier curve is the point (0,0) because of the term M0,0 and the terminal point of the Bezier curve is the point (10,80) which is listed at the end of the code fragment. Next, the fragment C75,150 150,10 specifies two control points (75,150) and (150,10) that are used for rendering the cubic Bezier curve. The control point (75,150) is used for drawing the beginning of the Bezier curve and the control point (150,10) is used for drawing the end of the Bezier curve.

Note that the uppercase letters M and C in a cubic Bezier curve refer to absolute points whereas the lowercase letters m and c refer to relative points.

## USING THE SVG skew FUNCTION

Consider the rectangles rendered in Figure 6.6.

**FIGURE 6.6**   Drawing rectangles with the SVG skew function.

The SVG document *skewedRect1.svg* in Listing 6.6 demonstrates how to use the SVG skew function in order to render a set of rectangles.

### Listing 6.6   skewedRect1.svg

```
<?xml version="1.0" encoding="iso-8859-1"?>
<!DOCTYPE svg PUBLIC "-//W3C//DTD SVG 20001102//EN"
```

```
     "http://www.w3.org/TR/2000/CR-SVG-20001102/DTD/svg-20001102.dtd">

     <svg width="100%" height="100%">

     <g transform="translate(100,100)">
     <rect
        x="0" y="0" width="150" height="50"
        style="fill:yellow;stroke:blue"/>
     </g>

     <g transform="translate(300,100)">
     <g transform="skewX(30)">
     <rect
        x="0" y="0" width="150" height="50"
        style="fill:green;stroke:blue"/>
     </g>
     </g>

     <g transform="translate(500,100)">
     <g transform="skewY(50)">
     <rect
        x="0" y="0" width="150" height="50"
        style="fill:blue;stroke:blue"/>
     </g>
     </g>

     </svg>
```

## Remarks

The SVG code in Listing 6.6 consists of three SVG g elements, each of which specifies an SVG transform function as well as an SVG rect element. The first SVG g element does not contain an SVG skew function, so it simply renders a standard rectangle.

The second SVG g element contains an SVG skew function skewX, which specifies a skewing with respect to the horizontal axis. The skew is accomplished by keeping the horizontal axis fixed while rotating the vertical axis counterclockwise by the specified number of degrees, which in this case is 30.

The third SVG g element specifies an SVG skew function skewY, which specifies a skewing with respect to the vertical axis. This skew is performed by keeping the vertical axis fixed and rotating the horizontal axis clockwise by the specified number of degrees, which in this case is 50.

Notice how the third rectangle appears "longer" than the first rectangle, which shows you that the SVG skewY function actually performs two things: a rotation and a scale of a geometric object.

## USING THE SVG matrix FUNCTION

Consider the rectangles rendered in Figure 6.7.

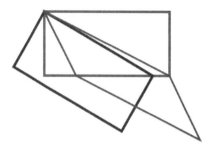

**FIGURE 6.7** Drawing rectangles with the SVG matrix function.

The SVG document *matrixRect1.svg* in Listing 6.7 demonstrates how to use the SVG matrix function in order to perform linear transformations on a rectangle in the plane.

**Listing 6.7** matrixRect1.svg

```
<?xml version="1.0" encoding="iso-8859-1"?>
<!DOCTYPE svg PUBLIC "-//W3C//DTD SVG 20001102//EN"
 "http://www.w3.org/TR/2000/CR-SVG-20001102/DTD/svg-20001102.dtd">

<svg width="100%" height="100%">
<g transform="translate(100,100)">
  <rect fill="none" stroke="red" stroke-width="4"
        width="200" height="100"/>

  <rect transform="matrix(.866 .5 -.5 .866 0 0)"
        fill="none" stroke="blue" stroke-width="4"
        width="200" height="100"/>

  <rect transform="matrix(1 .5 .5 1 0 0)"
        fill="none" stroke="green" stroke-width="4"
        width="200" height="100"/>
</g>
</svg>
```

## Remarks

The SVG code in Listing 6.7 renders three rectangles with width 200 and height 100, and whose perimeters are red, blue, and green, respectively. The first rectangle is rendered with the following SVG code:

```
<rect fill="none" stroke="red" stroke-width="4"
    width="200" height="100"/>
```

The second rectangle is rendered with the following SVG code:

```
<rect transform="matrix(.866 .5 -.5 .866 0 0)"
    fill="none" stroke="blue" stroke-width="4"
    width="200" height="100"/>
```

The SVG `matrix` function specified in the SVG code for the second rectangle represents a clockwise rotation of 30% of the associated rectangle. The mathematics for rotations is beyond the scope of this book. For those of you who are interested in the details, this topic is covered in books on linear algebra.

The third rectangle is rendered with the following SVG code:

```
<rect transform="matrix(.866 .5 -.5 .866 0 0)"
    fill="none" stroke="blue" stroke-width="4"
    width="200" height="100"/>
```

*← wrong*

The SVG `matrix` function specified in the SVG code for the third rectangle represents a combination of a skew and a rotation. Again, the mathematics can be found in a book on linear algebra.

## COMBINING MULTIPLE SVG FUNCTIONS

You can specify a set of SVG functions by means of a space-separated list or by means of a set of nested SVG g elements. For example, suppose you wanted to apply an SVG `translate` function followed by an SVG `scale` function to a rectangle. You can accomplish this pair of transformations with the following SVG code fragment:

```
<g transform="translate(100,100) scale(.5)">
<rect x="0" y="0" width="150" height="50"
    style="fill:yellow;stroke:blue"/>
</g>
```

You can accomplish the same pair of transformations with the following SVG code fragment as well:

```
<g transform="translate(100,100)">
  <g transform="scale(.5)">
    <rect x="0" y="0" width="150" height="50"
          style="fill:yellow;stroke:blue"/>
  </g>
</g>
```

# CYLINDERS AND THE SVG scale FUNCTION

Consider the two horizontal cylinders rendered in Figure 6.8.

**FIGURE 6.8** Drawing scaled cylinders with the SVG scale function.

The SVG document *hScaledSlantedGradientCylinderDotPattern3.svg* in Listing 6.8 demonstrates how to use the SVG scale function in order to render a cylinder and a scaled cylinder.

**Listing 6.8** hScaledSlantedGradientCylinderDotPattern3.svg

```
<?xml version="1.0" encoding="iso-8859-1"?>
<!DOCTYPE svg PUBLIC "-//W3C//DTD SVG 20001102//EN"
 "http://www.w3.org/TR/2000/CR-SVG-20001102/DTD/svg-20001102.dtd">

<svg width="100%" height="100%">

<defs>
  <linearGradient id="gradientDefinition1"
      x1="0" y1="0" x2="200" y2="0"
      gradientUnits="userSpaceOnUse">
    <stop offset="0%"   style="stop-color:#FF0000"/>
    <stop offset="100%" style="stop-color:#440000"/>
  </linearGradient>

  <pattern id="dotPattern"
```

```
                width="8" height="8"
                patternUnits="userSpaceOnUse">

        <circle id="circle1"
            cx="2" cy="2" r="2"
            style="fill:red;"/>
    </pattern>
</defs>

<g transform="translate(100,100)">
    <ellipse cx="0"   cy="50"
            rx="20" ry="50"
            stroke="blue" stroke-width="4"
            style="fill:url(#gradientDefinition1)"/>

    <rect x="0" y="0" width="300" height="100"
            style="fill:url(#gradientDefinition1)"/>

    <rect x="0" y="0" width="300" height="100"
            style="fill:url(#dotPattern)"/>

    <ellipse cx="300" cy="50"
            rx="20"  ry="50"
            stroke="blue" stroke-width="4"
            style="fill:yellow;"/>
</g>

<g transform="translate(100,100) scale(.5)">
    <ellipse cx="0"   cy="50"
            rx="20" ry="50"
            stroke="blue" stroke-width="4"
            style="fill:url(#gradientDefinition1)"/>

    <rect x="0" y="0" width="300" height="100"
            style="fill:url(#gradientDefinition1)"/>

    <rect x="0" y="0" width="300" height="100"
            style="fill:url(#dotPattern)"/>

    <ellipse cx="300" cy="50"
            rx="20"  ry="50"
            stroke="blue" stroke-width="4"
            style="fill:yellow;"/>
</g>
</svg>
```

## Remarks

The SVG code in Listing 6.8 consists of two SVG g elements, each of which renders a cylinder with gradient shading. The first SVG g element renders a cylinder by rendering the left-most ellipse, a rectangle, and then the right-most ellipse. Notice how the rectangle is actually rendered twice with different values for the `fill` attribute. The first rectangle is rendered with a `fill` attribute that references a linear gradient in the SVG `defs` element; the second rectangle is rendered on top of the first rectangle using a `fill` attribute that references an SVG `pattern` element. This creates the effect of a polka dot pattern rendered with a linear gradient. The second SVG g element uses the SVG `scale` function in order to render another cylinder that is a scaled version of the first cylinder. The SVG `scale` function makes it very easy to generate any number of scaled versions of an existing graphics image!

## HOURGLASSES WITH THE SVG scale AND skew FUNCTIONS

Consider the two hourglass figures rendered in Figure 6.9.

**FIGURE 6.9**   Drawing scaled skewed hourglass figures.

The SVG document *vScaledSkewedSlantedGradientHourGlass1.svg* in Listing 6.9 demonstrates how to use the SVG `scale` and `skew` functions in order to render skewed hourglass figures.

**Listing 6.9**  vScaledSkewedSlantedGradientHourGlass1.svg

```
<?xml version="1.0" encoding="iso-8859-1"?>
<!DOCTYPE svg PUBLIC "-//W3C//DTD SVG 20001102//EN"
 "http://www.w3.org/TR/2000/CR-SVG-20001102/DTD/svg-20001102.dtd">

<svg width="100%" height="100%">

<defs>
  <linearGradient id="gradientDefinition1"
     x1="0" y1="0" x2="100" y2="100"
     gradientUnits="userSpaceOnUse">
     <stop offset="0%"   style="stop-color:#FF0000"/>
     <stop offset="100%" style="stop-color:#000000"/>
  </linearGradient>

  <linearGradient id="gradientDefinition2"
     x1="0" y1="0" x2="300" y2="300"
     gradientUnits="userSpaceOnUse">
     <stop offset="0%"   style="stop-color:#FF0000"/>
     <stop offset="100%" style="stop-color:#000000"/>
  </linearGradient>
</defs>

<g transform="translate(150,20) skewX(30)">
   <ellipse cx="0"  cy="50"
            rx="100" ry="20"
            style="fill:url(#gradientDefinition1)"/>

   <polygon points="-100,50 100,50 0,200"
         style="fill:url(#gradientDefinition1)"/>

   <ellipse cx="0"  cy="50"
            rx="100" ry="20"
            style="fill:none;stroke:blue;stroke-width:2;"/>

   <polygon points="-100,350 100,350 0,200"
         style="fill:url(#gradientDefinition2)"/>

   <ellipse cx="0"  cy="350"
            rx="100" ry="20"
            style="fill:url(#gradientDefinition2)"/>

   <ellipse cx="0"  cy="350"
            rx="100" ry="20"
            style="fill:none;stroke:blue;stroke-width:2;"/>
```

```
      </g>

      <g transform="translate(150,20) skewX(30) scale(.5)">
        <ellipse cx="0"  cy="50"
                 rx="100" ry="20"
                 style="fill:url(#gradientDefinition1)"/>

        <polygon points="-100,50 100,50 0,200"
              style="fill:url(#gradientDefinition1)"/>

        <ellipse cx="0"  cy="50"
                 rx="100" ry="20"
               style="fill:none;stroke:blue;stroke-width:2;"/>

        <polygon points="-100,350 100,350 0,200"
              style="fill:url(#gradientDefinition2)"/>

        <ellipse cx="0"  cy="350"
                 rx="100" ry="20"
                 style="fill:url(#gradientDefinition2)"/>

        <ellipse cx="0"  cy="350"
                 rx="100" ry="20"
               style="fill:none;stroke:blue;stroke-width:2;"/>
      </g>

      </svg>
```

## Remarks

The SVG code in Listing 6.9 consists of two SVG g elements, each of which renders an hourglass figure with gradient shading. The first SVG g element renders a cone by rendering the top ellipse and a triangle with linear gradient shading, and then another ellipse that creates the blue circumference. This combination of components is "reflected" in order to create the lower half of the hourglass figure. The second SVG g element uses the SVG scale and skew functions in order to render a scaled and skewed hourglass figure that is derived from the first hourglass figure,

## KEY CONSTRUCTS

An SVG translate function can be defined with the following SVG snippet:

```
<g transform="translate(50,50)">
```

```
  <!-- other SVG elements here -->
</g>
```

An SVG rotate function can be defined with the following SVG snippet:

```
<g transform="translate(300,50)">
  <g transform="rotate(30)">

  <!-- other SVG elements here -->

  </g>
</g>
```

An SVG scale function applied to a rectangle can be defined with the following SVG snippet:

```
<g transform="scale(0.5) translate(50,50)">
  <rect
    fill="red"
    style="stroke:white"
    x="0" y="0" width="400" height="400">
  </rect>
</g>
```

A horizontal skew function can be defined with the following SVG snippet:

```
<g transform="translate(300,100)">
  <g transform="skewX(30)">

  <!-- other SVG elements here -->

  </g>
</g>
```

A vertical skew function can be defined with the following SVG snippet:

```
<g transform="translate(300,100)">
  <g transform="skewY(30)">

  <!-- other SVG elements here -->

  </g>
</g>
```

An SVG matrix function can be specified on a rectangle with the following SVG snippet:

```
<rect transform="matrix(.866 .5 -.5 .866 0 0)"
      fill="none" stroke="blue" stroke-width="4"
      width="200" height="100"/>
```

## CD-ROM LIBRARY

ON THE CD The folder for this chapter on the book's companion CD-ROM contains the following SVG documents that are required for rendering the graphics images in this chapter:

*translateRect1.svg*

*rotatedCheckerBoard1.svg*

*scaledCheckerBoard1.svg*

*multiScaledCheckerBoard1.svg*

*multiScaledCBezier3.svg*

*skewedRect1.svg*

*matrixRect1.svg*

*hScaledSlantedGradientCylinderDotPattern3.svg*

*vScaledSkewedSlantedGradientHourGlass1.svg*

## SUMMARY

This chapter focused on how to use SVG elements for applying transformations to graphics images. You can also "animate" these transformations to create animation effects in SVG documents. Although these animation effects require considerable effort in traditional programming languages, you may be surprised that these effects can be created simply by including a few lines of code. These animation effects are created via the SVG `animateTransform` element, which can be used in conjunction with the following SVG functions:

- the SVG `translate` function
- the SVG `rotate` function
- the SVG `scale` function
- the SVG `skew` function
- the SVG `matrix` function

# 7 SVG Filters

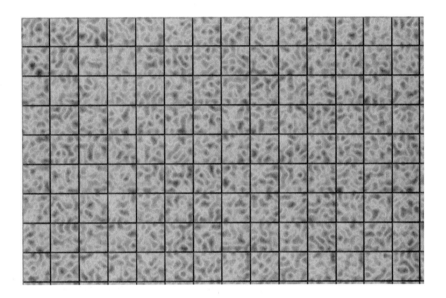

## OVERVIEW

This chapter demonstrates how to use the SVG `filter` element (which contains one or more *filter primitives*) in order to create a variety of filter effects. After you've finished this chapter, you'll have an appreciation for the rich textural patterns that can be created in SVG. This is another area where SVG positively shines and towers above the traditional programming languages. You will see examples of some of the SVG filter primitives (a complete list appears near the end of the chapter) combined with other SVG elements to render an interesting set of graphics images.

As an ancillary note, you need to be aware of the fact that the learning curve for this topic can be significant. While many of the features (e.g., rotate, translate, skew) of SVG are easy to use after you've seen an example of how to use them, a lot of the SVG filters are not intuitively obvious. As you delve into SVG filters, you'll see that some of them are extremely powerful and sophisticated, but sometimes it's not apparent where they would prove useful; that is, there is no *a priori* way of knowing how to generate interesting graphics images with every filter. This knowledge can only be acquired through practice and experimentation. All code and images for this chapter can be found on the companion CD-ROM in the Chapter 7 folder.

ON THE CD

## USING AN feGaussianBlur FILTER PRIMITIVE

Consider the rectangles rendered in Figure 7.1.

**FIGURE 7.1** An feGaussianBlur filter primitive.

The SVG document *rectBlurFilter1.svg* in Listing 7.1 demonstrates how to use the SVG filter element with the feGaussianBlur filter primitive in order to render a rectangle with a blurred filter effect.

**Listing 7.1**   rectBlurFilter1.svg

```
<?xml version="1.0" encoding="iso-8859-1"?>
<!DOCTYPE svg PUBLIC "-//W3C//DTD SVG 20001102//EN"
 "http://www.w3.org/TR/2000/CR-SVG-20001102/DTD/svg-20001102.dtd">

<svg width="100%" height="100%">
  <defs>
  <filter
     id="blurFilter1"
     filterUnits="objectBoundingBox"
     x="0" y="0"
     width="100%" height="100%">
     <feGaussianBlur stdDeviation="8"/>
  </filter>
```

```
    </defs>

<g transform="translate(50,50)">
  <rect
      x="0" y="0" width="100" height="100"
      filter="url(#blurFilter1)"
      fill="red" stroke="black" stroke-width="4"/>

  <rect
      x="200" y="0" width="100" height="100"
      fill="red" stroke="black" stroke-width="4"/>
</g>
</svg>
```

## Remarks

The SVG code in Listing 7.1 starts with an SVG defs element that contains an SVG filter element with a nested feGaussianBlur filter primitive, as shown in the following code fragment:

```
<filter
    id="blurFilter1"
    filterUnits="objectBoundingBox"
    x="0" y="0"
    width="100%" height="100%">
    <feGaussianBlur stdDeviation="8"/>
</filter>
```

The next element in Listing 7.1 is an SVG g element, which contains the SVG translate function that shifts the origin from the point (0,0) to the point (50,50), as listed below:

```
<g transform="translate(50,50)">
```

Next, the SVG g element renders two rectangles, the first of which appears below:

```
<rect
    x="0" y="0" width="100" height="100"
    filter="url(#blurFilter1)"
    fill="red" stroke="black" stroke-width="4"/>
```

The first rectangle is red, and it has a width of 100 pixels, a height of 100 pixels, and a black perimeter that is four pixels wide. The upper-left vertex of the rectangle is the point (0,0). The rectangle contains a filter attribute whose value is blurFilter1, which references a filter (containing an feGaussianBlur filter primitive) that is defined in the SVG defs element.

The SVG code for the second rectangle in the SVG g element is given below:

```
<rect
  x="200" y="0" width="100" height="100"
  fill="red" stroke="black" stroke-width="4"/>
```

The second rectangle is also red and has a width of 100 pixels, a height of 100 pixels, and a black perimeter that is four pixels wide. The upper-left vertex of the rectangle is the point (200,0). The rectangle contains a `filter` attribute whose value is `blurFilter1`, which references a blur filter that is defined in the SVG `defs` element.

Experiment with the `feGaussianBlur` filter primitive and observe how the rendered image is affected as you specify different values for the stdDeviation attribute.

## SHADOWS AND THE feGaussianBlur FILTER PRIMITIVE

Consider the rectangles rendered in Figure 7.2.

**FIGURE 7.2** An feGaussianBlur
with a shadow effect.

The SVG document *rectBlurShadowFilter1.svg* in Listing 7.2 demonstrates how to use the SVG `filter` element with an `feGaussianBlur` filter primitive in order to render a rectangle with a blurred shadow filter effect.

### Listing 7.2   rectBlurShadowFilter1.svg

```
<?xml version="1.0" encoding="iso-8859-1"?>
<!DOCTYPE svg PUBLIC "-//W3C//DTD SVG 20001102//EN"
 "http://www.w3.org/TR/2000/CR-SVG-20001102/DTD/svg-20001102.dtd">

<svg width="100%" height="100%">
  <defs>
  <filter
```

```
          id="blurFilter1"
          filterUnits="objectBoundingBox"
          x="0" y="0"
          width="100%" height="100%">
       <feGaussianBlur stdDeviation="8"/>
     </filter>
     </defs>

   <g transform="translate(100,100)">
     <rect
        x="10" y="10" width="100" height="100"
        filter="url(#blurFilter1)"
        fill="black" stroke="black" stroke-width="4"/>

     <rect
        x="0" y="0" width="100" height="100"
        filter="url(#blurFilter1)"
        fill="red" stroke="black" stroke-width="4"/>
   </g>
   </svg>
```

## Remarks

The SVG code in Listing 7.2 creates a blurred shadow effect by rendering two rectangles that differ only by the value of their fill attribute: one is red and the other is black. Notice that the SVG defs element contains an feGaussianBlur filter primitive that is the same as the feGaussianBlur filter primitive defined in Listing 7.1.

The rendering of the two rectangles occurs in the SVG g element, which specifies the SVG translate function that shifts the origin from the point (0,0) to the point (100,100). Next, the SVG g element renders two rectangles, the first of which is given below:

```
<rect
   x="10" y="10" width="100" height="100"
   filter="url(#blurFilter1)"
   fill="red" stroke="black" stroke-width="4"/>
```

This rectangle is red and has a width of 100 pixels, a height of 100 pixels, and a black perimeter that is four pixels wide. The upper-left vertex of the rectangle is the point (10,10). The rectangle contains a fill attribute whose value is blurFilter1, which references a blur filter that is defined in the SVG defs element.

The SVG code for the second rectangle in the SVG g element is :

```
<rect
   x="0" y="0" width="100" height="100"
   fill="red" stroke="black" stroke-width="4"/>
```

This rectangle is also red and has a width of 100 pixels, a height of 100 pixels, and a black perimeter that is four pixels wide. The upper-left vertex of the rectangle is the point (0,0). The rectangle contains a `fill` attribute whose value is `blurFilter1`, which references a blur filter that is defined in the SVG `defs` element. When you consider the type of image that this SVG document generates, the code is remarkably succinct. Obviously, the real work is taking place in the `feGaussianBlur` filter primitive, so you don't have to worry about the complexity of the underlying mathematics. This is only your second example of using an SVG filter primitive, and you already know how to create three-dimensional blur effects!

## CREATING AN `feGaussianBlur` FILTER PATTERN

Consider the image rendered in Figure 7.3.

**FIGURE 7.3** An `feGaussianBlur` filter pattern.

The SVG document *rectBlurFilterPattern1.svg* in Listing 7.3 demonstrates how to use the SVG `feGaussianBlur` filter primitive and the SVG `pattern` element in order to render a pattern of blurred filters.

## Listing 7.3 rectBlurFilterPattern1.svg

```
<?xml version="1.0" encoding="iso-8859-1"?>
<!DOCTYPE svg PUBLIC "-//W3C//DTD SVG 20001102//EN"
 "http://www.w3.org/TR/2000/CR-SVG-20001102/DTD/svg-20001102.dtd">

<svg width="100%" height="100%">
```

```
<defs>
  <filter
     id="blurFilter1"
     filterUnits="objectBoundingBox"
     x="0" y="0"
     width="55" height="25">
     <feGaussianBlur stdDeviation="8"/>
  </filter>

  <pattern id="multiPattern"
          width="60" height="30"
          patternUnits="userSpaceOnUse">

     <rect
        x="0" y="0"
        width="60" height="30"
        filter="url(#blurFilter1)"
        fill="red" stroke="black" stroke-width="4"/>
  </pattern>
</defs>

<g transform="translate(20,20)">
  <rect
     x="0" y="0" width="600" height="300"
     style="fill:url(#multiPattern)"
     fill="red" stroke="gray" stroke-width="2"/>
</g>
</svg>
```

### Remarks

The SVG code in Listing 7.3 renders a rectangular grid of rectangles. Each rectangle in the grid is rendered with a powder-like faded effect that seems palpable, reminiscent of certain paintings in modern, abstract art.

The rectangle in the SVG defs element has a width of 55 pixels and a height of 25 pixels; in every other respect, it is the same as the rectangle in the SVG defs element in Listing 7.1

The second part of the SVG defs element contains an SVG pattern element that is listed below:

```
<pattern id="multiPattern"
     width="60" height="30"
          patternUnits="userSpaceOnUse">

   <rect
      x="0" y="0"
```

```
            width="60" height="30"
            filter="url(#blurFilter1)"
            fill="red" stroke="black" stroke-width="4"/>
    </pattern>
```

Notice that the SVG `rect` element has a width of 60 pixels and a height of 30 pixels, which makes it slightly larger than the rectangle defined in the SVG `feGaussianBlur` filter primitive. This slight difference in dimensions underlies the way in which the textural effect is created.

The rendering is performed in an element that is nested inside the SVG `g` element, which contains an SVG `translate` function that shifts the origin from point (0,0) to point (20,20). Next, the SVG `g` element renders a rectangular grid with the following code fragment:

```
<rect
    x="0" y="0" width="600" height="300"
    style="fill:url(#multiPattern)"
    fill="red" stroke="gray" stroke-width="2"/>
```

The rectangular grid is 600 pixels wide and has a height of 300 pixels, with a gray perimeter that is two pixels wide. The rectangle contains a `fill` attribute whose value is `multiPattern`, which references an SVG `pattern` element defined in the SVG `defs` element, and that element (in turn) references an SVG `filter` element that contains an `feGaussianBlur` filter primitive (which is also defined in the SVG `defs` element).

## USING AN feFlood FILTER PRIMITIVE

Consider the image rendered in Figure 7.4.

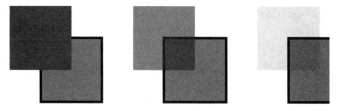

**FIGURE 7.4**  An `feFlood` filter primitive.

The SVG document *floodFilter1.svg* in Listing 7.4 demonstrates how to use an SVG `filter` element with an `feFlood` filter primitive.

**Listing 7.4**    floodFilter1.svg

```
<?xml version="1.0" encoding="iso-8859-1"?>
<!DOCTYPE svg PUBLIC "-//W3C//DTD SVG 20001102//EN"
 "http://www.w3.org/TR/2000/CR-SVG-20001102/DTD/svg-20001102.dtd">

<svg width="100%" height="100%">
  <defs>
  <filter
     id="floodFilter1"
     filterUnits="objectBoundingBox"
     x="0" y="0"
     width="100%" height="100%">
     <feFlood flood-color="blue" flood-opacity="1"/>
  </filter>

  <filter
     id="floodFilter2"
     filterUnits="objectBoundingBox"
     x="0" y="0"
     width="100%" height="100%">
     <feFlood flood-color="blue" flood-opacity=".5"/>
  </filter>

  <filter
     id="floodFilter3"
     filterUnits="objectBoundingBox"
     x="0" y="0"
     width="100%" height="100%">
     <feFlood flood-color="blue" flood-opacity=".1"/>
  </filter>
  <rect id="refRect1"
     width="100" height="100"
     fill="red" stroke="black" stroke-width="4"/>
  </defs>

  <g transform="translate(50,50)">
  <use xlink:href="#refRect1" x="50" y="50"/>
  <rect
     x="0"   y="0" width="100" height="100"
     filter="url(#floodFilter1)"
     fill="red" stroke="black" stroke-width="4"/>

  <use xlink:href="#refRect1" x="250" y="50"/>
  <rect
     x="200" y="0" width="100" height="100"
     filter="url(#floodFilter2)"
     fill="red" stroke="black" stroke-width="4"/>
```

```
<use xlink:href="#refRect1" x="450" y="50"/>
<rect
   x="400" y="0" width="100" height="100"
   filter="url(#floodFilter3)"
   fill="red" stroke="black" stroke-width="4"/>
</g>
</svg>
```

## Remarks

The SVG code in Listing 7.4 starts with an SVG defs element that contains the definition of three feFlood filter primitives that differ only by their opacity. The code for the first feFlood filter primitive is:

```
<filter
   id="floodFilter1"
   filterUnits="objectBoundingBox"
   x="0" y="0"
   width="100%" height="100%">
   <feFlood flood-color="blue" flood-opacity="1"/>
</filter>
```

If you look at the rendered graphics image, you'll see that the output that corresponds to this filter primitive looks like a blue rectangle.

The SVG g element contains an SVG translate function that shifts the origin from the point (0,0) to the point (50,50). Then, the SVG g element renders three pairs of overlapping rectangles. Now let's look at the code for the first pair of rectangles. The first rectangle (in the first pair) is rendered by referencing a rectangle defined in the SVG defs element by means of the following line of code:

```
<use xlink:href="#refRect1" x="50" y="50"/>
```

The second rectangle in the overlapping (first pair) of rectangles is drawn with the following code fragment:

```
<rect
   x="0"    y="0" width="100" height="100"
   filter="url(#floodFilter1)"
   fill="red" stroke="black" stroke-width="4"/>
```

The second rectangle contains a filter attribute whose value is floodFilter1, which references an feFlood filter primitive that is defined in the SVG defs element.

In a similar fashion, the SVG g element renders two more pairs of overlapping rectangles, each of which contains a different value for the opacity attribute.

## USING AN feImage FILTER PRIMITIVE

Consider the image rendered in Figure 7.5.

**FIGURE 7.5**    An feImage filter primitive.

The SVG document *imageFilter1.svg* in Listing 7.5 demonstrates how to use an feImage filter primitive that references an external image.

**Listing 7.5**    imageFilter1.svg

```
<?xml version="1.0" encoding="iso-8859-1"?>
<!DOCTYPE svg PUBLIC "-//W3C//DTD SVG 20001102//EN"
  "http://www.w3.org/TR/2000/CR-SVG-20001102/DTD/svg-20001102.dtd">

<svg width="100%" height="100%">
  <defs>

  <filter
     id="feImageFilter1"
     filterUnits="objectBoundingBox"
     x="0" y="0" width="100" height="100">
     <feImage xlink:href="simpleHouse1.gif"
       x="0" y="0"
       width="100" height="100"
       result="outputImage1"/>
  </filter>

  <filter
     id="feImageFilter2"
     filterUnits="objectBoundingBox"
     x="0" y="0" width="100" height="100">
     <feImage xlink:href="simpleHouse1.gif"
       x="200" y="0"
       width="200" height="50"
       result="outputImage2"/>
  </filter>
  </defs>

<g transform="translate(50,50)">
```

```
<rect
    x="0" y="0" width="100" height="100"
    filter="url(#feImageFilter1)"/>

<rect
    x="150" y="0" width="100" height="100"
    filter="url(#feImageFilter2)"/>
</g>
</svg>
```

## Remarks

The SVG code in Listing 7.5 renders an external GIF file and a scaled version of the same GIF file. The code starts with an SVG defs element that contains the definition of the filter (and its nested filter primitive) given below:

```
<filter
    id="feImageFilter1"
    filterUnits="objectBoundingBox"
    x="0" y="0" width="100" height="100">
    <feImage xlink:href="simpleHouse1.gif"
      x="0" y="0"
      width="100" height="100"
      result="outputImage1"/>
</filter>
```

This filter specifies a rectangle with a width of 100 pixels and a height of 100 pixels whose upper-left vertex is the origin. Notice how the GIF file itself is specified in the feImage filter primitive in the following fragment:

```
<feImage xlink:href="simpleHouse1.gif"
    x="0" y="0"
    width="100" height="100"
    result="outputImage1"/>
```

On the other hand, the rectangle in the second filter has a width of 200 pixels and a height of 50 pixels whose upper-left vertex is the point (200,100). The code for the second filter (and its nested filter primitive) is:

```
<filter
    id="feImageFilter2"
    filterUnits="objectBoundingBox"
    x="0" y="0" width="100" height="100">
    <feImage xlink:href="simpleHouse1.gif"
      x="200" y="0"
      width="200" height="50"
      result="outputImage2"/>
```

```
  </filter>
  </defs>
```

One other detail to observe is the `result` attribute that appears in both of the `feImage` filter primitives. The value of this attribute essentially provides a reference whereby the output of the current filter primitive can be used as the input for other filter primitives, thereby enabling you to create a chaining effect.

## USING AN feMerge FILTER PRIMITIVE

Consider the image rendered in Figure 7.6.

**FIGURE 7.6** An `feMerge` filter primitive.

The SVG document *mergeFilter1.svg* in Listing 7.6 demonstrates how to use an `feMerge` filter primitive.

**Listing 7.6**  mergeFilter1.svg

```
<?xml version="1.0" encoding="iso-8859-1"?>
<!DOCTYPE svg PUBLIC "-//W3C//DTD SVG 20001102//EN"
 "http://www.w3.org/TR/2000/CR-SVG-20001102/DTD/svg-20001102.dtd">

<svg width="100%" height="100%">
<defs>

<filter id="feMergeFilter1"
   filterUnits="objectBoundingBox"
   x="0" y="0" width="100" height="100">
   <feImage xlink:href="simpleHouse1.gif"
     x="0" y="0"
     width="100" height="100"
     result="outputImage1"/>

   <feGaussianBlur stdDeviation="5"
```

```
                              in="outputImage1"
                              baseFrequency="0.01"
                              result="imageOutput2"
                              x="0" y="0"
                              width="100" height="100"/>

          <feMerge>
            <feMergeNode in="imageOutput2"/>
            <feMergeNode in="simpleHouse1.gif"/>
          </feMerge>
       </filter>

     </defs>

     <g transform="translate(50,50)">
       <rect
           x="0" y="0" width="100" height="100"
           filter="url(#feMergeFilter1)"/>
     </g>
     </svg>
```

## Remarks

The SVG code in Listing 7.6 renders a GIF file that has been "processed" by an feGaussianBlur filter primitive; in this case the output is a blurry-looking image of a house. The feGaussian filter primitive (which is defined in an SVG defs element) is given below:

```
<feGaussianBlur stdDeviation="5"
                in="outputImage1"
                baseFrequency="0.01"
                result="imageOutput2"
                x="0" y="0"
                width="100" height="100"/>
```

The feMerge filter primitive, which is also in the SVG defs element, is defined with the following code fragment:

```
<feMerge>
  <feMergeNode in="imageOutput2"/>
  <feMergeNode in="simpleHouse1.gif"/>
</feMerge>
```

Finally, the result of applying the feMerge filter primitive occurs within the following code fragment:

```
<g transform="translate(50,50)">
  <rect
     x="0" y="0" width="100" height="100"
     filter="url(#feMergeFilter1)"/>
</g>
```

# USING AN feTurbulence FILTER PRIMITIVE

Consider the image rendered in Figure 7.7.

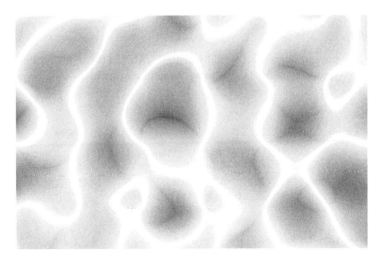

**FIGURE 7.7**  An feTurbulence filter primitive.

The SVG document *turbulenceFilter1.svg* in Listing 7.7 demonstrates how to use an feTurbulence filter primitive in order to create a turbulence effect.

**Listing 7.7**  turbulenceFilter1.svg

```
<?xml version="1.0" encoding="iso-8859-1"?>
<!DOCTYPE svg PUBLIC "-//W3C//DTD SVG 20001102//EN"
 "http://www.w3.org/TR/2000/CR-SVG-20001102/DTD/svg-20001102.dtd">

<svg width="100%" height="100%">
  <defs>
  <filter
     id="filter1"
```

```
        filterUnits="objectBoundingBox"
        x="0%" y="0%"
        width="100%" height="100%">
        <feTurbulence type="turbulence"
                      baseFrequency="0.01"
                      numOctaves="1"/>
    </filter>
    </defs>

    <rect
        x="0" y="0" width="800" height="400"
        filter="url(#filter1)"/>
    </svg>
```

## Remarks

The graphics image rendered by Listing 7.7 befits the name of the filter—it does indeed look turbulent! The feTurbulence filter primitive (which is defined in an SVG defs element) is:

```
<filter
    id="filter1"
    filterUnits="objectBoundingBox"
    x="0%" y="0%"
    width="100%" height="100%">
    <feTurbulence type="turbulence"
                  baseFrequency="0.01"
                  numOctaves="1"/>
</filter>
```

The feTurbulence filter primitive is "associated" with a rectangle by means of the following code fragment:

```
<rect
    x="0" y="0" width="800" height="400"
    filter="url(#filter1)"/>
```

Experiment with this filter by trying different combinations of values for the baseFrequency attribute and the numOctave attribute and see how the values of these attributes affect the graphics image. The feTurbulence filter primitive can be used for creating ethereal or impressionist-like effects, particularly when it's combined with other SVG elements. The next example shows how to combine an feTurbulence filter primitive with an SVG pattern element.

# feTurbulence **FILTER PRIMITIVES AND** pattern **ELEMENTS**

Consider the image rendered in Figure 7.8.

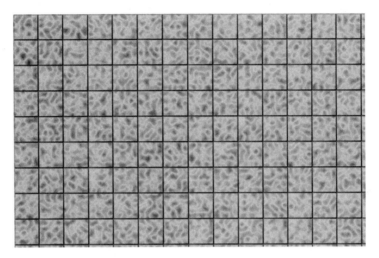

**FIGURE 7.8**    An feTurbulence filter primitive and an SVG pattern.

The SVG document *turbulenceFilterGrid1.svg* in Listing 7.8 demonstrates how to use the SVG pattern and linearGradient elements in combination with an feTurbulence filter primitive in order to create a grid-like turbulence pattern.

**Listing 7.8**    turbulenceFilterGrid1.svg

```
<?xml version="1.0" encoding="iso-8859-1"?>
<!DOCTYPE svg PUBLIC "-//W3C//DTD SVG 20001102//EN"
 "http://www.w3.org/TR/2000/CR-SVG-20001102/DTD/svg-20001102.dtd">

<svg width="100%" height="100%">
  <defs>
  <filter
     id="filter1"
     filterUnits="objectBoundingBox"
     x="0%" y="0%"
     width="100%" height="100%">
     <feTurbulence in="sourceAlpha"
                   type="turbulence"
                   baseFrequency="0.1"
                   numOctaves="1"
```

```
                        seed="0">
        </feTurbulence>
    </filter>

    <linearGradient id="gradientDefinition"
       x1="0" y1="0" x2="40" y2="40"
       gradientUnits="userSpaceOnUse">
       <stop offset="0%"   style="stop-color:#FF0000"/>
       <stop offset="100%" style="stop-color:#000000"/>
    </linearGradient>

    <pattern id="checkerPattern"
            width="40" height="40"
            patternUnits="userSpaceOnUse">

       <rect fill="url(#gradientDefinition)"
            x="0"   y="0"
            style="opacity:0.2"
            width="40" height="40"/>
    </pattern>
    </defs>

<g>
  <rect
     x="0" y="0" width="800" height="400"
     style="filter:url(#filter1)"/>

  <rect
     fill="url(#checkerPattern)"
     style="stroke:red"
     x="1" y="1" width="800" height="400"/>
</g>
</svg>
```

## Remarks

The SVG code in Listing 7.8 contains an SVG `defs` element that defines a filter containing an `feTurbulence` filter primitive, a linear color gradient, and an SVG `pattern` element that references the linear color gradient. The following code fragment renders the graphics image:

```
<g>
  <rect
     x="0" y="0" width="800" height="400"
     style="filter:url(#filter1)"/>

  <rect
     fill="url(#checkerPattern)"
```

```
        style="stroke:red"
        x="1" y="1" width="800" height="400"/>
   </g>
```

The first portion of the SVG code renders an SVG rect element that references an feTurbulence filter primitive, whose id attribute has value filter1, which is defined in the SVG defs element.

Next, the SVG code renders a rectangular grid of rectangles by specifying an SVG rect element that references an SVG pattern element, whose id attribute has value checkerPattern, which is also defined in the SVG defs element.

The combined effect of this combination is probably different from what you expected; indeed, this example demonstrates that you cannot always predict how filter primitives will "interact" with other user-defined patterns.

The key idea behind this graphics image is to specify an opacity attribute whose value is less than one. You can convince yourself that this is the case simply by setting the value of the opacity attribute to one, which will completely mask the feTurbulence filter primitive. You can experiment with other values for the opacity attribute to find other interesting combinations of an feTurbulence filter primitive and the SVG pattern element.

## QUADRATIC BEZIER CURVES AND feTurbulence FILTER PRIMITIVES

Consider the image rendered in Figure 7.9.

**FIGURE 7.9** A quadratic Bezier curve and a feTurbulence filter.

The SVG document *turbulenceFilterQBCP1.svg* in Listing 7.9 demonstrates how to combine an feTurbulence filter primitive with an SVG clip-path element.

**Listing 7.9**   turbulenceFilterQBCP1.svg

```
<?xml version="1.0" encoding="iso-8859-1"?>
<!DOCTYPE svg PUBLIC "-//W3C//DTD SVG 20001102//EN"
  "http://www.w3.org/TR/2000/CR-SVG-20001102/DTD/svg-20001102.dtd">

<svg width="100%" height="100%">
  <defs>
  <filter
     id="filter1"
     filterUnits="objectBoundingBox"
     x="0%" y="0%"
     width="100%" height="100%">
     <feTurbulence type="turbulence"
                   baseFrequency="0.01"
                   numOctaves="1"/>
  </filter>

  <clipPath id="clipPathDefinition"
            clipPathUnits="userSpaceOnUse">
    <path d="m0,0 Q100,0 200,200 T300,200"
          style="fill:red;stroke:blue;stroke-width:4;"/>
  </clipPath>

</defs>

<g transform="translate(50,50)"
   clip-path="url(#clipPathDefinition)"
             stroke="black" fill="none">

  <rect
     x="0" y="0" width="800" height="400"
     filter="url(#filter1)"/>

</g>
</svg>
```

## Remarks

The SVG code in Listing 7.9 combines an feTurbulence filter primitive with an SVG clip-path element that consists of a quadratic Bezier curve; both of these elements are defined inside an SVG defs element. You've already seen the feTurbulence filter primitive in previous examples in this chapter, and the Bezier curve was discussed in

Chapter 5. You can use this example as the basis for combining filter primitives with whatever clip path you have at hand in order to create subtle visual effects.

## feGaussianBlur FILTER TRIANGLES AND QUADRATIC BEZIER CURVES

Consider the image rendered in Figure 7.10.

**FIGURE 7.10** A blur filter triangle pattern with a quadratic Bezier curve.

The SVG document *triangleBlurFilterQBCP1.svg* in Listing 7.10 demonstrates how to combine an SVG filter element, a quadratic Bezier curve, and an SVG pattern element.

**Listing 7.10**   triangleBlurFilterQBCP1.svg

```
<?xml version="1.0" encoding="iso-8859-1"?>
<!DOCTYPE svg PUBLIC "-//W3C//DTD SVG 20001102//EN"
  "http://www.w3.org/TR/2000/CR-SVG-20001102/DTD/svg-20001102.dtd">

<svg width="100%" height="100%">

<defs>
  <filter
    id="blurFilter1"
```

```
                filterUnits="objectBoundingBox"
                x="0" y="0"
                width="60" height="15">
                <feGaussianBlur stdDeviation="8"/>
            </filter>

            <clipPath id="clipPathDefinition"
                    clipPathUnits="userSpaceOnUse">
              <path d="m0,0 Q100,0 200,200 T300,200"
                    style="fill:red;stroke:blue;stroke-width:4;"/>
            </clipPath>

            <pattern id="multiPattern"
                    width="60" height="30"
                    patternUnits="userSpaceOnUse">

              <polygon
                 points="0,0 60,0 60,30"
                 filter="url(#blurFilter1)"
                 fill="red" stroke="black" stroke-width="4"/>
            </pattern>
        </defs>

        <g transform="translate(20,20)"
          clip-path="url(#clipPathDefinition)"
                    stroke="black" fill="none">

          <rect
             style="fill:url(#multiPattern)"
             x="0" y="0" width="600" height="300"/>
        </g>
        </svg>
```

## Remarks

The SVG code in Listing 7.10 generates a rectangular pattern of blurred triangles that are enclosed by an SVG clip-path element that is defined by a quadratic Bezier curve. The image is visually pleasing because the filter blurs the perimeter of the rectangles and also because of the non-linear flow of the quadratic Bezier curve.

The SVG code in Listing 7.10 contains an SVG defs element that defines three elements: an feGaussianBlur filter primitive, an SVG clip-path element that defines a quadratic Bezier curve, and an SVG pattern element consisting of a triangle with the previously defined feGaussianBlur filter primitive applied to it. You can refer to previous examples for a detailed discussion of these three elements.

## feGaussianBlur **FILTER TRIANGLES AND CHECKERBOARDS**

Consider the image rendered in Figure 7.11.

**FIGURE 7.11** feGaussianBlur filter triangles and a checkerboard Pattern.

The SVG document *blurTriangleCheckerBoard1.svg* in Listing 7.11 demonstrates how to combine an feGaussianBlur filter primitive, a quadratic Bezier curve, and a checkerboard pattern that is based on an SVG pattern element.

**Listing 7.11** blurTriangleCheckerBoard1.svg

```
<?xml version="1.0" encoding="iso-8859-1"?>
<!DOCTYPE svg PUBLIC "-//W3C//DTD SVG 20001102//EN"
 "http://www.w3.org/TR/2000/CR-SVG-20001102/DTD/svg-20001102.dtd">

<svg width="100%" height="100%">
  <defs>
  <filter
     id="blurFilter1"
     filterUnits="objectBoundingBox"
     x="0" y="0"
     width="100%" height="100%">
     <feGaussianBlur stdDeviation="8"/>
  </filter>

  <pattern id="checkerPattern"
```

```
                    width="80" height="80"
                    patternUnits="userSpaceOnUse">

           <rect fill="red"
                 x="0"  y="0"  width="40" height="40"/>

           <polygon
              points="0,0 40,0 40,40"
              filter="url(#blurFilter1)"
              fill="blue" stroke="black" stroke-width="4"/>

           <rect fill="blue"
                 x="40" y="0"  width="40" height="40"/>

           <polygon
              points="40,0 80,0 80,40"
              filter="url(#blurFilter1)"
              fill="red" stroke="black" stroke-width="4"/>
           <rect fill="blue"
                 x="0"  y="40" width="40" height="40"/>

           <polygon
              points="0,40 40,40 40,80"
              filter="url(#blurFilter1)"
              fill="red" stroke="black" stroke-width="4"/>

           <rect fill="red"
                 x="40" y="40" width="40" height="40"/>

           <polygon
              points="40,40 80,40 80,80"
              filter="url(#blurFilter1)"
              fill="blue" stroke="black" stroke-width="4"/>
        </pattern>

        </defs>

   <g transform="translate(50,50)">
     <rect
        fill="url(#checkerPattern)"
        style="stroke:white"
        x="0" y="0" width="400" height="400"/>
   </g>
   </svg>
```

## Remarks

The SVG code in Listing 7.11 contains an SVG `defs` element that defines two familiar elements: an `feGaussianBlur` filter primitive and an SVG `pattern` element consisting of a "checkerboard" of triangles that are rendered with the `feGaussianBlur`
filter applied to it.

Listing 7.11 is actually quite straightforward, despite the fact that it's longer than
the other examples in this chapter. The reason for the apparent complexity is due to
the SVG `pattern` element—it contains four SVG `rect` elements and four SVG
`polygon` elements, each of which reference an SVG `blur` filter that is also defined in
the enclosing SVG `defs` element.

The graphics image rendered by Listing 7.11 resembles a grid of triangles that
have been daubed with paint. The unexpectedly rich textural pattern of red-on-blue
that alternates with blue-on-red somehow creates a "warm and fuzzy" effect.

## LIST OF SVG FILTER PRIMITIVES

The SVG `filter` primitives in this chapter give you a sample of what SVG can offer,
but it is by no means an exhaustive list. If you want to see the complete list of SVG
`filter` primitives, you can find them in Chapter 15 of the SVG specification. The list
of `filter` primitives is reproduced below:

```
feBlend
feColorMatrix
feComponentTransfer
feComposite
feConvolveMatrix
feDiffuseLIghting
feDisplacementMap
feFlood
feGaussianBlur
feImage
feMerge
feMorphology
feOffset
feSpecularLighting
feTile
feTurbulence
```

## KEY CONSTRUCTS

Apply an `feGaussianBlur` filter primitive to a rectangle with the following SVG
snippet:

```
<defs>
 <filter
    id="blurFilter1"
    filterUnits="objectBoundingBox"
    x="0" y="0"
    width="100%" height="100%">
    <feGaussianBlur stdDeviation="8"/>
 </filter>
 </defs>

<g transform="translate(50,50)">
 <rect
    x="0" y="0" width="100" height="100"
    filter="url(#blurFilter1)"
    fill="red" stroke="black" stroke-width="4"/>
</g>
```

Apply an feFlood filter primitive to a rectangle with the following SVG snippet:

```
<defs>
  <filter
    id="floodFilter1"
    filterUnits="objectBoundingBox"
    x="0" y="0"
    width="100%" height="100%">
    <feFlood flood-color="blue" flood-opacity="1"/>
  </filter>

  <rect id="refRect1"
    width="100" height="100"
    fill="red" stroke="black" stroke-width="4"/>
  </defs>

<g transform="translate(50,50)">
  <use xlink:href="#refRect1" x="50" y="50"/>
  <rect
    x="0"    y="0" width="100" height="100"
    filter="url(#floodFilter1)"
    fill="red" stroke="black" stroke-width="4"/>

</g>
```

Apply an feTurbulence filter primitive to a rectangle with the following SVG snippet:

```
<defs>
  <filter
```

```
        id="filter1"
        filterUnits="objectBoundingBox"
        x="0%" y="0%"
        width="100%" height="100%">
        <feTurbulence type="turbulence"
                      baseFrequency="0.01"
                      numOctaves="1"/>
    </filter>
    </defs>

    <rect
        x="0" y="0" width="800" height="400"
        filter="url(#filter1)"/>
</svg>
```

## CD-ROM LIBRARY

**ON THE CD**

The folder for this chapter on the book's companion CD-ROM contains the following SVG documents that are required for rendering the graphics images in this chapter:

*rectBlurFilter1.svg*

*rectBlurShadowFilter1.svg*

*rectBlurFilterPattern1.svg*

*floodFilter1.svg*

*imageFilter1.svg*

*mergeFilter1.svg*

*turbulenceFilter1.svg*

*turbulenceFilterGrid1.svg*

*turbulenceFilterQBCP1.svg*

*triangleBlurFilterQBCP1.svg*

*blurTriangleCheckerBoard1.svg*

## SUMMARY

This chapter focused on a subset of the available SVG `filter` primitives that can be used for creating unusual visual effects. Since the expressive power of filters is so vast, they require time and effort in order to master the various ways in which they can be employed. To that end, this chapter gave you some examples that illustrated how to use the following SVG `filter` primitives, as well as examples of how to combine some of them with an SVG `pattern` element:

- `feGaussianBlur`
- `feFlood`
- `feImage`
- `feMerge`
- `feTurbulence`

# 8 Displaying Text

Sample Text that follows a path specified by a Quadratic Bezier

## OVERVIEW

This chapter demonstrates how to use the SVG text element in order to render text strings. In addition to specifying attributes such as the font, size, and style of a text string, you can also scale, rotate, and skew a text string. Moreover, you can specify SVG elements, functions, and attributes when rendering a text string (such as filters and color gradients) that create very complex visual effects. Interesting clip-path effects can also be created with text. For example, this chapter shows you how to render a text string that follows the path of a Bezier curve. Imagine how difficult it would be to achieve this effect in other programming languages. All code and images for this chapter can be found on the companion CD-ROM in the Chapter 8 folder.

ON THE CD

**165**

## RENDERING A TEXT STRING

Consider the string of text rendered in Figure 8.1.

Sample Text

**FIGURE 8.1** A string
of text.

The SVG document *simpleText1.svg* in Listing 8.1 demonstrates how to use the
SVG text element in order to render a simple line of text.

**Listing 8.1** simpleText1.svg

```
<?xml version="1.0" encoding="iso-8859-1"?>
<!DOCTYPE svg PUBLIC "-//W3C//DTD SVG 20001102//EN"
 "http://www.w3.org/TR/2000/CR-SVG-20001102/DTD/svg-20001102.dtd">

<svg width="100%" height="100%">

<g transform="translate(100,100)">
  <text id="horizontalText" x="0" y="0"
        fill="red"
        font-size="18">
        Sample Text
  </text>
</g>
</svg>
```

### Remarks

The SVG code in Listing 8.1 renders the text string Sample Text with a fill value of
red and a font size of 18. The lower-left starting point for the string of text is (100,100)
because the SVG g element translates the origin to the point (100,100). The text string
is rendered above the point (100,100) in the sense that the bottom horizontal edge of
the text string "rests" on the horizontal line that passes through the point (100,100).
Note that this differs from an SVG rect element where the values of the x and y attributes specify the coordinates of a point that represents the upper-left corner of the
rendered rectangle.

## RENDERING A TEXT STRING WITH COLORED BORDERS

Consider the string of text rendered in Figure 8.2.

# Sample Text

**FIGURE 8.2**    A string of text with a colored border.

The SVG document *simpleText2.svg* in Listing 8.2 demonstrates how to use the SVG text element in order to render a simple line of text with a colored border.

### Listing 8.2    simpleText2.svg

```
<?xml version="1.0" encoding="iso-8859-1"?>
<!DOCTYPE svg PUBLIC "-//W3C//DTD SVG 20001102//EN"
 "http://www.w3.org/TR/2000/CR-SVG-20001102/DTD/svg-20001102.dtd">

<svg width="100%" height="100%">

<g transform="translate(100,150)">
  <text id="horizontalText" x="0" y="0"
        fill="red"
        stroke="blue"
        stroke-width="4"
        font-size="96">
        Sample Text
  </text>
</g>
</svg>
```

### Remarks

The SVG code in Listing 8.2 renders the text string Sample Text with a fill value of red and a font size of 96. The lower-left starting point for the string of text is (100,150) because the SVG g element translates the origin to the point (100,150). In this example, the text string is rendered so that the bottom horizontal edge of the text string Sample Text is on the horizontal line that passes through the point (100,150). The rendered text string is blue and has a thickness of four pixels because of the following combination of attribute values:

```
stroke="blue"
stroke-width="4"
```

## USING TEXT DECORATION WITH TEXT STRINGS

Consider the text strings rendered in Figure 8.3.

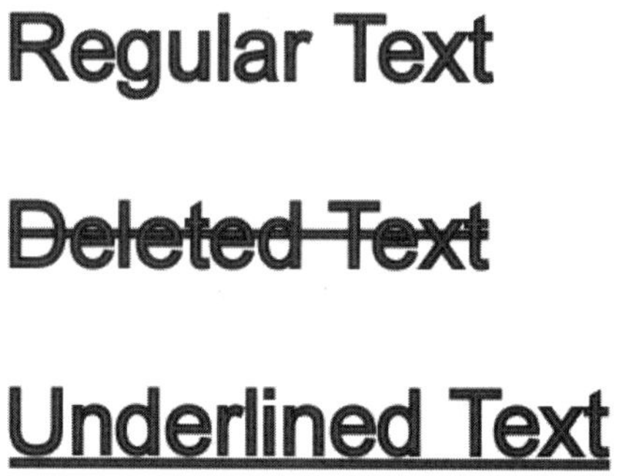

# Regular Text

# ~~Deleted Text~~

# <u>Underlined Text</u>

**FIGURE 8.3**   Text strings with text decoration.

The SVG document *textDecoration1.svg* in Listing 8.3 demonstrates how to use the SVG text element in order to display strike-through and underlined text.

### Listing 8.3   textDecoration1.svg

```
<?xml version="1.0" standalone="no"?>
<!DOCTYPE svg PUBLIC "-//W3C//DTD SVG 20010904//EN"
  "http://www.w3.org/TR/2001/REC-SVG-20010904/DTD/svg10.dtd">

<svg width="100%" height="100%"
    xmlns="http://www.w3.org/2000/svg">

  <g transform="translate(50,50)" font-size="48"
              fill="red" stroke="blue"
              stroke-width="2">

    <text x="0" y="50">Regular Text</text>
    <text x="0" y="150"
          text-decoration="line-through">Deleted Text</text>
    <text x="0" y="250"
          text-decoration="underline">Underlined Text</text>
```

```
      </g>
    </svg>
```

## Remarks

The SVG code in Listing 8.3 renders three text strings, all of which are rendered with a `fill` color of red and a blue `stroke width` of 2. This effect is achieved because the SVG g element has been specified as follows:

```
<g transform="translate(50,50)" font-size="48"
              fill="red" stroke="blue"
              stroke-width="2">
```

Since the SVG g element encloses all three SVG `text` elements, the specified attributes are inherited by the three SVG `text` elements. In addition, the SVG `translate` function shifts the origin from the point (0,0) to the point (50,50).

The first text string `Regular Text` is rendered without any additional adornment.

The second text string `Deleted Text` is rendered with a line through the middle of the text, thereby creating a strike-through effect.

The third line of text `Underlined Text` is rendered with a horizontal line that underscores this text string.

In Chapter 2 you also saw how to specify attributes of graphics images by means of internal or external stylesheets. In much the same fashion, such stylesheets can also be used for specifying attributes of rendered text.

## USING THE SVG `tspan` ELEMENT WITH TEXT STRINGS

Consider the text strings rendered in Figure 8.4.

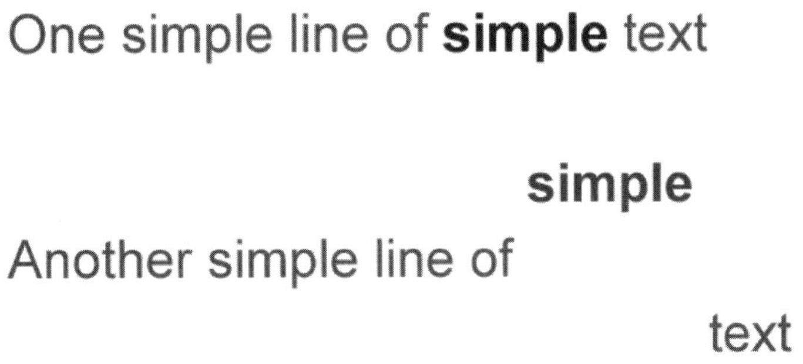

One simple line of **simple** text

**simple**

Another simple line of

text

**FIGURE 8.4**   Text strings with the `tspan` element.

The SVG document *tSpanText1.svg* in Listing 8.4 demonstrates how to use the SVG text element with the SVG tspan element in order to render text strings with different effects.

**Listing 8.4** tSpanText1.svg

```
<?xml version="1.0" standalone="no"?>
<!DOCTYPE svg PUBLIC "-//W3C//DTD SVG 20010904//EN"
  "http://www.w3.org/TR/2001/REC-SVG-20010904/DTD/svg10.dtd">

<svg width="100%" height="100%"
    xmlns="http://www.w3.org/2000/svg">

  <g transform="translate(10,10)">
    <text x="0" y="50" fill="red" font-size="36">
      One simple line of
        <tspan font-weight="bold"
               fill="blue">simple</tspan>
      text
    </text>

    <text x="0" y="200" fill="red" font-size="36">
      Another simple line of
        <tspan dx="0" dy="-50"
               font-weight="bold"
               fill="green">
          simple
        </tspan>
        <tspan dy="100">
            text
        </tspan>
    </text>
  </g>
</svg>
```

## Remarks

The SVG code in Listing 8.4 renders two text strings with several SVG tspan elements. The first text string, One simple line of simple text, is rendered with a font size of 36 and a fill color of red. The second occurrence of the word simple is enclosed in the SVG tspan element, which renders the text in bold and with a fill color of blue.

The second text string, Another simple line of simple text, is also rendered with a font size of 36 and a fill color of red. The second occurrence of the word simple is enclosed in the first SVG tspan element, which renders the text in bold and with a fill color of green. In addition, this SVG tspan element specifies the dy attribute with a value of -50, which causes the word simple to be shifted upward by 50 pixels. The second occurrence of the SVG `tspan` element encloses the word `text`, and it specifies the dy attribute with a value of 100, which causes the word `text` to be shifted downward by 100 pixels.

## RENDERING SHADOWED TEXT

Consider the text string rendered in Figure 8.5.

**FIGURE 8.5**   A string of shadowed text.

The SVG document *shadowText1.svg* in Listing 8.5 demonstrates how to use the SVG `text` element in order to render a text string with a shadow effect.

**Listing 8.5**   shadowText1.svg

```
<?xml version="1.0" encoding="iso-8859-1"?>
<!DOCTYPE svg PUBLIC "-//W3C//DTD SVG 20001102//EN"
 "http://www.w3.org/TR/2000/CR-SVG-20001102/DTD/svg-20001102.dtd">

<svg width="100%" height="100%">
<g transform="translate(50,150)">
  <text id="horizontalText" x="8" y="8"
        fill="black" stroke="black" stroke-width="4"
        font-size="72">
    Shadow Text
  </text>

  <text id="horizontalText" x="0" y="0"
        fill="red" stroke="black" stroke-width="4"
        font-size="72">
    Shadow Text
  </text>
</g>
</svg>
```

## Remarks

The SVG code in Listing 8.5 contains two SVG `text` elements, both of which render the same text string `Shadow Text` with a font size of 72. Notice how the shadow effect is achieved without using an SVG filter: first the text string is rendered as a background "shadow" effect using a `fill` value of black, and then the same text string is rendered again with a `fill` value of red. Observe that the first SVG `text` element contains the fragment:

```
x="8" y="8"
```

and the second SVG `text` element contains the fragment:

```
x="0" y="0"
```

Consequently, the first SVG `text` element is shifted 8 pixels to the right and 8 pixels downward with respect to the second SVG `text` element, thereby creating a shadow effect.

## RENDERING SHADOWED blur TEXT

Consider the string of text rendered in Figure 8.6.

**FIGURE 8.6**   A string of shadowed blur text.

The SVG document *shadowFilterText1.svg* in Listing 8.6 demonstrates how to use the SVG `text` element in order to render a simple line of shadowed blur text.

### Listing 8.6   shadowFilterText1.svg

```
<?xml version="1.0" encoding="iso-8859-1"?>
<!DOCTYPE svg PUBLIC "-//W3C//DTD SVG 20001102//EN"
 "http://www.w3.org/TR/2000/CR-SVG-20001102/DTD/svg-20001102.dtd">

<svg width="100%" height="100%">
 <defs>
```

```
<filter
    id="blurFilter1"
    filterUnits="objectBoundingBox"
    x="0" y="0"
    width="100%" height="100%">
    <feGaussianBlur stdDeviation="4"/>
</filter>
</defs>

<g transform="translate(50,150)">
<text id="horizontalText" x="15" y="15"
      filter="url(#blurFilter1)"
      fill="red" stroke="black" stroke-width="2"
      font-size="72">
    Shadow Text
</text>

<text id="horizontalText" x="0" y="0"
      fill="red" stroke="black" stroke-width="4"
      font-size="72">
    Shadow Text
</text>
</g>
</svg>
```

## Remarks

The SVG code in Listing 8.6 renders the text string Shadow Text with a fill value of red and a font size of 72. The first text string is rendered with a filter attribute that references a so-called *blur filter* that is defined in the SVG defs element. Next, the same text string is rendered again with a fill value of red. Notice how the shadow effect is combined with an SVG filter. Specifically, the first SVG text element contains the fragment:

```
x="15" y="15"
```

and the second SVG text element contains the fragment:

```
x="0" y="0"
```

Consequently, the first SVG text element is shifted 15 pixels to the right and 15 pixels downward with respect to the second SVG text element, thereby creating a shadow effect.

## ROTATING A TEXT STRING COUNTERCLOCKWISE

Consider the string of rotated text rendered in Figure 8.7.

Counter clockwise Rotated Text

**FIGURE 8.7** A rotated
string of text.

The SVG document *rotatedTextCCW1.svg* in Listing 8.7 demonstrates how to use the SVG text element together with the SVG rotate function in order to render a line of text that has been rotated in the counterclockwise direction.

**Listing 8.7** rotatedTextCCW1.svg

```
<?xml version="1.0" encoding="iso-8859-1"?>
<!DOCTYPE svg PUBLIC "-//W3C//DTD SVG 20001102//EN"
 "http://www.w3.org/TR/2000/CR-SVG-20001102/DTD/svg-20001102.dtd">

<svg width="100%" height="100%">

<g transform="translate(100,300)">
  <text id="simpleText" x="0" y="0"
        transform="rotate(-90)"
        fill="red"
        font-size="18">
        Counter clockwise Rotated Text
  </text>
</g>
</svg>
```

## Remarks

The SVG code in Listing 8.7 is quite straightforward. First the SVG g element translates the origin from the point (0,0) to the point (100,300), and then it renders the text string `Counter Clockwise Rotated Text` with a `fill` value of red and a font size of 18.  The text string is rotated counterclockwise by means of the following line:

```
transform="rotate(-90)"
```

*Rotations are negative in the counterclockwise direction, which is why the integer in the SVG* rotate *function is -90 instead of 90.*

## DISPLAYING TEXT WITH LINEAR GRADIENTS

Consider the text string rendered in Figure 8.8.

# Gradient Text

**FIGURE 8.8**    A text string with a linear gradient.

The SVG document *linearGradientText1.svg* in Listing 8.8 demonstrates how to use the SVG elements `text` and `linearGradient` in order to render a text string with a linear color gradient.

### Listing 8.8    linearGradientText1.svg

```
<?xml version="1.0" encoding="iso-8859-1"?>
<!DOCTYPE svg PUBLIC "-//W3C//DTD SVG 20001102//EN"
 "http://www.w3.org/TR/2000/CR-SVG-20001102/DTD/svg-20001102.dtd">

<svg width="100%" height="100%">
<defs>
  <linearGradient id="gradientDefinition"
    x1="0" y1="0" x2="300" y2="0"
    gradientUnits="userSpaceOnUse">
    <stop offset="0%"   style="stop-color:#FFFF00"/>
    <stop offset="100%" style="stop-color:#000000"/>
  </linearGradient>
</defs>

<g transform="translate(50,150)">
```

```
      <text id="horizontalText" x="0" y="0"
            fill="url(#gradientDefinition)"
            font-size="96">
            Gradient Text
      </text>
   </g>
</svg>
```

## Remarks

The SVG code in Listing 8.8 renders the text string `Gradient Text` with a `font-size` of 96 and a `fill` attribute that refers to an element whose `id` value is `gradient-Definition` and which is defined as a linear gradient in the SVG `defs` element. The linear gradient has a start color of yellow and a stop color of black. The dimensions of the enclosing rectangle for the linear gradient are specified by the following fragment:

```
x1="0" y1="0" x2="300" y2="0"
```

On the other hand, if you specify something like,

```
x1="0" y1="0" x2="100" y2="500"
```

you'll see a text string where most of the linear gradient is concentrated on the first two letters of the rendered text string. Experiment with different values for the attributes in order to achieve the effect that you want.

## DISPLAYING TEXT WITH OPACITY

Consider the text string rendered in Figure 8.9

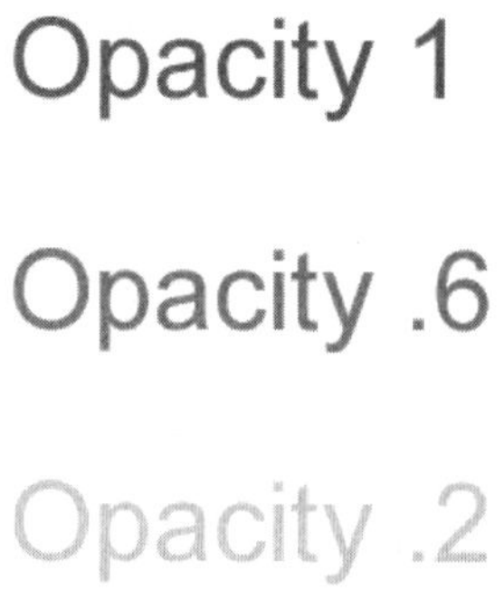

Opacity 1

Opacity .6

Opacity .2

**FIGURE 8.9** Text strings with different `opacity` values.

The SVG document *opacityText1.svg* in Listing 8.9 demonstrates how to use the SVG text element with different opacity values when displaying text strings.

**Listing 8.9** opacityText1.svg

```
<?xml version="1.0" encoding="iso-8859-1"?>
<!DOCTYPE svg PUBLIC "-//W3C//DTD SVG 20001102//EN"
 "http://www.w3.org/TR/2000/CR-SVG-20001102/DTD/svg-20001102.dtd">

<svg width="100%" height="100%">

<g transform="translate(50,100)">
  <text id="horizontalText" x="0" y="0"
        fill="red"
        font-size="48">
        Opacity 1
  </text>

  <text id="horizontalText" x="0" y="100"
        fill="red"
        font-size="48"
        opacity=".6">
        Opacity .6
  </text>

  <text id="horizontalText" x="0" y="200"
        fill="red"
        font-size="48"
        opacity=".2">
        Opacity .2
  </text>
</g>
</svg>
```

## Remarks

The SVG code in Listing 8.9 renders three horizontal text strings, all of which have a font size of 48 and a fill value of red. The three values of the opacity attribute are 1 (which is the default value), .6, and .2. The smaller the value of the opacity attribute, the fainter the rendered text string. Thus, the string with opacity .2 is fainter than the one with opacity .6, which in turn is fainter than the string with opacity 1. You can specify lower values for the opacity attribute in situations where you are overlaying multiple text strings with various SVG functions (e.g., rotate, skew, etc.) in conjunction with animation and you want to create specific artistic effects.

## DISPLAYING TEXT WITH blur FILTERS

Consider the two text strings rendered in Figure 8.10.

**FIGURE 8.10**   A text string with a blur filter.

The SVG document *blurFilterText1.svg* in Listing 8.10 demonstrates how to use the SVG elements text and blur in order to render a text string with a blur filter.

**Listing 8.10**   blurFilterText1.svg

```
<?xml version="1.0" encoding="iso-8859-1"?>
<!DOCTYPE svg PUBLIC "-//W3C//DTD SVG 20001102//EN"
 "http://www.w3.org/TR/2000/CR-SVG-20001102/DTD/svg-20001102.dtd">

<svg width="100%" height="100%">
  <defs>
  <filter
     id="blurFilter1"
     filterUnits="objectBoundingBox"
     x="0" y="0"
     width="100%" height="100%">
     <feGaussianBlur stdDeviation="4"/>
  </filter>
  </defs>

<g transform="translate(50,100)">

  <text id="normalText" x="0" y="0"
       fill="red" stroke="black" stroke-width="4"
       font-size="72">
     Normal Text
  </text>

  <text id="horizontalText" x="0" y="100"
       filter="url(#blurFilter1)"
```

```
            fill="red" stroke="black" stroke-width="4"
            font-size="72">
         Blurred Text
      </text>
   </g>
</svg>
```

### Remarks

The SVG code in Listing 8.10 renders two horizontal text strings, both of which have a `font-size` of 72 and a `fill` value of red. The upper horizontal text string has a black border with a thickness of four pixels, while the lower horizontal text string references an element with a `filter` value of blurFilter1. This filter is defined in the SVG `defs` element and is a filter of type `feGaussianBlur`.

## TEXT FOLLOWING A SPECIFIED PATH

Consider the text string rendered in Figure 8.11.

**FIGURE 8.11**    Text following a specified path.

The SVG document *textOnQBezierPath1.svg* in Listing 8.11 demonstrates how to use the SVG `textPath` element and the SVG `text` element in order to display a text string that follows a path.

**Listing 8.11**   textOnQBezierPath1.svg

```
<?xml version="1.0" encoding="iso-8859-1"?>
<!DOCTYPE svg PUBLIC "-//W3C//DTD SVG 20001102//EN"
 "http://www.w3.org/TR/2000/CR-SVG-20001102/DTD/svg-20001102.dtd">

<svg width="100%" height="100%">

<defs>
  <path id="pathDefinition"
        d="m0,0 Q100,0 200,200 T300,200 z"/>
</defs>

<g transform="translate(100,100)">
  <text id="textStyle" fill="red"
      stroke="blue" stroke-width="2"
      font-size="24">

  <textPath xlink:href="#pathDefinition">
      Sample Text that follows a path specified by a Quadratic
          Bezier curve
  </textPath>
  </text>
</g>
</svg>
```

### Remarks

The SVG code in Listing 8.11 contains the SVG `textPath` element that contains a horizontal text string which has a font size of 24 and a `fill` value of red. The SVG `textPath` element text refers to an `id` with value `pathDefinition`, which is defined as a quadratic Bezier curve by means of the SVG `path` element inside the SVG `defs` element. (Got it?)

## KEY CONSTRUCTS

A text string can be rendered with the following SVG snippet:

```
<g transform="translate(100,100)">
  <text id="horizontalText" x="0" y="0"
        fill="red"
        font-size="18">
        Sample Text
```

```
    </text>
  </g>
```

A text string can be rotated counterclockwise 90% with the following SVG snippet:

```
<g transform="translate(100,300)">
  <text id="simpleText" x="0" y="0"
        transform="rotate(-90)"
        fill="red"
        font-size="18">
        Counter clockwise Rotated Text
  </text>
</g>
```

A text string with an SVG `blur` filter can be rendered with the following SVG snippet:

```
<defs>
  <filter
      id="blurFilter1"
      filterUnits="objectBoundingBox"
      x="0" y="0"
      width="100%" height="100%">
      <feGaussianBlur stdDeviation="4"/>
  </filter>
</defs>

<g transform="translate(50,100)">
  <text id="horizontalText" x="0" y="100"
        filter="url(#blurFilter1)"
        fill="red" stroke="black" stroke-width="4"
        font-size="72">
      Blurred Text
  </text>
</g>
```

A text string can follow a Bezier curve with the following SVG snippet:

```
<defs>
  <path id="pathDefinition"
        d="m0,0 Q100,0 200,200 T300,200 z"/>
</defs>

<g transform="translate(100,100)">
  <text id="textStyle" fill="red"
```

```
            stroke="blue" stroke-width="2"
            font-size="24">

        <textPath xlink:href="#pathDefinition">
            Sample Text that follows a path specified by a Quadratic
                Bezier curve
        </textPath>
        </text>
    </g>
```

## CD-ROM LIBRARY

ON THE CD

The folder for this chapter on the book's companion CD-ROM contains the following SVG documents that are required for rendering the graphics images in this chapter:

*simpleText1.svg*

*simpleText2.svg*

*textDecoration1.svg*

*tSpanText1.svg*

*shadowText1.svg*

*shadowFilterText1.svg*

*linearGradientText1.svg*

*opacityText1.svg*

*blurFilterText1.svg*

*textOnQBezierPath1.svg*

## SUMMARY

This chapter focused on presenting various techniques for rendering text with different shading effects. In case you are unfamiliar with these shading effects, you can find examples of them in previous chapters. The examples in this chapter demonstrated how to combine the SVG text element with the SVG elements listed below:

- the SVG text element to display text strings
- the SVG rotate element to rotate text strings
- the SVG linearGradient element to display text with linear gradients

- the SVG `opacity` primitive
- the SVG `feGaussianBlur` element to display text with a blur effect
- the SVG `scale` element to display scaled text
- the SVG `textPath` element to render text strings along a path

# 9 Simple SVG Animation

## OVERVIEW

This chapter demonstrates how to use the SVG `animate`, `animateColor`, and `animateTransform` elements in conjunction with other SVG elements in order to generate a variety of graphics images with animation effects. One obvious fact about animation-based graphics images is that they look much better when you view them in action—and in color—than they do in a static image. Therefore, it's a good idea to launch the code examples in this chapter (as well as later chapters containing animation) in your SVG viewer as you examine the SVG code.

The SVG `animate` element allows you to modify an attribute of an SVG element. For example, you can modify the `width` attribute of an SVG `rectangle` element in order to make it expand or shrink based on the range of values specified.

The SVG `animateColor` element allows you to specify a pair of colors (that represent the start color and end color for an SVG element) as well as a `duration` attribute that specifies the time interval during which the color changes take place.

The SVG `animateTransform` element is very powerful because it allows you to perform animation involving one or more of the SVG functions. For instance, you can rotate a triangle or a rectangle around its center or around one of its vertices. You can also rotate circles or ellipses around their centers as well as around one of the vertices of the rectangles that enclose them.

Yet another type of animation involves specifying an SVG `clip-path` that serves as the path on which a particular object will travel. This chapter contains an example of an ellipse that rotates around its center as it travels along the path of a Bezier curve. Incidentally, the clip path for animation is the same as the clip paths in Chapter 7 that were used as a "window" in order to restrict the displayed portion of a graphics object.

In addition to providing simultaneous animation of multiple elements, SVG allows you to "chain" animation events so that the start time for one element coincides with the "end time" of another element. SVG also allows you to specify a value for a `repeatCount` attribute that controls the number of times an animation effect is repeated. The combination of these animation-related features gives you the foundation for creating realistic, powerful, and sophisticated animation effects. All code and images for this chapter can be found on the companion CD-ROM in the Chapter 9 folder.

ON THE CD

## ANIMATING TRANSFORMATIONS

The SVG `animateTransform` element has a `type` attribute whose allowable values are `translate`, `scale`, `rotate`, `skewX`, or `skewY`. Other attributes of the SVG `animate-Transform` element are `from`, `to`, and `dur`, which correspond to the start location, end location, and duration, respectively, of the transformation in question. The SVG documents in this chapter will give you specific examples of different ways of assigning values to the attributes of the SVG `animateTransform` element.

## ROTATING A LINE SEGMENT

Consider the snapshots of the line segment in Figure 9.1 and Figure 9.2.

**FIGURE 9.1**   A snapshot of a
rotating line segment.

**FIGURE 9.2**   Another snapshot
of a rotating line segment.

The SVG document *rotatingLineSegment1.svg* in Listing 9.1 demonstrates how to
use the SVG animateTransform element in order to rotate a line segment.

**Listing 9.1**   rotatingLineSegment1.svg

```
<?xml version="1.0" encoding="iso-8859-1"?>
<!DOCTYPE svg PUBLIC "-//W3C//DTD SVG 20001102//EN"
 "http://www.w3.org/TR/2000/CR-SVG-20001102/DTD/svg-20001102.dtd">

<svg width="100%" height="100%">
  <g transform="translate(200,180)">
    <line x1="0" y1="0"
       x2="150"   y2="0"
       stroke-dasharray="4 4 4 4"
       stroke="blue" stroke-width="8"/>

    <line x1="0" y1="0"
       x2="150"   y2="0"
       stroke-dasharray="8 8 8 8"
       stroke="red" stroke-width="8">
       <animateTransform attributeName="transform"
                     attributeType="XML"
                     type="rotate"
                     from="0" to="360" dur="4s"/>
    </line>
  </g>
</svg>
```

## Remarks

Listing 9.1 specifies two line segments: the first line segment is stationary while the
second line segment rotates clockwise one revolution during a four-second interval by
means of the following SVG animateTransform element:

```
<animateTransform attributeName="transform"
                  attributeType="XML"
                  type="rotate"
                  from="0" to="360" dur="4s"/>
```

Let's take a closer look at the purpose of the attributes in the preceding SVG element.

The `attributeType` attribute can be either CSS or XML; in the former case, it refers to a CSS property of the SVG element, and in the latter case, it refers to an attribute of the SVG element.

The `type` attribute has a value of `rotate`, which means that the transformation will be a rotation.

The `from` attribute specifies the starting angle for the rotation and has a value of 0, whereas the `to` attribute specifies the final angle for the rotation and has a value of 360. The `dur` attribute specifies a value of 4s, which means that the animation will last for four seconds.

The angle of rotation is measured in degrees, and the positive direction for rotations is *clockwise*. If you double-click on this file, you will see a rotating line segment that immediately begins rotating around a center point that coincides with the left end point of the line segment and lasts for four seconds.

## ROTATING RECTANGLES

Consider the snapshots of the rotating rectangles rendered in Figure 9.3 and Figure 9.4.

**FIGURE 9.3**    A snapshot of rotating rectangles.

**FIGURE 9.4**    Another snapshot of rotating rectangles.

The SVG document *rotatingRect1.svg* in Listing 9.2 demonstrates how to use the SVG animateTransform element in order to rotate a pair of rectangles.

**Listing 9.2**    rotatingRect1.svg

```
<?xml version="1.0" encoding="iso-8859-1"?>
<!DOCTYPE svg PUBLIC "-//W3C//DTD SVG 20001102//EN"
 "http://www.w3.org/TR/2000/CR-SVG-20001102/DTD/svg- 20001102.dtd">

<svg width="100%" height="100%">

<!-- rotation point: upper-left vertex -->
<g transform="translate(150,150)">
  <rect x="0" y="0"
        width="100" height="50"
        stroke-dasharray="4 4 4 4"
        fill="red" stroke="green" stroke-width="4">
        <animateTransform attributeName="transform"
                          attributeType="XML"
                          type="rotate" fill="freeze"
                          from="0" to="360" dur="4s"/>
  </rect>

  <ellipse cx="0" cy="0"
           rx="4" ry="4"
           style="fill:blue;stroke:none"/>
</g>

<!-- rotation point: center -->
<g transform="translate(400,150)">
  <rect x="-50" y="-25"
        width="100" height="50"
        stroke-dasharray="8 8 8 8"
        fill="yellow" stroke="green" stroke-width="4">
        <animateTransform attributeName="transform"
                          attributeType="XML"
                          type="rotate" fill="freeze"
                          from="0" to="360" dur="4s"/>
  </rect>

  <ellipse cx="0" cy="0"
           rx="4" ry="4"
           style="fill:blue;stroke:none"/>
</g>
</svg>
```

## Remarks

The SVG code in Listing 9.2 demonstrates how to use the SVG `animateTransform` element in order to rotate a pair of rectangles, one through its center, and the other through one of its vertices. The first rectangle is defined as follows:

```
<rect x="0" y="0"
      width="100" height="50"
      style="fill:red;stroke:green;stroke-width:4;">
```

The preceding SVG `rect` element defines a red rectangle with width 100 and height 50 and a green perimeter with a width of four pixels. This rectangle is rotated via the following SVG `animateTransform` element:

```
<animateTransform attributeName="transform"
                  attributeType="XML"
                  type="rotate" fill="freeze"
                  from="0" to="360" dur="4s"/>
```

The `attributeType` attribute can be either CSS or XML; in the former case, it refers to a CSS property of the SVG element, and in the latter case it refers to an attribute of the SVG element.

The `type` attribute has a value of `rotate`, which means that the transformation will be a rotation.

The `fill` attribute has a value of `freeze`, which means that the associated graphics element will not return to its original position when the animation effect is finished.

The `from` attribute specifies the starting angle for the rotation and has a value of 0, whereas the `to` attribute specifies the final angle for the rotation and has a value of 360.

The `dur` attribute specifies a value of `4s`, which means that the animation will last for four seconds.

The angle of rotation is measured in degrees, and keep in mind that the positive direction for rotations is *clockwise*. If you double-click on this file, you will see a rotating rectangle that immediately begins rotating clockwise around a center point that coincides with the upper-left vertex of the rectangle and lasts for four seconds.

The second rectangle is defined as follows:

```
<g transform="translate(400,150)">
 <rect x="-50" y="-25"
       width="100" height="50"
       style="fill:yellow;stroke:green;stroke-width:4;">
```

The preceding SVG `rect` element defines a yellow rectangle with width 100 and height 50 and a green perimeter with a width of four pixels. This rectangle is rotated via the following SVG `animateTransform` element:

```
<animateTransform attributeName="transform"
                  attributeType="XML"
                  type="rotate" fill="freeze"
                  from="0" to="360" dur="4s"/>
```

The attribute values for the second rectangle are similar in nature to those for the first rectangle.

Notice that two stationary circles are rendered via the SVG `ellipse` element. The first circle has a center that coincides with the upper-left vertex of the left rectangle, and the second circle has a center that coincides with the center of the right rectangle.

## COUNTER ROTATING ELLIPSES

Consider the snapshots of the rotating ellipses rendered in Figure 9.5 and Figure 9.6.

**FIGURE 9.5**   A snapshot of rotating ellipses.

**FIGURE 9.6**   Another snapshot of rotating ellipses.

The SVG document *rotatingOppositeEllipses1.svg* in Listing 9.3 demonstrates how to use the SVG `animateTransform` element in order to render a pair of rotating ellipses that rotate in opposite directions.

### Listing 9.3   rotatingOppositeEllipses1.svg

```
<?xml version="1.0" encoding="iso-8859-1"?>
<!DOCTYPE svg PUBLIC "-//W3C//DTD SVG 20001102//EN"
 "http://www.w3.org/TR/2000/CR-SVG-20001102/DTD/svg-20001102.dtd">
  <svg width="100%" height="100%">
  <defs>
    <ellipse id="ellipseDefinition"
```

```
                     cx="0" cy="0" rx="100" ry="50"
                     style="stroke-width:4;"/>
</defs>

<g transform="translate(300,200)">
  <!-- clockwise rotation -->
  <g>
    <animateTransform begin="0s" dur="8s"
                      type="rotate"
     from="0 0 0" to="360 0 0"
     attributeName="transform"/>

    <g transform="translate(0,0)">
      <use xlink:href="#ellipseDefinition"
           x="0" y="0"
           stroke-dasharray="4 4 4 4"
           stroke="green"
           style="fill:red;"
           transform="rotate(0)"/>
    </g>

      <circle cx="100" cy="100" r="12"
           fill="green"
           stroke-dasharray="8 8 8 8"
           style="stroke:blue;stroke-width:4;"/>
  </g>

  <!-- counter clockwise rotation -->
  <g>
    <animateTransform begin="0s" dur="8s"
                      type="rotate"
     from="360 0 0" to="0 0 0"
     attributeName="transform"/>

    <g transform="translate(0,0)">
      <use xlink:href="#ellipseDefinition"
           x="0" y="0"
           stroke="red"
           stroke-dasharray="4 4 4 4"
           style="fill:blue;"
           transform="rotate(90)"/>
    </g>
  </g>
</g>
</svg>
```

## Remarks

The SVG code in Listing 9.3 contains two SVG g elements, each of which contains a rotating ellipse. The animation of the first ellipse is defined by the following segment:

```
<animateTransform begin="0s" dur="8s" type="rotate"
    from="0 0 0" to="360 0 0"
    attributeName="transform"/>
```

Notice that both the from attribute and the to attribute for this rotation effect contain three numbers instead of just one number. Specifically, the from attribute has a value of "0 0 0", where the first number represents an angle of 0 and the second and third numbers correspond to the coordinates of the point (0,0) of rotation. The to attribute has a value of "360 0 0", which represents an angle of 360° and the point (0,0) of rotation. Thus, this transformation will result in a clockwise rotation from 0° to 360° about the center point (0,0) for a period of eight seconds.

The animation of the second ellipse is defined by the following segment:

```
<animateTransform begin="0s" dur="8s" type="rotate"
    from="360 0 0" to="0 0 0"
    attributeName="transform"/>
```

This animation specifies rotations by means of three numbers, where the first number represents an angle and the second and third numbers correspond to the coordinates of the point of rotation. In this case, the rotation is specified in terms of a from attribute with value "360 0 0" and a to attribute with value "0 0 0", which corresponds to a rotation from counterclockwise 360° to 0° about the center point (0,0) for a period of eight seconds. The overall effect is a pair of ellipses rotating in opposite directions.

## RECTANGLES AND MULTIPLE ANIMATION EFFECTS

Consider the snapshot of the rectangle in Figure 9.7 and Figure 9.8.

**FIGURE 9.7**   A snapshot of a rectangle with multiple animation effects.

**FIGURE 9.8** Another snapshot of a rectangle with multiple animation effects.

The SVG document *animateRect1.svg* in Listing 9.4 demonstrates how to use multiple SVG animate elements in order to render a rectangle with multiple changing attributes.

**Listing 9.4** animateRect1.svg

```
<?xml version="1.0" standalone="no"?>
<!DOCTYPE svg PUBLIC "-//W3C//DTD SVG 20010904//EN"
  "http://www.w3.org/TR/2001/REC-SVG-20010904/DTD/svg10.dtd">

<svg width="100%" height="100%"
    xmlns="http://www.w3.org/2000/svg">

  <rect fill="red" stroke-width="1" stroke="blue"
      x="300" y="100" width="300" height="100">

    <animate attributeName="stroke" attributeType="XML"
           begin="1s" dur="5s"
           fill="freeze" from="blue" to="yellow"/>

    <animate attributeName="stroke-width"
           attributeType="XML"
           begin="1s" dur="5s"
           fill="freeze" from="1" to="40"/>

    <animate attributeName="x" attributeType="XML"
           begin="1s" dur="5s"
           fill="freeze" from="300" to="100"/>

    <animate attributeName="y" attributeType="XML"
           begin="2s" dur="5s"
           fill="freeze" from="100" to="50"/>
```

```
        <animate attributeName="width" attributeType="XML"
                begin="3s" dur="5s"
                fill="freeze" from="300" to="500"/>

        <animate attributeName="height" attributeType="XML"
                begin="4s" dur="5s"
                fill="freeze" from="100" to="300"/>
    </rect>
</svg>
```

## Remarks

The SVG code in Listing 9.4 contains six SVG `animate` elements that are applied to a rectangle in order to create an animation effect. The initial rectangle has a width of 300, a height of 100, and a blue perimeter that is one pixel wide; its upper-left vertex is located at the point (300,100), as specified in the following code fragment:

```
<rect fill="red" stroke-width="1" stroke="blue"
    x="300" y="100" width="300" height="100">
```

The first SVG `animate` element starts after one second and lasts for five seconds, during which time the color of the perimeter of the rectangle changes from blue to yellow:

```
<animate attributeName="stroke" attributeType="XML"
        begin="1s" dur="5s"
        fill="freeze" from="blue" to="yellow"/>
```

The second SVG `animate` element starts after one second and lasts for five seconds, during which time the width of the perimeter increases from one pixel to forty pixels:

```
<animate attributeName="stroke-width"
        attributeType="XML"
        begin="1s" dur="5s"
        fill="freeze" from="1" to="40"/>
```

The third SVG `animate` element starts after one second and lasts for five seconds, during which time the x-coordinate of the upper-left vertex of the rectangle changes from 300 to 100:

```
<animate attributeName="x" attributeType="XML"
        begin="1s" dur="5s"
        fill="freeze" from="300" to="100"/>
```

The fourth SVG `animate` element starts after two seconds and lasts for five seconds, during which time the y-coordinate of the upper-left vertex of the rectangle changes from 100 to 50:

```
<animate attributeName="y" attributeType="XML"
         begin="2s" dur="5s"
         fill="freeze" from="100" to="50"/>
```

The fifth SVG `animate` element starts after three seconds and lasts for five seconds, during which time the width of the rectangle from 300 to 100:

```
<animate attributeName="width" attributeType="XML"
         begin="3s" dur="5s"
         fill="freeze" from="300" to="500"/>
```

The sixth and final SVG `animate` element starts after four seconds and lasts for five seconds, during which time the height of the rectangle changes from 100 to 300:

```
<animate attributeName="height" attributeType="XML"
         begin="4s" dur="5s"
         fill="freeze" from="100" to="300"/>
```

## CHAINED ANIMATION EFFECTS

Consider the snapshots of a set of moving rectangles that belong to a group of chained animation effect in Figure 9.9 and Figure 9.10.

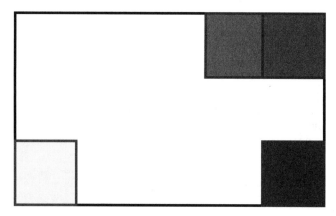

**FIGURE 9.9** A snapshot of multiple rectangles and chained animation effects.

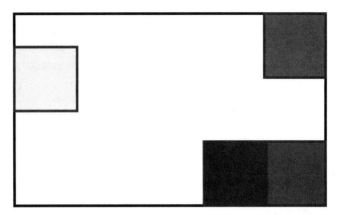

**FIGURE 9.10**   Another snapshot of multiple rectangles and chained animation effects.

The SVG document *chainedAnimateMultiRect1.svg* in Listing 9.5 demonstrates how to use multiple SVG animate elements in order to render a set of moving rectangles according to a specified time sequence.

**Listing 9.5**   chainedAnimateMultiRect1.svg

```
<?xml version="1.0" standalone="no"?>
<!DOCTYPE svg PUBLIC "-//W3C//DTD SVG 20010904//EN"
  "http://www.w3.org/TR/2001/REC-SVG-20010904/DTD/svg10.dtd">

<svg width="100%" height="100%"
     xmlns="http://www.w3.org/2000/svg">

<g transform="translate(50,50)">
  <rect width="500" height="400"
        fill="none" stroke-width="4" stroke="black"/>
</g>

<g transform="translate(50,50)">
  <rect id="rect1" x="0" y="0" width="100" height="100"
        stroke-width="4" stroke="blue" fill="red">
        <animate id="rect1b"
                attributeName="x" attributeType="XML"
                begin="0s" dur="2s"
                fill="freeze" from="0" to="400"/>
  </rect>

  <rect id="rect2" x="400" y="0" width="100" height="100"
        stroke-width="4" stroke="blue" fill="green">
```

```
            <animate id="rect2b"
                    attributeName="y" attributeType="XML"
                    begin="rect1b.end" dur="4s"
                    fill="freeze" from="0" to="200"/>
    </rect>

    <rect id="rect3" x="400" y="200"
          width="100" height="100"
          stroke-width="4" stroke="blue" fill="blue">
        <animate id="rect3b"
                attributeName="x" attributeType="XML"
                begin="rect2b.end+2s" dur="4s"
                fill="freeze" from="400" to="0"/>
    </rect>

    <rect id="rect4" x="0" y="200" width="100" height="100"
          stroke-width="4" stroke="blue" fill="yellow">
        <animate id="rect4b"
                attributeName="y" attributeType="XML"
                begin="rect2b.end" dur="4s"
                fill="freeze" from="200" to="0"/>
    </rect>
</g>
</svg>
```

## Remarks

Listing 9.5 renders an outer "anchor rectangle," and it contains four SVG animate elements that are applied to four rectangles (all of which reference the same rectangle defined in the SVG defs element) in order to create an animation effect. However, in this example, the start and stop points for the shifting rectangles are linked together as described in the following four steps.

1. The first animation effect shifts the rectangle in the upper-left corner of the anchor rectangle horizontally to the right until it overlays the rectangle in the upper-right corner of the anchor rectangle with the following fragment:

```
<rect id="rect1" x="0" y="0" width="100" height="100"
      stroke-width="4" stroke="blue" fill="red">
    <animate id="rect1b"
            attributeName="x" attributeType="XML"
            begin="0s" dur="2s"
            fill="freeze" from="0" to="400"/>
</rect>
```

2. The second animation starts immediately after the first animation effect has completed, and it shifts the rectangle in the upper-right corner of the anchor

rectangle vertically downward until it overlays the rectangle in the lower-right corner of the anchor rectangle with the following fragment:

```
<rect id="rect2" x="400" y="0" width="100" height="100"
      stroke-width="4" stroke="blue" fill="green">
      <animate id="rect2b"
               attributeName="y" attributeType="XML"
               begin="rect1b.end" dur="4s"
               fill="freeze" from="0" to="200"/>
</rect>
```

3.  The third animation starts two seconds after the second animation effect has completed, and it shifts the rectangle in the lower-right corner of the anchor rectangle horizontally toward the left until it overlays the rectangle in the upper-left corner of the anchor rectangle.

```
<rect id="rect3" x="400" y="200"
      width="100" height="100"
      stroke-width="4" stroke="blue" fill="blue">
      <animate id="rect3b"
               attributeName="x" attributeType="XML"
               begin="rect2b.end+2s" dur="4s"
               fill="freeze" from="400" to="0"/>
</rect>
```

4.  The fourth animation starts immediately after the second animation effect has completed, and it shifts the rectangle in the lower-left corner of the anchor rectangle vertically upward until it overlays the rectangle in the upper-left corner of the anchor rectangle with the following fragment.

```
<rect id="rect4" x="0" y="200" width="100" height="100"
      stroke-width="4" stroke="blue" fill="yellow">
      <animate id="rect4b"
               attributeName="y" attributeType="XML"
               begin="rect2b.end" dur="4s"
               fill="freeze" from="200" to="0"/>
</rect>
```

# CONTINUOUS ROTATION OF A TEXT STRING

Consider the snapshots of a rotating string of text rendered in Figure 9.11 and Figure 9.12.

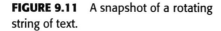

**FIGURE 9.11** A snapshot of a rotating string of text.

**FIGURE 9.12** Another snapshot of a rotating string of text.

The SVG document *rotatingTextPair1.svg* in Listing 9.6 demonstrates how to combine the SVG text element and the SVG animateTransform attribute in order to rotate two text strings 360% in the clockwise direction at different rates.

**Listing 9.6**   rotatingTextPair1.svg

```
<?xml version="1.0" encoding="iso-8859-1"?>
<!DOCTYPE svg PUBLIC "-//W3C//DTD SVG 20001102//EN"
 "http://www.w3.org/TR/2000/CR-SVG-20001102/DTD/svg-20001102.dtd">

<svg width="100%" height="100%">
<g transform="translate(0,0)">
   <text id="background" x="200" y="200"
        fill="red" fill-opacity="1"
        font-size="24">
     Rotating text
   </text>

  <animateTransform
        begin="0s" dur="4s" type="rotate"
        from="0 200 200" to="360 200 200"
        fill="freeze"
        attributeName="transform"/>
</g>

<g transform="translate(0,0)">
   <text id="background" x="200" y="200"
        fill="red" fill-opacity="1"
        font-size="24">
```

```
      Rotating text
    </text>

  <animateTransform
      begin="0s" dur="8s" type="rotate"
      from="0 200 200" to="360 200 200"
      fill="freeze"
      attributeName="transform"/>
 </g>
 </svg>
```

## Remarks

The SVG code in Listing 9.6 renders two text strings, both of which have the value
Rotating Text, with a fill value of red and a font size of 24. The first SVG g element
rotates the text string about the center point (200, 200) for four seconds by means of
the following code:

```
<animateTransform
    begin="0s" dur="4s" type="rotate"
    from="0 200 200" to="360 200 200"
    fill="freeze"
    attributeName="transform"/>
```

On the other hand, the second SVG g element rotates the text string about the
center point (200,200) for eight seconds:

```
<animateTransform
    begin="0s" dur="8s" type="rotate"
    from="0 200 200" to="360 200 200"
    fill="freeze"
    attributeName="transform"/>
```

Since the second SVG g element rotates its enclosed text string at half the speed
of the first SVG g element, the two rotating strings create the impression of a delayed
and slightly overlapping effect.

## MULTIPLE ANIMATION EFFECTS

Consider the snapshots of a rotating text string in Figure 9.13 and Figure 9.14.

**FIGURE 9.13** A snapshot of a text string undergoing multiple animation effects.

**FIGURE 9.14** Another snapshot of a text string undergoing multiple animation effects.

The SVG document *animateText1.svg* in Listing 9.7 demonstrates how to render a string of text with multiple animation effects.

**Listing 9.7**   animateText1.svg

```
<?xml version="1.0" encoding="iso-8859-1"?>
<!DOCTYPE svg PUBLIC "-//W3C//DTD SVG 20010904//EN"
  "http://www.w3.org/TR/2001/REC-SVG-20010904/DTD/svg10.dtd">

<svg width="100%" height="100%"
    xmlns="http://www.w3.org/2000/svg">

  <g transform="translate(100,100)">
    <text x="0" y="0" font-size="48" visibility="hidden"
        stroke="black" stroke-width="2">
      Animating Text
      <set attributeName="visibility"
          attributeType="CSS" to="visible"
          begin="2s" dur="5s" fill="freeze"/>

      <animateMotion path="M0,0 L50,150"
          begin="2s" dur="5s" fill="freeze"/>

      <animateColor attributeName="fill"
          attributeType="CSS"
          from="yellow" to="red"
          begin="2s" dur="8s" fill="freeze"/>

      <animateTransform attributeName="transform"
          attributeType="XML"
          type="rotate" from="-90" to="0"
          begin="2s" dur="5s" fill="freeze"/>
```

```
        <animateTransform attributeName="transform"
            attributeType="XML"
            type="scale" from=".5" to="1.5" additive="sum"
            begin="2s" dur="5s" fill="freeze"/>
    </text>
  </g>
</svg>
```

## Remarks

The SVG code in Listing 9.7 simultaneously rotates and scales a text string while changing the color of that string—rather impressive, especially when you consider the fact that this SVG document is only about half a page in length. The SVG `text` element has four SVG animation-related elements associated with it, two of which are new to you. Let's first look at the SVG `animateMotion` element listed below:

```
<animateMotion path="M0,0 L50,150"
    begin="2s" dur="5s" fill="freeze"/>
```

The preceding SVG `path` attribute specifies a line segment whose starting point is (0,0) and whose end point is (50,150), which starts its rotation two seconds after the document is loaded (`begin="2s"`) and then rotates for five seconds (`dur="5s"`), after which it will not return to its original position (`fill="freeze"`).

Now take a look at the SVG `animateColor` element given below:

```
<animateColor attributeName="fill"
    attributeType="CSS"
    from="yellow" to="red"
    begin="2s" dur="8s" fill="freeze"/>
```

The SVG `atttributeType` attribute has a value of `CSS`, which means that the effect pertains to a CSS attribute associated with the SVG `text` element; in this case, it's the color of the text.

The `animateColor` element will start changing color two seconds after the document has been loaded (`begin="2s"`) and during a span of eight seconds (`dur="8"`) the color will start with yellow (`from=" yellow"`) and end with the color red (`to="red"`) and then remain in that position (`fill=" freeze"`).

The last two SVG animate effects have already been described in previous examples, so you can refer to them in case you've forgotten how they work.

## KEY CONSTRUCTS

A line segment can be rotated with the following SVG snippet:

```
<g transform="translate(200,200)">
  <line x1="0"    y1="0"
     x2="100" y2="0"
     style="stroke:green;stroke-width:4;">
     <animateTransform attributeName="transform"
                       attributeType="XML"
                       type="rotate"
                       from="0" to="360" dur="4s"/>
</g>
```

Rotating a rectangle around its upper-left vertex can be done with the following SVG snippet:

```
<g transform="translate(150,150)">
  <rect x="0" y="0"
       width="100" height="50"
       style="fill:red;stroke:green;stroke-width:4;">
       <animateTransform attributeName="transform"
                         attributeType="XML"
                         type="rotate" fill="freeze"
                         from="0" to="360" dur="4s"/>
  </rect>

  <ellipse cx="0" cy="0"
          rx="4" ry="4"
          style="fill:blue;stroke:none"/>
</g>
```

Rotating a rectangle around its center can be handled with the following SVG snippet:

```
<g transform="translate(400,150)">
  <rect x="-50" y="-25"
       width="100" height="50"
       style="fill:yellow;stroke:green;stroke-width:4;">
       <animateTransform attributeName="transform"
                         attributeType="XML"
                         type="rotate" fill="freeze"
                         from="0" to="360" dur="4s"/>
  </rect>
  <ellipse cx="0" cy="0"
          rx="4" ry="4"
          style="fill:blue;stroke:none"/>
</g>
```

Simple scaling animation with a text string can be done with the following SVG snippet:

```
<g transform="translate(50,200)">
 <text id="horizontalText" x="0" y="0"
       fill="green"
       font-size="96">

       <animateTransform attributeName="transform"
                  attributeType="XML" type="scale"
                  from="0" to="1"
                  begin="0s" dur="4s"/>
    Sample Text
 </text>
</g>
```

## CD-ROM LIBRARY

The folder for this chapter on the book's companion CD-ROM contains the following SVG documents that are required for rendering the graphics images in this chapter:

*rotatingLineSegment1.svg*

*rotatingRect1.svg*

*rotatingRectCP1.svg*

*vMovingEllipseScaleGradientCP1.svg*

*rotatingOppositeEllipses1.svg*

*rotatingEllipsesQBCP2.svg*

*animateRect1.svg*

*animateMultiRect1.svg*

*chainedAnimateMultiRect1.svg*

*rotatingTextPair1.svg*

*animateText1.svg*

## SUMMARY

This chapter showed you how to use the SVG elements animate, animateColor, animateMotion, and animateTransform. The code examples in this chapter demonstrated how to use these SVG elements in order to do the following:

■ rotate line segments
■ rotate a rectangle around a vertex

- rotate a rectangle around its center
- rotate a pair of strings around a common point
- scale a text string
- perform multiple transformations on a text string

# 10  SVG for Bar Charts and Line Graphs

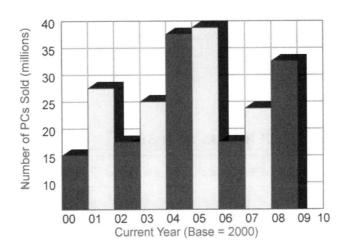

## OVERVIEW

This chapter demonstrates how you can use SVG elements for creating labeled bar charts and line graphs. SVG is extremely well suited for creating SVG documents whose contents are rendered as charts and graphs. Although the charts and graphs in this chapter are created manually and are based on hard-coded data, you can apply XSL stylesheets to XML documents in order to generate charts and graphs. As you will see later in Chapter 17, XSLT enables you to separate data from presentation, which is advantageous for transforming a set of frequently changing data into various types of graphs, including your own custom-formatted charts or graphs. Currently there are numerous books entirely devoted to XSLT (including several excellent ones); you can read the XSLT appendix in this book if you need to familiarize yourself with this topic. The book *XSLT in 21 Days* by Michiel van Otegem is a very good starting point, followed by *Mastering XSLT* by Chuck White. The book *XSLT and Xpath on the Edge* by Jeni Tennison provides an excellent source of XSL stylesheets.

The first part of this chapter starts with rendering bar sets. As simple as that may seem, bar sets form the basis for creating much more sophisticated bar charts. This iteration-based approach for rendering charts and graphs (which is influenced by eXtreme Programming) will serve you particularly well in this chapter for the following reason: visually appealing charts can require a great deal of code that can be logically partitioned into "components" that can be implemented in ECMAScript functions.

The second part of the chapter extends the concepts introduced in the first part by showing you how to render single and multiple line graphs and how to create three-dimensional effects. After you have learned how to use ECMAScript functions, you will see how to produce these graphs using modularized functions, as well as graphs that implement your specific needs and requirements. All code and images for this chapter can be found on the companion CD-ROM in the Chapter 10 folder.

ON THE CD

## DRAWING HOMOGENEOUS BAR SETS

Consider the set of equal-sized rectangles rendered in Figure 10.1.

**FIGURE 10.1**  A bar set.

The SVG document *barSet1.svg* in Listing 10.1 demonstrates how to draw a bar set of rectangles of equal width and height that alternate the colors red and blue.

### Listing 10.1  barSet1.svg

```
<?xml version="1.0" encoding="iso-8859-1"?>
<!DOCTYPE svg PUBLIC "-//W3C//DTD SVG 20001102//EN"
"http://www.w3.org/TR/2000/CR-SVG-20001102/DTD/svg-20001102.dtd">

<svg width="100%" height="100%">

<defs>
```

```
<rect id="blot1"
   x="0" y="0" width="40" height="200" stroke="white"/>
</defs>

<g transform="translate(40,100)">
  <use x="0"   y="0" fill="blue" xlink:href="#blot1"/>
  <use x="40"  y="0" fill="red"  xlink:href="#blot1"/>
  <use x="80"  y="0" fill="blue" xlink:href="#blot1"/>
  <use x="120" y="0" fill="red"  xlink:href="#blot1"/>
  <use x="160" y="0" fill="blue" xlink:href="#blot1"/>
  <use x="200" y="0" fill="red"  xlink:href="#blot1"/>
  <use x="240" y="0" fill="blue" xlink:href="#blot1"/>
  <use x="280" y="0" fill="red"  xlink:href="#blot1"/>
</g>
</svg>
```

## Remarks

The SVG code in Listing 10.1 is straightforward. The SVG code starts with an SVG `defs` element that defines an SVG `rect` element whose `id` attribute has a value of `blot1`. Next, the SVG code contains an SVG `g` element with multiple SVG `use` elements. Each SVG `use` element references the SVG `rect` element defined in the SVG `defs` element. Notice that the x-coordinate is incremented by 40 pixels, which produces a set of contiguous rectangles. In this book a set of contiguous rectangles that have the same width and height will be informally referred to as a "homogeneous bar set."

## DRAWING VARIABLE BAR SETS

Consider the set of contiguous rectangles in Figure 10.2.

The SVG document *barSet2.svg* in Listing 10.2 demonstrates how to draw a bar set of rectangles with different heights.

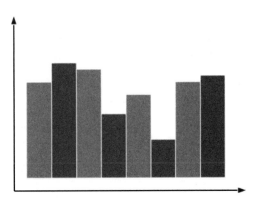

**FIGURE 10.2**   A variable bar set.

**Listing 10.2** barSet2.svg

```
<?xml version="1.0" encoding="iso-8859-1"?>
<!DOCTYPE svg PUBLIC "-//W3C//DTD SVG 20001102//EN"
"http://www.w3.org/TR/2000/CR-SVG-20001102/DTD/svg-20001102.dtd">

<svg width="100%" height="100%">

<g transform="translate(80,100)">
  <!-- draw vertical axis -->
  <line x1="-20" y1="-40"
        x2="-20" y2="220"
        style="stroke:black;stroke-width:2;"/>

  <!-- draw horizontal axis -->
  <line x1="-20" y1="220"
        x2="340" y2="220"
        style="stroke:black;stroke-width:2;"/>

  <!-- vertical tip: cc from lower-left vertex -->
  <polygon points="-25,-40 -15,-40 -20,-55"
          style="fill:black;stroke:white"/>

  <!-- horizontal tip: cc from lower-left vertex -->
  <polygon points="340,225 355,220 340,215"
          style="fill:black;stroke:white"/>

  <!-- draw bar set -->
  <rect x="0" y="50" width="40" height="150"
        style="fill:red;stroke:white"/>

  <rect x="40" y="20" width="40" height="180"
        style="fill:blue;stroke:white"/>

  <rect x="80" y="30" width="40" height="170"
        style="fill:red;stroke:white"/>

  <rect x="120" y="100" width="40" height="100"
        style="fill:blue;stroke:white"/>

  <rect x="160" y="70" width="40" height="130"
        style="fill:red;stroke:white"/>

  <rect x="200" y="140" width="40" height="60"
        style="fill:blue;stroke:white"/>

  <rect x="240" y="50" width="40" height="150"
```

```
        style="fill:red;stroke:white"/>

    <rect x="280" y="40" width="40" height="160"
        style="fill:blue;stroke:white"/>
  </g>
  </svg>
```

## Remarks

The SVG code in Listing 10.2 is more complicated than the SVG code in Listing 10.1 because of code for rendering the triangular end points of the horizontal and vertical axes. The first part of Listing 10.2 uses an SVG line element for drawing a vertical axis and a horizontal axis, followed by an SVG polygon element for rendering the triangular tip of both axes. Next, the SVG code contains a set of SVG rect elements that render a set of contiguous rectangles of varying heights. Notice that every rectangle has a width of 40, and that the x-coordinate is incremented by 40 pixels, which produces a set of contiguous rectangles. Since the rectangles have different heights, the value of the y attribute and the height attribute varies from rectangle to rectangle. Moreover, the sum of these two values is always 200 for the following reason: each rectangle in this set of rectangles has the same value for the y-coordinate of the lower horizontal line segment that represents the "base" of each rectangle.

## DRAWING LABELED RECTANGULAR GRIDS

Consider the labeled grid in Figure 10.3.

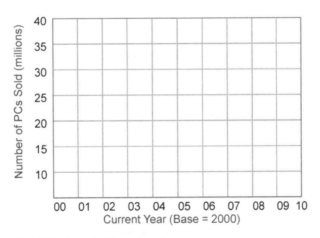

**FIGURE 10.3**  A labeled grid.

The SVG document *labeledGrid1.svg* in Listing 10.3 demonstrates how to render a grid with labeled vertical and horizontal axes.

### Listing 10.3   labeledGrid1.svg

```
<?xml version="1.0" encoding="iso-8859-1"?>
<!DOCTYPE svg PUBLIC "-//W3C//DTD SVG 20001102//EN"
"http://www.w3.org/TR/2000/CR-SVG-20001102/DTD/svg-20001102.dtd">

<svg width="100%" height="100%">
  <defs>
    <pattern id="gridPattern"
             width="40" height="40"
             patternUnits="userSpaceOnUse">

      <rect x="0" y="0"
            width="40" height="40"
            style="fill:none;stroke:blue;
            stroke-width:1;fill-opacity:.5;"/>
    </pattern>
  </defs>

  <!-- *** render background grid *** -->
  <g transform="translate(80,30)">
    <rect fill="url(#gridPattern)"
          style="stroke:red;fill-opacity:.2"
          x="0" y="0" width="400" height="280">
    </rect>
  </g>

  <!-- *** text label (vertical axis) *** -->
  <g transform="translate(30,300)">
    <text id="verticalLabel" x="20" y="0"
          transform="rotate(-90)"
          fill="red"
          font-size="18">
          Number of PCs Sold (millions)
    </text>
  </g>

  <!-- *** unit label (vertical axis) *** -->
  <g transform="translate(50,280)">
    <text id="horizontalLabel" x="0" y="0"
          fill="blue" fill-opacity="1"
          font-size="18">10</text>
  </g>
```

```
<g transform="translate(50,240)">
  <text id="horizontalLabel" x="0" y="0"
        fill="blue" fill-opacity="1"
        font-size="18">15</text>
</g>

<g transform="translate(50,200)">
  <text id="horizontalLabel" x="0" y="0"
        fill="blue" fill-opacity="1"
        font-size="18">20</text>
</g>

<g transform="translate(50,160)">
  <text id="horizontalLabel" x="0" y="0"
        fill="blue" fill-opacity="1"
        font-size="18">25</text>
</g>
 <g transform="translate(50,120)">
  <text id="horizontalLabel" x="0" y="0"
        fill="blue" fill-opacity="1"
        font-size="18">30</text>
</g>

<g transform="translate(50,80)">
  <text id="horizontalLabel" x="0" y="0"
        fill="blue" fill-opacity="1"
        font-size="18">35</text>
</g>

<g transform="translate(50,40)">
  <text id="horizontalLabel" x="0" y="0"
        fill="blue" fill-opacity="1"
        font-size="18">40</text>
</g>

<!-- *** text label (horizontal axis) *** -->
<g transform="translate(160,350)">
  <text id="horizontalLabel" x="0" y="0"
        fill="red" fill-opacity="1"
        font-size="18">
        Current Year (Base = 2000)
  </text>
</g>

<!-- *** unit label (horizontal axis) *** -->
<g transform="translate(80,330)">
  <text id="horizontalLabel" x="0" y="0"
        fill="blue" fill-opacity="1"
```

```
              font-size="18">00</text>
      </g>

      <g transform="translate(120,330)">
        <text id="horizontalLabel" x="0" y="0"
              fill="blue" fill-opacity="1"
              font-size="18">01</text>
      </g>

      <g transform="translate(160,330)">
        <text id="horizontalLabel" x="0" y="0"
              fill="blue" fill-opacity="1"
              font-size="18">02</text>
      </g>
        <!-- similar blocks omitted for brevity -->
      </svg>
```

## Remarks

**ON THE CD**

Although the SVG code in Listing 10.3 contains much more code than Listing 10.2, much of the code is very similar in nature. Some of the code has been omitted for brevity, and you can find the complete code for *labelledGrid1.svg* in the folder for this chapter on the accompanying CD-ROM. You can see how the SVG code has been labeled with comments that make it easier to understand as well as simplifying code maintenance.

The first part of Listing 10.3 contains an SVG defs element for defining a grid-like pattern that is used in step 1 in order to render a background grid for the graph.

Step 2 of the SVG code contains a rotated line segment and a rotated text string that labels the vertical axis.

Step 3 of the SVG code renders a set of short horizontal line segments as the "hash" marks for the vertical axis.

Step 4 of the SVG code renders a text string that labels the horizontal axis.

Step 5 of the SVG code renders a set of short vertical line segments as the "hash" marks for the horizontal axis.

Now that you understand how to create a labeled grid in SVG, you can use this code as a "template" for your own graphs. You can easily make your own custom enhancements (e.g., dotted internal line segments with differing colors) in order to tailor the appearance of this grid to each of your custom graphs.

## DRAWING BAR CHARTS

Consider the bar graph shown in Figure 10.4.

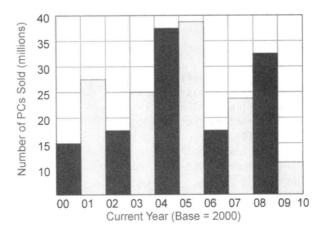

**FIGURE 10.4** A bar graph.

The SVG document *barGraph1.svg* in Listing 10.4 demonstrates how to draw a bar graph.

**Listing 10.4** barGraph1.svg

```
<?xml version="1.0" encoding="iso-8859-1"?>
<!DOCTYPE svg PUBLIC "-//W3C//DTD SVG 20001102//EN"
"http://www.w3.org/TR/2000/CR-SVG-20001102/DTD/svg-20001102.dtd">

<svg width="100%" height="100%">
<!-- *** STEP 1:  define grid pattern *** -->
  <defs>
    <pattern id="gridPattern"
          width="40" height="40"
          patternUnits="userSpaceOnUse">

    <rect x="0" y="0"
          width="40" height="40"
          style="fill:none;stroke:blue;
          stroke-width:1;fill-opacity:.5;"/>
    </pattern>
  </defs>
<!-- *** STEP 2:  render background grid *** -->
<g transform="translate(80,30)">
  <rect fill="url(#gridPattern)"
          style="stroke:red;fill-opacity:.2"
```

```
              x="0" y="0" width="400" height="280">
   </rect>
</g>


<!-- *** STEP 3:  vertical text labels *** -->
<g transform="translate(30,300)">
  <text id="verticalLabel" x="20" y="0"
        transform="rotate(-90)"
        fill="red"
        font-size="18">
        Number of PCs Sold (millions)
  </text>
</g>


<!-- *** STEP 4:  label vertical axis *** -->
<g transform="translate(50,280)">
  <text id="horizontalLabel" x="0" y="0"
        fill="blue" fill-opacity="1"
        font-size="18">10</text>
</g>

<g transform="translate(50,240)">
  <text id="horizontalLabel" x="0" y="0"
        fill="blue" fill-opacity="1"
        font-size="18">15</text>
</g>

 <!-- details omitted for brevity --->

<!-- *** STEP 5:  horizontal axis label *** -->
<g transform="translate(160,350)">
  <text id="horizontalLabel" x="0" y="0"
        fill="red" fill-opacity="1"
        font-size="18">
        Current Year (Base = 2000)
  </text>
</g>


<!-- *** STEP 6:  label horizontal axis *** -->
<g transform="translate(80,330)">
  <text id="horizontalLabel" x="0" y="0"
        fill="blue" fill-opacity="1"
        font-size="18">00</text>
</g>

<g transform="translate(120,330)">
  <text id="horizontalLabel" x="0" y="0"
        fill="blue" fill-opacity="1"
```

```
            font-size="18">01</text>
    </g>

    <g transform="translate(160,330)">
      <text id="horizontalLabel" x="0" y="0"
            fill="blue" fill-opacity="1"
            font-size="18">02</text>
    </g>

    <g transform="translate(200,330)">
      <text id="horizontalLabel" x="0" y="0"
            fill="blue" fill-opacity="1"
            font-size="18">03</text>
    </g>
    <!- details omitted for brevity -->

    <!-- *** STEP 7:  render histogram *** -->
    <g transform="translate(80,30)">
      <rect x="0" y="200" width="40" height="80"
            style="fill:green;stroke:green;fill-opacity:1;"/>
    </g>

    <g transform="translate(80,30)">
      <rect x="40" y="100" width="40" height="180"
          style="fill:yellow;stroke:green;fill-opacity:1;"/>
    </g>

    <!-- details omitted for brevity -->

    <g transform="translate(80,30)">
      <rect x="360" y="230" width="40" height="50"
          style="fill:yellow;stroke:green;fill-opacity:1;"/>
    </g>
    </svg>
```

## Remarks

ON THE CD

The SVG code in Listing 10.4 is similar in nature to the code in Listing 10.2. Some of the code has been omitted for brevity, and you can find the complete code for *bar-Graph1.svg* in the folder for this chapter on the accompanying CD-ROM. You can see how the SVG code has been labeled with comments that make it easier to understand as well as simplify code maintenance.

Step 1 of Listing 10.4 contains an SVG `defs` element for defining a grid-like pattern that is used to render a background grid for the graph.

Step 2 renders the background grid patten.

Step 3 of the SVG code contains a rotated line segment and a rotated text string that labels the vertical axis.

Step 4 of the SVG code renders a set of short horizontal line segments as the "hash" marks for the vertical axis.

Step 5 of the SVG code renders a text string that labels the horizontal axis.

Step 6 of the SVG code renders a set of short vertical line segments as the "hash" marks for the horizontal axis.

Step 7 of the SVG code consists of a set of SVG `rect` elements that render the actual bar graph. If you count the number of lines in this file, you'll see that almost three-quarters of the code is devoted to setting up the graph, and roughly one-quarter of the code is for rendering the actual graph itself. The set of SVG `rect` elements in Listing 10.4 is similar to the set in Listing 10.3. In this case, the sum of the values of the `height` attribute and the `y` attribute in the SVG `rect` elements is 400.

You have now reached the point where you can create a bar graph that can be adapted to a variety of situations. One way to embellish this graph is to create a three-dimensional effect, which is the subject of the next example.

## DRAWING BAR CHARTS WITH 3D EFFECTS

Consider the three-dimensional bar graph shown in Figure 10.5.

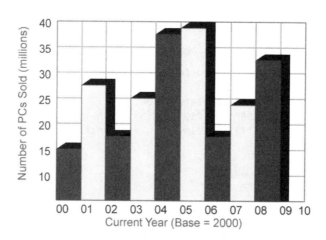

**FIGURE 10.5** A bar graph with a three-dimensional effect.

The SVG document *barGraph3D1.svg* in Listing 10.5 demonstrates how to draw a bar graph with a three-dimensional effect.

**Listing 10.5**   barGraph3D1.svg

```
<?xml version="1.0" encoding="iso-8859-1"?>
<!DOCTYPE svg PUBLIC "-//W3C//DTD SVG 20001102//EN"
"http://www.w3.org/TR/2000/CR-SVG-20001102/DTD/svg-20001102.dtd">

    <svg width="100%" height="100%">
    <!-- *** STEP 1:  define grid pattern *** -->
    <defs>
      <pattern id="gridPattern"
            width="40" height="40"
            patternUnits="userSpaceOnUse">

       <rect x="0" y="0"
             width="40" height="40"
             style="fill:none;stroke:blue;
             stroke-width:1;fill-opacity:.5;"/>
      </pattern>

     <polygon id="topShadow"
             points="0,0 40,0 55,-10 15,-10"
             style="fill:black;fill-opacity:.8;"/>
    </defs>

   <!-- steps omitted for brevity -->

   <!-- *** STEP 7:  render histogram *** -->
   <g transform="translate(80,30)">
    <use xlink:href="#topShadow" x="0" y="200"/>

    <polygon points="40,200 55,190 55,270 40,280"
            style="fill:black;fill-opacity:.8;"/>

    <rect x="0" y="200" width="40" height="80"
         style="fill:green;stroke:green;fill-opacity:1;"/>
   </g>

   <g transform="translate(80,30)">
     <use xlink:href="#topShadow" x="40" y="100"/>

     <polygon points="80,100 95,90 95,170 80,180"
             style="fill:black;fill-opacity:.8;"/>

     <rect x="40" y="100" width="40" height="180"
          style="fill:yellow;stroke:green;fill-opacity:1;"/>
   </g>

   <g transform="translate(80,30)">
```

```
<use xlink:href="#topShadow" x="80" y="180"/>

<polygon points="100,180 135,170 135,280 120,280"
         style="fill:black;fill-opacity:.8;"/>

<rect x="80" y="180" width="40" height="100"
      style="fill:green;stroke:green;fill-opacity:1;"/>
</g>

<!-- similar blocks omitted for brevity -->
</svg>
```

## Remarks

ON THE CD

Listing 10.5 extends the previous example by adding the appropriate SVG elements in order to create a three-dimensional effect. As in previous examples, some of the code has been omitted for brevity, and you can find the complete code for *barGraph3D1.svg* in the folder for this chapter on the accompanying CD-ROM.

The first five steps of Listing 10.5 are similar to previous examples, so they will not be covered in detail in this example. The new code in the SVG defs element contains an SVG polygon element used for creating a shadow effect, as shown in the code fragment below:

```
<polygon id="topShadow"
         points="0,0 40,0 55,-10 15,-10"
         style="fill:black;fill-opacity:.8;"/>
```

Step 7 of the SVG code consists of a set of SVG rect elements that render the actual bar graph. If you count the number of lines in Listing 10.5 and in Listing 10.4, you'll see that roughly the same amount of code is devoted to setting up the graphs. In this example, rendering a three-dimensional effect means that more code is required for rendering the actual graph than the amount of code for rendering the graph in Listing 10.3. In this example, the sum of the values of the height attribute and the y attribute in the SVG rect elements is 400. The SVG code for each SVG rect element in this step also contains the following code:

```
<use xlink:href="#topShadow" x="80" y="300"/>
```

The preceding SVG code references an SVG polygon element whose id attribute has value topShadow, which is defined in the SVG defs element of Listing 10.5. Its purpose is to add shading in order to create a three-dimensional effect.

This example is a simple illustration of enhancing the "template" for the two-dimensional bar graph in order to create a three-dimensional effect. This "component-based" approach to creating charts and graphs will enable you to leverage your existing code and develop a consistent coding style.

## DRAWING SIMPLE LINE GRAPHS

Consider the line graph in Figure 10.6.

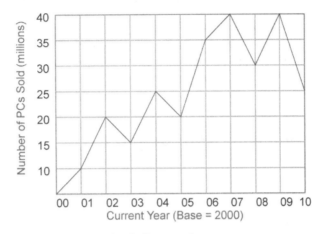

**FIGURE 10.6** A simple line graph.

The SVG document *simpleLineGraph1.svg* in Listing 10.6 demonstrates how to render a simple line graph.

### Listing 10.6  simpleLineGraph1.svg

```
<?xml version="1.0" encoding="iso-8859-1"?>
<!DOCTYPE svg PUBLIC "-//W3C//DTD SVG 20001102//EN"
"http://www.w3.org/TR/2000/CR-SVG-20001102/DTD/svg-
20001102.dtd">

<!-- steps omitted for brevity -->
<!-- *** STEP 7:  render line graph *** -->
<g transform="translate(80,30)">
<path
  d="m0,280
    140,-40 40,-80  40,40  40,-80
    40,40  40,-120 40,-40 40,80
    40,-80 40,120"
  style="fill:none;stroke:green;fill-opacity:1;"/>
  </g>
</svg>
```

## Remarks

ON THE CD

The SVG code in Listing 10.6 leverages the code for the labeled grid in order to create a line graph. The copy of Listing 10.6 on the accompanying CD-ROM contains the complete code for rendering the corresponding bar chart. The first six steps in Listing 10.6 contain the same code as the previous examples, so they will not be covered in detail again. Step 7 of the SVG code contains the key idea for creating a line graph; that is, an SVG `polygon` element that specifies the points on the line graph. You might be surprised to learn that creating a line graph is much simpler than a bar graph; the line graph is rendered with fewer than ten lines of code!

## DRAWING MULTIPLE LINE GRAPHS

Consider the line graphs in Figure 10.7.

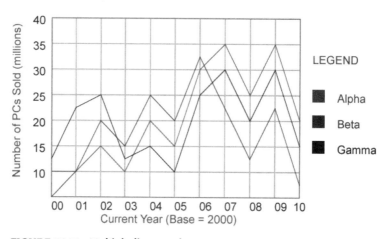

**FIGURE 10.7**   Multiple line graphs.

The SVG document *multiLineGraph1.svg* in Listing 10.7 demonstrates how to render a set of line graphs.

## Listing 10.7    multiLineGraph1.svg

```
<?xml version="1.0" encoding="iso-8859-1"?>
<!DOCTYPE svg PUBLIC "-//W3C//DTD SVG 20001102//EN"
"http://www.w3.org/TR/2000/CR-SVG-20001102/DTD/svg-
   20001102.dtd">
```

```
<!-- *** STEP 7:  render line graphs *** -->

<!-- Company Name: Alpha -->
<g transform="translate(80,30)">
<path
   d="m0,240
      140,0   40,-40  40,40   40,-80
      40,40   40,-120 40,-40  40,80
      40,-80  40,120"
  style="fill:none;stroke:red;fill-opacity:1;"/>
</g>

<!-- Company Name: Beta -->
<g transform="translate(80,30)">
<path
  d="m0,280
     140,-40 40,-80   40,40   40,-80
     40,40   40,-100  40,80   40,80
     40,-80  40,120"
  style="fill:none;stroke:green;fill-opacity:1;"/>
</g>

<!-- Company Name: Gamma -->
<g transform="translate(80,30)">
<path
  d="m0,220
     140,-80 40,-20   40,100 40,-20
     40,40   40,-120 40,-40  40,80
     40,-80  40,120"
  style="fill:none;stroke:blue;fill-opacity:1;"/>
</g>

<!-- *** STEP 8:  company legend *** -->
<g transform="translate(500,100)">
  <text id="verticalLabel" x="0" y="0"
        fill="red"
        font-size="18">
        LEGEND
  </text>

  <rect fill="red"
        x="0" y="40" width="20" height="20"/>

  <text id="verticalLabel" x="40" y="60"
        fill="red"
        font-size="18">
        Alpha
```

```
        </text>

    <rect fill="green"
          x="0" y="80" width="20" height="20"/>

      <text id="verticalLabel" x="40" y="100"
            fill="green"
            font-size="18">
            Beta
      </text>
      <rect fill="blue"
            x="0" y="120" width="20" height="20"/>

      <text id="verticalLabel" x="40" y="140"
            fill="blue"
            font-size="18">
            Gamma
      </text>
    </g>
    </svg>
```

## Remarks

ON THE CD

The SVG code in Listing 10.7 extends the previous example by showing you how to render multiple line graphs in the same SVG document. You can find the complete code for *multiLineGraph1.svg* in the folder for this chapter on the accompanying CD-ROM.

Step 7 of the SVG code consists of three SVG polygon elements that render the actual line graph for three fictional companies named Alpha, Beta, and Gamma.

Step 8 of the SVG code consists of a *legend* that consists of three colored squares that correspond to the three fictional company names. The color of each square is the association between each company and its corresponding line graph.

You can use different colors in conjunction with the various attributes of the SVG line element (such as the stroke-dasharray and stroke-width) in order to render line graphs that create a nice contrasting effect.

## KEY CONSTRUCTS

A homogeneous bar set can be rendered with the following SVG code:

```
<defs>
<rect id="blot1"
    x="0" y="0" width="40" height="200" stroke="white"/>
</defs>
```

```
<g transform="translate(40,100)">
  <use x="0"    y="0" fill="blue" xlink:href="#blot1"/>
  <use x="40"   y="0" fill="red"  xlink:href="#blot1"/>
  <use x="80"   y="0" fill="blue" xlink:href="#blot1"/>
  <use x="120"  y="0" fill="red"  xlink:href="#blot1"/>
  <use x="160"  y="0" fill="blue" xlink:href="#blot1"/>
  <use x="200"  y="0" fill="red"  xlink:href="#blot1"/>
  <use x="240"  y="0" fill="blue" xlink:href="#blot1"/>
  <use x="280"  y="0" fill="red"  xlink:href="#blot1"/>
</g>
```

# CD-ROM LIBRARY

ON THE CD

The folder for this chapter on the book's companion CD-ROM contains the SVG documents that are required for viewing the following graphics images:

*barSet1.svg*

*barSet2.svg*

*labeledGrid1.svg*

*barGraph1.svg*

*barGraph3D1.svg*

*simpleLineGraph1.svg*

*multiLineGraph1.svg*

*equalSectorsPie1.svg*

*equalSectorsShadowPie1.svg*

*filledLineGraph1.svg*

*multi4Pipe1LineGraph3.svg*

*multiLine4Pipe1Graph3.svg*

*multiLineGraph2.svg*

*multiLineGraph3.svg*

*scaledEqualSectorsPie1.svg*

*scaledUnequalSectorsPie1.svg*

*simpleLineGraph2.svg*

*simpleLineGraph3.svg*

*unequalSectorsPie1.svg*

*unequalSectorsShadowPie1.svg*

## SUMMARY

This chapter focused on rendering bar sets, bar graphs, single line graphs, and multiple line graphs in SVG. These types of charts and graphs leverage some of the knowledge that you gained in previous chapters, such as SVG `rect` and `polygon` elements, gradient shading, and rendering rotated text. This chapter also provided an example of creating a three-dimensional effect by means of a simple shading technique. The

*ON THE CD* examples on the CD-ROM for this chapter will further illustrate the fact that SVG is a superb tool for rendering graphs and charts. Creating charts and graphs in SVG provides a fine example of one cornerstone of the XP style of programming, which entails building a solid foundation with a small and simple set of features. After you have a created a robust foundation of code, you can add new features in an iterative, incremental fashion. Graphs and charts are ideal in terms of "deconstructing" them into a set of logically-related components, which greatly simplifies the task of making fine-grained adjustments to the relative positions of the elements within a given component.

**PLATE 1** Archimedean Spiral.

**PLATE 2** Modulus-based Archimedean reflected ellipses.

**PLATE 3** Tubular set of Archimedean ellipses.

**PLATE 4** Triangle-enhanced set of Archimedean ellipses.

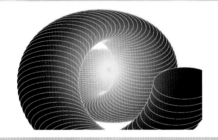

**PLATE 5** Archimedean radial gradient spiral.

**PLATE 6** Cardioid set of partial-view elliptic arcs.

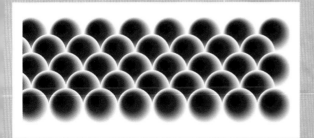

**PLATE 7** Blue circle grid with frost-like shading effect.

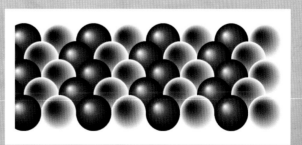

**PLATE 8** Black and white circle grid with frost-like shading effect.

**PLATE 9**  Set of rotated triangles.

**PLATE 10**  Cochleoid set of arcs and rectangles with shading.

**PLATE 11**  Cochleoid set of elliptic arcs and Venetian shading.

**PLATE 12**  Cochleoid set of double elliptic arcs.

**PLATE 13**  Cosine-based Loop of dotted ellipses.

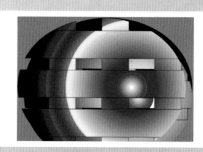

**PLATE 14**  Rectangles with extreme radial gradient shading.

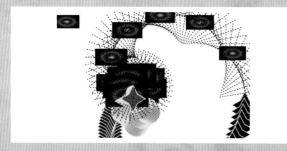

**PLATE 15**  Cochleoid with rectangles, diamonds, and line segments.

**PLATE 16**  Double cubic bezier curve.

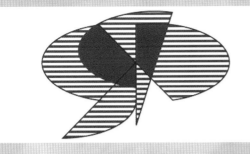

**PLATE 17**   Overlapping striped elliptic arcs.

**PLATE 18**   Overlapping Venetian striped elliptic arcs.

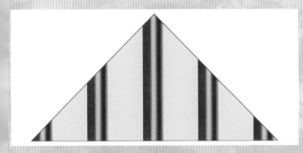

**PLATE 19**   Triangle with simple linear gradient shading.

**PLATE 20**   Metallic-colored color effect.

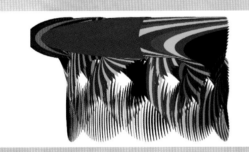

**PLATE 21**   Lissajous pattern of ellipses with Venetian shading.

**PLATE 22**   Multiple Bezier curves with a common start point.

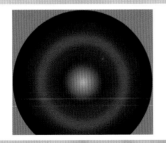

**PLATE 23**   Metallic-colored color effect from radial gradient.

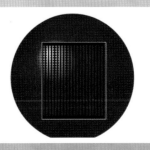

**PLATE 24**   Grid-like overlay of a circle with 3D shading.

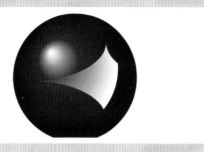

**PLATE 25** Cut-out section of a circle with 3D shading.

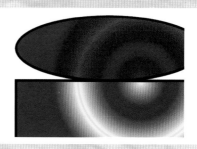

**PLATE 26** "Extreme" radial gradient shading.

**PLATE 27** Scaled grid-like overlay of a circle with 3D shading.

**PLATE 28** Double-coiled ellipses with radial gradient shading.

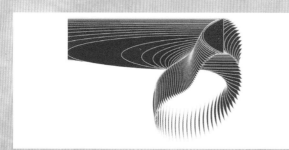

**PLATE 29** Sine-based ellipses with perturbation-style pattern.

**PLATE 30** Sine-based mesh with tetrahedra and Venetian shading.

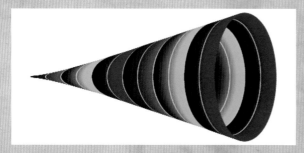

**PLATE 31** Cone with venetian-shaded sections.

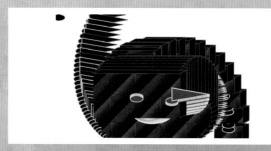

**PLATE 32** Lituus curve with ellipses, triangles, and Venetian shading.

# 11 HTML, ECMAScript, and SVG DOM

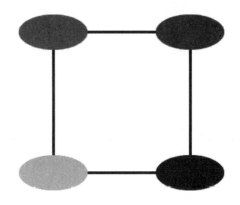

## OVERVIEW

The aim of this chapter is to familiarize you with the SVG DOM and the ECMAScript features that are necessary for manipulating SVG elements. As such, the first part of this chapter (which is fairly short) provides examples of embedding SVG code in HTML pages. The second part of this chapter (also fairly short) introduces you to EC-MAScript functions and provides you with the necessary techniques for processing mouse events in SVG. For example, you'll see how simple it is to associate a graphics image with a hyperlink that navigates to the specified URL after clicking inside that image with your mouse.

The third part of the chapter introduces you to SVG DOM and provides examples of deleting, adding, and updating SVG elements via ECMAScript functions. The code examples in this section delve into more detail vis-à-vis ECMAScript functions. Since the SVG Document Object Model (DOM) hierarchy is accessible through EC-MAScript, you can modify individual attributes of an SVG element. For example, you can detect a mouse click over an ellipse and then (based on some logic of your choice) determine whether to increase or decrease the values of the attributes cx, cy, rx, and ry that are associated with that ellipse. If you label all the elements in your SVG code with an id attribute, it is a straightforward process to check for the presence of multiple SVG elements, regardless of whether or not you clicked on them with your mouse. Moreover, you'll see how easy it is to dynamically create new SVG elements and delete existing elements. Once you gain access to the SVG elements, you will have the freedom to create a remarkable panoply of visual effects with SVG. All code and images for this chapter can be found on the companion CD-ROM in the Chapter 11 folder.

ON THE CD

## PROTECTING SVG CODE

People who have strong feelings about this subject tend to be in one of two camps: either they feel that everything should be visible to anyone or they want the ability to prevent people from viewing their code (sometimes written for the purpose of earning a living). Both positions arguably have merit (though that statement itself would probably be contested).

Currently, there is no guaranteed way to prevent people from looking at your SVG code. Placing SVG code in separate ".js" files will prevent the code from being visible via "view source," but the code is loaded into memory (in unencrypted form) so it's possible to write functions that will display the contents of all your ECMAScript code. You can encrypt code in external files or place the code in a "zip" file but once the code is loaded into memory, it is accessible in unencrypted form. You can prevent the uninitiated from accessing your code, but people who are determined to view the source code in plain text can obtain the requisite knowledge to do so.

## EMBEDDING SVG IN HTML PAGES

Consider the SVG rectangle displayed in Figure 11.1.

The SVG document *displayRect1.svg* in Listing 11.1 contains the SVG code for rendering a rectangle, and Listing 11.2 contains the HTML code that launches the SVG code.

**FIGURE 11.1**    An SVG document
to display an SVG rectangle.

**Listing 11.1**    displayRect1.svg

```
<?xml version="1.0" encoding="iso-8859-1"?>
<!DOCTYPE svg PUBLIC "-//W3C//DTD SVG 20001102//EN"
 "http://www.w3.org/TR/2000/CR-SVG-20001102/DTD/svg-20001102.dtd">

<svg width="100%" height="100%">
  <g transform="translate(50,50)">
    <rect x="10" cy="10"
          width="60" height="100"
          style="stroke:blue;stroke-width:4;fill:red;"/>
  </g>
</svg>
```

**Listing 11.2**    displayRect1.html

```
<html>
  <head></head>

  <body BGCOLOR="#CCCCCC">
    <embed width="500" height="400"
           src="displayRect1.svg" type="image/svg">
  </body>
</html>
```

### Remarks

The SVG code in Listing 11.1 renders a red rectangle with a blue border because of the following code fragment:

```
<rect x="10" cy="10"
      width="60" height="100"
      style="stroke:blue;stroke-width:4;fill:red;"/>
```

The HTML code in Listing 11.2 is very straightforward. Below is the HTML tag required for launching the SVG document *displayRect1.svg*:

```
<embed width="500" height="400"
       src="displayRect1.svg" type="image/svg">
```

Now you can embed SVG documents in your HTML pages with a minimum of effort!

## HTML PAGES WITH IMAGES EMBEDDED IN SVG

Consider the image displayed in Figure 11.2.

**FIGURE 11.2** An HTML page with a scaled image in an SVG document.

The SVG document *scaledImage1.svg* in Listing 11.3 demonstrates how to render a scaled embedded image, and Listing 11.4 contains the HTML code that launches the SVG code in Listing 11.3.

### Listing 11.3   scaledImage1.svg

```
<?xml version="1.0" encoding="iso-8859-1"?>
<!DOCTYPE svg PUBLIC "-//W3C//DTD SVG 20001102//EN"
 "http://www.w3.org/TR/2000/CR-SVG-20001102/DTD/svg-20001102.dtd">

<svg width="100%" height="100%">
 <defs>
    <filter
        id="feImageFilter1"
        filterUnits="objectBoundingBox"
        x="0" y="0" width="200" height="200">
        <feImage xlink:href="simpleHouse1.gif"
          x="0" y="0"
          width="200" height="200"
          result="outputImage1"/>
    </filter>
```

```
      <filter
         id="feImageFilter2"
         filterUnits="objectBoundingBox"
         x="0" y="0" width="200" height="200">
         <feImage xlink:href="simpleHouse1.gif"
           x="200" y="0"
           width="200" height="200"
           result="outputImage2"/>
      </filter>
  </defs>

  <g transform="translate(50,50)">
    <rect x="0" y="0" width="200" height="200"
         filter="url(#feImageFilter1)"/>
  </g>
  <g transform="translate(250,50) scale(.5)">
    <rect x="0" y="0" width="100" height="100"
         filter="url(#feImageFilter1)"/>
  </g>
  </svg>
```

**Listing 11.4**   scaledImage1.html

```
<html>
 <head></head>

  <body BGCOLOR="#CCCCCC">
    <embed width="500" height="400"
          src="scaledImage1.svg" type="image/svg">
  </body>
</htmlL>
```

## Remarks

The SVG code in Listing 11.3 renders a picture of a house because of the SVG rectangle element in the following code fragment, which references an SVG filter element that explicitly references a GIF file on the file system:

```
<rect x="0" y="0" width="200" height="200"
      filter="url(#feImageFilter1)"/>
```

The HTML code in Listing 11.4 contains an HTML tag that launches the SVG document *scaledImage1.svg*, as listed below:

```
<embed width="500" height="400"
      src="scaledImage1.svg" type="image/svg">
```

Obviously you don't need SVG code for displaying images: you can bypass the SVG code and simply use the appropriate HTML tag; still, the functionality is available should you decide to make use of it.

## URL-ENABLED ELLIPSES

Consider the ellipses rendered in Figure 11.3.

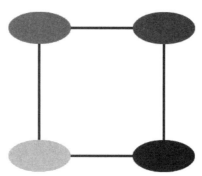

**FIGURE 11.3**   URL-enabled ellipses.

The SVG document *hyperLinkEllipses1.svg* in Listing 11.5 demonstrates how to use the SVG onclick element in order to resize a circle and change its color.

**Listing 11.5**   hyperLinkEllipses1.svg

```
<?xml version="1.0" standalone="no"?>
<!DOCTYPE svg PUBLIC "-//W3C//DTD SVG 20010904//EN"
  "http://www.w3.org/TR/2001/REC-SVG-20010904/DTD/svg10.dtd">

<svg width="100%" height="100%"
    xmlns="http://www.w3.org/2000/svg"
    xmlns:xlink="http://www.w3.org/1999/xlink">

<g transform="translate(100,50)">
  <text font-size="24" color="black">
    Click on any ellipse:
  </text>
```

```
  </g>

  <g transform="translate(100,100)">
    <rect x="0" y="0" width="200" height="200"
          fill="none" stroke="blue"  stroke-width="4"/>

    <a xlink:href="http://www.w3.org">
      <ellipse fill="red" cx="0" cy="0"
               rx="50" ry="25"/>
    </a>

    <a xlink:href="http://www.w3.org">
      <ellipse fill="green" cx="200" cy="0"
               rx="50" ry="25"/>
    </a>

    <a xlink:href="http://www.w3.org">
      <ellipse fill="blue" cx="200" cy="200"
               rx="50" ry="25"/>
    </a>

    <a xlink:href="http://www.w3.org">
      <ellipse fill="yellow" cx="0" cy="200"
               rx="50" ry="25"/>
    </a>
  </g>
</svg>
```

## Remarks

Listing 11.5 starts by displaying a message with the following code fragment:

```
<g transform="translate(100,50)">
  <text font-size="24" color="black">
    Click on any ellipse:
  </text>
</g>
```

Next, Listing 11.5 renders an "anchor rectangle" with the following SVG code fragment:

```
<rect x="0" y="0" width="200" height="200"
      fill="none" stroke="blue" stroke-width="4"/>
```

Lastly, Listing 11.5 renders an ellipse that is centered on each of the four vertices of the anchor rectangle. For example, the following code fragment renders an ellipse whose center is the upper-left vertex of the anchor rectangle:

```
<a xlink:href="http://www.w3.org">
    <ellipse fill="red" cx="0" cy="0"
             rx="50" ry="25"/>
</a>
```

When you click on the ellipse with your mouse, your browser will be directed to the URL *http://www.w3.org* because it is associated with the ellipse by means of the SVG a element.

This example used an ellipse for the purpose of illustrating the SVG a element; in general, though, SVG allows you great flexibility in terms of the graphics image that you wish to associate with an URL. Depending on your needs, you can easily create SVG documents with lots of fancy "URL-enabled" graphics images.

## HANDLING MOUSE-OVER EVENTS

Consider the "mouse-aware" rectangle rendered in Figure 11.4.

**FIGURE 11.4** A mouse-aware rectangle.

The SVG document *mouseOverRect1.svg* in Listing 11.6 demonstrates how to use the SVG mouseover element in order to change the color of a rectangle.

**Listing 11.6**   mouseOverRect1.svg

```
<?xml version="1.0" encoding="iso-8859-1"?>
<!DOCTYPE svg PUBLIC "-//W3C//DTD SVG 20001102//EN"
 "http://www.w3.org/TR/2000/CR-SVG-20001102/DTD/svg-20001102.dtd">

<svg width="100%" height="100%">
<g transform="translate(100,100)">
<rect
    x="0" y="0" width="200" height="100"
    style="fill:red;stroke:blue;stroke-width:4;">
    <set begin="mouseover" end="mouseout"
```

```
        attributeName="fill" from="#FF0000" to="#FFFF00"/>
    </rect>
    </g>
    </svg>
```

## Remarks

Listing 11.6 contains an SVG rect element that specifies the color, location, and dimensions of the rectangle by means of the following code fragment:

```
<rect
    x="0" y="0" width="200" height="100"
    style="fill:red;stroke:blue;stroke-width:4;">
```

When you move your mouse anywhere in the interior of the rectangle, the color changes from red to yellow. When you move your mouse outside the rectangle, its color reverts to red. This color change is produced by the following code fragment that is specified in the same SVG rect element:

```
<set begin="mouseover" end="mouseout"
    attributeName="fill" from="#FF0000" to="#FFFF00"/>
```

SVG makes it very easy to associate mouse events with SVG elements, and you can process those mouse events in order to extract the information that you need. The next example shows you how to make a "mouse-aware" rectangle disappear when you click your mouse inside the rectangle.

## HIDING RECTANGLES

Consider the "mouse-aware" rectangle rendered in Figure 11.5.

**FIGURE 11.5**   A mouse-aware rectangle.

The SVG document *invisibleRect1.svg* in Listing 11.7 demonstrates how to use the SVG mouseover element in order to hide a rectangle.

**Listing 11.7**   invisibleRect1.svg

```
<?xml version="1.0" encoding="iso-8859-1"?>
<!DOCTYPE svg PUBLIC "-//W3C//DTD SVG 20001102//EN"
 "http://www.w3.org/TR/2000/CR-SVG-20001102/DTD/svg-20001102.dtd">

<svg width="100%" height="100%">

<g transform="translate(100,100)">
<rect
   x="0" y="0" width="200" height="100"
   style="fill:red;stroke:blue;stroke-width:4;">
   <set begin="mouseover" end="mouseout"
    attributeName="fill" from="#FF0000" to="#000000"/>
   <set attributeName="visibility" attributeType="XML"
    to="hidden" begin="1s" dur="3s"/>
</rect>
</g>
</svg>
```

## Remarks

The SVG code in Listing 11.7 renders a red rectangle via the following code fragment:

```
<rect
   x="0" y="0" width="200" height="100"
   style="fill:red;stroke:blue;stroke-width:4;">
```

When you move your mouse anywhere in the interior of the rectangle, the color changes from red to black. When you move your mouse outside the rectangle, its color reverts to red. This color change is produced by the following line of code:

```
<set begin="mouseover" end="mouseout"
 attributeName="fill" from="#FF0000" to="#000000"/>
```

Notice the other feature of this example: one second after the SVG document is loaded, this rectangle will disappear for three seconds and then reappear on the screen. The following lines of code produce this disappearance effect:

```
<set attributeName="visibility" attributeType="XML"
 to="hidden" begin="1s" dur="3s"/>
```

This example demonstrates how to associate two mouse-related events with the same SVG element, and you can specify additional mouse events in a similar manner. Despite having seen only a few examples of mouse-based events, you're already in a position to create interesting visual effects that combine graphics images and mouse-clicks!

## MOUSE CLICKS AND GRADIENT COLORS

Consider the circle rendered in Figure 11.6.

**FIGURE 11.6**   A circle whose color
changes after a mouse click.

The SVG document *circleGradient1.svg* in Listing 11.8 demonstrates how to handle mouse clicks in order to render a circle with a gradient color set.

**Listing 11.8**   circleGradient1.svg

```
<?xml version="1.0" encoding="iso-8859-1"?>
<!DOCTYPE svg PUBLIC "-//W3C//DTD SVG 20001102//EN"
 "http://www.w3.org/TR/2000/CR-SVG-20001102/DTD/svg-20001102.dtd">

<svg width="100%" height="100%">

<defs>
   <animateColor
      id="circleGradient1"
      xlink:href="#shape"
      attributeName="fill"
      values="rgb(255,0,0);rgb(0,255,255);
              rgb(0,128,151);rgb(255,0,0)"
      dur="3s" begin="indefinite"/>
</defs>

<a xlink:href="#circleGradient1">
   <circle id="shape"
           cx="100" cy="100" r="50"
           style="fill:rgb(255,255,0)"/>
</a>
</svg>
```

### Remarks

The SVG code in Listing 11.8 renders a yellow circle via the following code fragment:

```
<circle id="shape"
        cx="100" cy="100" r="50"
        style="fill:rgb(255,255,0)"/>
```

When you click on the circle with your mouse, the color of the circle changes through a range of colors for three seconds. The range of colors is specified in the values attribute in the following code fragment that is defined in the SVG defs element:

```
<animateColor
  id="circleGradient1"
    xlink:href="#shape"
    attributeName="fill"
    values="rgb(255,0,0);rgb(0,255,255);
            rgb(0,128,151);rgb(255,0,0)"
    dur="3s" begin="indefinite"/>
```

The association between the SVG circle element and the SVG animateColor element is made by embedding the SVG circle element inside a link element, as shown below:

```
<a xlink:href="#circleGradient1">
   <circle id="shape"
           cx="100" cy="100" r="50"
           style="fill:rgb(255,255,0)"/>
</a>
```

This example shows how to combine graphics images, mouse events, and animation.

## DETERMINING ATTRIBUTE VALUES OF SVG ELEMENTS

Consider the rectangle rendered in Figure 11.7.

Click inside the rectangle:

**FIGURE 11.7** Displaying attribute values of SVG elements.

The SVG document *elementAttributes1.svg* in Listing 11.9 demonstrates how to use the SVG `onclick` element in order to invoke an ECMAScript function that displays the values of the attributes of an SVG `rect` element.

**Listing 11.9**   elementAttributes1.svg

```
<?xml version="1.0" standalone="no"?>
<!DOCTYPE svg PUBLIC "-//W3C//DTD SVG 20010904//EN"
  "http://www.w3.org/TR/2001/REC-SVG-20010904/DTD/svg10.dtd">

<svg width="100%" height="100%"
    xmlns="http://www.w3.org/2000/svg"
    xmlns:xlink="http://www.w3.org/1999/xlink">

  <!-- *** JavaScript code starts here *** -->
  <script type="text/ecmascript">
  <![CDATA[
    // Remove rectangle and add circle
    function showAttributes(event)
    {
       var msg = "";

       var theRect   = event.target;
       var theParent = theRect.parentNode;

       var theID     = theRect.getAttribute("id");
       var xPosition = theRect.getAttribute("x");
       var yPosition = theRect.getAttribute("y");
       var theWidth  = theRect.getAttribute("width");
       var theHeight = theRect.getAttribute("height");

       msg += "Rectangle ID: " + theID     + "\n";
       msg += "x coordinate: " + xPosition + "\n";
       msg += "y coordinate: " + yPosition + "\n";
       msg += "width:        " + theWidth  + "\n";
       msg += "height:       " + theHeight + "\n";

       alert(msg);
    }

  ]]> </script>

  <!-- *** SVG code starts here *** -->
  <g transform="translate(50,50)">
     <text id="text1" font-size="24" fill="blue">
     Click inside the rectangle:
     </text>
```

```
    </g>

    <g transform="translate(50,100)">
      <rect id="rect1" fill="red"
            onclick="showAttributes(evt)"
            x="10" y="10" width="200" height="100"/>
    </g>
  </svg>
```

## Remarks

The SVG code in Listing 11.9 renders a red rectangle by means of the following code fragment:

```
<rect id="rect1" fill="red"
      onclick="showAttributes(evt)"
      x="10" y="10" width="200" height="100"/>
```

When you click on the rectangle with your mouse, the ECMAScript function showAttributes() is invoked, which will extract the values of the various attributes of the rectangle and then display the result in an ECMAScript alert box. This technique is useful when you are debugging your SVG code, particularly when you are dynamically constructing complex string patterns, which may involve elements such as SVG path elements or SVG polygon elements.

You might be wondering why the ECMAScript function showAttributes() is invoked with the variable evt, which is nowhere to be found in the SVG document. The variable evt is a special variable that contains a reference to an event. This variable is always available to you, and you must invoke your ECMAScript functions with this variable whenever you want to process mouse-based events.

Notice how the ECMAScript code begins with the following lines:

```
<script type="text/ecmascript">
<![CDATA[
```

The ECMAScript function begins with a comment line followed by the function definition:

```
// Remove rectangle and add circle
function remove(event)
{
```

The ECMAScript function starts by defining an empty string variable msg:

```
var msg = "";
```

The next pair of statements retrieve the clicked rectangle and its parent object:

```
var theRect   = event.target;
var theParent = theRect.parentNode;
```

The next five statements retrieve the values of the attributes id, x, y, width, and height of the clicked rectangle:

```
var theID    = theRect.getAttribute("id");
var xPosition = theRect.getAttribute("x");
var yPosition = theRect.getAttribute("y");
var theWidth = theRect.getAttribute("width");
var theHeight = theRect.getAttribute("height");
```

The last assignment statement concatenates the values of the preceding variables in preparation for display:

```
msg += "Rectangle ID: " + theID   + "\n";
msg += "x coordinate: " + xPosition + "\n";
msg += "y coordinate: " + yPosition + "\n";
msg += "width:        " + theWidth  + "\n";
msg += "height:       " + theHeight + "\n";
```

The final statement produces an alert box that contains a string with the values of the attributes of the clicked rectangle:

```
alert(msg);
```

The end of the ECMAScript function and the CDATA section consists of the following pair of lines:

```
   }
]]> </script>
```

The SVG code for rendering a text string and a rectangle is:

```
<g transform="translate(50,50)">
  <text id="text1" font-size="24" fill="blue">
    Click inside the rectangle:
  </text>
</g>

<g transform="translate(50,100)">
   <rect id="rect1" onclick="remove(evt)" fill="red"
        x="10" y="10" width="200" height="100"/>
</g>
```

The actual amount of SVG code is only a small percentage of the ECMAScript code in Listing 11.9. Later, in Chapter 13 and Chapter 14, you'll see examples of ECMAScript functions that are much longer than the ECMAScript in Listing 11.9; in fact, you can write ECMAScript functions that contain hundreds or thousands of lines of code! Rest assured, though, that the SVG code in this book utilizes a small subset of ECMAScript.

## MOUSE CLICKS AND RESIZING CIRCLES

Consider the mouse-aware circle rendered in Figure 11.8.

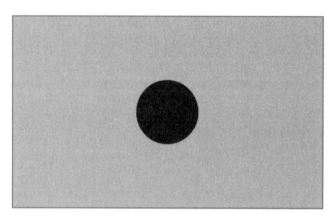

**FIGURE 11.8**   A circle whose radius changes after a mouse click.

The SVG document *resizeCircle1.svg* in Listing 11.10 demonstrates how to use the SVG onclick element in order to resize a circle and change its color.

### Listing 11.10   resizeCircle1.svg

```
<?xml version="1.0" standalone="no"?>
<!DOCTYPE svg PUBLIC "-//W3C//DTD SVG 20010904//EN"
  "http://www.w3.org/TR/2001/REC-SVG-20010904/DTD/svg10.dtd">

<svg width="100%" height="100%"
```

```
          xmlns="http://www.w3.org/2000/svg">

  <desc>Capture mouse click events</desc>

  <!-- script for updating the visible circle -->
  <script type="text/ecmascript"> <![CDATA[
    function mouseClick1(evt)
    {
        var circle = evt.target;
        var currentRadius = circle.getAttribute("r");

        if(currentRadius == 50)
        {
           circle.setAttribute("r", currentRadius*2);
           circle.setAttribute("fill", "#FF0000");
        }
        else
        {
           circle.setAttribute("r", currentRadius*0.5);
           circle.setAttribute("fill", "#FFFF00");
        }
    }
  ]]> </script>

  <g transform="translate(50,40)">
     <text x="0" y="0" font-size="30">
       Click inside the circle
     </text>
  </g>

  <!-- rectangular background -->
  <g transform="translate(20,90)">
     <rect x="0" y="0" width="500" height="300"
           fill="#CCCCCC" stroke="blue"/>

     <!-- Handle mouse click via script function -->
     <circle onclick="mouseClick1(evt)"
             cx="250" cy="150" r="50" fill="blue"/>
  </g>
</svg>
```

## Remarks

The logic for updating the circle rendered in Listing 11.10 is contained in the following ECMAScript function:

```
function mouseClick1(evt)
{
```

```
var circle = evt.target;
var currentRadius = circle.getAttribute("r");

if(currentRadius == 100)
{
   circle.setAttribute("r", currentRadius*2);
   circle.setAttribute("fill", "#FF0000");
}
else
{
   circle.setAttribute("r", currentRadius*0.5);
   circle.setAttribute("fill", "#FFFF00");
}
}
```

When you click inside the circle, here's what happens: the variable `circle` is assigned a reference to the object representing the clicked circle, thereby allowing you to extract the value of the attribute r as shown below:

```
var circle = evt.target;
var currentRadius = circle.getAttribute("r");
```

The "`if/else`" logic in the ECMAScript code contains the logic for setting the new value for the r attribute (i.e., the radius of the circle) and the `fill` attribute of the circle.

## MOUSE CLICKS AND SCALED ELLIPSES

Consider the ellipse rendered in Figure 11.9.

## Click on the moving ellipse

**FIGURE 11.9**   A mouse-aware scaling ellipse.

The SVG document *scalingEllipse1.svg* in Listing 11.11 demonstrates how to use the SVG onclick element in order to resize a scaling ellipse.

**Listing 11.11**    scalingEllipse1.svg

```
<?xml version="1.0" standalone="no"?>
<!DOCTYPE svg PUBLIC "-//W3C//DTD SVG 20010904//EN"
  "http://www.w3.org/TR/2001/REC-SVG-20010904/DTD/svg10.dtd">

<svg width="100%" height="100%"
    xmlns="http://www.w3.org/2000/svg">

  <desc>Capture mouse click events</desc>

  <!-- script for updating the visible ellipse -->
  <script type="text/ecmascript">
  <![CDATA[
    function mouseClick1(event)
    {
       var ellipse = event.target;
       var currentXRadius = ellipse.getAttribute("rx");

       if(currentXRadius == 120)
       {
          ellipse.setAttribute("rx", currentXRadius*2);
          ellipse.setAttribute("fill", "#FF0000");
       }
       else
       {
          ellipse.setAttribute("rx", currentXRadius*0.5);
          ellipse.setAttribute("fill", "#FFFF00");
       }
    }
  ]]> </script>

  <g transform="translate(20,50)">
     <text x="0" y="0" font-size="30">
     Click on the moving ellipse
     </text>
  </g>

  <!-- rectangular background -->
  <g transform="translate(50,100)">
     <rect x="0" y="0" width="500" height="400"
          fill="#CCCCCC" stroke="blue"/>

     <!-- Handle mouse click via script function -->
```

```
            <ellipse onclick="mouseClick1(evt)"
                    cx="250" cy="200" rx="120" ry="60"
                    fill="blue">
                <animateTransform attributeName="transform"
                                    attributeType="XML"
                                    type="scale"
                                    from="0" to="1"
                                    begin="0s" dur="4s"/>
        </ellipse>
    </g>
</svg>
```

## Remarks

When you click inside the moving ellipse, the ECMAScript function mouseClick1()
is executed; the contents of this function are given below:

```
function mouseClick1(event)
{
    var ellipse = event.target;
    var currentXRadius = ellipse.getAttribute("rx");

    if(currentXRadius == 120)
    {
        ellipse.setAttribute("rx", currentXRadius*2);
        ellipse.setAttribute("fill", "#FF0000");
    }
    else
    {
        ellipse.setAttribute("rx", currentXRadius*0.5);
        ellipse.setAttribute("fill", "#FFFF00");
    }
}
```

The function mouseClick1() initializes the variable ellipse with an object. The
variable currentXRadius is assigned the value of the rx attribute of the variable ellipse with the following line of code:

```
var currentXRadius = ellipse.getAttribute("rx");
```

Next, the "if/then" logic determines which block of code to execute in order to
assign values to the rx attribute (i.e., the horizontal axis for the ellipse) and the fill
attribute:

```
if(currentXRadius == 120)
{
    ellipse.setAttribute("rx", currentXRadius*2);
```

```
      ellipse.setAttribute("fill", "#FF0000");
   }
   else
   {
      ellipse.setAttribute("rx", currentXRadius*0.5);
      ellipse.setAttribute("fill", "#FFFF00");
   }
```

The examples that you have seen in this chapter demonstrated how to associate mouse-related events with SVG elements and then use `getAttribute`/`setAttribute` in ECMAScript functions in order to dynamically update attributes of SVG elements.

## KEY CONSTRUCTS

An SVG document can be launched in an HTML page with the following HTML fragment:

```
<embed width="500" height="400"
       src="displayRect1.svg" type="image/svg">
```

The following SVG fragment specifies an URL-enabled ellipse:

```
<a xlink:href="http://www.w3.org">
   <ellipse fill="red" cx="0" cy="0"
            rx="50" ry="25"/>
</a>
```

The following SVG fragment specifies a "mouse-aware" rectangle:

```
<rect
  x="0" y="0" width="200" height="100"
  style="fill:red;stroke:blue;stroke-width:4;">
  <set begin="mouseover" end="mouseout"
   attributeName="fill" from="#FFFF00" to="#000000"/>
</rect>
```

The following SVG fragment specifies a "mouse-aware" rectangle that becomes invisible when you move your mouse over the rectangle:

```
<rect
  x="0" y="0" width="200" height="100"
  style="fill:red;stroke:blue;stroke-width:4;">
  <set begin="mouseover" end="mouseout"
   attributeName="fill" from="#FFFF00" to="#000000"/>
```

```
<set attributeName="visibility" attributeType="XML"
  to="hidden" begin="1s" dur="3s"/>
</rect>
```

The following ECMAScript function changes the radius of a rendered circle:

```
function mouseClick1(evt)
{
   var circle = evt.target;
   var currentRadius = circle.getAttribute("r");

   if(currentRadius == 100)
   {
      circle.setAttribute("r", currentRadius*2);
      circle.setAttribute("fill", "#FF0000");
   }
   else
   {
      circle.setAttribute("r", currentRadius*0.5);
      circle.setAttribute("fill", "#FFFF00");
   }
}
```

# CD-ROM LIBRARY

ON THE CD
The folder for this chapter on the book's companion CD-ROM contains the SVG documents that are required for viewing the following graphics images:

*displayRect1.svg*

*displayRect1.html*

*scaledImage1.html*

*scaledImage1.svg*

*simpleHouse1.gif*

*hyperLinkEllipses1.svg*

*mouseOverRect1.svg*

*invisibleRect1.svg*

*circleGradient1.svg*

*elementAttributes1.svg*

*resizeCircle1.svg*

*scalingEllipse1.svg*

*deleteElement1.svg*

*mouseCoordinates1.svg*

*rotatingImage1.html*

*rotatingImage1.svg*

*scalingImage1.html*

*scalingImage1.svg*

*skewedImage1.html*

*skewedImage1.svg*

## SUMMARY

This chapter focused on how to embed SVG documents in HTML pages, manipulate the DOM of an SVG document, and associate mouse-related events with SVG elements. The examples in this chapter showed you how to do the following:

- launch SVG documents from an HTML page
- URL-enable an ellipse
- define "mouse-aware" rectangles
- access and modify SVG elements
- define ECMAScript functions for modifying circles

ON THE CD

You also saw how to create simple animation effects triggered by mouse events that produce color gradient effects. The code samples for this chapter that are on the CD-ROM provide additional examples of writing ECMAScript functions that manipulate SVG elements embedded in SVG documents.

# 12 Interactive SVG and ECMAScript

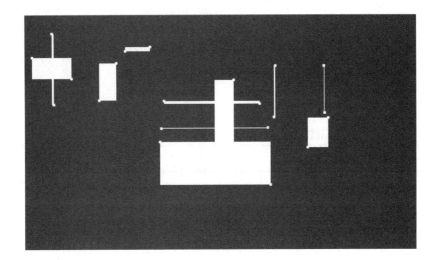

## OVERVIEW

The concepts in this chapter extend the knowledge that you gained in the previous chapter, so if you are unfamiliar with the SVG DOM, now would be a good time to read (or at least skim) the contents of the previous chapter. At this point, you have seen many examples of defining SVG "primitives" and techniques for combining them in order to produce interesting and colorful graphics images. Hopefully, you feel comfortable with the built-in animation techniques available in SVG that allow you to manipulate various attributes (e.g., width, height, radius, etc). However, attributes of some SVG elements, such as the points attribute of the SVG path element, are more easily modified via ECMAScript functions. The examples in the first part of this chapter will demonstrate how to make such modifications. Once you get a reference to an SVG element, it's easy to change the attributes of that element.

One very important aspect of SVG, particularly with regard to animation, is the ability to dynamically create new SVG elements. Creating such elements on the fly is actually quite straightforward; however, the dynamic generation of tens of thousands of SVG elements will obviously affect both memory and performance. Although the concepts and techniques in this chapter might seem simple (or perhaps even trivial), they provide you with a knowledge base for developing more sophisticated SVG animation that can be handled via ECMAScript functions. As you'll see in Chapter 14, ECMAScript functions allow you not only to compute values of trigonometric functions (e.g., sine, cosine, tangent, and combinations thereof) and mathematical functions, but also give you the ability to make recursive function calls. All code and images for this chapter can be found on the companion CD-ROM in the Chapter 12 folder.

ON THE CD

## SVG CODE TEMPLATE FOR THIS CHAPTER

If you are relatively new to ECMAScript, it might be helpful to look at a high-level overview of the structure of the code samples in this chapter. All the SVG documents in this chapter have an ECMAScript function that is executed whenever a particular mouse event occurs that is associated with an SVG element (which makes it "mouse aware"). Structurally all the examples have a format that is similar to the one listed below, where the ellipsis ("...") indicates that some information has been omitted:

```
<?xml version="1.0" standalone="no"?>
<!DOCTYPE ....>

<svg ....>
  <script type="text/ecmascript">
    <![CDATA[
    // global variables here

    function doSomething(event)
    {
        // some code goes here
    }

  ]]> </script>

<g transform="translate(10,10)">
 <!-- 'rect' is an example (not mandatory) -->
  <rect onclick="doSomething(evt)" .../>
 </g>
</svg>
```

The key idea in the preceding template involves "associating" the ECMAScript function doSomething() with an SVG rect element, and this function is invoked when you click your mouse inside the rectangle. The exact nature of what happens inside this function depends on the code that you include in this function. You can specify other ECMAScript functions that are executed when you click on different SVG elements. For example, the following code fragment associates an ECMAScript function with an SVG polygon element and a different function with an SVG rect element:

```
<g transform="translate(10,10)">
  <polygon onclick="doSomething1(evt)" .../>
  <rect    onclick="doSomething2(evt)" .../>
</g>
```

In the preceding fragment, the ECMAScript function doSomething1() will be invoked when you click inside the polygon and the ECMAScript function doSomething2() will be invoked when you click inside the rectangle.

You can also specify the same ECMAScript function for multiple SVG elements; in this scenario, you'll obviously need some mechanism for determining the specific SVG element that is associated with the mouse click event. Until you become highly proficient in ECMAScript functions, though, it's probably easier to invoke different functions for different SVG elements.

SVG can handle much more than just mouse click events; if you read Chapter 18 (section 4) of the SVG specification, you will find the following mouse-related events:

- onmousedown
- onmouseup
- onmouseover
- onmousemove
- onmouseout

Note that the onclick mouse event consists of an onmousedown event followed by an onmouseup event. The onmouseover mouse event is useful for detecting the fact that your mouse is inside the region defined by an SVG element contained in your SVG document, and this event can trigger the execution of an ECMAScript function that will perform the appropriate actions. The onmouseout mouse event can trigger the execution of an ECMAScript function when your mouse exits the region that belongs to one of your SVG elements. This chapter will focus on presenting various situations where you want to process a "mouse click" event. Now let's examine some complete examples in order to understand how to manipulate the contents of an SVG document.

## UPDATING ATTRIBUTES OF SVG path ELEMENTS

Consider the rectangle rendered in Figure 12.1.

# Click inside the polygon:

**FIGURE 12.1** A modifiable
path-based rectangle.

The SVG document *changePath1.svg* in Listing 12.1 demonstrates how to define an ECMAScript function that updates the points in an SVG path element.

### Listing 12.1 changePath1.svg

```
<?xml version="1.0" standalone="no"?>
<!DOCTYPE svg PUBLIC "-//W3C//DTD SVG 20010904//EN"
  "http://www.w3.org/TR/2001/REC-SVG-20010904/DTD/svg10.dtd">

<svg width="100%" height="100%"
     xmlns="http://www.w3.org/2000/svg">

  <!-- Capture mouse clicks and update path -->
  <script type="text/ecmascript">
   <![CDATA[
   var clickCount = 0.;
   var newPath    = "";
   var points     = "";
   var pathNode    = null;

   function clickPath1(event)
   {
      pathNode    = event.target;
      points = pathNode.getAttribute("points");
      ++clickCount;

      if( clickCount % 2 == 0 )
      {
         str = "100,100 300,100 300,200 200,200"
```

```
            pathNode.setAttribute("points", str);
            pathNode.setAttribute("fill", 'red');
        }
        else
        {
            str = "250,100 300,100 300,200 200,200"
            pathNode.setAttribute("points", str);
            pathNode.setAttribute("fill", 'green');
        }
    }

  ]]> </script>

<!-- ===================================== -->
<g transform="translate(10,10)">
  <rect x="0" y="0"
        width="800" height="500"
        fill="none" stroke="none"/>

  <!-- Specify function to handle mouse -->
  <!-- click and update the path -->
  <polygon onclick="clickPath1(evt)"
           points="200,100 300,100 300,200 200,200"
           fill="blue"/>

  <!-- Display text message -->
  <text x="250" y="50"
        font-family="Verdana"
        font-size="25" text-anchor="middle">
    Click inside the polygon:
  </text>
</g>
</svg>
```

## Remarks

The SVG code in Listing 12.1 renders a polygon with the following code fragment:

```
<polygon onclick="clickPath1(evt)"
         points="200,100 300,100 300,200 200,200"
         fill="blue"/>
```

This polygon is initially a blue rectangle, and it is "mouse-aware" because of the following onclick attribute:

```
onclick="clickPath1(evt)"
```

When you click inside the rectangle, the ECMAScript function `mouseClick1()` is executed, which accesses the SVG `path` element and then the contents of the `points` attribute with the following statements:

```
var pathNode = event.target;
var points = pathNode.getAttribute("points");
```

The global ECMAScript variable `clickCount` is incremented each time you click on your mouse inside the polygon by means of a simple statement:

```
++clickCount;
```

The preceding line of code is typical in languages such as Java, C/C++ (as well as ECMAScript), and it will be used throughout this book. If you are not familiar with this construct, you can think of it as being essentially equivalent (ignoring the concepts of post-increment and pre-increment) to the following:

```
clickCount += 1;
```

The "`if`/`else`" portion of the ECMAScript code determines which block of code to execute. Each block assigns a value to the ECMAScript variable `str` that is used for assigning a value to the `points` attribute of an SVG `path` element that represents a quadrilateral. The `fill` attribute of the SVG `path` element is assigned a hard-coded value of "red" or "green," depending on the block of code, as shown below:

```
if( clickCount % 2 == 0 )
{
   str = "100,100 300,100 300,200 200,200"
   pathNode.setAttribute("points", str);
   pathNode.setAttribute("fill", 'red');
}
else
{
   str = "250,100 300,100 300,200 200,200"
   pathNode.setAttribute("points", str);
   pathNode.setAttribute("fill", 'green');
}
```

If you have an SVG document with multiple geometric objects, you have the ability to specify a different ECMAScript function for each geometric object, based on the type of processing that you need to do.

The text message is rendered with the following code fragment:

```
<text x="250" y="50"
      font-family="Verdana"
      font-size="25" text-anchor="middle">
```

```
    Click inside the path
</text>
```

As obvious as it may seem, you need to provide some type of instruction for users, otherwise they'll be presented with a pair of toggling quadrilaterals without realizing that they are expected to click on their mouse!

## UPDATING ATTRIBUTES OF SVG `circle` ELEMENTS

Consider the pair of circles rendered in Figure 12.2.

Click inside either circle

**FIGURE 12.2**   A mouse-aware pair of circles.

The SVG document *shiftCircles2.svg* in Listing 12.2 demonstrates how to define an ECMAScript function that can update the coordinates of an SVG `circle` element.

**Listing 12.2**   shiftCircles2.svg

```
<?xml version="1.0" standalone="no"?>
<!DOCTYPE svg PUBLIC "-//W3C//DTD SVG 20010904//EN"
 "http://www.w3.org/TR/2001/REC-SVG-20010904/DTD/svg10.dtd">

<svg width="100%" height="100%"
    xmlns="http://www.w3.org/2000/svg">

 <!-- Capture mouse clicks and update circle -->
 <script type="text/ecmascript">
  <![CDATA[
```

```
    var currentX = 0.;

    function clickLeftCircle(event)
    {
       var circle = event.target;
       var currentX = circle.getAttribute("cx");

       if(currentX < 250)
       {
          circle.setAttribute("cx", currentX*1.1);
       }
       else
       {
          circle.setAttribute("cx", "150");
       }
    }

    function clickRightCircle(event)
    {
       var circle = event.target;
       var currentFill = circle.getAttribute("fill");

       if(currentFill == 'red')
       {
          circle.setAttribute("fill", "blue");
       }
       else
       {
          circle.setAttribute("fill", "red");
       }
    }

 ]]> </script>

<!-- =================================== -->
<g transform="translate(10,10)">
 <!-- red outline of a rectangle -->
 <rect x="0" y="0"
       width="800" height="500"
       fill="none" stroke="none"/>

 <!-- Specify function to handle mouse   -->
 <!-- clicks and update the left circle -->
 <circle onclick="clickLeftCircle(evt)"
         cx="150" cy="250" r="50"
         fill="blue"/>

 <!-- clicks and update the right circle -->
```

```
<circle onclick="clickRightCircle(evt)"
        cx="350" cy="250" r="50"
        fill="red"/>

<!-- Display text message -->
<text x="250" y="50"
      font-family="Verdana"
      font-size="25" text-anchor="middle">
  Click inside either circle
</text>
</g>
</svg>
```

## Remarks

The SVG document in Listing 12.2 extends the concept presented in Listing 12.1 by defining two "mouse-aware" circles:

```
<!-- Specify function to handle mouse  -->
<!-- clicks and update the left circle -->
<circle onclick="clickLeftCircle(evt)"
        cx="150" cy="250" r="50"
        fill="blue"/>

<!-- clicks and update the right circle -->
<circle onclick="clickRightCircle(evt)"
        cx="350" cy="250" r="50"
        fill="red"/>
```

The ECMAScript function clickLeftCircle() is associated with the left circle and the ECMAScript function clickRightCircle() is associated with the right circle. As usual, both ECMAScript functions are invoked with the built-in variable evt. Each time you click inside the left circle, the ECMAScript function clickLeft-Circle() is executed; this function is listed below:

```
function clickLeftCircle(event)
{
    var circle = event.target;
    var currentX = circle.getAttribute("cx");

    if(currentX < 250)
    {
        circle.setAttribute("cx", currentX*1.1);
    }
    else
    {
```

```
                    circle.setAttribute("cx", "150");
            }
    }
```

The ECMAScript function `clickLeftCircle()` first assigns a reference to the variable `circle`, and then assigns the value of the `cx` attribute to the variable `currentX`. While the value of the variable `currentX` is less than 250, the "if" logic multiplies the value of `currentX` by 1.1, which shifts the left circle toward the right. When the value of the variable `currentX` reaches a value of 250 or greater, the code in the "`else`" logic assigns the value 150 to the variable `currentX`, which shifts the left circle back to its original position.

Each time you click inside the right circle, the ECMAScript function `clickRightCircle()` is executed, which simply alternates the color of the right circle between red and blue by updating the value of the `fill` attribute appropriately.

## DYNAMICALLY REMOVING AN SVG ELEMENT

Consider the rectangle rendered in Figure 12.3.

Click inside the rectangle:

**FIGURE 12.3**   Removing a rectangle.

The SVG document *deleteElement1.svg* in Listing 12.3 demonstrates how to use the SVG `onclick` attribute in order to invoke an ECMAScript function that removes an SVG `rect` element.

### Listing 12.3   deleteElement1.svg

```
<?xml version="1.0" standalone="no"?>
<!DOCTYPE svg PUBLIC "-//W3C//DTD SVG 20010904//EN"
  "http://www.w3.org/TR/2001/REC-SVG-20010904/DTD/svg10.dtd">

<svg width="100%" height="100%"
    xmlns="http://www.w3.org/2000/svg"
```

```
        xmlns:xlink="http://www.w3.org/1999/xlink">

    <!-- *** ECMAScript code starts here *** -->
    <script type="text/ecmascript">
    <![CDATA[
      // Capture mouse click and remove rectangle
      function remove(event)
      {
         var rectangle = event.target;
         var parent    = rectangle.parentNode;
         parent.removeChild(rectangle);
      }
    ]]> </script>

    <!-- ================================== -->
    <g transform="translate(50,50)">
       <text font-size="24" fill="blue">
         Click inside the rectangle:
       </text>
    </g>

    <g transform="translate(50,100)">
       <rect onclick="remove(evt)" fill="red"
             x="0" y="0" width="200" height="100"/>
    </g>
</svg>
```

## Remarks

The SVG document in Listing 12.3 defines a "mouse-aware" rectangle with the following code fragment:

```
<g transform="translate(50,100)">
   <rect onclick="remove(evt)" fill="red"
         x="0" y="0" width="200" height="100"/>
</g>
```

When you click inside the rectangle, the ECMAScript function remove() is invoked (with the built-in variable evt). This function removes the SVG rect element by executing the following lines of code:

```
function remove(event)
{
   var rectNode = event.target;
   var parent   = rectNode.parentNode;
   parent.removeChild(rectNode);
}
```

The text message that provides instructions for users, telling them to click inside the rendered rectangle with their mouse, is given below:

```
<g transform="translate(50,50)">
  <text font-size="24" fill="blue">
    Click inside the rectangle:
  </text>
</g>
```

This simple example shows you how easy it is to remove an SVG element from the DOM that is associated with an SVG document. The next example shows you how to remove an SVG element and then add an SVG element to a DOM.

## ADDING AN SVG ELEMENT VIA ECMASCRIPT

Consider the rectangle rendered in Figure 12.4.

Click inside the rectangle:

**FIGURE 12.4**   Adding a circle.

The SVG document *addElement1.svg* in Listing 12.4 demonstrates how to use the SVG onclick element in order to invoke an ECMAScript function that removes an SVG rect element and adds an SVG circle element.

**Listing 12.4**   addElement1.svg

```
<?xml version="1.0" standalone="no"?>
<!DOCTYPE svg PUBLIC "-//W3C//DTD SVG 20010904//EN"
 "http://www.w3.org/TR/2001/REC-SVG-20010904/DTD/svg10.dtd">

<svg width="100%" height="100%"
    xmlns="http://www.w3.org/2000/svg"
    xmlns:xlink="http://www.w3.org/1999/xlink">
```

```
<script type="text/ecmascript">
<![CDATA[
  var rectNode = null;
  var parent   = null;
  var svgDocument = null;

  // Remove rectangle and add circle
  function remove(event)
  {
     // remove the rectangle...
     rectNode = event.target;
     parent   = rectNode.parentNode;
     parent.removeChild(rectNode);

     svgDocument = parent.getOwnerDocument();

     // and add a circle...
     circleNode = svgDocument.createElement("circle");

     circleNode.setAttribute("style","fill:blue");
     circleNode.setAttribute("cx", "100");
     circleNode.setAttribute("cy", "100");
     circleNode.setAttribute("r",  "100");

     parent.appendChild(circleNode);
  }

]]> </script>

<!-- ==================================== -->
<g transform="translate(50,50)">
  <text id="text1" font-size="24" fill="blue">
    Click inside the rectangle:
  </text>
</g>

<g transform="translate(50,100)">
  <rect onclick="remove(evt)" fill="red"
        x="0" y="0" width="200" height="100"/>
</g>
</svg>
```

## Remarks

The SVG document in Listing 12.4 demonstrates how to remove an existing SVG element and replace it with a newly created SVG element. The SVG rect element is made "mouse-aware" with the following code fragment:

```
<g transform="translate(50,100)">
  <rect onclick="remove(evt)" fill="red"
        x="0" y="0" width="200" height="100"/>
</g>
```

When you click inside this rectangle with your mouse, the ECMAScript function remove() is invoked with the built-in variable evt, which then removes the SVG rect element by executing the following lines of code:

```
// remove the rectangle...
rectNode = event.target;
parent   = rectNode.parentNode;
parent.removeChild(rectNode);
```

The reference to the current SVG document, obtained by the following line of code, is needed in order to create a new SVG circle element:

```
svgDocument = parent.getOwnerDocument();
```

Next, the ECMAScript function remove() creates a new SVG circle element with the following code fragment:

```
// and add a circle...
circleNode = svgDocument.createElement("circle");
```

Finally, the ECMAScript function remove() assigns values to the attributes style, cx, cy, and r of the newly created circle and then adds the new SVG circle element as a child of the parent node:

```
circleNode.setAttribute("style","fill:blue");
circleNode.setAttribute("cx", "100");
circleNode.setAttribute("cy", "100");
circleNode.setAttribute("r", "100");

parent.appendChild(circleNode);
```

The text message that provides instructions for users (telling them to click inside the rendered rectangle with their mouse) is:

```
<g transform="translate(50,50)">
  <text font-size="24" fill="blue">
    Click inside the rectangle:
  </text>
</g>
```

The SVG code in Listing 12.4 gives you the techniques for creating more sophisticated SVG documents that require removing or adding multiple SVG elements. One such example is the SVG document in Listing 12.5, which shows you how to keep track of multiple SVG elements.

## UPDATING AN SVG ELEMENT VIA ECMASCRIPT

Consider the set of rectangles rendered in Figure 12.5.

**FIGURE 12.5** Dynamically updating multiple SVG elements.

The SVG document *updateRectangles1.svg* in Listing 12.5 demonstrates how to define an ECMAScript function in order to dynamically populate the screen with a grid of colored rectangles.

**Listing 12.5** updateRectangles1.svg

```
<?xml version="1.0" standalone="no"?>
<!DOCTYPE svg PUBLIC "-//W3C//DTD SVG 20010904//EN"
    "http://www.w3.org/TR/2001/REC-SVG-20010904/DTD/svg10.dtd">

<svg width="100%" height="100%"
    xmlns="http://www.w3.org/2000/svg">

  <script type="text/ecmascript">
  <![CDATA[
```

```
var rectID     = "";
var style      = "";
var color      = "";
var idStr      = "";
var idVal      = 0.;
var altVal1    = 0.;
var altVal2    = 0.;

var rect        = null;
var altRect1    = null;
var altRect2    = null;
var parent      = null;
var svgDocument = null;


function mouseClick1(evt)
{
   rect    = evt.target;
   parent = rect.parentNode;
   svgDocument = parent.getOwnerDocument();

   rectID   = rect.getAttribute("id");
   idVal    = 1.*rectID.substr(4);

   altVal1  = (idVal+1)%4;
   altID1   = "rect" + altVal1;

   altVal2  = (idVal+2)%4;
   altID2   = "rect" + altVal2;

   altRect1 = svgDocument.getElementById(altID1);
   style    = altRect1.getAttribute("style");
   color    = style.substr(5,3);

   if( color == "red" )
   {
      altRect1.setAttribute("style", "fill:blue");
   }
   else
   {
      altRect1.setAttribute("style", "fill:red");
   }

   altRect2 = svgDocument.getElementById(altID2);
   style    = altRect2.getAttribute("style");
   color    = style.substr(5,3);

   if( color == "red" )
```

```
          {
              altRect2.setAttribute("style", "fill:blue");
          }
          else
          {
              altRect2.setAttribute("style", "fill:red");
          }
      }

]]> </script>

<!-- ==================================== -->
<g transform="translate(50,50)">
   <text x="0" y="0" font-size="30">
     Click inside any rectangle:
   </text>
</g>

<g id="gc" transform="translate(50,100)">
   <!-- first row -->
   <rect id="rect0" style="fill:red"
          width="100" height="100" x="0"   y="0"
          onclick="mouseClick1(evt)"/>

   <rect id="rect1" style="fill:blue"
          width="100" height="100" x="200" y="0"
          onclick="mouseClick1(evt)"/>

   <!-- second row -->
   <rect id="rect3" style="fill:red"
          width="100" height="100" x="0"   y="150"
          onclick="mouseClick1(evt)"/>

   <rect id="rect2" style="fill:blue"
          width="100" height="100" x="200" y="150"
          onclick="mouseClick1(evt)"/>
</g>
</svg>
```

## Remarks

Listing 12.5 is definitely more complicated than the previous examples! In order to simplify the description of the code, here's a high-level description of the logic: whenever you click on one of the four rectangles, extract the value of its id attribute in order to update the fill attribute of the two "subsequent" rectangles, where the "subsequent" rectangles means the next two rectangles that are encountered while moving in a clockwise fashion. For example, if you click on the rectangle whose id attribute has value rect1, then the next two subsequent rectangles have id attribute values of rect2 and rect3. Similarly, if you click on the rectangle whose id attribute has value rect3, then the next two subsequent rectangles have id attribute values of rect0 and rect1.

Now let's examine the logic of the code in more detail.

First, the text message that provides instructions for users, telling them to click inside the rendered rectangle with their mouse, is given below:

```
<g transform="translate(50,50)">
   <text x="0" y="0" font-size="30">
     Click inside the grid
   </text>
</g>
```

Next, the SVG code that makes the four rectangles "mouse-aware" is given below:

```
<!-- first row -->
<rect id="rect0" style="fill:red"
      width="100" height="100" x="0"   y="0"
      onclick="mouseClick1(evt)"/>

<rect id="rect1" style="fill:blue"
      width="100" height="100" x="200" y="0"
      onclick="mouseClick1(evt)"/>

<!-- second row -->
<rect id="rect3" style="fill:red"
       width="100" height="100" x="0"   y="200"
       onclick="mouseClick1(evt)"/>

<rect id="rect2" style="fill:blue"
      width="100" height="100" x="200" y="200"
          onclick="mouseClick1(evt)"/>
```

When you click on one of the four rectangles with your mouse, the ECMAScript function mouseClick1() is invoked with the built-in variable evt. The following pair of lines in the ECMAScript function mouseClick1() determine the value of the id attribute of the currently clicked rectangle:

```
rectID  = rect.getAttribute("id");
idVal   = 1.*rectID.substr(4);
```

The next thing that must be done is to compute the value of the id attribute of the two subsequent rectangles, and that's accomplished with the following four lines of code:

```
altVal1 = (idVal+1)%4;
altID1  = "rect" + altVal1;

altVal2 = (idVal+2)%4;
altID2  = "rect" + altVal2;
```

Notice how the following "if/else" code block sets the value of the style attribute of the first subsequent rectangle:

```
if( color == "red" )
{
    altRect1.setAttribute("style", "fill:blue");
}
else
{
    altRect1.setAttribute("style", "fill:red");
}
```

In a similar fashion, the following code updates the value of the style attribute of the second subsequent rectangle:

```
altRect2 = svgDocument.getElementById(altID2);
style    = altRect2.getAttribute("style");
color    = style.substr(5,3);

if( color == "red" )
{
    altRect2.setAttribute("style", "fill:blue");
}
else
{
    altRect2.setAttribute("style", "fill:red");
}
```

Now that you've read the explanation of the code in Listing 12.5, you can see that it really isn't that complicated. You might even have noticed that this is an example where the explanation is lengthier and more involved than the actual code!

## INTERACTIVELY ADDING SVG ELEMENTS

Consider the grid of rectangles rendered in Figure 12.6.

# Click inside the grid

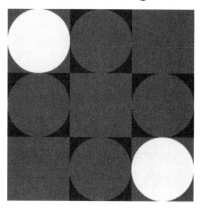

**FIGURE 12.6** Adding circles to a grid
of rectangles.

The SVG document *XsOsBoard2.svg* in Listing 12.6 demonstrates how to use the
SVG onclick element in order to invoke an ECMAScript function that adds an SVG
circle element based on the value of the id attribute of the clicked rectangle.

**Listing 12.6** XsOsBoard2.svg

```
<?xml version="1.0" standalone="no"?>
<!DOCTYPE svg PUBLIC "-//W3C//DTD SVG 20010904//EN"
"http://www.w3.org/TR/2001/REC-SVG- 20010904/DTD/svg10.dtd">

<svg width="100%" height="100%" onload="init(evt)"
    xmlns="http://www.w3.org/2000/svg">

 <desc>Capture mouse click events</desc>

 <script type="text/ecmascript">
   <![CDATA[
     function init(evt) {}

     function mouseClick1(evt)
     {
        var rect      = evt.target;
        var parent    = rect.parentNode;
        var svgDocument = parent.getOwnerDocument();
```

```
      var rectID = rect.getAttribute("id");
      var xPos   = rect.getAttribute("x");
      var yPos   = rect.getAttribute("y");
      var width  = rect.getAttribute("width");
      var height = rect.getAttribute("height");

      var cx     = 1.*xPos;
      var cy     = 1.*yPos;

      cx        += 1.*width/2;
      cy        += 1.*height/2;

      var style = "";

      var idVal = 1.*rectID.substr(4);

      if(idVal % 2 == 0) { style = "fill:red"; }
      else               { style = "fill:yellow"; }

      circleNode = svgDocument.createElement("circle");

      circleNode.setAttribute("x",     xPos);
      circleNode.setAttribute("y",     yPos);
      circleNode.setAttribute("cx",    cx);
      circleNode.setAttribute("cy",    cy);
      circleNode.setAttribute("style", style);
      circleNode.setAttribute("r",     width/2);

      parent.appendChild(circleNode);
   }

]]> </script>

<!-- ================================== -->
<g transform="translate(50,50)">
   <text x="0" y="0" font-size="30">
     Click inside the grid
   </text>
</g>

<!-- rectangular background -->
<g id="gc" transform="translate(50,70)">

   <!-- first row -->
   <rect id="rect1" fill="red"
         width="100" height="100" x="0"   y="0"
         onclick="mouseClick1(evt)"/>
```

```
                  <rect id="rect2" fill="blue"
                        width="100" height="100" x="100" y="0"
                        onclick="mouseClick1(evt)"/>

                  <rect id="rect3" fill="red"
                        width="100" height="100" x="200" y="0"
                        onclick="mouseClick1(evt)"/>

                  <!-- second row -->
                  <rect id="rect4" fill="blue"
                        width="100" height="100" x="0"   y="100"
                        onclick="mouseClick1(evt)"/>

                  <rect id="rect5" fill="red"
                        width="100" height="100" x="100" y="100"
                        onclick="mouseClick1(evt)"/>

                  <rect id="rect6" fill="blue"
                        width="100" height="100" x="200" y="100"
                        onclick="mouseClick1(evt)"/>

                  <!-- third row -->
                  <rect id="rect7" fill="red"
                        width="100" height="100" x="0"   y="200"
                        onclick="mouseClick1(evt)"/>

                  <rect id="rect8" fill="blue"
                        width="100" height="100" x="100" y="200"
                        onclick="mouseClick1(evt)"/>

                  <rect id="rect9" fill="red"
                        width="100" height="100" x="200" y="200"
                        onclick="mouseClick1(evt)"/>
            </g>
            </svg>
```

## Remarks

As you've probably surmised, the SVG document in Listing 12.6 is the starting point for a game of "TicTacToe." The code starts by creating a 3x3 rectangular grid of "mouse-aware" rectangles. For brevity, only the code fragment for the upper-left rectangle is given below:

```
<rect id="rect1" fill="red"
      width="100" height="100" x="0" y="0"
      onclick="mouseClick1(evt)"/>
```

Each time you click on your mouse on one of the nine "mouse-aware" rectangles, the ECMAScript function `mouseClick1()` is invoked with the built-in variable `evt`. This ECMAScript function determines the values of the attributes of the associated rectangle and uses them in order to assign appropriate values to the attributes of a dynamically created SVG `circle` element that is superimposed on the existing rectangle. The code fragment for the SVG `circle` element is:

```
circleNode = svgDocument.createElement("circle");

circleNode.setAttribute("x",     xPos);
circleNode.setAttribute("y",     yPos);
circleNode.setAttribute("cx",    cx);
circleNode.setAttribute("cy",    cy);
circleNode.setAttribute("style", style);
circleNode.setAttribute("r",     width/2);
```

The color of a new circle is either green or white, based on whether or not the integer-valued suffix of the `id` attribute of the clicked rectangle is even or odd. For example, if the clicked rectangle has an `id` value of `rect2`, `rect4`, `rect6`, or `rect8`, then its integer-valued suffix is 2, 4, 6, or 8, respectively, which means that the newly added circle will be green. The other rectangles have `id` values of `rect1`, `rect3`, `rect5`, `rect7`, or `rect9`, which means that their integer-valued suffix is 1, 3, 5, 7, or 9, respectively, and therefore they will be drawn as white circles. The code for making this determination is quite easy and it's listed below. Keep in mind that `rectID` is the value of the `id` attribute of the clicked rectangle:

```
var idVal  = 1.*rectID.substr(4);

if(idVal % 2 == 0) { style = "fill:green"; }
else               { style = "fill:white"; }
```

## DYNAMICALLY ADDING MULTIPLE SVG rect ELEMENTS

Consider the overlapping white rectangles rendered in Figure 12.7.

The SVG document *overlayWhiteRectangles1.svg* in Listing 12.7 demonstrates how to use the SVG `onclick` element in order to invoke an ECMAScript function that dynamically creates and renders an SVG `rect` element whose dimensions are based on the points on the screen that are associated with the user-initiated mouse clicks.

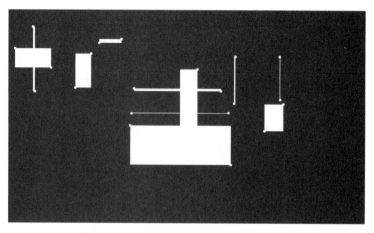

**FIGURE 12.7** Overlaying a rectangle with dynamic rectangles.

**Listing 12.7** overlayWhiteRectangles1.svg

```
<?xml version="1.0" standalone="no"?>
<!DOCTYPE svg PUBLIC "-//W3C//DTD SVG 20010904//EN"
  "http://www.w3.org/TR/2001/REC-SVG-20010904/DTD/svg10.dtd">

<svg width="100%" height="100%"
    xmlns="http://www.w3.org/2000/svg"
    xmlns:xlink="http://www.w3.org/1999/xlink">

  <script type="text/ecmascript">
  <![CDATA[
    var pointCount  = 0.;
    var width       = 0.;
    var height      = 0.;
    var xCoord      = 0.;
    var yCoord      = 0.;
    var xPosition   = 0.;
    var yPosition   = 0.;
    var xCoords     = Array(2);
    var yCoords     = Array(2);
    var cRadius     = 2.;

    var rectNode    = null;
    var circleNode  = null;
    var rectangle   = null;
    var parent      = null;
```

```
var svgDocument = null;


// Capture mouse click
function mouseClick1(event)
{
   xCoord = event.getClientX();
   yCoord = event.getClientY();

   xCoords[pointCount] = xCoord;
   yCoords[pointCount] = yCoord;
   addPointCircle(event);
   ++pointCount;

   if( pointCount == 2 )
   {
      addRectangle(event);
      pointCount = 0;
   }

} // mouseClick1

function addPointCircle(event)
{
   rectangle   = event.target;
   parent      = rectangle.parentNode;
   svgDocument = parent.getOwnerDocument();

   // add a new circle...
   circleNode = svgDocument.createElement("circle");
   circleNode.setAttribute("cx",
                             xCoords[pointCount]);

   circleNode.setAttribute("cy",
                             yCoords[pointCount]);

   circleNode.setAttribute("r", cRadius);
   circleNode.setAttribute("style", "fill:white");
   parent.appendChild(circleNode);

} // addPointCircle

function addRectangle(event)
{
   rectangle   = event.target;
   parent      = rectangle.parentNode;
   svgDocument = parent.getOwnerDocument();
```

```
        computeDimensions(event);

        // add a new rectangle...
        rectNode = svgDocument.createElement("rect");

        rectNode.setAttribute("x",      xPosition);
        rectNode.setAttribute("y",      yPosition);
        rectNode.setAttribute("width",  width);
        rectNode.setAttribute("height", height);
        rectNode.setAttribute("style", "fill:white");

        parent.appendChild(rectNode);
    }

    function computeDimensions(event)
    {
        width  = Math.abs(xCoords[1]-xCoords[0]);
        height = Math.abs(yCoords[1]-yCoords[0]);

        xPosition = xCoords[0]-xCoords[1] <= 0 ?
                    xCoords[0] : xCoords[1];

        yPosition = yCoords[0]-yCoords[1] <= 0 ?
                    yCoords[0] : yCoords[1];

    } // computeDimensions

]]> </script>

<!-- =================================== -->
<g transform="translate(0,0)">
    <rect onclick="mouseClick1(evt)" fill="blue"
                stroke="red" stroke-width="2"
          x="0" y="0" width="800" height="400"/>

    <text x="50" y="450"
          font-size="24" font-color="red">
      Click on two points inside the rectangle
    </text>
</g>

<g transform="translate(50,50)">
    <text font-size="24" fill="white">
      Click on two points:
    </text>
</g>
</svg>
```

## Remarks

The logic of the ECMAScript code in Listing 12.7 is as follows: each time you click on a pair of points, a white rectangle is created with those two points as diagonal vertices of the rectangle, and then that rectangle is added to the existing graphics image. The logic that determines when (and where) to add a new rectangle is contained in the ECMAScript function mouseClick1(), which is invoked each time you click on your mouse. This function is supplied with the built-in variable evt, as listed below:

```
// Capture mouse click
function mouseClick1(event)
{
   xCoord = event.getClientX();
   yCoord = event.getClientY();

   xCoords[pointCount] = xCoord;
   yCoords[pointCount] = yCoord;
   addPointCircle(event);
   ++pointCount;

   if( pointCount == 2 )
   {
      addRectangle(event);
      pointCount = 0;
   }

} // mouseClick1
```

Each time you click your mouse, the ECMAScript function mouseClick1() determines the x-coordinate and the y-coordinate of the point where you clicked on your mouse, and these values are stored in an array, After you've clicked your mouse twice, the ECMAScript function addRectangle() is invoked in order to create an SVG rect element that is populated with appropriate values for the attributes x, y, width, height, and style, as seen in the following code fragment:

```
computeDimensions(event);

// add a new rectangle...
rectNode = svgDocument.createElement("rect");

rectNode.setAttribute("x",      xPosition);
rectNode.setAttribute("y",      yPosition);
rectNode.setAttribute("width",  width);
rectNode.setAttribute("height", height);
rectNode.setAttribute("style", "fill:white");

parent.appendChild(rectNode);
```

Before a new rectangle is created, the ECMAScript function `addRectangle()` invokes the ECMAScript function `computeDimensions()` in order to compute dimensions of the new rectangle:

```
function computeDimensions(event)
{
   width      = Math.abs(xCoords[1]-xCoords[0]);
   height     = Math.abs(yCoords[1]-yCoords[0]);

   xPosition = xCoords[0]-xCoords[1] <= 0 ?
               xCoords[0] : xCoords[1];

   yPosition = yCoords[0]-yCoords[1] <= 0 ?
               yCoords[0] : yCoords[1];

} // computeDimensions
```

The width and the height of the new rectangle are computed as follows:

```
width      = Math.abs(xCoords[1]-xCoords[0]);
height     = Math.abs(yCoords[1]-yCoords[0]);
```

The ECMAScript function `Math.abs()` ensures that the value of the `width` and `height` attributes are non-negative.

After the dimensions of the new rectangle have been computed, the SVG attributes of the new rectangle are assigned values in the ECMAScript function `addRectangle()`. This logic is executed each time you click on your mouse, and you'll see a new rectangle after an even number of mouse clicks.

## KEY CONSTRUCTS

The following ECMAScript function changes the vertices of a quadrilateral that is specified by an existing SVG `path` element:

```
function clickPath1(event)
{
   var pathNode = event.target;
   var points = pathNode.getAttribute("points");
   clickCount += 1;

   if( clickCount % 2 == 0 )
   {
      str = "100,100 300,100 300,200 200,200"
      pathNode.setAttribute("points", str);
```

```
      pathNode.setAttribute("fill", 'red');
   }
   else
   {
      str = "250,100 300,100 300,200 200,200"
      pathNode.setAttribute("points", str);
      pathNode.setAttribute("fill", 'green');
   }
```

The following ECMAScript function changes the radius of an existing SVG circle element when you click on the circle with your mouse:

```
function clickLeftCircle(event)
{

   var circle = event.target;
   var currentX = circle.getAttribute("cx");

   if(currentX < 250)
   {
      circle.setAttribute("cx", currentX*1.1);
   }
   else
   {
      circle.setAttribute("cx", "150");
   }
}
```

The following ECMAScript function removes an existing rectangle when you click on the rectangle with your mouse:

```
function remove(event)
{
   var rectNode = event.target;
   var parent   = rectNode.parentNode;
   parent.removeChild(rectNode);
}
```

The following code fragment can be included in an ECMAScript function in order to create a new circle:

```
circleNode = svgDocument.createElement("circle");

circleNode.setAttribute("x",    xPos);
circleNode.setAttribute("y",    yPos);
circleNode.setAttribute("cx",   cx);
circleNode.setAttribute("cy",   cy);
```

```
circleNode.setAttribute("style", style);
circleNode.setAttribute("r",     width/2);

parent.appendChild(circleNode);
```

## CD-ROM LIBRARY

ON THE CD

The folder for this chapter on the book's companion CD-ROM contains the SVG documents that are required for viewing the following graphics images:

*changePath1.svg*

*shiftCircles2.svg*

*deleteElement1.svg*

*addElement1.svg*

*updateRectangles1.svg*

*XsOsBoard2.svg*

*overlayWhiteRectangles1.svg*

*dynamicCBezierCurves1.svg*

*dynamicQBezierCurves1.svg*

*overlayQBezierCurve1.svg*

*overlayWhitePolygons1.svg*

*populateCircles1.svg*

*tiltedDigits1.svg*

*XsOsBoard3.svg*

*XsOsBoardRemove1.svg*

## SUMMARY

This chapter focused on showing you how to dynamically add or remove SVG elements from the DOM of an SVG document. This type of dynamic update also relied on the ability to capture the following mouse-related events:

- the SVG mouseover element to start animation effects
- the SVG mouseout element to end animation effects

- the SVG `onclick` element and ECMAScript functions for updating or deleting existing SVG elements
- the SVG `onclick` element and ECMAScript functions for dynamically creating new SVG elements
- graphics images and hyperlinks

# 13 ECMAScript and SVG Animation

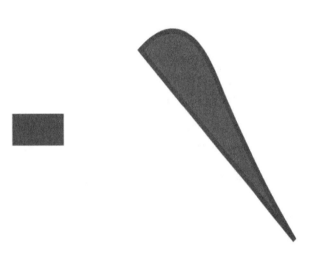

This chapter demonstrates how to define and use ECMAScript functions in order to create SVG animation effects. In previous chapters you've seen how to create SVG animation effects based on the SVG elements `animate`, `animateColor`, and `animate-Transform`, which provide an indirect mechanism for modifying the values of the attributes associated with SVG elements (e.g., `width`, `height`, `x`, and `y` attributes of a rectangle). However, these animation-related SVG elements do not provide direct access to the points inside an SVG `path` element. Since the SVG `path` element is used for defining Bezier curves and other sophisticated graphics images, you cannot easily modify the definitions of such images by the aforementioned set of SVG animation-based elements.

Fortunately, the SVG DOM provides you with a mechanism for directly accessing and modifying attributes such as the path attribute of an SVG element. These modifications are performed in ECMAScript functions, where you can also invoke a plethora of mathematical functions as well as trigonometric functions (among others) in order to create sophisticated animation effects that are not directly available in SVG. The techniques presented in this chapter can also be used to render polynomials, rational functions, and polar equations. Keep in mind that ECMAScript functions can easily become very lengthy when they perform many computations that involve mathematical functions or trigonometric functions. Consequently, the SVG examples in this chapter are longer than those in previous chapters.

By necessity, this chapter requires an understanding of ECMAScript functions, mathematical functions, and trigonometry. Now would be a good time (if you haven't done so already) to review the relevant material in the associated appendices in this book.

The SVG examples in this chapter have a very similar style: a large block of global variables is declared at the top of the code, followed by a set of ECMAScript functions. Initially you might find yourself progressing rather slowly through the code. This is understandable because you need to familiarize yourself with the ECMAScript variable names and the overall flow of logic. Since the style of the examples is consistent, each example serves to further reinforce your understanding of the overall form as well as purpose of the SVG code. By the end of this chapter, you'll not only become comfortable with the code, you'll also be able to understand the supplemental examples more quickly and more easily. In addition, most (if not all) of the techniques presented in this chapter can easily be adapted for rendering mathematical functions such as polynomials and rational functions. All code and images for this chapter can be found on the companion CD-ROM in the Chapter 13 folder.

ON THE CD

## SVG PERFORMANCE

As you probably already know, the rendering of SVG-based graphics images can be very CPU-intensive, particularly when the SVG document contains a significant amount of dynamically generated SVG. Roughly 20% of the SVG code in this book was developed and tested on a 166MHz PC, and the remainder (which includes virtually all of the examples with ECMAScript code) was developed and tested on a 2GHz Pentium 4. Generally, the most CPU-intensive SVG code in this book involves code that contains many dynamically generated SVG elements such as Bezier curves, elliptic arcs, and filters that are often accompanied by many dynamically generated color gradients. Other examples of CPU-intensive code involve the SVG skew element combined with many dynamically generated SVG elements. As you peruse the examples on the CD-ROM and launch them in a browser session, you will be able to determine which examples are suitable for your hardware configuration. Another point to keep in mind is that some software applications require a relatively low color resolution in order to function properly, in which case the SVG code will not appear as sharp and rich. For best viewing results, make sure that you maximize the number of colors displayed while rendering the SVG code.

## ERROR CHECKING IN SVG DOCUMENTS

All the SVG code in this book has been verified to work on a PC with Internet Explorer. If you have significant ECMAScript experience, you'll notice that some error checking has been omitted from the ECMAScript functions. For example, you could enhance the code in the init() function so that it checks whether or not each variable is null after it has been assigned a reference to some other object. This error checking was omitted because the focus of this book is to present techniques for rendering graphics and to do so in a manner that is as clear and simple as possible. You can easily add the additional error checking if you are working in a production environment, where you might want to display a message in an ECMAScript pop-up alert in the event of an error.

## SVG CODE TEMPLATE FOR THIS CHAPTER

The animation-based examples in this chapter contain at least three ECMAScript functions: an init() function that is executed immediately after the SVG document is loaded into memory, a drawPath() function (or some function with a comparable name) that is invoked from the init() function, and a stopAnimation() function that stops the animation. The stopAnimation() function is executed after some event occurs, which is typically a mouse click on a "mouse aware" SVG element. Structurally the SVG documents have a format that is similar to the one below:

```
<?xml version="1.0" standalone="no"?>
<!DOCTYPE ....>

<svg onload="init(evt)" ...>

<script type="text/ecmascript">
 <![CDATA[
 // global variables here

 function init(event)
 {
    // initialization code goes here
    // some more code here

    drawPath(event);
```

```
    }
    function drawPath(event)
    {
        // some code goes here

        if( someEventHappens )
        {
            stopAnimation(event);
        }
    }

    function stopAnimation(event)
    {
        window.clearTimeout(theTimeout);
    }

    ]]> </script>

    <g transform="translate(10,10)">
        <polygon id="thePolygon"
                onclick="stopAnimation(evt)" .../>

    </g>
</svg>
```

The preceding fragment contains the following line, whose purpose is to invoke the function init() immediately after the SVG document is loaded into memory:

```
<svg onload="init(evt)" ...>
```

The init() function performs some initialization and then invokes another function, such as drawPath(), in order to perform some type of animation.

The other function, appropriately named stopAnimation(), is invoked when you click inside an SVG polygon element. Note that the particular SVG element is not restricted to polygons; the SVG element can be a rectangle, circle, or other geometric object.

## GLOBAL VERSUS LOCAL VARIABLES

One significant point pertains to the use of global variables in the SVG examples in this book. As a general programming practice, it's preferable to use local variables so that you can avoid the side effects that can occur when modifying global variables (and at the same time make your code reusable).

The rationale behind using global variables, all of which are listed near the beginning of each SVG document, is that this approach enables you to focus as much as possible on the details of generating a particular graphics image. The problems that can occur with global variables will not occur in the examples in this book because the code is essentially "stand-alone"; that is, it's not part of a "library" that can be invoked with ECMAScript functions in other SVG documents. Once you have firmly grasped the logic and the purpose of the code in each example, it will be much easier to refactor the code by replacing global variables with local variables.

## ECMASCRIPT AND SIMPLE SVG path ANIMATION

Consider the oscillating quadrilateral rendered in Figure 13.1.

## Click inside the quadrilateral to stop animation

**FIGURE 13.1**  A toggling quadrilateral.

The SVG document *togglePath1.svg* in Listing 13.1 demonstrates how to define an ECMAScript function in order to stop a "toggling" quadrilateral.

**Listing 13.1**    togglePath1.svg

```
<?xml version="1.0" standalone="no"?>
<!DOCTYPE svg PUBLIC "-//W3C//DTD SVG 20010904//EN"
  "http://www.w3.org/TR/2001/REC-SVG-20010904/DTD/svg10.dtd">

<svg width="100%" height="100%" onload="init(evt)"
     xmlns="http://www.w3.org/2000/svg">

  <script type="text/ecmascript">
    <![CDATA[
    var toggleCount = 0.;
    var shortPause  = 100.;
```

```
var points      = "";

var polyNode    = null;
var theTimeout  = null;
var svgDocument = null;
var target      = null;
var gcNode      = null;

function init(event)
{
   target = event.getTarget();
   svgDocument = target.getOwnerDocument();
   gcNode = svgDocument.getElementById("gc");

   theTimeout = setTimeout("window.drawPath()",
                               shortPause);
}
function updateToggleCount()
{
   toggleCount += 1;
}

function drawPath()
{
   polyNode = svgDocument.getElementById(
                               "thePolygon");
   points = polyNode.getAttribute("points");

   updateToggleCount();

   if( toggleCount % 2 == 0 )
   {
      points = "100,100 300,100 300,200 200,200"
      polyNode.setAttribute("points", points);
      polyNode.setAttribute("fill", 'red');
   }
   else
   {
      points = "250,100 300,100 300,200 200,200"
      polyNode.setAttribute("points", points);
      polyNode.setAttribute("fill", 'green');
   }

   theTimeout = setTimeout("drawPath()",
                               shortPause);
}

function stopAnimation(event)
```

```
        {
            window.clearTimeout(theTimeout);
        }

    ]]> </script>

    <!-- ============================ -->
    <g id="gc" transform="translate(10,10)">
        <rect x="0" y="0"
              width="800" height="500"
              fill="none" stroke="none"/>

        <!-- render blue quadrilateral -->
        <polygon id="thePolygon"
                 onclick="stopAnimation(evt)"
                 points="200,100 300,100 300,200 200,200"
                 fill="blue"/>

        <!-- Display text message -->
        <text x="300" y="50"
              font-family="Verdana"
              font-size="25" text-anchor="middle">
          Click inside the quadrilateral to stop animation
        </text>
    </g>
</svg>
```

## Remarks

The SVG code in Listing 13.1 demonstrates how to render two quadrilaterals in an alternating fashion, thereby creating a "toggling" effect that continues until you click inside one of the quadrilaterals. The code in this example starts with the definition of a set of global variables as listed below:

```
var toggleCount = 0.;
var shortPause  = 100.;
var points      = "";

var polyNode    = null;
var theTimeout  = null;
var svgDocument = null;
var target      = null;
var gcNode      = null;
```

The variable `toggleCount` is incremented each time a quadrilateral is rendered, and its value controls which of the two quadrilaterals will be rendered.

The variable `shortPause` is measured in milliseconds, and it is used as an internal delay between the rendering of successive quadrilaterals.

The variable `points` is a string variable that will contain the set of points that specify the vertices of the rendered polygon.

The variable `polyNode` is used as a "reference" to the SVG `polygon` element whose id attribute has the value `thePolygon`.

The variable `theTimeout` is used for clearing the timer in order to switch off the animation when you click inside one of the quadrilaterals with your mouse.

Before discussing the variables `document`, `target`, and `gcNode` that are initialized in the ECMAScript function `init()`, observe that the animation sequence for this example is initiated by the following code fragment:

```
<svg width="100%" height="100%" onload="init(evt)"
     xmlns="http://www.w3.org/2000/svg">
```

The value of the `onload` attribute specifies an ECMAScript function that will be executed as soon as the SVG document is loaded. In this case, the ECMAScript function is `init()`, and its contents are listed below:

```
function init(event)
{
    target = event.getTarget();
    svgDocument = target.getOwnerDocument();
    gcNode = svgDocument.getElementById("gc");

    theTimeout = setTimeout("window.drawPath()",
                            shortPause);
}
```

The variable `target` is initialized by the following line of code:

```
target = event.getTarget();
```

The variable `gcNode` is initialized by the following line of code:

```
gcNode = svgDocument.getElementById("gc");
```

The ECMAScript function `drawPath()` contains the code for updating the points in the existing SVG `polygon` element (whose gc attribute has the value `thePolygon`). The first part of this function is shown below:

```
polyNode = svgDocument.getElementById(
                       "thePolygon");
points = polyNode.getAttribute("points");

updateToggleCount();
```

This function calls the ECMAScript function updateToggleCount(), which simply increments the value of the variable toggleCount.

The following "if/else" block of code sets the new value for the points attribute, depending on whether toggleCount is even or odd:

```
if( toggleCount % 2 == 0 )
{
   points = "100,100 300,100 300,200 200,200"
   polyNode.setAttribute("fill", 'red');
}
else
{
   points = "250,100 300,100 300,200 200,200"
   polyNode.setAttribute("points", points);
   polyNode.setAttribute("fill", 'green');
}
```

The next statement causes the drawPath() function to call itself after a delay of shortPause milliseconds:

```
theTimeout = setTimeout("drawPath()",
                        shortPause);
```

The last ECMAScript function is stopAnimation(), which stops the animation:

```
function stopAnimation()
{
   window.clearTimeout(theTimeout);
}
```

The following "mouse aware" SVG rectangle invokes the function stopAnimation() with the built-in variable evt when you click inside the rectangle with your mouse:

```
<!-- render blue quadrilateral -->
<polygon id="thePolygon"
         onclick="stopAnimation(evt)"
         points="200,100 300,100 300,200 200,200"
         fill="blue"/>
```

The last section of code in this SVG document displays a text string that tells users how they can stop the animation:

```
<!-- Display text message -->
  <text x="300" y="50"
```

```
        font-family="Verdana"
        font-size="25" text-anchor="middle">
    Click inside the quadrilateral to stop animation
  </text>
```

# ANIMATION AND DYNAMIC CREATION OF SVG ELEMENTS

Consider the set of circles rendered in Figure 13.2.

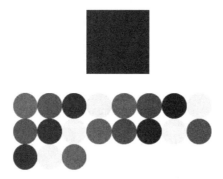

Click inside the rectangle to stop animation

**FIGURE 13.2**   Dynamically adding a grid of circles.

The SVG document *populateCircles2.svg* in Listing 13.2 demonstrates how to define an ECMAScript function in order to use mouse clicks to control the populating of a grid of circles.

### Listing 13.2   populateCircles2.svg

```
<?xml version="1.0" standalone="no"?>
<!DOCTYPE svg PUBLIC "-//W3C//DTD SVG 20010904//EN"
  "http://www.w3.org/TR/2001/REC-SVG-20010904/DTD/svg10.dtd">

  <script type="text/ecmascript">
   <![CDATA[
   var startX      = 100.;
   var startY      = 250.;
   var xPosition   = 0.;
   var yPosition   = 0.;
```

```
var rowCount      = 4.;
var columnCount   = 8.;
var theRow        = 0.;
var theColumn     = 0.;
var fillColor     = "";

var shortPause    = 100.;
var circleRadius  = 20.;
var circleColors  = ['red','green',
                     'blue','yellow'];

var circleNode    = null;
var theTimeout    = null;
var svgDocument   = null;
var target        = null;
var gcNode        = null;


function init(event)
{
   target    = event.getTarget();
   svgDocument = target.getOwnerDocument();
   gcNode    = svgDocument.getElementById("gc");

   theTimeout = setTimeout(
                   "window.populateCircles()",
                   shortPause);
}

function populateCircles(event)
{
   circleNode = svgDocument.createElement("circle");

   xPosition  = startX+2*circleRadius*theColumn;
   yPosition  = startY+2*circleRadius*theRow;

   circleNode.setAttribute("cx", xPosition);
   circleNode.setAttribute("cy", yPosition);

   fillColor  = "fill:";
   fillColor += circleColors[(theRow+theColumn)%4];

   circleNode.setAttribute("style", fillColor);
   circleNode.setAttribute("r",     circleRadius);

   gcNode.appendChild(circleNode);

   theTimeout = setTimeout(
```

```
                              "window.populateCircles()",
                              shortPause);

        if( ++theColumn >= columnCount )
        {
           theColumn = 0;
           ++theRow;
        }

        if( theRow >= rowCount )
        {
           stopAnimation(event);
        }

     } // populateCircles

     function stopAnimation(event)
     {
        window.clearTimeout(theTimeout);
     }

  ]]> </script>

  <!-- ============================ -->
  <g id="gc" transform="translate(10,10)">
    <rect x="0" y="0"
          width="800" height="500"
          fill="none" stroke="none"/>

    <!-- render blue quadrilateral -->
    <polygon id="thePolygon"
             onclick="stopAnimation(evt)"
             points="200,100 300,100 300,200 200,200"
             fill="blue"/>

    <!-- Display text message -->
    <text x="300" y="50"
          font-family="Verdana"
          font-size="25" text-anchor="middle">
      Click inside the rectangle to stop animation
    </text>
  </g>
</svg>
```

## Remarks

The SVG code in Listing 13.2 combines mouse events with an animation effect by adding a set of circles, one row at a time, until a 4x8 grid of circles is rendered. While these circles are being rendered, you can stop the animation simply by clicking on the blue rectangle above the rendered set of circles. The code in this example starts with the definition of a number of ECMAScript global variables. The first set of global variables is given below:

```
var startX       = 100.;
var startY       = 250.;
var xPosition    = 0.;
var yPosition    = 0.;
var rowCount     = 4.;
var columnCount  = 8.;
var theRow       = 0.;
var theColumn    = 0.;
var fillColor    = "";
```

The variables startX and startY specify the x-coordinate and the y-coordinate of the upper-left vertex that contains the rectangular grid of circles.

The variables xPosition and yPosition specify the x-coordinate and the y-coordinate of the center of each new circle that is added to the rectangular grid of circles.

The variables rowCount and columnCount specify the number of rows and the number of columns for the rectangular grid of circles.

The variables theRow and theColumn specify the current row and the current column of the current circle.

The variable fillColor is a dynamically constructed string that specifies the "style" of the current circle.

The second set of global variables is given below:

```
var shortPause   = 100.;
var circleRadius = 20.;
var circleColors = ['red','green',
                    'blue','yellow'];
```

The variable shortPause has a value of 100, which represents the number of milliseconds between the rendering of successive circles in the rectangular grid of circles.

The variable circleRadius has a value of 20, which is the radius of all the circles in the rectangular grid of circles.

The variable circleColors is an array of strings representing the colors red, green, blue, and yellow. These colors are used for coloring all the circles in the rectangular grid of circles.

The third set of global variables is:

```
var circleNode   = null;
var theTimeout   = null;
var svgDocument  = null;
```

```
var target      = null;
var gcNode      = null;
```

The variable circleNode is used for creating each circle that is added to the rectangular grid of circles.

The variables theTimeout, svgDocument, target, and gcNode are assigned their usual values in the ECMAScript function init().

The ECMAScript function populateCircles() performs the actual work of adding the circles to the rectangular grid of circles. The first part of this function creates a new SVG circle element, populates the cx, cy, style, and r attributes, and then adds this element to the DOM:

```
circleNode = svgDocument.createElement("circle");
circleID   = "circle"+theRow+"_"+theColumn;

xPosition  = startX+2*circleRadius*theColumn;
yPosition  = startY+2*circleRadius*theRow;

circleNode.setAttribute("cx", xPosition);
circleNode.setAttribute("cy", yPosition);

fillColor  = "fill:";
fillColor += circleColors[(theRow+theColumn)%4];

circleNode.setAttribute("style", fillColor);
circleNode.setAttribute("r",     circleRadius);

gcNode.appendChild(circleNode);
```

Next, the variable theTimeout is assigned a value, followed by the end-of-row logic:

```
theTimeout = setTimeout("window.populateCircles()",
                        shortPause);

if( ++theColumn >= columnCount )
{
   theColumn = 0;
   ++theRow;
}
```

The last block of code checks if the value of theRow exceeds the value of rowCount, which represents a fully populated rectangular array of circles; if so, the ECMAScript function stopAnimation() is invoked:

```
if( theRow >= rowCount )
{
   stopAnimation(event);
}
```

The ECMAScript function `stopAnimation()` contains one line of code in order to stop the animation:

```
function stopAnimation(event)
{
   window.clearTimeout(theTimeout);
}
```

There are two cases in which the animation will stop: the first case is when the rectangular grid of circles is filled with circles, and the second case is when you click on the "mouse aware" blue rectangle at the top of the screen, which is defined as follows:

```
<polygon id="thePolygon"
         onclick="stopAnimation(evt)"
         points="200,100 300,100 300,200 200,200"
         fill="blue"/>
```

When you click on the blue rectangle, the ECMAScript function `stopAnimation()` is invoked, which stops the animation. If you click on the blue rectangle after the rectangular grid of circles has been completely filled, you obviously won't see any difference.

The last section of the SVG document displays a text message that explains how to stop the animation, as listed below:

```
<text x="300" y="50"
      font-family="Verdana"
      font-size="25" text-anchor="middle">
   Click inside the rectangle to stop animation
</text>
```

## ANIMATION AND MODIFYING QUADRATIC BEZIER CURVES

Consider the Bezier-based animation in Figure 13.3.

The SVG document *dynamicQBezier1.svg* in Listing 13.3 demonstrates how to define an ECMAScript function in order to dynamically update a Bezier curve and the values of its attributes.

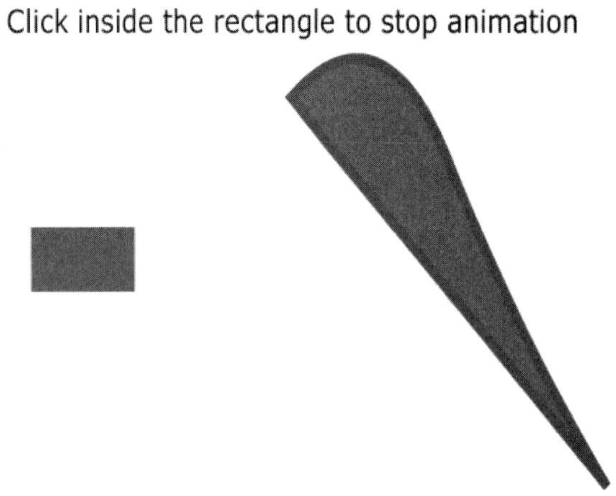

Click inside the rectangle to stop animation

**FIGURE 13.3** A dynamically modified quadratic Bezier curve.

**Listing 13.3** dynamicQBezier1.svg

```
<?xml version="1.0" standalone="no"?>
<!DOCTYPE svg PUBLIC "-//W3C//DTD SVG 20010904//EN"
  "http://www.w3.org/TR/2001/REC-SVG-20010904/DTD/svg10.dtd">


<svg width="100%" height="100%" onload="init(evt)"
     xmlns="http://www.w3.org/2000/svg">

  <script type="text/ecmascript">
   <![CDATA[
   var basePointX      = 300.;
   var basePointY      = 100.;
   var endPointX       = 600.;
   var endPointY       = 400.;
   var middlePointX    = (basePointX+endPointX)/2.;
   var middlePointY    = (basePointY+endPointY)/2-100.;

   var xOffset         = 0.0;
   var yOffset         = 0.0;
   var multiplier1     = 2.0;
   var multiplier2     = 3.0;
   var theta           = 0.0;
   var startTheta      = 0.0;
   var shiftTheta      = 1.0;
   var maxTheta        = 2*Math.PI;
   var displayCount    = 0.;
```

```
var shortPause      = 100.;
var constant1       = 200.0;
var constant2       = -80.0;
var fillColor       = "";
var fillColors      = ['red','green',
                       'blue','yellow'];
var colorCount      = 4.;
var strokeColor     = "";
var strokeWidth     = 1.;
var strokeDelta     = 2.;
var strokeDirection = 1.;
var minStrokeWidth  = 2.;
var maxStrokeWidth  = 12.;
var pathString      = "";

var pathNode        = null;
var theTimeout      = null;
var svgDocument     = null;
var target          = null;
var gcNode          = null;


function init(event)
{
   target    = event.getTarget();
   svgDocument = target.getOwnerDocument();
   gcNode    = svgDocument.getElementById("gc");

   pathNode = svgDocument.createElement("path");
   pathNode.setAttribute("style",
          "stroke-width:4; stroke:red; fill:none");

   gcNode.appendChild(pathNode);

   theTimeout = setTimeout("window.renderBezier()",
                           shortPause);
}

function updateCoordinates()
{
   displayCount += 1;

   strokeWidth += strokeDelta*strokeDirection;

   if( strokeWidth > maxStrokeWidth )
   {
      strokeWidth = maxStrokeWidth;
```

```
        strokeDirection *= -1;
    }

    if( strokeWidth < minStrokeWidth )
    {
        strokeWidth = minStrokeWidth;
        strokeDirection *= -1;
    }

} // updateCoordinates


function renderBezier()
{
    pathNode = svgDocument.getElementById("thePath");

    updateCoordinates();

    /////////////////////////////////////////////
    // sample string for quadratic Bezier curves:
    // d="m0,0 Q100,0 200,200 T300,200 z"
    /////////////////////////////////////////////
    // construct the string for the path points
    pathString = "M"+basePointX+","+basePointY;

    xOffset    = basePointX+constant1*Math.cos(
                    multiplier1*(theta+startTheta));

    yOffset    = basePointY+constant2*Math.sin(
                    multiplier2*(theta+startTheta));

    pathString += " Q" + xOffset + "," + yOffset;

    pathString += " "+middlePointX+","+middlePointY;
    pathString += " T"+endPointX+","+endPointY+"z";

    startTheta += shiftTheta;

    pathNode.setAttribute("d", pathString);

    fillColor  = fillColors[displayCount%colorCount];
    pathNode.setAttribute("fill", fillColor);

    strokeColor = "stroke-width:"+
                    strokeWidth+";stroke:";
    strokeColor += fillColors[
                    (displayCount+1)%colorCount];
```

```
        pathNode.setAttribute("style", strokeColor);

        theTimeout = setTimeout("window.renderBezier()",
                                shortPause);

        if( ++theta >= maxTheta )
        {
           theta = 0;
        }
    }

    function stopAnimation()
    {
        window.clearTimeout(theTimeout);
    }

]]> </script>

<!-- ============================ -->
<g id="gc" transform="translate(10,10)">
  <!-- render outer rectangle -->
  <rect x="0" y="0"
        width="800" height="500"
        fill="none" stroke="none"/>

  <!-- render mouse-handling rectangle -->
  <rect id="theRectangle"
        x="50" y="200"
        width="100" height="50"
        onclick="stopAnimation()"
        fill="green"/>

  <!-- render the polar equation -->
  <path id="thePath"
        onclick="stopAnimation()"
        d="m200,100 300,100 300,200 200,200 z"
        fill="blue"/>

  <!-- display text message -->
  <text x="300" y="50"
        font-family="Verdana"
        font-size="25" text-anchor="middle">
    Click inside the rectangle to stop animation
  </text>
</g>
</svg>
```

## Remarks

The SVG code in Listing 13.3 renders a quadratic Bezier curve that is updated dynamically in order to produce an oscillating effect. You can stop the animation by clicking on the blue rectangle rendered to the left of the Bezier curve.

The code in this example starts with the definition of a number of ECMAScript global variables. The first set of global variables is given below:

```
var basePointX      = 300.;
var basePointY      = 100.;
var endPointX       = 600.;
var endPointY       = 400.;
var middlePointX    = (basePointX+endPointX)/2.;
var middlePointY    = (basePointY+endPointY)/2-100.;
```

The global variables basePointX and basePointY specify the x-coordinate and the y-coordinate of the upper-left corner of the set of rendered ellipses.

The global variables endPointX and endPointY specify the x-coordinate and the y-coordinate of the end point of the quadratic Bezier curve.

The global variables middlePointX and middlePointY specify the x-coordinate and the y-coordinate of the middle point of the quadratic Bezier curve.

The second set of global variables is:

```
var xOffset         = 0.0;
var yOffset         = 0.0;
var multiplier1     = 2.0;
var multiplier2     = 3.0;
var theta           = 0.0;
var startTheta      = 0.0;
var shiftTheta      = 1.0;
var maxTheta        = 2*Math.PI;
var displayCount    = 0.;
var shortPause      = 100.;
var constant1       = 200.0;
var constant2       = -80.0;
```

The global variables xOffset and yOffset specify the x-coordinate and the y-coordinate of the Q point in the SVG path element that defines the current quadratic Bezier curve.

The global variable theta is used for computing trigonometric quantities that are in turn used for updating the current values of the variables xOffset and yOffset as given below:

```
xOffset = basePointX+constant1*Math.cos(
                multiplier1*(theta+startTheta));
```

```
yOffset = basePointY+constant2*Math.sin(
                  multiplier2*(theta+startTheta));
```

The global variables startTheta, shiftTheta, and maxTheta specify the initial value, increment value, and maximum value of the variable theta.

The global variable displayCount is incremented each time a quadratic Bezier curve is displayed, and its value is used as an index into the array fillColors, which contains a set of colors.

The third set of global variables is given below:

```
var fillColor       = "";
var fillColors      = ['red','green',
                         'blue','yellow'];
var colorCount      = 4.;
var strokeColor     = "";
var strokeWidth     = 1.;
var strokeDelta     = 2.;
var strokeDirection = 1.;
var minStrokeWidth  = 2.;
var maxStrokeWidth  = 12.;
var pathString      = "";
```

The global variable fillColor is used for specifying the color of the current Bezier curve.

The global variable fillColors is an array that consists of the colors red, green, blue, and yellow.

The value of the global variable colorCount equals the number of elements in the array fillColors.

The global variable strokeDelta specifies the increment value for the variable strokeWidth.

The global variable strokeDirection is either 1 or -1, which is used for either increasing or decreasing the value of the variable strokeWidth.

The global variables minStrokeWidth and maxStrokeWidth specify the minimum and maximum allowable values for the variable strokeWidth.

The global variable pathString is a string that stores the actual points for the current quadratic Bezier curve, and it is used for setting the value of the d attribute.

The fourth and final set of global variables is given below:

```
var pathNode     = null;
var theTimeout   = null;
var document     = null;
var target       = null;
var gcNode       = null;
```

The global variable `pathNode` is a reference to a dynamically created SVG `path` element that represents the current quadratic Bezier curve.

The variables `theTimeout`, `svgDocument`, `target`, and `gcNode` are assigned their usual values in the ECMAScript function `init()`.

In addition, the `init()` function does two important things. First, it creates an SVG `path` element that is added to the current SVG document by means of the following code fragment:

```
pathNode = svgDocument.createElement("path");
pathNode.setAttribute("style",
        "stroke-width:4; stroke:red; fill:none");
gcNode.appendChild(pathNode);

theTimeout = setTimeout("window.renderBezier()",
                        shortPause);
```

Second, the `init()` function invokes the ECMAScript function `renderBezier()`, which contains the code for dynamically updating the quadratic Bezier curve. The code in the function `renderBezier()` begins by assigning a reference to the variable `pathNode` with the following line of code:

```
pathNode = svgDocument.getElementById("thePath");
```

Next, the function `renderBezier()` invokes the ECMAScript function `updateCoordinates()`, which updates the value of the variables `displayCount` and `strokeWidth`, with the following line of code:

```
updateCoordinates();
```

In order to better understand how the function `renderBezier()` constructs the value of the `d` attribute, look at the sample string given below:

```
// d="M0,0 Q100,0 200,200 T300,200 z"
```

The code for constructing the initial point associated with the M term consists of the following line:

```
pathString = "M"+basePointX+","+basePointY;
```

The code for constructing the Q term contains the following lines of code:

```
xOffset    = basePointX+constant1*Math.cos(
                    multiplier1*(theta+startTheta));

yOffset    = basePointY+constant2*Math.sin(
```

```
                    multiplier2*(theta+startTheta));

pathString += " Q" + xOffset + "," + yOffset;
```

The code for constructing the "middle" point contains one line of code:

```
pathString += " "+middlePointX+","+middlePointY;
```

The code for constructing the T term contains one line of code:

```
pathString += " T"+endPointX+","+endPointY+"z";
```

Next, the `renderBezier()` function sets the value of the d attribute, determines the color of the current quadratic Bezier curve, determines the stroke color, and sets the `style` attribute, all of which is performed in the following code fragment:

```
path.NodesetAttribute("d", pathString);

fillColor   = fillColors[displayCount%colorCount];
pathNode.setAttribute("fill", fillColor);

strokeColor = "stroke-width:"+strokeWidth+";stroke:";
strokeColor += fillColors[(displayCount+1)%colorCount];

pathNode.setAttribute("style", strokeColor);
```

The `renderBezier()` function invokes the following line of code in order to call itself after a delay of `shortPause` milliseconds:

```
theTimeout = setTimeout("window.renderBezier()",
                        shortPause);
```

The last ECMAScript function is `stopAnimation()`, which stops the animation:

```
function stopAnimation()
{
    window.clearTimeout(theTimeout);
}
```

The following SVG "mouse-aware" rectangle is rendered to the left of the dynamically updated quadratic Bezier curve, and the ECMAScript function `stopAnimation()` is invoked when you click inside this rectangle with your mouse:

```
<rect id="theRectangle"
      x="50" y="200"
```

```
      width="100" height="50"
      onclick="stopAnimation()"
      fill="green"/>
```

## KEY CONSTRUCTS

You can create *animation effects* in ECMAScript functions by specifying four things. First, you need a time-out period (measured in milliseconds), such as the following global variable:

```
var shortPause  = 100.;
```

Second, you need to specify the function that will be invoked after a delay of shortPause milliseconds:

```
theTimeout = setTimeout("window.renderBezier()",
                        shortPause);
```

Third, you need invoke the code that stops the animation, which you can embed in a simple ECMAScript function as follows:

```
function stopAnimation()
{
   window.clearTimeout(theTimeout);
}
```

Fourth, you need to specify a mechanism by which the preceding function will be invoked in order to stop the animation. In the current example, this mechanism is provided by clicking on the rectangle defined below:

```
<rect id="theRectangle"
      x="50" y="200"
      width="100" height="50"
      onclick="stopAnimation()"
      fill="green"/>
```

## CD-ROM LIBRARY

ON THE CD

The folder for this chapter on the book's companion CD-ROM contains the SVG documents that are required for viewing the following graphics images:

*togglePath1.svg*
*populateCircles2.svg*
*dynamicQBezier1.svg*

## SUMMARY

This chapter showed you techniques for directly accessing the `path` attribute of an SVG element so that you can generate more sophisticated SVG animation effects. The examples in this chapter used ECMAScript in order to create these animation effects:

- accessing SVG `path` elements in ECMAScript functions
- invoking trigonometric functions in ECMAScript functions
- creating Bezier curves dynamically

# 14

# ECMAScript and Polar Equations

## OVERVIEW

This chapter demonstrates how to define and use ECMAScript functions in order to create SVG documents that are based on polar equations. In this chapter, you will see that there are many ways to manipulate polar equations; the more interesting graphics images are actually a combination of polar equations with other geometric objects, such as ellipses, as well as different color gradients.

The SVG code presented in this chapter uses more complicated ECMAScript functions and also tends to be longer than the examples in previous chapters. In some cases, you'll also see a significant performance penalty. For instance, the CD-ROM for this chapter contains *Steiner1.svg*, which generates a graphics image that is based on

ON THE CD

a Steiner equation. The code in *Steiner1.svg* dynamically creates and adds more than 30,000 SVG rect elements in an ECMAScript function, so there's a significant delay involved on most PCs. When the code in *Steiner1.svg* was converted to a Java class, the Java code performed roughly 20 times faster than the SVG code on the same PC! Even though Java code is interpreted byte-code, it does not have the overhead of EC-MAScript, nor does it need to dynamically create SVG elements. Incidentally, when you launch *Steiner1.svg*, it might be interesting to watch the memory consumption on your PC while you wait for the SVG viewer to render the graphics image. All code and images for this chapter can be found on the companion CD-ROM in the Chapter 14 folder.

ON THE CD

## MATHEMATICAL TERMINOLOGY

The second half of this book (and most of the supplementary code on the companion CD-ROM) contains many graphics images that are based on mathematical equations. You will often see modifications and enhancements of these equations in order to generate a greater variety of interesting graphics images. In such cases, the graphics images are still named after the original equation in order to convey the source of the key idea that underlies the image in question. In other cases, the graphics images depart substantially from the strict mathematical interpretation of the equation. The names of these graphics images are meant to give you an indication of the "spirit" of the original mathematical equation, even though the generalization may depart considerably from the original equation. Many times the mathematical term for the given graphics image simply does not exist, which necessitates a mechanism for describing the images in a reasonable fashion. While it might be more correct to use the name "gradientGeneralizedConeBasedOnASetOfEllipses.svg" for an SVG document, it's unnecessarily unwieldy; on the other hand, the simpler and shorter name "ellipticConeGradient.svg" conveys just as much information about the nature of the contents of the SVG document, provided that you keep in mind that you are dealing with a generalization rather than the strict mathematical definition.

## SVG CODE TEMPLATE FOR THIS CHAPTER

The examples in this chapter have at least two ECMAScript functions: an init() function that is executed immediately after the SVG document is loaded into memory, and a drawSpiral() function that is invoked from the init() function. Structurally the SVG documents have a format that is similar to the one listed below:

```
<?xml version="1.0" standalone="no"?>
<!DOCTYPE ....>
```

```
<svg onload="init(evt)" ...>

  <script type="text/ecmascript">
  <![CDATA[
  // global variables here

  function init(event)
  {
      target = event.getTarget();
      svgDocument = target.getOwnerDocument();
      gcNode = svgDocument.getElementById("gc");

      drawSpiral();
  }

  function drawSpiral(event)
  {
      for(angle=0; angle<maxAngle; angle+=angleDelta)
      {
          // do something here
      }
  }
  ]]> </script>

  <g id="gc" transform="translate(10,10)">
    <rect x="0" y="0"
          width="800" height="500"
          fill="none" stroke="none"/>
  </g>
</svg>
```

The preceding fragment contains the following line in order to invoke the function init() immediately after the SVG document is loaded into memory:

```
<svg onload="init(evt)" ...>
```

The init() function performs some initialization and then invokes another function, often called drawSpiral(), that dynamically creates SVG elements. The other detail to notice is the following line:

```
<g id="gc" transform="translate(10,10)">
```

ON THE CD

This particular SVG g element is used *very* extensively in the examples for the remainder of this book and also the examples on the CD-ROM. Please note that the presence of this element is not mandatory; you can dynamically create this element and then add additional SVG elements as children of this element. The rationale for this construct is that it enables you to add other elements inside the SVG g element easily and quickly, and you can leverage those new elements with a minimum amount of code modification to the ECMAScript contained in the SVG document. For example, suppose you have already created another animation effect and you want to test the effect of combining both of them with a particular SVG document. You can do something like the following:

```
<g id="gc" transform="translate(10,10)">
  <rect x="0" y="0"
        width="800" height="500"
        fill="none" stroke="none"/>

  <!-- some fancy graphics here -->
  ...
  <!-- more fancy graphics here -->
  ...
</g>
```

The preceding fragment will cause your "fancy graphics" to appear prior to anything that is dynamically created in an ECMAScript function. Indeed, this technique enables you to add some very large code fragments very easily and without having to write any of the corresponding ECMAScript code. This approach allows you to quickly "mix and match" in order to test many different combinations of graphics objects and color-related effects. After you have decided which block of code to include in your SVG document, you can refactor the document, whereby the hard-coded block of code is replaced by an ECMAScript function that dynamically creates the necessary SVG elements.

Incidentally, this approach is also a prime example of leveraging both "native" SVG code and ECMAScript functions in a manner that exploits what each of them does best. The proportion of ECMAScript code versus SVG code in your SVG documents will depend on various factors, such as the type of available code, your needs, and your proficiency in writing ECMAScript functions.

Another (slightly different) situation can arise where you have a sophisticated gradient shading pattern that you want to incorporate in order to alter the appearance of some existing SVG elements in your code. You can easily incorporate the existing SVG code in the following manner:

```
<defs>
  <!-- dazzling gradient shading definition -->
</defs>

<g id="gc" transform="translate(10,10)">
  <rect x="0" y="0"
        width="800" height="500"
```

```
                    fill="none" stroke="none"/>
    </g>
```

In the preceding code fragment, you would also specify an `id` attribute for the gradient that you've defined in the SVG `defs` element so that you can reference that definition as part of the `style` attribute for an SVG element that you've created inside an ECMAScript function. Again, after having decided which code you want to include in your SVG document, you can perform the appropriate refactoring of the code. In case you're not quite sure how this is done, you'll see subsequent examples that will make this point clear.

What about performance? The insertion of dynamically created SVG elements to the SVG DOM is a time-consuming process. An alternative to this technique of using a hard-coded SVG `g` element involves dynamically constructing an SVG `g` element *without* adding this element to the SVG DOM. First create the dynamic elements, adding them to the new SVG `g` element in order to create a hierarchical structure of new elements, and then—as a final step—add the top-level dynamic SVG `g` element to the SVG DOM. You can experiment with this technique on several SVG documents and see if there is an appreciable difference in rendering time.

## GENERATING SINE-BASED PETALS

Consider the set of sine-based petals in Figure 14.1.

**FIGURE 14.1** A set of sine-based petals.

The SVG document *sineCirclePetals1.svg* in Listing 14.1 demonstrates how to define an ECMAScript function in order to dynamically generate a set of sine-based petals.

**Listing 14.1**   sineCirclePetals1.svg

```
<?xml version="1.0" standalone="no"?>
<!DOCTYPE svg PUBLIC "-//W3C//DTD SVG 20010904//EN"
  "http://www.w3.org/TR/2001/REC-SVG-20010904/DTD/svg10.dtd">

<svg width="100%" height="100%" onload="init(evt)"
    xmlns="http://www.w3.org/2000/svg">

  <script type="text/ecmascript">
   <![CDATA[
   var basePointX    = 300.;
   var basePointY    = 250.;
   var currentX      = 0.;
   var currentY      = 0.;
   var offsetX       = 0.;
   var offsetY       = 0.;
   var radius        = 0.;
   var smallRadius   = 2.;
   var Constant      = 200.;
   var branches      = 5.;
   var angle         = 0.;
   var maxAngle      = 360.;
   var angleDelta    = 1.;
   var strokeWidth   = 2.;
   var style         = "";

   var circleNode    = null;
   var svgDocument   = null;
   var target        = null;
   var gcNode        = null;

   function init(event)
   {
      target = event.getTarget();
      svgDocument = target.getOwnerDocument();
      gcNode = svgDocument.getElementById("gc");

      drawSpiral();
   }

   function drawSpiral()
   {
```

```
        for(angle=0; angle<maxAngle; angle+=angleDelta)
        {
            radius = Constant*Math.sin(
                            branches*angle*Math.PI/180);

            offsetX = radius*Math.cos(angle*Math.PI/180);
            offsetY = radius*Math.sin(angle*Math.PI/180);

            currentX = basePointX+offsetX;
            currentY = basePointY-offsetY;

            circleNode = svgDocument.createElement(
                                        "circle");

            style  = "fill:red;";
            style += "stroke-width:"+strokeWidth;

            circleNode.setAttribute("style",style);
            circleNode.setAttribute("cx", currentX);
            circleNode.setAttribute("cy", currentY);
            circleNode.setAttribute("r",  smallRadius);

            gcNode.appendChild(circleNode);
        }

    } // drawSpiral

  ]]> </script>

<!-- ============================= -->
<g id="gc" transform="translate(10,10)">
  <rect x="0" y="0"
        width="800" height="500"
        fill="none" stroke="none"/>
</g>
</svg>
```

## Remarks

The SVG code in Listing 14.1 starts with a block of global ECMAScript variables, followed by the ECMAScript function init(), whose purpose is to initialize the global variables svgDocument, target, and gcNode and then invoke the ECMAScript function drawSpiral(), which performs the required computations.

Listing 14.1 illustrates a technique that is used in virtually all the SVG examples in this book: the global variable gcNode serves as the parent of all the SVG elements that are dynamically created in the drawSpiral() function.

Notice that the ECMAScript function drawSpiral() contains a loop for dynamically creating SVG circle elements that are added to the DOM. The first part of the loop contains code that calculates the x-coordinate and the y-coordinate of each new circle, as shown below:

```
radius = Constant*Math.sin(
                    branches*angle*Math.PI/180);

offsetX = radius*Math.cos(angle*Math.PI/180);
offsetY = radius*Math.sin(angle*Math.PI/180);

currentX = basePointX+offsetX;
currentY = basePointY-offsetY;
```

The value of the variable `radius` is computed as the product of the global variable `Constant` (which has a constant value) and a `sine` function that depends on the variables `branches` and `angle`. The value of radius is then used for calculating the values of the variables `offsetX` and `offsetY` (which also depend on `sine` and `cosine` values).

The second part of the loop contains code for dynamically creating, initializing, and adding a circle to the SVG DOM, as shown below:

```
circleNode = document.createElement("circle");

style  = "fill:red;";
style += "stroke-width:"+strokeWidth;

circleNode.setAttribute("style",style);
circleNode.setAttribute("cx", currentX);
circleNode.setAttribute("cy", currentY);
circleNode.setAttribute("r",  smallRadius);

gcNode.appendChild(circleNode);
```

The preceding code fragment assigns the variable `circleNode` a reference to a dynamically created SVG `circle` element. Next, values are assigned to the attributes `style`, `cx`, `cy`, and `r`, after which the newly created SVG `circle` element is added to the SVG DOM by means of the last statement in the code block above.

Make sure that you pay close attention to the manner in which dynamically created SVG elements are assigned to the SVG DOM:

```
gcNode.appendChild(circleNode);
```

Recall that the global variable `gcNode` is initialized in the `init()` function, and it is a reference to a statically defined SVG `rect` element that is defined at the bottom of the SVG document.

The last section of Listing 14.1 renders a rectangle whose id attribute has the value gc, which is the static SVG element that serves as the "graphics context" for the SVG document:

```
<g id="gc" transform="translate(10,10)">
  <rect x="0" y="0"
        width="800" height="500"
        fill="none" stroke="none"/>
</g>
```

## GENERATING A SINE-BASED WIRE FRAME EFFECT

Consider the image in Figure 14.2.

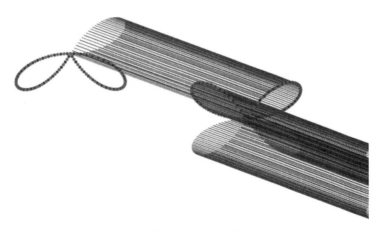

**FIGURE 14.2**   A sine-based wire frame effect.

The SVG document *sinePetalsWireFrame4.svg* in Listing 14.2 demonstrates how to define an ECMAScript function in order to dynamically generate a sine-based wireframe.

**Listing 14.2**   sinePetalsWireFrame4.svg

```
<?xml version="1.0" standalone="no"?>
<!DOCTYPE svg PUBLIC "-//W3C//DTD SVG 20010904//EN"
  "http://www.w3.org/TR/2001/REC-SVG-20010904/DTD/svg10.dtd">

<svg width="100%" height="100%" onload="init(evt)"
```

```
            xmlns="http://www.w3.org/2000/svg">

       <script type="text/ecmascript">
        <![CDATA[
        var basePointX    = 400.;
        var basePointY    = 200.;
        var currentX      = 0.;
        var currentY      = 0.;
        var offsetX       = 0.;
        var offsetY       = 0.;
        var slantX        = 0.;
        var slantY        = 0.;
        var slantAngle    = 20.;
        var slantLength   = 300.;
        var minorAxis     = 80.;
        var majorAxis     = 20.;
        var radius        = 0.;
        var smallRadius   = 2.;
        var Constant      = 100.;
        var branches      = 3.;
        var angle         = 0.;
        var maxAngle      = 60.;
        var angleDelta    = 1.;
        var hGap          = 1.;
        var strokeWidth   = 1.;
        var fillColor     = "black";
        var style         = "";

        var circleColors  = ['red','green','blue',
                             'yellow','white','magenta'];
        var colorCount    = 6.;

        var lineNode      = null;
        var circleNode    = null;
        var svgDocument   = null;
        var target        = null;
        var gcNode        = null;

        function init(event)
        {
           slantX = slantLength*Math.cos(
                           slantAngle*Math.PI/180);

           slantY = slantLength*Math.sin(
                           slantAngle*Math.PI/180);

           target = event.getTarget();
           svgDocument = target.getOwnerDocument();
```

```
        gcNode = svgDocument.getElementById("gc");

    drawSpiral();
}

function drawSpiral()
{
    for(angle=0; angle<maxAngle; angle+=angleDelta)
    {
        radius = Constant*Math.sin(
                        branches*angle*Math.PI/180);

        offsetX = radius*Math.cos(angle*Math.PI/180);
        offsetY = radius*Math.sin(angle*Math.PI/180);

        currentX = basePointX+offsetX;
        currentY = basePointY-offsetY;
        addCircle(currentX, currentY);

        currentX = basePointX-offsetX;
        currentY = basePointY-offsetY;
        addCircle(currentX, currentY);

        currentX = basePointX+offsetX-slantX;
        currentY = basePointY+offsetY-slantY;
        addCircle(currentX, currentY);

        currentX = basePointX-offsetX-slantX;
        currentY = basePointY+offsetY-slantY;
        addCircle(currentX, currentY);

        if( angle % hGap == 0 )
        {
            currentX = basePointX+offsetX;
            currentY = basePointY-offsetY;
            addLine(currentX,
                    currentY,
                    currentX-slantX,
                    currentY-slantY);

            currentX = basePointX-offsetX;
            currentY = basePointY+offsetY;
            addLine(currentX,
                    currentY,
                    currentX+slantX,
                    currentY+slantY);
            currentX = basePointX+offsetX;
            currentY = basePointY+offsetY;
```

```
                    addLine(currentX,
                            currentY,
                            currentX+slantX,
                            currentY+slantY);

                currentX = basePointX-offsetX;
                currentY = basePointY-offsetY;
                addLine(currentX,
                        currentY,
                        currentX+slantX,
                        currentY+slantY);
        }
    }

} // drawSpiral

function addCircle(currentX, currentY)
{
    circleNode = svgDocument.createElement("circle");

    fillColor = circleColors[2*(angle%2)];
    style  = "fill:"+fillColor+";stroke:";
    style += circleColors[angle%2];
    style += ";stroke-width:"+strokeWidth;

    circleNode.setAttribute("style",style);
    circleNode.setAttribute("cx", currentX);
    circleNode.setAttribute("cy", currentY);
    circleNode.setAttribute("r",  smallRadius);

    gcNode.appendChild(circleNode);
} // addCircle

function addLine(x1, y1, x2, y2)
{
    style  = "stroke:"+circleColors[2*(angle%2)];
    style += ";stroke-width:"+strokeWidth;

    lineNode = svgDocument.createElement("line");
    lineNode.setAttribute("style",style);
    lineNode.setAttribute("x1", x1);
    lineNode.setAttribute("y1", y1);
    lineNode.setAttribute("x2", x2);
    lineNode.setAttribute("y2", y2);

    gcNode.appendChild(lineNode);
```

```
      } // addLine

  ]]> </script>

<!-- ============================ -->
<g id="gc" transform="translate(10,10)">
  <rect x="0" y="0"
        width="800" height="500"
        fill="none" stroke="none"/>
</g>
</svg>
```

## Remarks

The SVG code in Listing 14.2 starts with a block of global ECMAScript variables, followed by the ECMAScript function `init()` that initializes the global variables `svgDocument`, `target`, and `gcNode`. The function `init()` also initializes the variables `slantX` and `slantY` as follows:

```
slantX = slantLength*Math.cos(
                   slantAngle*Math.PI/180);

slantY = slantLength*Math.sin(
                   slantAngle*Math.PI/180);
```

The variables `slantX` and `slantY` are used for rendering slanted line segments in the function `addLines()` and they provide a good example of variables that can be initialized once because they have fixed values. In situations where you define ECMAScript functions that dynamically generate hundreds or even thousands of SVG elements, you can improve performance by placing unchanging variables outside of code loops. If you wish, you could also add a new ECMAScript function called something like `initializeVariables()` that can be invoked from the `init()` function. Since there is flexibility of coding style in this regard, code your functions in a manner that is comfortable and convenient for you.

The ECMAScript function `drawSpiral()` contains a loop that first calculates the values of `radius`, `offsetX`, and `offsetY` that are used for determining the x-coordinate and the y-coordinate of the center of each new circle. These variables are calculated in a manner that is similar to the code in Listing 14.1, as shown below:

```
radius = Constant*Math.sin(
                   branches*angle*Math.PI/180);

offsetX = radius*Math.cos(angle*Math.PI/180);
offsetY = radius*Math.sin(angle*Math.PI/180);
```

Next, the ECMAScript function drawSpiral() calculates the x-coordinate and the y-coordinate of the center of four new circles and then invokes the ECMAScript function addCircle() four times as shown below:

```
currentX = basePointX+offsetX;
currentY = basePointY-offsetY;
addCircle(currentX, currentY);

currentX = basePointX-offsetX;
currentY = basePointY-offsetY;
addCircle(currentX, currentY);

currentX = basePointX+offsetX-slantX;
currentY = basePointY+offsetY-slantY;
addCircle(currentX, currentY);

currentX = basePointX-offsetX-slantX;
currentY = basePointY+offsetY-slantY;
addCircle(currentX, currentY);
```

The preceding code fragment is grouped into four sub-blocks of code, each of which assigns values to the variables currentX and currentY and then invokes the addCircle() function. This code style is advantageous because it makes it easy to modify existing sub-blocks of code and to add new sub-blocks. Moreover, the name of the ECMAScript function makes its purpose obvious; while this detail might seem minor, it becomes increasingly important when you have an SVG document consisting of thousands of lines of code in dozens of functions.

The second part of the loop contains a conditional block of code for adding four line segments to the DOM. The calculation of the variables currentX and currentY is similar to the first part of this loop, as listed below:

```
if( angle % hGap == 0 )
{
  currentX = basePointX+offsetX;
  currentY = basePointY-offsetY;
  addLine(currentX,
          currentY,
          currentX-slantX,
          currentY-slantY);

  currentX = basePointX-offsetX;
  currentY = basePointY+offsetY;
  addLine(currentX,
          currentY,
          currentX+slantX,
          currentY+slantY);
```

```
      currentX = basePointX+offsetX;
      currentY = basePointY+offsetY;
      addLine(currentX,
              currentY,
              currentX+slantX,
              currentY+slantY);

      currentX = basePointX-offsetX;
      currentY = basePointY-offsetY;
      addLine(currentX,
              currentY,
              currentX+slantX,
              currentY+slantY);
   }
```

Once again, this code style simplifies the process of understanding the EC-MAScript function because its purpose is readily discernible by looking at the layout of the code.

The ECMAScript function addCircle() contains the code for creating a new SVG circle element and assigning values to the attributes style, cx, cy, and r:

```
function addCircle(currentX, currentY)
{
   circleNode = svgDocument.createElement("circle");

   fillColor = circleColors[2*(angle%2)];
   style  = "fill:"+fillColor+";stroke:";
   style += circleColors[angle%2];
   style += ";stroke-width:"+strokeWidth;

   circleNode.setAttribute("style",style);
   circleNode.setAttribute("cx", currentX);
   circleNode.setAttribute("cy", currentY);
   circleNode.setAttribute("r",  smallRadius);

   gcNode.appendChild(circleNode);

} // addCircle
```

Notice the technique that is used for assigning a value to the style attribute:

```
fillColor = circleColors[2*(angle%2)];
style  = "fill:"+fillColor+";stroke:";
style += circleColors[angle%2];
style += ";stroke-width:"+strokeWidth;
```

Since the global `style` variable is a string variable, you can concatenate its constituent parts in any order; just make sure that you include a semi-colon (";") in all the required locations! Remember the earlier example involving an ECMAScript `alert` function that displayed attribute values? The `style` variable is an ideal candidate for display when you get errors in this part of the code. (As you become increasingly proficient in writing SVG code, you'll use this technique less frequently.)

The ECMAScript function `addLine()` contains the code for creating a new SVG `line` element and assigning values to the attributes `style`, `x1`, `y1`, `x2`, and `y2`:

```
function addLine(x1, y1, x2, y2)
{
   style  = "stroke:"+circleColors[2*(angle%2)];
   style += ";stroke-width:"+strokeWidth;

   lineNode = document.createElement("line");
   lineNode.setAttribute("style",style);
   lineNode.setAttribute("x1", x1);
   lineNode.setAttribute("y1", y1);
   lineNode.setAttribute("x2", x2);
   lineNode.setAttribute("y2", y2);

   gcNode.appendChild(lineNode);

} // addLine
```

The last portion of the SVG document renders a rectangle whose `id` attribute has the value `gc`, which is used for adding the sine-based petals:

```
<g id="gc" transform="translate(10,10)">
  <rect x="0" y="0"
        width="800" height="500"
        fill="none" stroke="none"/>
</g>
```

## MULTI-FIXED POINT MESH PATTERN AND ARCHIMEDEAN SPIRALS

Consider the image in Figure 14.3.

The SVG document *multiArchimedesEllipses2FP4.svg* in Listing 14.3 demonstrates how to define an ECMAScript function in order to dynamically generate multiple Archimedean spirals with a mesh pattern generated with multiple fixed points.

**FIGURE 14.3**    Multi-fixed point mesh pattern and Archimedean spirals.

## Listing 14.3    multiArchimedesEllipses2FP4.svg

```
<?xml version="1.0" standalone="no"?>
<!DOCTYPE svg PUBLIC "-//W3C//DTD SVG 20010904//EN"
  "http://www.w3.org/TR/2001/REC-SVG-20010904/DTD/svg10.dtd">

<svg width="100%" height="100%" onload="init(evt)"
    xmlns="http://www.w3.org/2000/svg">

  <script type="text/ecmascript">
   <![CDATA[
   var basePointX   = 400.;
   var basePointY   = 250.;
   var currentX     = 0.;
   var currentY     = 0.;
   var offsetX      = 0.;
   var offsetY      = 0.;
   var fpCount      = 4.;
   var fixedPointsX = Array(fpCount);
   var fixedPointsY = Array(fpCount);
   var index        = 0.;
   var radius       = 0.;
   var minorAxis    = 4.;
   var majorAxis    = 8.;
   var spiralCount  = 4.;
   var constants    = Array(spiralCount);
   var angle        = 0.;
   var maxAngle     = 720.;
```

```
var angleDelta    = 2.;
var shortPause    = 0.;
var eStrokeWidth  = 1.;
var lStrokeWidth  = 1.;
var fillColor     = "";
var style         = "";
var ellipseColors = ['red','green',
                     'blue','yellow'];
var colorCount    = 4;

var ellipseNode   = null;
var svgDocument   = null;
var target        = null;
var gcNode        = null;

function init(event)
{
   target = event.getTarget();
   svgDocument = target.getOwnerDocument();
   gcNode = svgDocument.getElementById("gc");

   initializeFixedPoints();
   drawSpiral();
}

function initializeFixedPoints()
{
   fixedPointsX[0] = 700.;
   fixedPointsY[0] = 100.;
   fixedPointsX[1] = 100.;
   fixedPointsY[1] = 100.;
   fixedPointsX[2] = 100.;
   fixedPointsY[2] = 400.;
   fixedPointsX[3] = 700.;
   fixedPointsY[3] = 400.;

} // initializeFixedPoints

function drawSpiral()
{
   constants[0] = 0.25;
   constants[1] = 0.50;
   constants[2] = 0.75;
   constants[3] = 1.00;

   for(angle=0; angle<maxAngle; angle+=angleDelta)
   {
      for(var c=0; c<spiralCount; c++)
```

```
    {
        radius = constants[c]*angle;

        offsetX = radius*Math.cos(
                      angle*Math.PI/180);
        offsetY = radius*Math.sin(
                      angle*Math.PI/180);

        currentX = basePointX+offsetX;
        currentY = basePointY-offsetY;

        ellipseNode = svgDocument.createElement(
                                    "ellipse");

        fillColor = ellipseColors[
                        (c+angle)%colorCount];

        style  = "fill:"+fillColor;
        style += ";stroke:red;";
        style += "stroke-width:"+eStrokeWidth;

        ellipseNode.setAttribute("style",style);
        ellipseNode.setAttribute("cx", currentX);
        ellipseNode.setAttribute("cy", currentY);
        ellipseNode.setAttribute("rx", majorAxis);
        ellipseNode.setAttribute("ry", minorAxis);

        gcNode.appendChild(ellipseNode);
    }

    for(var v=0; v<fpCount; v++)
    {
        addLineFP(currentX,
                  currentY,
                  fixedPointsX[v],
                  fixedPointsY[v]);
    }
}

function addLineFP(currentX, currentY, fpX, fpY)
{
    index = Math.abs(currentX+currentY);
    fillColor = ellipseColors[index%2];

    style  = "stroke:"+fillColor;
    style += ";stroke-width:"+lStrokeWidth;

    lineNode = svgDocument.createElement("line");
```

```
                    lineNode.setAttribute("style",style);
                    lineNode.setAttribute("x1", fpX);
                    lineNode.setAttribute("y1", fpY);
                    lineNode.setAttribute("x2", currentX);
                    lineNode.setAttribute("y2", currentY);

                    gcNode.appendChild(lineNode);

               } // addLineFP

          } // drawSpiral

     ]]> </script>

   <!-- ============================ -->
   <g id="gc" transform="translate(10,10)">
     <rect x="0" y="0"
           width="800" height="500"
           fill="none" stroke="none"/>
   </g>
   </svg>
```

## Remarks

The SVG code in Listing 14.3 starts with a block of global ECMAScript variables, followed by the ECMAScript function `init()` that initializes the global variables `svgDocument`, `target`, and `gcNode`.

The `init()` function also invokes the function `initializeFixedPoints()`, which contains the code for populating the arrays `fixedPointsX` and `fixedPointsY` with the x-coordinate and the y-coordinate of four fixed points, respectively. The function `initializeFixedPoints()` is listed below:

```
function initializeFixedPoints()
{
   fixedPointsX[0] = 700.;
   fixedPointsY[0] = 100.;
   fixedPointsX[1] = 100.;
   fixedPointsY[1] = 100.;
   fixedPointsX[2] = 100.;
   fixedPointsY[2] = 400.;
   fixedPointsX[3] = 700.;
   fixedPointsY[3] = 400.;

} // initializeFixedPoints
```

The preceding function stores the x-coordinates of four fixed points in one array and the y-coordinates of the fixed points in another array. You can create your own variations of this example by using a different technique for assigning values to these fixed points. One variant involves generating random values as follows:

```
function initializeFixedPoints()
{
   for(var v=0; v<4; v++)
   {
      fixedPointsX[v] = 700*Math.random();
      fixedPointsY[v] = 700*Math.random();
   }

} // initializeFixedPoints
```

The first part of the ECMAScript function drawSpiral() initializes four constants that are used as coefficients for four different Archimedean spirals:

```
constants[0] = 0.25;
constants[1] = 0.50;
constants[2] = 0.75;
constants[3] = 1.00;
```

Since the values in the array constants are constant values, you can obviously perform the initialization of this array in the init() function or in some other convenient location.

Next, the function drawSpiral() contains a nested loop that first calculates the values of radius, offsetX, and offsetY that are used for determining the x-coordinate and the y-coordinate of the center of each new circle. These variables are calculated in a manner that is similar to the code in Listing 14.1, as shown below:

```
radius  = constants[c]*angle;

offsetX = radius*Math.cos(angle*Math.PI/180);
offsetY = radius*Math.sin(angle*Math.PI/180);

currentX = basePointX+offsetX;
currentY = basePointY-offsetY;
```

Now that values for the x-coordinate and the y-coordinate of the current point have been calculated, drawSpiral() dynamically creates a new ellipse and assigns values to the attributes style, cx, cy, rx, and ry, as shown below:

```
ellipseNode = document.createElement("ellipse");

fillColor = ellipseColors[(c+angle)%colorCount];

style  = "fill:"+fillColor;
```

```
style += ";stroke:red;";
style += "stroke-width:"+eStrokeWidth;

ellipseNode.setAttribute("style",style);
ellipseNode.setAttribute("cx", currentX);
ellipseNode.setAttribute("cy", currentY);
ellipseNode.setAttribute("rx", majorAxis);
ellipseNode.setAttribute("ry", minorAxis);

gcNode.appendChild(ellipseNode);
```

The last portion of the ECMAScript function drawSpiral() contains a loop that is inside the outer loop (but outside the nested loop) that adds line segments by invoking the ECMAScript function addLineFP():

```
for(var v=0; v<fpCount; v++)
{
    addLineFP(currentX,
             currentY,
             fixedPointsX[v],
             fixedPointsY[v]);
}
```

The ECMAScript function addLineFP() contains the code for creating a new SVG line element and assigning values to the line-related attributes style, x1, y1, x2, and y2:

```
function addLineFP(currentX, currentY, fpX, fpY)
{
    index = Math.abs(currentX+currentY);
    fillColor = ellipseColors[index%2];

    style  = "stroke:"+fillColor;
    style += ";stroke-width:"+lStrokeWidth;

    lineNode = document.createElement("line");
    lineNode.setAttribute("style",style);
    lineNode.setAttribute("x1", fpX);
    lineNode.setAttribute("y1", fpY);
    lineNode.setAttribute("x2", currentX);
    lineNode.setAttribute("y2", currentY);

    gcNode.appendChild(lineNode);

} // addLineFP
```

The last portion of the SVG document renders a rectangle whose id attribute has the value gc, which is used for adding the ellipses and the line segments:

```
<!-- ============================ -->
<g id="gc" transform="translate(10,10)">
  <rect x="0" y="0"
        width="800" height="500"
        fill="none" stroke="none"/>
</g>
```

This example concludes the discussion of ECMAScript functions for this chapter, and you'll probably be happy to know that you are now able to understand virtually all the code samples on the CD-ROM!

## CD-ROM LIBRARY

The folder for this chapter on the book's companion CD-ROM contains the SVG documents that are required for viewing the following graphics images:

*sineCirclePetals1.svg*

*sinePetalWireFrame4.svg*

*multiArchimedesEllipses2FP4.svg*

*archimedesEllipses2Ref4.svg*

*cissoidRectanglesDouble2.svg*

*cochleoidEllipsesExpandingRectangles2.svg*

*cochleoidEllipsesLines1.svg*

*cochleoidEllipsesLines2.svg*

*conchoidEllipsesExpandingRectangles4.svg*

*conchoidEllipsesSVenetianMultiRectExpandingRectangles4.svg*

*lissajousLEllipsesSV5.svg*

*lituusEllipsesExpanding23D2Rectangles4.svg*

*lituusEllipsesExpandingSVenetianMultiRectangles4.svg*

*lituusEllipsesLinesFP1.svg*

*sineCCosineCExpanding3D3Rectangles2.svg*

*sineCCosineCRectangles2.svg*

*Steiner1.svg*

*twistingCosineLoop1Ellipses2.svg*

## SUMMARY

This chapter focused on defining ECMAScript functions for rendering graphics images that are based on trigonometric functions or polar equations. The examples demonstrated how to create images that are derived from the following:

- sine functions and ellipses
- Lituus curves
- the Spiral of Archimedes

# 15 SVG and Pie Charts

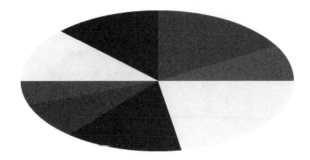

## OVERVIEW

This chapter demonstrates how to use ECMAScript in order to create circular and elliptic pie charts that also incorporate mouse-handling events. As in the two previous chapters, the ECMAScript functions in this chapter dynamically create SVG elements. In the case of pie charts, these elements are SVG path elements whose contents consist of computed points in the plane. The first example shows you how to render a circular pie chart, after which it is very straightforward to modify the pie chart code in order to render an elliptic pie chart. You can also make another simple modification to create a rotating circular pie chart, as shown later in this chapter. A third modification to the circular pie chart code allows you to make it "mouse-aware" so that you can rotate the pie chart either clockwise or counterclockwise. Therefore, your primary goal in this chapter is to focus on understanding the code for the circular pie chart because that example will enable you to grasp the other examples more easily.

Some of the examples in this chapter have long sections of similar SVG code that are not displayed because their inclusion would make the code more difficult to understand. If you want to see the code in its entirety, you can find the unedited files on the companion CD-ROM. All code and images for this chapter can be found on the companion CD-ROM in the Chapter 15 folder.

ON THE CD

## DRAWING CIRCULAR PIE CHARTS

Consider the circular pie chart rendered in Figure 15.1.

**FIGURE 15.1** A circular pie chart.

The SVG document *circularPieChart1.svg* in Listing 15.1 demonstrates how to draw a circular pie chart.

### Listing 15.1    circularPieChart1.svg

```
<?xml version="1.0" standalone="no"?>
<!DOCTYPE svg PUBLIC "-//W3C//DTD SVG 20010904//EN"
  "http://www.w3.org/TR/2001/REC-SVG-20010904/DTD/svg10.dtd">

<svg width="100%" height="100%" onload="init(evt)"
    xmlns="http://www.w3.org/2000/svg">

 <script type="text/ecmascript">
   <![CDATA[
    var width        = 800.;
    var height       = 500.;
```

```
var basePointX      = 300.;
var basePointY      = 150.;
var currentX        = 0.0;
var currentY        = 0.0;
var offsetX1        = 0.0;
var offsetY1        = 0.0;
var offsetX2        = 0.0;
var offsetY2        = 0.0;
var radius          = 100.;
var angleSum1       = 0.;
var angleSum2       = 0.;
var vertexCount     = 8.;
var xPts            = Array(vertexCount);
var yPts            = Array(vertexCount);
var angles          = Array(vertexCount);
var pointPath       = "";
var circleColors    = ['red','green',
                        'blue','yellow'];
var colorCount      = 4.;

var pieNode         = null;
var svgDocument     = null;
var target          = null;
var gcNode          = null;


function init(event)
{
   target = event.getTarget();
   svgDocument = target.getOwnerDocument();
   gcNode = svgDocument.getElementById("gc");

   initializeChart();
   drawChart();
}

function initializeChart()
{
   angles[0] = 30.;
   angles[1] = 60.;
   angles[2] = 45.;
   angles[3] = 45.;
   angles[4] = 20.;
   angles[5] = 30.;
   angles[6] = 50.;
   angles[7] = 80.;

} // initializeChart
```

```
function drawChart()
{
   for(var v=0; v<vertexCount; v++)
   {
      angleSum2 = angleSum1 + angles[v];

      offsetX1 = radius*Math.cos(
                         angleSum1*Math.PI/180);

      offsetY1 = radius*Math.sin(
                         angleSum1*Math.PI/180);

      offsetX2 = radius*Math.cos(
                         angleSum2*Math.PI/180);

      offsetY2 = radius*Math.sin(
                         angleSum2*Math.PI/180);

      currentX = basePointX+offsetX2;
      currentY = basePointY-offsetY2;

      // the vertical offset must be subtracted,
      // so we need to "flip" the sign of offsetY1
      offsetY1 *= -1;

      pointPath = "M"+basePointX+","+basePointY;
      pointPath += " l"+offsetX1+","+offsetY1;
      pointPath += " A"+radius+","+radius+" 0 0 0 ";
      pointPath += currentX+","+currentY;
      pointPath += " L"+basePointX+","+
                         basePointY+"z";

      fillColor  = "fill:"+
                      circleColors[v%colorCount];

      pieNode = svgDocument.createElement("path");
      pieNode.setAttribute("d",    pointPath);
      pieNode.setAttribute("style",fillColor);

      gcNode.appendChild(pieNode);

      angleSum1 += angles[v];
   }

} // drawPattern
]]> </script>
```

```
<!-- ============================= -->
<g id="gc" transform="translate(10,10)">
  <rect x="0" y="0"
        width="800" height="500"
        fill="none" stroke="none"/>
</g>
</svg>
```

## Remarks

The SVG code in Listing 15.1 starts with a block of global ECMAScript variables, followed by the ECMAScript function init() that initializes the variables svgDocument, target, and gcNode. The init() function invokes the ECMAScript function initializeChart(), which assigns a value (measured in degrees) to each sector of the pie chart as listed below:

```
function initializeChart()
{
    angles[0] = 30.;
    angles[1] = 60.;
    angles[2] = 45.;
    angles[3] = 45.;
    angles[4] = 20.;
    angles[5] = 30.;
    angles[6] = 50.;
    angles[7] = 80.;

} // initializeChart
```

The last line of the init() function invokes drawChart(), which performs all the necessary calculations for determining the coordinates of the circular pie sectors.

The first portion of drawChart() updates the current cumulative angle and then computes the x-coordinates and the y-coordinates of the two "end points" (of the current circular arc) that lie on the circumference of the outer circle:

```
angleSum2 = angleSum1 + angles[v];

offsetX1 = radius*Math.cos(angleSum1*Math.PI/180);
offsetY1 = radius*Math.sin(angleSum1*Math.PI/180);
offsetX2 = radius*Math.cos(angleSum2*Math.PI/180);
offsetY2 = radius*Math.sin(angleSum2*Math.PI/180);
```

The argument to the functions Math.cos() and Math.sin() is interpreted as a radian value; therefore, you must multiply the variables angleSum1 and angleSum2 (which represent degree values) by the constant Math.PI/180.

Next, drawChart() constructs the string pointPath that will be used in an SVG path element:

```
currentX = basePointX+offsetX2;
currentY = basePointY-offsetY2;

// the vertical offset must be subtracted,
// so we need to "flip" the sign of offsetY1
offsetY1 *= -1;

pointPath = "M"+basePointX+","+basePointY;
pointPath += " l"+offsetX1+","+offsetY1;
pointPath += " A"+radius+","+radius+" 0 0 0 ";
pointPath += currentX+","+currentY;
pointPath += " L"+basePointX+","+
                    basePointY+"z";
```

The following line of code emphasizes the fact that the vertical offset must be subtracted or its sign must be inverted:

```
offsetY1 *= -1;
```

An alternative would be to embed the negative sign as follows:

```
pointPath += " l"+offsetX1+","+(-offsetY1);
```

Both techniques have advantage and disadvantages; select one that suits your needs and then use it consistently in your code.

The last portion of drawChart() dynamically creates an SVG path element and assigns values to the attributes path and style:

```
fillColor = "fill:"+circleColors[v%colorCount];

pieNode = svgDocument.createElement("path");
pieNode.setAttribute("d",     pointPath);
pieNode.setAttribute("style",fillColor);

gcNode.appendChild(pieNode);

angleSum1 += angles[v];
```

Notice how the current "color index" is determined in the following line of code:

```
fillColor = "fill:"+circleColors[v%colorCount];
```

The term v%colorCount ensures that the index into the color array circleColors will not exceed the number of elements in the array. You will see this technique (as well as some other variants) used in many examples in this book.

SVG makes it very easy to create a "separation" effect between adjacent pie slices; simply add the following code to drawChart():

```
var style       = "";
var strokeWidth = 4.;
var strokeColor = 'white';

stroke   = "stroke:"+strokeColor+";";
stroke  += "stroke-width:"+strokeWidth+";";

fillColor = "fill:"+circleColors[v%colorCount];

style = stroke+fillColor;
pieNode.setAttribute("style",style);
```

If you want to create a "dotted" effect, you can add this line of code:

```
style += "stroke-dasharray:2 2 2 2";
```

Instead of hard-coding the value of the attribute stroke-dasharray, you can use a more flexible approach (which is used extensively in this book):

```
var dashStyle = "2 2 2 2";
....
style += "stroke-dasharray:"+dashStyle;
```

If you use the preceding technique, make sure that you include semi-colons (";") in the proper locations, or you will see the following type of message in the status bar of your browser:

```
bad CSS property or descriptor declaration
```

If you are dynamically concatenating multiple strings together in order to define the value of the style attribute, you can display the value of this attribute in an ECMAScript alert() function as follows:

```
if( count == 0 )
{
    alert("style "+style);
}
```

The if statement is useful when you need to display the value of the style attribute inside a for loop that has a large number of iterations.

Another variation of the code involves creating a shadow-like three-dimensional effect; this change requires adding the following code to the function drawChart():

```
function drawChart()
{
   circleNode = svgDocument.createElement("circle");
   circleNode.setAttribute("cx",   basePointX+10);
   circleNode.setAttribute("cy",   basePointY+10);
   circleNode.setAttribute("r",    radius);
   circleNode.setAttribute("style","fill:black;");

   gcNode.appendChild(circleNode);

   // the remaining code is the same....
}
```

ON THE CD
The complete code for the preceding modifications is available on the CD-ROM in the SVG files *circularPieChart2.svg* and *circularPieChartShadow1.svg*.

## CONVERTING DATA FOR CIRCULAR PIE CHARTS

The SVG code in Listing 15.2 defines an array of values that represent the angle subtended by circular arcs. What would you do if you had a set of numeric data instead of the pre-computed angles for the corresponding circular arc? The code below shows you how to convert numeric data into the corresponding angles in order to create the associated circular pie chart.

The SVG document *circularPieChartData1.svg* in Listing 15.2 demonstrates how to draw a circular pie chart.

### Listing 15.2  circularPieChartData1.svg

```
<?xml version="1.0" standalone="no"?>

   function initializeDataPoints()
   {
      dataPoints[0] = 100.;
      dataPoints[1] = 200.;
      dataPoints[2] = 300.;
      dataPoints[3] = 450.;
      dataPoints[4] = 250.;
      dataPoints[5] = 350.;
      dataPoints[6] = 500.;
      dataPoints[7] = 275.;

      dataSum = 0.;
```

```
          for(var v=0; v<vertexCount; v++)
          {
             dataSum += dataPoints[v];
          }
      }

      function initializeChart()
      {
          initializeDataPoints();

          for(var v=0; v<vertexCount; v++)
          {
             angles[v] = 360.*dataPoints[v]/dataSum;
          }

      } // initializeChart
```

## Remarks

The code in Listing 15.2 contains the ECMAScript function `initializeChart()` that invokes the ECMAScript function `initializeDataPoints()`, which in turn initializes an array with numeric values, while the former computes the associated angle values. The section of code that computes the corresponding angle value is given below:

```
for(var v=0; v<vertexCount; v++)
{
    angles[v] = 360.*dataPoints[v]/dataSum;
}
```

The preceding loop assigns each pie slice the number of degrees that is proportionate to the sum of all the pie chart values.

ON THE CD

The file *circularPieChartData1.svg*, which can be found on the CD-ROM, is a complete listing that computes a set of angles based on a set of numeric data and then renders a circular pie chart.

## DRAWING ELLIPTIC PIE CHARTS

Consider the elliptic pie chart shown in Figure 15.2.

The SVG document *ellipticPieChart1.svg* in Listing 15.3 demonstrates how to draw an elliptic pie chart.

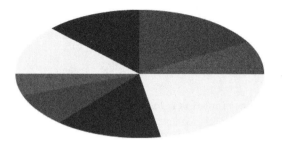

**FIGURE 15.2** An elliptic pie chart.

## Listing 15.3   ellipticPieChart1.svg

```
<?xml version="1.0" standalone="no"?>
<!DOCTYPE svg PUBLIC "-//W3C//DTD SVG 20010904//EN"
  "http://www.w3.org/TR/2001/REC-SVG-20010904/DTD/svg10.dtd">

<svg width="100%" height="100%" onload="init(evt)"
    xmlns="http://www.w3.org/2000/svg">

  <script type="text/ecmascript">
   <![CDATA[
    var basePointX    = 300.;
    var basePointY    = 150.;
    var currentX      = 0.0;
    var currentY      = 0.0;
    var offsetX1      = 0.0;
    var offsetY1      = 0.0;
    var offsetX2      = 0.0;
    var offsetY2      = 0.0;
    var minorAxis     = 100.;
    var majorAxis     = 200.;
    var angleSum1     = 0.;
    var angleSum2     = 0.;
    var vertexCount   = 8.;
    var xPts          = Array(vertexCount);
    var yPts          = Array(vertexCount);
    var angles        = Array(vertexCount);
    var pointPath     = "";
    var ellipseColors = ['red','green',
                          'blue','yellow'];
    var colorCount    = 4.;

    var pieNode       = null;
    var svgDocument   = null;
    var target        = null;
```

```
var gcNode          = null;


function init(event)
{
   target = event.getTarget();
   svgDocument = target.getOwnerDocument();
   gcNode = svgDocument.getElementById("gc");

   initializeChart();
   drawChart();
}

function initializeChart()
{
   angles[0] = 30.;
   angles[1] = 60.;
   angles[2] = 45.;
   angles[3] = 45.;
   angles[4] = 20.;
   angles[5] = 30.;
   angles[6] = 50.;
   angles[7] = 80.;

} // initializeChart

function drawChart()
{
   for(var v=0; v<vertexCount; v++)
   {
      angleSum2 = angleSum1 + angles[v];

      offsetX1 = majorAxis*Math.cos(
                          angleSum1*Math.PI/180);

      offsetY1 = minorAxis*Math.sin(
                          angleSum1*Math.PI/180);

      offsetX2 = majorAxis*Math.cos(
                          angleSum2*Math.PI/180);

      offsetY2 = minorAxis*Math.sin(
                          angleSum2*Math.PI/180);

      currentX = basePointX+offsetX2;
      currentY = basePointY-offsetY2;

      // the vertical offset must be subtracted,
```

```
                        // so we need to "flip" the sign of offsetY1
                        offsetY1 *= -1;

                        pointPath = "M"+basePointX+","+basePointY;
                        pointPath += " l"+offsetX1+","+offsetY1;
                        pointPath += " A"+majorAxis+","+
                                          minorAxis+" 0 0 0 ";

                        pointPath += currentX+","+currentY;
                        pointPath += " L"+basePointX+","+
                                          basePointY+"z";

                        fillColor  = "fill:"+
                                        ellipseColors[v%colorCount];

                        pieNode = svgDocument.createElement("path");
                        pieNode.setAttribute("d",    pointPath);
                        pieNode.setAttribute("style",fillColor);

                        gcNode.appendChild(pieNode);

                        angleSum1 += angles[v];
                    }

             } // drawPattern
        ]]> </script>

     <!-- ============================ -->
     <g id="gc" transform="translate(10,10)">
       <rect x="0" y="0"
             width="800" height="500"
             fill="none" stroke="none"/>
     </g>
     </svg>
```

## Remarks

The SVG code in Listing 15.3 is based on the code for generating a circular pie chart. The actual changes are as follows: replace the variable radius with the variables majorAxis for the horizontal axis and minorAxis for the vertical axis:

```
var minorAxis  = 100.;
var majorAxis  = 200.;

offsetX1 = majorAxis*Math.cos(angleSum1*PI/180);
offsetY1 = minorAxis*Math.sin(angleSum1*PI/180);
```

```
offsetX2 = majorAxis*Math.cos(angleSum2*PI/180);
offsetY2 = minorAxis*Math.sin(angleSum2*PI/180);
```

With the preceding changes, you have now converted a circular pie chart into an elliptic pie chart.

Since a circle is a special case of an ellipse, you can generate a circular pie chart in the preceding code by assigning the same value to minorAxis and majorAxis.

As you saw in the case of a circular pie chart, you can easily create a "separation" effect between adjacent pie elliptic slices by adding the following code in the function drawChart():

```
var style      = "";
var strokeWidth = 4.;
var strokeColor = 'white';

stroke   = "stroke:"+strokeColor+";";
stroke  += "stroke-width:"+strokeWidth+";";

fillColor = "fill:"+ellipseColors[v%colorCount];

style = stroke+fillColor;
pieNode.setAttribute("style",style);
```

Another simple variation of the code involves creating a shadow-like three-dimensional effect for the elliptic pie chart; this change requires adding the following code to the function drawChart():

```
function drawChart()
{
    ellipseNode = svgDocument.createElement("ellipse");

    ellipseNode.setAttribute("cx",   basePointX+10);
    ellipseNode.setAttribute("cy",   basePointY+10);
    ellipseNode.setAttribute("rx",   majorAxis);
    ellipseNode.setAttribute("ry",   minorAxis);
    ellipseNode.setAttribute("style","fill:black;");

    // the remaining code is the same....
}
```

The complete code for the preceding modifications is available on the CD-ROM in the SVG documents *ellipticPieChart2.svg* and *ellipticPieChartShadow1.svg*.

## ROTATING CIRCULAR PIE CHARTS

Consider the circular pie chart rendered in Figure 15.3.

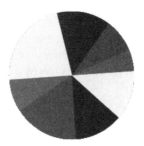

**FIGURE 15.3** A rotating
circular pie chart.

The SVG document *rotatingCircularPieChart1.svg* in Listing 15.4 demonstrates
how to draw a rotating circular pie chart.

**Listing 15.4** rotatingCircularPieChart1.svg

```
<?xml version="1.0" standalone="no"?>
<!DOCTYPE svg PUBLIC "-//W3C//DTD SVG 20010904//EN"
  "http://www.w3.org/TR/2001/REC-SVG-20010904/DTD/svg10.dtd">

<svg width="100%" height="100%" onload="init(evt)"
    xmlns="http://www.w3.org/2000/svg">

  <script type="text/ecmascript">
    <![CDATA[
    var basePointX     = 300.;
    var basePointY     = 150.;
    var currentX       = 0.0;
    var currentY       = 0.0;
    var offsetX1        = 0.0;
    var offsetY1        = 0.0;
    var offsetX2        = 0.0;
    var offsetY2        = 0.0;
    var shortPause     = 80.;
    var radius         = 100.;
    var startAngle     = 0.;
    var angleDelta     = 8.;
    var angleDirection = 1.;
    var maxAngle       = 180.;
    var angleSum1      = 0.;
```

```
var angleSum2      = 0.;
var vertexCount    = 8.;
var xPts           = Array(vertexCount);
var yPts           = Array(vertexCount);
var angles         = Array(vertexCount);
var pointPath      = "";
var circleColors   = ['red','green',
                        'blue','yellow'];
var colorCount     = 4.;

var pieNode        = null;
var theTimeout     = null;
var svgDocument    = null;
var target         = null;
var gcNode         = null;


function init(event)
{
   target = event.getTarget();
   svgDocument = target.getOwnerDocument();
   gcNode = svgDocument.getElementById("gc");

   initializeChart(event);
   drawChart(event);
}

function initializeChart(event)
{
   angles[0] = 30.;
   angles[1] = 60.;
   angles[2] = 45.;
   angles[3] = 45.;
   angles[4] = 20.;
   angles[5] = 30.;
   angles[6] = 50.;
   angles[7] = 80.;

} // initializeChart

function updateCoordinates()
{
   startAngle += angleDelta*angleDirection;

} // updateCoordinates

function drawChart(event)
{
```

```
for(var v=0; v<vertexCount; v++)
{
  angleSum2 = angleSum1+angles[v];

  offsetX1 = radius*Math.cos(
          (startAngle+angleSum1)*Math.PI/180);

  offsetY1 = radius*Math.sin(
          (startAngle+angleSum1)*Math.PI/180);

  offsetX2 = radius*Math.cos(
          (startAngle+angleSum2)*Math.PI/180);

  offsetY2 = radius*Math.sin(
          (startAngle+angleSum2)*Math.PI/180);

  currentX = basePointX+offsetX2;
  currentY = basePointY-offsetY2;

  // the vertical offset must be subtracted,
  // so we need to "flip" the sign of offsetY1
  offsetY1 *= -1;

  pointPath = "M"+basePointX+","+basePointY;
  pointPath += " l"+offsetX1+","+offsetY1;
  pointPath += " A"+radius+","+radius+" 0 0 ";
  pointPath += currentX+","+currentY;
  pointPath += " L"+basePointX+","+
                  basePointY+"z";

  fillColor  = "fill:"+
              circleColors[v%colorCount];

  pieNode = svgDocument.createElement("path");
  pieNode.setAttribute("d",    pointPath);
  pieNode.setAttribute("style",fillColor);

  gcNode.appendChild(pieNode);

  angleSum1 += angles[v];
}

theTimeout = setTimeout(
            "window.drawChart()",
            shortPause);

if( startAngle > maxAngle )
{
```

```
                    stopAnimation(event);
             }

             updateCoordinates();

        } // drawChart

        function stopAnimation(event)
        {
            window.clearTimeout(theTimeout);
        }

    ]]> </script>

<!-- ============================= -->
<g id="gc" transform="translate(10,10)">
    <rect x="0" y="0"
          width="800" height="500"
          fill="none" stroke="none"/>
</g>
</svg>
```

## Remarks

Although Listing 15.4 contains code that is similar to a static pie chart, let's examine the logic of the code. The key idea involves the variable startAngle, which is the start angle for the display of the rotated pie chart. Since this variable is incremented by the amount angleDelta*angleDirection each time the pie chart is refreshed, the result is a rotating pie chart. The variable shortPause (which equals 80 in this example) controls the rate at which the pie chart is refreshed; note that this value is interpreted in milliseconds. The setTimeout() function waits for shortPause milliseconds before invoking the drawChart() function. When the value of startAngle exceeds the value of maxAngle (which happens to be 180 in this example), the stopAnimation() function is invoked, which stops the animation.

Now let's return to the details of Listing 15.4. The SVG code starts with a block of global ECMAScript variables, followed by the ECMAScript function init() that initializes the variables theTimeout, svgDocument, target, and gcNode.

The init() function invokes the ECMAScript function initializeChart(), which assigns a value (measured in degrees) to each sector of the pie chart as listed below:

```
function initializeChart(event)
{
    angles[0] = 30.;
    angles[1] = 60.;
    angles[2] = 45.;
    angles[3] = 45.;
```

```
        angles[4] = 20.;
        angles[5] = 30.;
        angles[6] = 50.;
        angles[7] = 80.;

   } // initializeChart
```

The last line of the `init()` function invokes the function `drawChart()`, which performs all the necessary calculations for determining the coordinates of the circular pie sectors.

The first part of the function `drawChart()` updates the current cumulative angle and then computes the x-coordinates and the y-coordinates of the two "end points" of the current circular arc that lie on the circumference of the outer circle:

```
angleSum2 = angleSum1 + angles[v];

offsetX1 = radius*Math.cos(angleSum1*Math.PI/180);
offsetY1 = radius*Math.sin(angleSum1*Math.PI/180);
offsetX2 = radius*Math.cos(angleSum2*Math.PI/180);
offsetY2 = radius*Math.sin(angleSum2*Math.PI/180);
```

Next, `drawChart()` constructs the string `pointPath` that will be used in an SVG path element:

```
currentX = basePointX+offsetX2;
currentY = basePointY-offsetY2;

// the vertical offset must be subtracted,
// so we need to "flip" the sign of offsetY1
offsetY1 *= -1;

pointPath = "M"+basePointX+","+basePointY;
pointPath += " l"+offsetX1+","+offsetY1;
pointPath += " A"+radius+","+radius+" 0 0 0 ";
pointPath += currentX+","+currentY;
pointPath += " L"+basePointX+","+
                     basePointY+"z";
```

The next section of code in `drawChart()` dynamically creates an SVG path element and assigns values to the attributes path and style:

```
fillColor  = "fill:"+circleColors[v%colorCount];

pieNode = svgDocument.createElement("path");
pieNode.setAttribute("d",     pointPath);
pieNode.setAttribute("style",fillColor);
```

```
gcNode.appendChild(pieNode);
```

The next part of drawChart() causes this function to call itself after a pause of shortPause milliseconds:

```
theTimeout = setTimeout("window.drawChart()",
                        shortPause);
```

The following conditional code block in drawChart() invokes the function stopAnimation() in order to stop the animation effect:

```
if( startAngle > maxAngle )
{
    stopAnimation(event);
}
```

The last portion of the function drawChart() invokes the ECMAScript function updateCoordinates(), which updates the value of angleSum1 in order to create the rotating animation effect:

```
function updateCoordinates()
{
    startAngle += angleDelta*angleDirection;

} // updateCoordinates
```

If you were watching closely, or if you've written this type of code in other languages, you might have noticed that the code can easily be modified to alternate the direction of rotation. The following type of code block can accomplish this:

```
startAngle += angleDelta*angleDirection;

if( startAngle >= maxAngle )
{
    angleDirection *= -1;
    startAngle = maxAngle;
    ++changeDirection;
}

if( startAngle <= minAngle )
{
    angleDirection *= -1;
    startAngle = minAngle;
    ++changeDirection;
```

```
}

if(changeDirection > maxChangeCount )
{
    stopAnimation(event);
}
```

This code block requires the following new variables with sample initial values:

```
var changeDirection = 0.;
var minAngle        = 0.;
var maxChangeCount  = 10.;
```

## MOUSE-CONTROLLED ROTATING CIRCULAR PIE CHARTS

Consider the circular pie chart and the two rectangles rendered in Figure 15.4.

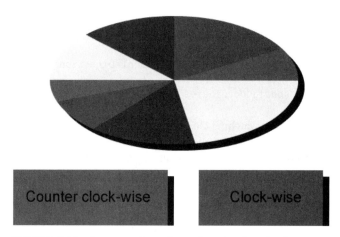

**FIGURE 15.4** A mouse-based rotating circular pie chart.

The SVG document *mouseCircularPieChartShadow1.svg* in Listing 15.5 demonstrates how to rotate a circular pie chart either clockwise or counterclockwise before rendering the pie chart.

**Listing 15.5**    mouseCircularPieChartShadow1.svg

```
<?xml version="1.0" standalone="no"?>
<!DOCTYPE svg PUBLIC "-//W3C//DTD SVG 20010904//EN"
  "http://www.w3.org/TR/2001/REC-SVG-20010904/DTD/svg10.dtd">

<svg width="100%" height="100%" onload="init(evt)"
     xmlns="http://www.w3.org/2000/svg">

  <script type="text/ecmascript">
   <![CDATA[
    var basePointX    = 300.;
    var basePointY    = 150.;
    var currentX      = 0.0;
    var currentY      = 0.0;
    var offsetX1      = 0.0;
    var offsetY1      = 0.0;
    var offsetX2      = 0.0;
    var offsetY2      = 0.0;
    var radius        = 100.;
    var startAngle    = 0.;
    var angleDelta    = 8.;
    var angleDirection = 1.;
    var maxAngle      = 180.;
    var angleSum1     = 0.;
    var angleSum2     = 0.;
    var vertexCount   = 8.;
    var xPts          = Array(vertexCount);
    var yPts          = Array(vertexCount);
    var angles        = Array(vertexCount);
    var pointPath     = "";
    var circleColors  = ['red','green',
                         'blue','yellow'];
    var colorCount    = 4.;

    var pieNode       = null;
    var circleNode    = null;
    var svgDocument   = null;
    var target        = null;
    var gcNode        = null;


    function init(event)
    {
       target = event.getTarget();
       svgDocument = target.getOwnerDocument();
       gcNode = svgDocument.getElementById("gc");
```

```
      initializeChart();
      drawChart(event);
   }

   function initializeChart()
   {
      angles[0] = 30.;
      angles[1] = 60.;
      angles[2] = 45.;
      angles[3] = 45.;
      angles[4] = 20.;
      angles[5] = 30.;
      angles[6] = 50.;
      angles[7] = 80.;

   } // initializeChart

   function rotateCounterClockwise(event)
   {
      startAngle += angleDelta*angleDirection;
      if( startAngle > 360 ) startAngle = 0;

      drawChart(event);
   }

   function rotateClockwise(event)
   {
      startAngle -= angleDelta*angleDirection;
      if( startAngle < 0 ) startAngle += 360;

      drawChart(event);
   }

   function drawChart(event)
   {
      circleNode = svgDocument.createElement("circle");
      circleNode.setAttribute("cx",    basePointX+10);
      circleNode.setAttribute("cy",    basePointY+10);
      circleNode.setAttribute("r",     radius);
      circleNode.setAttribute("style","fill:black;");

      parent.appendChild(circleNode);

      for(var v=0; v<vertexCount; v++)
      {
         angleSum2 = angleSum1+angles[v];
```

```
            offsetX1 = radius*Math.cos(
                    (startAngle+angleSum1)*Math.PI/180);

            offsetY1 = radius*Math.sin(
                    (startAngle+angleSum1)*Math.PI/180);

            offsetX2 = radius*Math.cos(
                    (startAngle+angleSum2)*Math.PI/180);

            offsetY2 = radius*Math.sin(
                    (startAngle+angleSum2)*Math.PI/180);

            currentX = basePointX+offsetX2;
            currentY = basePointY-offsetY2;

            // the vertical offset must be subtracted,
            // so we need to "flip" the sign of offsetY1
            offsetY1 *= -1;

            pointPath = "M"+basePointX+","+basePointY;
            pointPath += " l"+offsetX1+","+offsetY1;
            pointPath += " A"+radius+","+radius+" 0 0 ";
            pointPath += currentX+","+currentY;
            pointPath += " L"+basePointX+","+
                              basePointY+"z";

            fillColor  = "fill:"+
                          circleColors[v%colorCount];

            pieNode = svgDocument.createElement("path");
            pieNode.setAttribute("d",    pointPath);
            pieNode.setAttribute("style",fillColor);

            gcNode.appendChild(pieNode);

            angleSum1 += angles[v];
        }
    } // drawChart

]]> </script>

<!-- ============================ -->
<g id="gc" transform="translate(10,10)">
    <rect x="0" y="0"
         width="800" height="500"
         fill="none" stroke="red"/>
  </g>
```

```
<g transform="translate(50,300)">
    <rect fill="black" x="10" y="10"
          width="250" height="100"/>

    <rect onclick="rotateCounterClockwise(evt)"
          fill="red" x="0" y="0"
          width="250" height="100"/>

    <text font-size="24" x="20" y="50">
       Counter clock-wise
    </text>

    <rect fill="black" x="310" y="10"
          width="200" height="100"/>

    <rect onclick="rotateClockwise(evt)"
          fill="red" x="300" y="0"
          width="200" height="100"/>

    <text font-size="24" x="350" y="50">
       Clock-wise
    </text>
</g>
</svg>
```

## Remarks

The SVG code in Listing 15.5 for rendering a circular chart is the same as the code in
Listing 15.1. This example also contains two "mouse-aware" rectangles that are used
for rotating the pie chart clockwise and counterclockwise:

```
<rect onclick="rotateCounterClockwise(evt)"
      fill="red" x="0" y="0"
      width="250" height="100"/>

<text font-size="24" x="20" y="50">
   Counter clock-wise
</text>

<rect fill="black" x="310" y="10"
      width="200" height="100"/>

<rect onclick="rotateClockwise(evt)"
      fill="red" x="300" y="0"
      width="200" height="100"/>

 <text font-size="24" x="350" y="50">
```

```
            Clock-wise
    </text>
```

When you click your mouse inside the left rectangle, the pie chart will rotate counterclockwise, and when you click in the right rectangle, the rotation is clockwise. The ECMAScript functions that make this possible are given below:

```
    function rotateCounterClockwise(event)
    {
        startAngle += angleDelta*angleDirection;
        if( startAngle > 360 ) startAngle = 0;

        drawChart(event);
    }

    function rotateClockwise(event)
    {
        startAngle -= angleDelta*angleDirection;
        if( startAngle < 0 ) startAngle += 360;

        drawChart(event);
    }
```

As you can see, the previous functions either increment or decrement the value of the variable startAngle and ensure that its value lies between 0 and 360. Next, the ECMAScript function drawChart() is invoked, which then renders the rotated pie chart.

**ON THE CD**

The CD-ROM for this chapter contains the SVG document *circular-PieChartWedge1.svg* that renders a "mouse-aware" circular pie chart that allows you to "explode" individual wedges of the pie chart.

## KEY CONSTRUCTS

Circular and elliptic pie charts in SVG involve three things: 1) initializing an array with a set of angle values, 2) using the sine and cosine functions in order to calculate the points on a circle or an ellipse, and 3) dynamically creating a set of elliptic arcs whose angle spans are commensurate with their fractional value of the total value.

You can make the elliptic arcs "mouse aware" by specifying an ECMAScript function in the onclick attribute (or another mouse-related event of your choice) that is included as part of the definition of each dynamically created elliptic arc.

## CD-ROM LIBRARY

ON THE CD

The folder for this chapter on the book's companion CD-ROM contains the SVG documents that are required for viewing the following graphics images:

*circularPieChart1.svg*

*circularPieChart2.svg*

*circularPieChartShadow1.svg*

*circularPieChartData1.svg*

*ellipticPieChart1.svg*

*ellipticPieChart2.svg*

*ellipticPieChartShadow1.svg*

*rotatingCircularPieChart1.svg*

*mouseCircularPieChartShadow1.svg*

*circularPieChartWedge1.svg*

## SUMMARY

This chapter focused on how to write ECMAScript functions that render circular and elliptic pie charts. The examples in this chapter and on the CD-ROM also contain techniques for rendering the following types of charts:

- rotating circular pie charts
- mouse-aware circular pie charts
- mouse-aware circular pie charts with exploded wedges

# 16 ECMAScript, Recursion, and SVG

## OVERVIEW

As you may already know, recursion plays an important role in computer science, partly because its expressive power can yield compact and elegant algorithms that are far superior to their iteration-based counterparts. In fact, deceptively simple and succinct recursion-based algorithms can produce surprisingly beautiful graphics images. When producing such images with SVG, though, the cost of doing so often involves greater memory and slower performance. Moreover, there are situations when you can use a simple iterative algorithm that is much faster than an equivalent recursive algorithm; two examples of this scenario involve the calculation of Fibonacci numbers and the factorial value of a non-negative integer.

When you combine recursion with ECMAScript and SVG, the performance can be slower than the Java equivalent by a factor of five or more, despite the fact that Java is an interpreted language. In this chapter, the file names that contain the string "triangle " or "Sierpinski " are the fastest: they require two or three seconds on a 2GHz Pentium-4 PC. The remaining examples in this chapter are *very* compute-intensive, and they will probably cause a slower PC to "hang" or require far too much time to render the SVG contents.

This chapter contains various examples of generating recursion-based SVG graphics images. The first example, which renders a set of nested triangles, contains the necessary logic and ECMAScript code that can be enhanced in order to render a Sierpinski curve that is presented in the second example. All code and images for this chapter can be found on the companion CD-ROM in the Chapter 16 folder.

ON THE CD

## HIGH-LEVEL TEMPLATE FOR CODE EXAMPLES

Listing 16.1 contains the outline of the format for most of the examples in this chapter that will help you visualize the flow of logic that underlies the code.

**Listing 16.1**  A high-level code template for this chapter

```
// global variables here...

function init(event)
{
   // initialization here...
   initializeTriangle();
}

function initializeTriangle()
{
   drawPattern(level, xPts, yPts);

} // initializeTriangle

function drawPattern(level, oldXPts, oldYPts)
{
   if( level >= 0 )
   {
      // assign values to newXPts and newYPts
      // and then do some more things here...

      gcNode.appendChild(triangleNode);
      drawPattern(level-1, newXPts, newYPts);
   }
```

```
} // drawPattern
```

## Remarks

Listing 16.1 can be summarized in the following manner: "repeatedly invoke the function `drawPattern()` until some condition is no longer true." Note that although this listing contains references to `triangleNode` and `initializeTriangle()`, you are obviously not restricted to triangles; in general, these entities can be replaced by polygons or other geometric objects of your choice.

# RENDERING NESTED TRIANGLES VIA RECURSION

Consider the image displayed in Figure 16.1, which is a recursion-based example that implements the code template in Listing 16.1.

**FIGURE 16.1**   A set of nested triangles.

The SVG document *nestedTriangles1.svg* in Listing 16.2 demonstrates how to define an SVG document that generates a set of nested triangles.

**Listing 16.2**   nestedTriangles1.svg

```
<?xml version="1.0" standalone="no"?>
<!DOCTYPE svg PUBLIC "-//W3C//DTD SVG 20010904//EN"
"http://www.w3.org/TR/2001/REC-SVG-20010904/DTD/svg10.dtd">

<svg width="100%" height="100%" onload="init(evt)"
  xmlns="http://www.w3.org/2000/svg">

<script type="text/ecmascript">
 <![CDATA[
  var width        = 800.;
  var height       = 500.;
```

```
var basePointX    = 300.;
var basePointY    = 0.;
var currentX      = 0.;
var currentY      = 0.;
var offsetX       = 0.0;
var offsetY       = 0.0;
var level         = 5.;
var triangleWidth  = 800.;
var triangleHeight = 300.;
var vertexCount   = 3.;
var xPts          = Array(vertexCount);
var yPts          = Array(vertexCount);
var newXPts       = Array(vertexCount);
var newYPts       = Array(vertexCount);
var pointPath     = "";
var ellipseColors = ['red','green',
                       'blue','yellow'];
var colorCount    = 4.;

var triangleNode  = null;
var svgDocument   = null;
var target        = null;
var gcNode        = null;


function init(event)
{
   target = event.getTarget();
   svgDocument = target.getOwnerDocument();
   gcNode = svgDocument.getElementById("gc");

   initializeTriangle();
   drawPattern(level, xPts, yPts);
}

function initializeTriangle()
{
   // clockwise from top vertex...
   xPts[0] = basePointX;
   yPts[0] = basePointY;

   xPts[1] = basePointX+triangleWidth/2;
   yPts[1] = basePointY+triangleHeight;

   xPts[2] = basePointX-triangleWidth/2;
   yPts[2] = basePointY+triangleHeight;

} // initializeTriangle
```

```
function drawPattern(level, oldXPts, oldYPts)
{
  if( level >= 0 )
  {
                    // arrays for inner triangle...
      newXPts = Array(vertexCount);
      newYPts = Array(vertexCount);

      for(v=0; v<vertexCount; v++)
      {
          // clockwise from upper-left vertex...
          newXPts[v] = (oldXPts[v]+
                      oldXPts[(v+1)%vertexCount])/2;

          newYPts[v] = (oldYPts[v]+
                      oldYPts[(v+1)%vertexCount])/2;
      }

      pointPath = "";
      for(var v=0; v<vertexCount; v++)
      {
          pointPath += newXPts[v]+","+newYPts[v]+" ";
      }

      fillColor  = "fill:";
      fillColor += ellipseColors[level%colorCount];

      triangleNode = svgDocument.createElement(
                                          "polygon");

      triangleNode.setAttribute("points",pointPath);
      triangleNode.setAttribute("style", fillColor);

      gcNode.appendChild(triangleNode);
      drawPattern(level-1, newXPts, newYPts);
  }

} // drawPattern
]]> </script>

<!-- ============================= -->
<g id="gc" transform="translate(10,10)">
  <rect x="0" y="0"
        width="800" height="500"
        fill="none" stroke="none"/>
</g>
</svg>
```

## Remarks

The key idea in Listing 16.2 involves creating a new triangle whose vertices are the midpoints of the sides of the current triangle, as illustrated in the following code fragment:

```
    // arrays for inner triangle...
newXPts = Array(vertexCount);
newYPts = Array(vertexCount);

for(var v=0; v<vertexCount; v++)
{
   // clockwise from upper-left vertex...
   newXPts[v] = (oldXPts[v]+
                 oldXPts[(v+1)%vertexCount])/2;

   newYPts[v] = (oldYPts[v]+
                 oldYPts[(v+1)%vertexCount])/2;
}
```

If you use the same arrays for the current triangle and the nested triangle instead of creating new arrays for the vertices of the nested triangle, you will clobber the values of the vertices of the current triangle and the result will not be what you expected. If you are curious, though, try replacing the existing loop with the code fragment given below:

```
for(var v=0; v<vertexCount; v++)
{
   // clockwise from upper-left vertex...
   oldXPts[v] = (oldXPts[v]+
                 oldXPts[(v+1)%vertexCount])/2;

   oldYPts[v] = (oldYPts[v]+
                 oldYPts[(v+1)%vertexCount])/2;
}
```

Don't forget to replace the other occurrences of newXPts and newYPts with oldXPts and oldYPts, respectively.

## RENDERING SIERPINSKI CURVES

Informally, a Sierpinski triangle involves the creation of half-sized sub-triangles of an equilateral ("all sides equal") triangle. The following example shows you how to use recursion in order to successively sub-divide a set of triangles that are "derived" from an initial triangle. Consider the image displayed in Figure 16.2.

**FIGURE 16.2**   A Sierpinski curve.

The SVG document *Sierpinski2.svg* in Listing 16.3 demonstrates how to define an SVG document that generates a Sierpinski curve.

**Listing 16.3**   Sierpinski2.svg

```
<?xml version="1.0" standalone-"no"?>
<!DOCTYPE svg PUBLIC "-//W3C//DTD SVG 20010904//EN"
 "http://www.w3.org/TR/2001/REC-SVG-20010904/DTD/svg10.dt d">

<svg width="100%" height="100%" onload="init(evt)"
  xmlns="http://www.w3.org/2000/svg">

 <script type="text/ecmascript">
 <![CDATA[
 var width         = 800.;
 var height        = 500.;
 var basePointX    = 350.;
 var basePointY    = 50.;
 var currentX      = 0.;
 var currentY      = 0.;
 var offsetX       = 0.0;
 var offsetY       = 0.0;
 var level         = 5.;
 var triangleWidth = 600.;
 var triangleHeight = 300.;
 var vertexCount   = 3.;
 var xPts          = Array(vertexCount);
 var yPts          = Array(vertexCount);
 var pointPath     = "";
 var ellipseColors = ['red','green',
```

```
                                'blue','yellow'];
      var colorCount      = 4.;

      var triangleNode    = null;
      var svgDocument     = null;
      var target          = null;
      var gcNode          = null;


      function init(event)
      {
         target = event.getTarget();
         svgDocument = target.getOwnerDocument();
         gcNode = svgDocument.getElementById("gc");

         initializeTriangle();
         drawPattern(level, xPts, yPts);
      }

      function initializeTriangle()
      {
         // clockwise from top vertex...
         xPts[0] = basePointX;
         yPts[0] = basePointY;

         xPts[1] = basePointX+triangleWidth/2;
         yPts[1] = basePointY+triangleHeight;

         xPts[2] = basePointX-triangleWidth/2;
         yPts[2] = basePointY+triangleHeight;

      } // initializeTriangle

      function drawPattern(level, oldXPts, oldYPts)
      {
         var innerXPts = Array(vertexCount);
         var innerYPts = Array(vertexCount);

         var upperXPts = Array(vertexCount);
         var upperYPts = Array(vertexCount);

         var leftXPts  = Array(vertexCount);
         var leftYPts  = Array(vertexCount);
         var rightXPts = Array(vertexCount);
         var rightYPts = Array(vertexCount);

         if( level >= 0 )
         {
```

```
for(var v=0; v<vertexCount; v++)
{
   // clockwise from upper-left vertex...
   innerXPts[v] =
    (oldXPts[v]+oldXPts[(v+1)%vertexCount])/2;

   innerYPts[v] =
    (oldYPts[v]+oldYPts[(v+1)%vertexCount])/2;
}

pointPath = "";
for(var v=0; v<vertexCount; v++)
{
   pointPath += innerXPts[v]+","+
                innerYPts[v]+" ";
}

fillColor  = "fill:";
fillColor += ellipseColors[level%colorCount];

triangleNode = svgDocument.createElement(
                                  "polygon");

triangleNode.setAttribute("points",pointPath);
triangleNode.setAttribute("style", fillColor);

gcNode.appendChild(triangleNode);
drawPattern(level-1, innerXPts, innerYPts);
// clockwise from top vertex (upper triangle)
upperXPts[0] = oldXPts[0];
upperYPts[0] = oldYPts[0];

upperXPts[1] = innerXPts[0];
upperYPts[1] = innerYPts[0];

upperXPts[2] = innerXPts[2];
upperYPts[2] = innerYPts[2];
drawPattern(level-1, upperXPts, upperYPts);

// clockwise from top vertex (left triangle)
leftXPts[0] = innerXPts[2];
leftYPts[0] = innerYPts[2];

leftXPts[1] = innerXPts[1];
leftYPts[1] = innerYPts[1];

leftXPts[2] = oldXPts[2];
leftYPts[2] = oldYPts[2];
```

```
                drawPattern(level-1, leftXPts, leftYPts);

                // clockwise from top vertex (right triangle)
                rightXPts[0] = innerXPts[0];
                rightYPts[0] = innerYPts[0];

                rightXPts[1] = oldXPts[1];
                rightYPts[1] = oldYPts[1];

                rightXPts[2] = innerXPts[1];
                rightYPts[2] = innerYPts[1];
                drawPattern(level-1, rightXPts, rightYPts);
            }

        } // drawPattern
    ]]> </script>

    <!-- ============================= -->
    <g id="gc" transform="translate(10,10)">
        <rect x="0" y="0"
                width="800" height="500"
                fill="none" stroke="none"/>
    </g>
</svg>
```

## Remarks

Listing 16.3 extends the technique presented in Listing 16.2. Instead of recursively computing the coordinates of a triangle whose coordinates are the midpoints of the sides of the current triangle, this example sub-divides the current triangle into four triangles, and then recursively invokes the function drawPattern() with each of those four triangles. This seemingly minor detail produces a much richer visual effect because of the recursion that is performed.

You can enhance this example by introducing a "shift" term for the rendered triangles, thereby creating a more abstract effect. For example, you could do something like this:

```
var factor = 0.9;
.....
shiftX = (oldXPts[0]+oldXPts[2])/factor;
shiftY = (oldYPts[0]+oldYPts[2])/factor;

for(var v=0; v<vertexCount; v++)
{
    // clockwise from upper-left vertex...
    innerXPts[v] = shiftX+
            (oldXPts[v]+oldXPts[(v+1)%vertexCount])/2;
```

```
        innerYPts[v] = shiftY+
                (oldYPts[v]+oldYPts[(v+1)%vertexCount])/2;
    }
```

As you experiment with different colors and various "shifting" techniques (such as randomly generated values), you will see that some combinations are much more interesting than others are. This is actually very common and will even happen to people who have a well-developed ability to visualize or anticipate the combined effect of recursion and code variations. The best way to learn is through experimentation and by reading other examples of recursion-based code.

## RENDERING ELLIPSES WITH RECURSION

Consider the set of ellipses displayed in Figure 16.3.

**FIGURE 16.3**   A set of recursion-based ellipses.

The SVG document *nestedShadowEllipses1.svg* in Listing 16.4 demonstrates how to define an SVG document that generates a set of recursion-based ellipses.

**Listing 16.4**   nestedShadowEllipses1.svg

```
<?xml version="1.0" standalone="no"?>
<!DOCTYPE svg PUBLIC "-//W3C//DTD SVG 20010904//EN"
```

```
                "http://www.w3.org/TR/2001/REC-SVG-20010904/DTD/svg10.dtd">

                <svg width="100%" height="100%" onload="init(evt)"
                  xmlns="http://www.w3.org/2000/svg">

                <script type="text/ecmascript">
                 <![CDATA[
                  var width          = 800.;
                  var height         = 500.;
                  var basePointX     = 300.;
                  var basePointY     = 180.;
                  var currentX       = 0.;
                  var currentY       = 0.;
                  var shiftX         = 15.;
                  var shiftY         = 15.;
                  var scale          = 0.90;
                  var maxLevel       = 10.;
                  var level          = maxLevel;
                  var majorAxis      = 200.;
                  var minorAxis      = 100.;
                  var pointPath      = "";
                  var ellipseColors  = ['red','green','blue',
                                        'white','yellow','red',
                                        'magenta','black','green'];
                  var colorCount     = 9.;

                  var style          = "";
                  var strokeWidth    = 1.;
                  var dashStyle      = "4 4 4 4";

                  var ellipseNode    = null;
                  var svgDocument    = null;
                  var target         = null;
                  var gcNode         = null;


                  function init(event)
                  {
                     target = event.getTarget();
                     svgDocument = target.getOwnerDocument();
                     gcNode = svgDocument.getElementById("gc");

                     drawPattern(maxLevel,
                                 basePointX, basePointY,
                                 majorAxis, minorAxis);
                  }

                  function drawPattern(level, xCoord, yCoord,
```

```
                    majorAxis, minorAxis)
{
  if( level >= 0 )
  {
    // draw "shadow" ellipse...
    style = "fill:black;";

    ellipseNode = svgDocument.createElement(
                                    "ellipse");

    ellipseNode.setAttribute("cx", xCoord+shiftX);
    ellipseNode.setAttribute("cy", yCoord+shiftY);
    ellipseNode.setAttribute("rx", majorAxis);
    ellipseNode.setAttribute("ry", minorAxis);
    ellipseNode.setAttribute("style", style);

    gcNode.appendChild(ellipseNode);

    drawPattern(level-1, xCoord, yCoord,
                scale*minorAxis, scale*majorAxis);

    // draw white ellipse...
    style  = "fill:none";
    style += ";stroke:white";
    style += ";stroke-width:"+strokeWidth;
    style += ";stroke-dasharray:"+dashStyle;

    ellipseNode = svgDocument.createElement(
                                    "ellipse");

    ellipseNode.setAttribute("cx", xCoord+shiftX);
    ellipseNode.setAttribute("cy", yCoord+shiftY);
    ellipseNode.setAttribute("rx", majorAxis-shiftX);
    ellipseNode.setAttribute("ry", minorAxis-shiftY);
    ellipseNode.setAttribute("style", style);

    gcNode.appendChild(ellipseNode);

    // draw "regular" ellipse...
    style  = "fill:";
    style += ellipseColors[level%colorCount];

    ellipseNode = svgDocument.createElement(
                                    "ellipse");
    ellipseNode.setAttribute("cx", xCoord);
    ellipseNode.setAttribute("cy", yCoord);
    ellipseNode.setAttribute("rx", majorAxis);
    ellipseNode.setAttribute("ry", minorAxis);
```

```
            ellipseNode.setAttribute("style", style);

            gcNode.appendChild(ellipseNode);

            drawPattern(level-1, xCoord, yCoord,
                        scale*minorAxis, scale*majorAxis);
        }

    } // drawPattern
  ]]> </script>

  <!-- ============================ -->
  <g id="gc" transform="translate(10,10)">
    <rect x="0" y="0"
          width="800" height="500"
          fill="none" stroke="none"/>
  </g>
</svg>
```

## Remarks

Listing 16.4 demonstrates a simple yet useful point regarding recursively invoked functions: you can embed all sorts of non-recursive elements in them. In Listing 16.4, a "shadow" ellipse is rendered as a dark ellipse, followed by a recursive invocation, then a dashed white ellipse is followed by yet another recursive invocation. Obviously you are not limited to rendering only ellipses; you could also include recursive invocations of other geometric objects (such as polygons), or even have two functions recursively invoke each other. As you can see, there is virtually no limit to the variations you can add to recursively invoked functions, but remember that you can make a relatively small change in your code that can significantly reduce the performance. In the SVG/ECMAScript environment, the most significant performance decrease tends to occur with recursion that involves rendering a large number of ellipses, elliptic arcs, or Bezier curves (or some combination thereof), whereas performance will not be adversely affected to the same extent when you render a comparable number of polygons. This performance difference tends to be true even when recursion is not involved, but in such cases you need to dynamically generate a much greater number of objects in order to produce a performance penalty that is comparable to that of the absented recursion.

## KEY CONSTRUCTS

Generating "midpoint" nested objects that are in the polygon "family" (in a manner of speaking) rely on the following type of code fragment:

```
       // arrays for inner polygon...
newXPts = Array(vertexCount);
newYPts = Array(vertexCount);

for(var v=0; v<vertexCount; v++)
{
    // clockwise from upper-left vertex...
    newXPts[v] = (oldXPts[v]+
                 oldXPts[(v+1)%vertexCount])/2;

    newYPts[v] = (oldYPts[v]+
                 oldYPts[(v+1)%vertexCount])/2;
}
```

Recursion is a very useful technique for rendering visually rich and complex patterns that are based on simple geometric objects such as triangles and ellipses.

Performance is always a key factor when you write recursively invoked ECMAScript functions, and in some cases you might need to find an iteration-based equivalent algorithm that produces the desired results.


## CD-ROM LIBRARY

ON THE CD
The folder for this chapter on the book's companion CD-ROM contains the SVG documents that are required for viewing the following graphics images:

*nestedTriangles1.svg*

*Sierpinski2.svg*

*nestedShadowEllipses1.svg*


## SUMMARY

This chapter introduced you to recursion, which can be used for rendering very exotic graphics images. The examples in this chapter showed you how to use recursion in ECMAScript functions in order to render various geometric objects, including the well-known Sierpinski curve. Remember that most of the examples in this chapter are very CPU-intensive, even on a 2GHz Pentium-4 PC, and therefore it would be better not to launch them on slower machines.

# 17 Generating SVG Documents

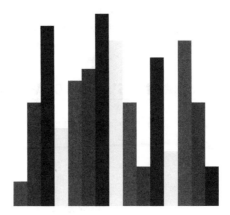

## OVERVIEW

The first part of this chapter shows you various techniques for generating SVG documents via Perl scripts and Unix shell scripts that can be invoked manually from the command line for your PC or in a Unix environment. Such scripts can also be executed on a regularly scheduled basis through some type of scheduler (e.g., the Unix cron utility). If you are unfamiliar with Perl, you can read the Perl appendix (Appendix C) in the back of this book. The second part of this chapter contains examples of applying XSLT to XML documents in order to generate SVG documents. If you are unfamiliar with XSLT, you might want to read the accompanying appendix. All code

ON THE CD

and images for this chapter can be found on the companion CD-ROM in the Chapter 17 folder.

## GENERATING XML DOCUMENTS FROM TEXT FILES

Converting text files to XML is a task that can be performed via custom code by means of various scripting languages. Although a delimited flat file with employee information sounds generic, the conversion requires custom code that is closely tied to the format and content of the text file. Since our primary focus is on generating SVG

ON THE CD

documents, check the CD-ROM for this chapter to see examples of Unix shell scripts and Perl scripts that convert a text file with employee data into an XML document.

## GENERATING A SIMPLE SVG DOCUMENT WITH PERL

Consider the red rectangle displayed in Figure 17.1.

**FIGURE 17.1** A red rectangle.

The Perl script *simplePerl1.pl* in Listing 17.1 generates an SVG document that renders a rectangle.

### Listing 17.1   simplePerl1.pl

```
print "<svg>\n";
print "  <g transform=\"translate(50,50)\">\n";
print "  <rect x=\"0\" y=\"50\"  width=\"20\"
height=\"50\"\n";
print "          style=\"fill:red\"/>\n";
print "  </g>\n";
print "</svg>\n";
```

The SVG document script *simplePerl1.svg* in Listing 17.2 is the output of the Perl script in Listing 17.1.

**Listing 17.2**   simplePerl1.svg

```
<svg>
 <g transform="translate(50,50)">
   <rect x="0" y="50"  width="20" height="50"
         style="fill:red"/>
 </g>
</svg>
```

## Remarks

After you have added the directory containing the Perl executable to your PATH variable, you can generate the SVG document displayed in Listing 17.2 by invoking Perl
from the command line as follows:

```
perl -w simplePerl1.pl >simplePerl1.svg
```

The Perl script in Listing 17.2 contains of a set of print statements that print
each line of SVG code. While this is acceptable for very small SVG documents, this
technique becomes cumbersome with SVG documents that are more than a page in
length. A slightly better approach is demonstrated in the next example.

## GENERATING A SIMPLE SVG DOCUMENT WITH PERL FUNCTIONS

The Perl script *simplePerl2.pl* in Listing 17.3 uses Perl 4A-style invocation of Perl
functions in order to generate an SVG document that renders a rectangle. (If you're
using Perl 5.x, you can remove the ampersands.)

**Listing 17.3**   simplePerl2.pl

```
&generateHeader();
&generateRectangle(0, 288, 20, 112,"fill:red");
&generateFooter();

sub generateHeader()
{
    print "<svg>\n";
}

sub generateRectangle($$$$)
{
    my($x,$y,$width,$height,$style) = @_;
```

```
    print "  <g transform=\"translate(50,50)\">\n";
    print "   <rect x=\"$x\" y=\"$y\" width=\"$width\"
height=\"$height\"\n";
    print "         style=\"$style\"/>\n";
    print "  </g>\n";
}

sub generateFooter()
{
    print "</svg>\n";
}
```

The SVG document *simplePerl2.svg* in Listing 17.4 is the output of the Perl script in Listing 17.3.

### Listing 17.4    simplePerl2.svg

```
<svg>
  <g transform="translate(50,50)">
    <rect x="0" y="288"  width="20" height="112"
          style="fill:red"/>
  </g>
</svg>
```

## Remarks

After you have added the directory containing the Perl executable to your PATH variable, you can generate the SVG document displayed in Listing 17.4 by invoking Perl from the command line as follows:

```
perl -w simplePerl2.pl >simplePerl2.svg
```

The Perl script in Listing 17.3 is an improvement over Listing 17.1 because it uses Perl functions to render the initial <svg> tag, the SVG rect element, and the closing SVG </svg> tag. You can obviously add more function calls in order to generate additional rectangles. For example, you could modify the Perl script in Listing 17.3 so that it adds two more rectangles as follows:

```
&generateHeader();
&generateRectangle(0,  288, 20, 112,"fill:red");
&generateRectangle(40, 288, 20, 112,"fill:green");
&generateRectangle(80, 288, 20, 112,"fill:blue");
&generateFooter();
```

The modified Perl script will generate the following output from the command line:

```
<svg>
  <g transform="translate(50,50)">
   <rect x="0" y="288"  width="20" height="112"
      style="fill:red"/>
  </g>
  <g transform="translate(50,50)">
   <rect x="40" y="288"  width="20" height="112"
        style="fill:green"/>
  </g>
  <g transform="translate(50,50)">
   <rect x="80" y="288"  width="20" height="112"
        style="fill:blue"/>
  </g>
</svg>
```

## GENERATING BAR SETS WITH PERL

Consider the bar set displayed in Figure 17.2.

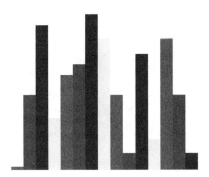

**FIGURE 17.2**   A bar set.

The text file *barSet1.txt* in Listing 17.5 contains a list of numbers that represent the height of the rectangles in the bar set displayed in Figure 17.2.

**Listing 17.5**   barSet1.txt

```
112
224
333
188
255
```

272
350
312
224
133
288
155
312
224
133

The Perl script *barSet1.pl* in Listing 17.6 generates an SVG document that renders a bar set.

## Listing 17.6   barSet1.pl

```
# STEP 1:  initialize variables
my($fileName)    = "barSet1.txt";
my($index)       = 0;
my($height)      = 0;
my($color)       = "";
my($barWidth)    = 20;
my($xPosition)   = 0;
my($yPosition)   = 0;
my($baseLine)    = 400;

my(@barColors)   = ("red", "green", "blue", "yellow");
my($colorCount)  = scalar(@barColors);

my(@dataValues);


# STEP 2:  does input file exist?
open(INPUT_FILE, "<$fileName") ||
       die "Cannot open $fileName: $!\n";

(@dataValues) = <INPUT_FILE>;
chomp (@dataValues);

# STEP 3:  print header information
print "<svg>\n";
print "  <g transform=\"translate(50,50)\">\n";

# STEP 4:  generate bar-related information
foreach $index (0..$#dataValues)
{
  $height    = $dataValues[$index];
```

```
    $color     = $barColors[$index%$colorCount];
    $yPosition = $baseLine-$height;

    print "  <rect x=\"$xPosition\" y=\"$yPosition\" ";
    print " width=\"$barWidth\" height=\"$height\"\n";
    print "            style=\"fill:$color\"/>\n";

    $xPosition += $barWidth;
}

# STEP 5:  print trailer information
print "  </g>\n";
print "</svg>\n";

# STEP 6:  close input file
close(INPUT_FILE);
```

## Remarks

Make sure that the directory with the Perl executable is included in your PATH variable, and then type the following at the command line:

```
perl barSet1.pl >barSet1.svg
```

The SVG document *barSet1.svg* in Listing 17.7 is generated by the Perl script in Listing 17.6.

## Listing 17.7   barSet1.svg

```
<svg>
<g transform="translate(50,50)">
 <rect x="0"  y="288"  width="20" height="112"
       style="fill:red"/>
 <rect x="20" y="176"  width="20" height="224"
       style="fill:green"/>
 <rect x="40" y="67"   width="20" height="333"
       style="fill:blue"/>
 <rect x="60" y="212"  width="20" height="188"
       style="fill:yellow"/>
 <rect x="80" y="145"  width="20" height="255"
       style="fill:red"/>
 <rect x="100" y="128"  width="20" height="272"
       style="fill:green"/>
 <rect x="120" y="50"   width="20" height="350"
       style="fill:blue"/>
 <rect x="140" y="88"   width="20" height="312"
       style="fill:yellow"/>
```

```
<rect x="160" y="176"  width="20" height="224"
      style="fill:red"/>
<rect x="180" y="267"  width="20" height="133"
      style="fill:green"/>
<rect x="200" y="112"  width="20" height="288"
      style="fill:blue"/>
<rect x="220" y="245"  width="20" height="155"
      style="fill:yellow"/>
<rect x="240" y="88"  width="20" height="312"
      style="fill:red"/>
<rect x="260" y="176"  width="20" height="224"
      style="fill:green"/>
<rect x="280" y="267"  width="20" height="133"
      style="fill:blue"/>
</g>
</svg>
```

### Remarks

The Perl script in Listing 17.6 can be easily enhanced so that the heights of the rectangles in the bar set are scaled between 0 and 100. These enhancements will always generate a reasonably sized bar set based on an input file that contains positive numbers. The CD-ROM contains *barSet2.pl* which will generate a scaled bar set. Note that there are other enhancements that can be added to the Perl script as well, such as ensuring that all the numbers in the text file are positive and ensuring that every line consists of digits only. However, these latter enhancements are data integrity issues, and therefore they won't be covered in this book.

ON THE CD

## GENERATING BAR SETS WITH UNIX SCRIPTS

The text file *barSet1.txt* Listing 17.8 contains a list of numbers that represent the height of the rectangles in the bar set displayed in Figure 17.3.

### Listing 17.8   barSet1.txt

```
112
224
333
188
255
272
350
312
224
```

```
133
288
155
312
224
133
```

The shell script *barSet1.sh* in Listing 17.9 demonstrates how to read the contents of a text file in order to generate an SVG document with a bar set.

Consider the bar set displayed in Figure 17.3.

**FIGURE 17.3**    A bar set.

The Unix shell script *barSet1.sh* in Listing 17.9 generates an SVG document that renders the bar set in Figure 17.3.

**Listing 17.9**    barSet1.sh

```
# STEP 1:  initialize variables
fileName="barSet1.txt"
index=0
count=0
height=0
color=""
barWidth=20
xPosition=0
yPosition=0
baseLine=400

# STEP 2:  does input file exist?
if [ ! -f $fileName ]
```

```
then
  echo "Cannot open $fileName"
else
  # STEP 3:  print header information
  echo "<svg>"
  echo "  <g transform=\"translate(50,50)\">"

  # STEP 4:  generate bar-related information
  for height in `cat $fileName`
  do
    index=`expr $count % 4`

    if [ "$index" -eq "0" ]
    then
      color="red"
    elif [ "$index" -eq "1" ]
    then
      color="green"
    elif [ "$index" -eq "2" ]
    then
      color="blue"
    elif [ "$index" -eq "3" ]
    then
      color="yellow"
    fi

    yPosition=`expr $baseLine - $height`

    subline1=" <rect x=\"$xPosition\" y=\"$yPosition\" "
    subline2=" width=\"$barWidth\" height=\"$height\""
    subline3=" style=\"fill:$color\"/>"

    fullline="${subline1} ${subline2}"
    echo $fullline
    echo $subline3

    xPosition=`expr $xPosition + $barWidth`
    count=`expr $count + 1`
  done

  # STEP 5:  print trailer information
  echo "  </g>"
  echo "</svg>"
fi
```

## Remarks

Listing 17.9 is a straightforward Unix shell script. The Unix echo statement is analogous to the Perl print statement, and the if / then / fi construct is analogous to the Perl if statement. You need to make the shell script executable by typing something like this:

```
chmod +x barSet1.sh
```

or you can explicitly set the octal values like this:

```
chmod 755 barSet.sh
```

Next, add the current directory to the PATH variables like this:

```
PATH=.:$PATH; export PATH (Bourne shell)
export PATH=.:$PATH
```

and then you can redirect the output of the Unix shell script to an SVG file as follows:

```
barSet1.sh >unixBarSet1.svg
```

The SVG document *unixBarSet1.svg* in Listing 17.10 is generated by the Unix shell script *barSet1.sh* in Listing 17.9

### Listing 17.10   unixBarSet1.svg

```
<svg>
  <g transform="translate(50,50)">
  <rect x="0" y="288" width="20" height="112"
        style="fill:red"/>
  <rect x="20" y="176" width="20" height="224"
        style="fill:green"/>
  <rect x="40" y="67" width="20" height="333"
        style="fill:blue"/>
  <rect x="60" y="212" width="20" height="188"
        style="fill:yellow"/>
  <rect x="80" y="145" width="20" height="255"
        style="fill:red"/>
  <rect x="100" y="128" width="20" height="272"
        style="fill:green"/>
  <rect x="120" y="50" width="20" height="350"
        style="fill:blue"/>
  <rect x="140" y="88" width="20" height="312"
        style="fill:yellow"/>
```

```
      <rect x="160" y="176" width="20" height="224"
          style="fill:red"/>
      <rect x="180" y="267" width="20" height="133"
          style="fill:green"/>
      <rect x="200" y="112" width="20" height="288"
          style="fill:blue"/>
      <rect x="220" y="245" width="20" height="155"
          style="fill:yellow"/>
      <rect x="240" y="88" width="20" height="312"
          style="fill:red"/>
      <rect x="260" y="176" width="20" height="224"
          style="fill:green"/>
      <rect x="280" y="267" width="20" height="133"
          style="fill:blue"/>
    </g>
</svg>
```

## CONVERTING PROPRIETARY FILES TO SVG WITH PERL

The text file *proprietary1.xyz* (note the suffix of this file) in Listing 17.11 contains a proprietary format for a fictitious company.

### Listing 17.11 proprietary1.xyz

```
##########################################
# This file is based on a proprietary
# format for a fictitious company XYZ
#
# Supported objects include the following:
# circle
# rectangle
# polygon
#
##########################################

START DEFINITION
ID:   CIRCLEO
TYPE: CIRCLE
centerx:100
centery:80
radius:20
style
{
fill:blue
```

```
stroke:yellow
stroke-width:2
}
END DEFINITION

START DEFINITION
ID:   RECT0
TYPE: RECT
width:200
height:100
xcoordinate:200
ycoordinate:200
style
{
fill:red
stroke:green
stroke-width:4
}
END DEFINITION
```

The SVG document *proprietary1.svg* in Listing 17.12 is generated when the Perl script *convert1.pl* is invoked on the text file *proprietary1.xyz*.

## Listing 17.12   proprietary1.svg

```
<svg width="100%" height="100%">
<g>
<circle id="CIRCLE0"
style="stroke:yellow;fill:blue;stroke-width:2;"
cx="100"
cy="80"
r="20"
/>

<rect id="RECT0"
style="stroke:green;fill:red;stroke-width:4;"
y="200"
height="100"
width="200"
x="200"
/>

</g>
</svg>
```

## Remarks

You can generate the SVG document from the following command:

```
perl -w convert1.pl >proprietary1.svg
```

The Perl script *convert1.pl* will not be covered because it contains 300 lines of code; it uses Perl arrays, hashes, functions, and file manipulation. If you read the Perl appendix, you will be able to understand the code. You can find this script in the folder for this chapter on the CD-ROM.

# GENERATING SVG WITH XSLT

You need to install an XSLT processor on your machine so that you can apply XSL stylesheets to XML documents. If you haven't already done so, copy the Instant Saxon executable on the CD-ROM to a convenient directory on your PC and then add this directory to your PATH variable. An example of invoking this executable is given below:

```
saxon abc.xml abc.xsl >abc.svg
```

The preceding invocation applies the XSL stylesheet *abc.xsl* to the XML document *abc.xml* and then redirects the output to the file abc.svg.

If you want to see the list of options that you can use with saxon, you can type the following,

```
saxon -?
```

and you will see something like this:

```
No source file name
SAXON 6.2.2 from Michael Kay
Usage: saxon [options] source-doc style-doc {param=value}...
Options:
  -a            Use xml-stylesheet PI, not style-doc argument
  -ds           Use standard tree data structure
  -dt           Use tinytree data structure (default)
  -o filename   Send output to named file or directory
  -m classname  Use specified Emitter class for xsl:message
output
  -r classname  Use specified URIResolver class
  -t            Display version and timing information
  -T            Set standard TraceListener
```

```
-TL classname    Set a specific TraceListener
-u               Names are URLs not filenames
-w0              Recover silently from recoverable errors
-w1              Report recoverable errors and continue (default)
-w2              Treat recoverable errors as fatal
-x classname     Use specified SAX parser for source file
-y classname     Use specified SAX parser for stylesheet
-?               Display this message
```

XSLT is an extremely powerful tool that can require a substantial amount of time and effort to gain a high level of mastery. With that in mind, let's start with a relatively easy example of an XML file containing a set of object tags that we can "map" to an SVG document by means of an XSL stylesheet. Listing 17.13 contains the sample XML document *xsltToSVG1.xml*, which specifies a rectangle, a polygon, and an ellipse by way of standard XML tags; Listing 17.14 contains the XSL stylesheet *xsltToSVG1.xsl* that can be applied to *xsltToSVG1.xml* in order to generate an SVG document.

**Listing 17.13**   xsltToSVG1.xml

```xml
<?xml version="1.0"?>
<objects>
  <object>
    <type>rect</type>
    <x>50</x>
    <y>50</y>
    <width>100</width>
    <height>50</height>
    <style>fill:red</style>
  </object>

  <object>
    <type>polygon</type>
    <points>300,50 450,50 350,100 300,150</points>
    <style>fill:blue</style>
  </object>

  <object>
    <type>ellipse</type>
    <cx>300</cx>
    <cy>100</cy>
    <rx>100</rx>
    <ry>50</ry>
    <style>fill:blue</style>
  </object>
</objects>
```

## Remarks

The first point to observe in Listing 17.13 is the objects tag and the object tag; these were chosen in an arbitrary manner as a generic mechanism for including multiple SVG-like elements. In this particular case, Listing 17.13 contains the necessary attributes for specifying three SVG elements: a rectangle, a polygon, and an ellipse.

### Listing 17.14   xsltToSVG1.xsl

```
<?xml version="1.0"?>
<xsl:stylesheet
    xmlns:xsl="http://www.w3.org/1999/XSL/Transform"
    version="1.0">

<xsl:template match="/">
 <svg>
  <g>
    <xsl:apply-templates/>
  </g>
 </svg>
</xsl:template>

<xsl:template match="objects/object">
 <xsl:for-each select=".">
   <xsl:choose>
     <xsl:when test="./type = 'rect'">
       <xsl:call-template name="createRectangle"/>
     </xsl:when>

     <xsl:when test="./type = 'polygon'">
      <xsl:call-template name="createPolygon"/>
     </xsl:when>
   </xsl:choose>
 </xsl:for-each>
</xsl:template>

<xsl:template name="createRectangle">
  <xsl:variable name="x"      select="./x"/>
  <xsl:variable name="y"      select="./y"/>
  <xsl:variable name="width"  select="./width"/>
  <xsl:variable name="height" select="./height"/>
  <xsl:variable name="style"  select="./style"/>

  <rect x="{$x}"           y="{$y}"
        width="{$width}" height="{$height}"
        style="{$style}"/>
```

```
    </xsl:template>

    <xsl:template name="createPolygon">
      <xsl:variable name="points" select="./points"/>
      <xsl:variable name="style"  select="./style"/>

      <polygon points="{$points}" style="{$style}"/>
    </xsl:template>
  </xsl:stylesheet>
```

## Remarks

Listing 17.14 starts by matching the root element ("/"), generating the outermost SVG element, and then invoking the main loop of the XSL stylesheet via the XSL code in bold, as listed below:

```
<xsl:template match="/">
  <svg>
    <g>
      <xsl:apply-templates/>
    </g>
  </svg>
</xsl:template>
```

The main loop in Listing 17.14 is executed by means of the following type of XSL statement,

```
<xsl:for-each select=".">
  <!- add processing logic for each node here ->
</xsl:for-each>
```

and the logic that decides which XSL template to invoke is based on the content of each type element, as shown below:

```
<xsl:template match="objects/object">
  <xsl:for-each select=".">
    <xsl:choose>
      <xsl:when test="./type = 'rect'">
       <xsl:call-template name="createRectangle"/>
      </xsl:when>

      <xsl:when test="./type = 'polygon'">
        <xsl:call-template name="createPolygon"/>
      </xsl:when>
    </xsl:choose>
  </xsl:for-each>
</xsl:template>
```

Notice that the `<xsl:when>` logic in the preceding loop only checks for object elements that contain a type element whose value is either rect or polygon (hence, the ellipse element is ignored). Whenever one of these two matching elements is encountered, an XSL template is explicitly invoked: one template generates an SVG rect element and the other template generates an SVG polygon element.

The createRectangle template for generating an SVG rect element is:

```
<xsl:template name="createRectangle">
  <xsl:variable name="x"      select="./x"/>
  <xsl:variable name="y"      select="./y"/>
  <xsl:variable name="width"  select="./width"/>
  <xsl:variable name="height" select="./height"/>
  <xsl:variable name="style"  select="./style"/>

  <rect x="{$x}"           y="{$y}"
        width="{$width}" height="{$height}"
        style="{$style}"/>
</xsl:template>
```

The createRectangle template requires the value of five elements from the XML document: the x-coordinate and y-coordinate of the upper-left corner of the rectangle, the width and height of the rectangle, and the style attribute of the rectangle.

The createPolygon template for generating an SVG polygon element is:

```
<xsl:template name="createPolygon">
  <xsl:variable name="points" select="./points"/>
  <xsl:variable name="style"  select="./style"/>

  <polygon points="{$points}" style="{$style}"/>
</xsl:template>
```

The createPolygon template is shorter than the createRectangle template because it only requires the points element and the style element from the XML document.

Although Listing 17.14 contains a significant amount of XSL code, it has been organized in a structured fashion to make it easier for you to understand the logic of each component. Incidentally, a good exercise would be to write the corresponding code required for processing an SVG ellipse element. When you are done, add your own SVG-based elements to the XML document—and the corresponding code in the XSL stylesheet. It will help you attain a good comfort level with the XSL code.

## GENERATING BAR CHARTS WITH XSLT

The next example involves an XML file whose first element consists of the maximum of a set of bar heights, followed by the set of elements that correspond to the vertical bars in a bar graph. We will use this information in order to "map" the vertical bars to a set of SVG `rect` elements by means of an XSL stylesheet. Keep in mind that each bar element contains the height and width of the rectangle; thus, our code needs to determine the correct values for the upper-left vertex of the vertical bar in order to generate the correct attributes for the corresponding SVG `rect` element.

Listing 17.15 contains the sample XML document *xsltGraph1.xml*, which specifies a rectangle, a polygon, and an ellipse by means of standard XML tags, and Listing 17.16 contains the XSL stylesheet *xsltGraph1.xsl* that can be applied *to xsltGraph1.xml* in order to generate an SVG document.

### Listing 17.15   xsltGraph1.xml

```
<?xml version="1.0"?>
 <objects>
   <maxValue>250</maxValue>
   <object>
     <width>40</width>
     <height>100</height>
     <style>fill:red</style>
   </object>

   <object>
     <width>40</width>
     <height>150</height>
     <style>fill:green</style>
   </object>

   <object>
     <width>40</width>
     <height>175</height>
     <style>fill:blue</style>
   </object>

   <object>
     <width>40</width>
     <height>195</height>
     <style>fill:yellow</style>
   </object>

   <object>
```

```
      <width>40</width>
      <height>125</height>
      <style>fill:blue</style>
    </object>

    <object>
      <width>40</width>
      <height>50</height>
      <style>fill:red</style>
    </object>

    <object>
      <width>40</width>
      <height>120</height>
      <style>fill:cyan</style>
    </object>

    <object>
      <width>40</width>
      <height>180</height>
      <style>fill:magenta</style>
    </object>

    <object>
      <width>40</width>
      <height>90</height>
      <style>fill:green</style>
    </object>
</objects>
```

**Listing 17.16**  xsltGraph1.xsl

```
<?xml version="1.0"?>
 <xsl:stylesheet
      xmlns:xsl="http://www.w3.org/1999/XSL/Transform"
      version="1.0">

<xsl:variable name="maxValue"
              select="/objects/maxValue"/>
<xsl:variable name="count"
              select="0"/>

<xsl:template match="/">
  <svg>
    <g>
      <xsl:apply-templates/>
```

```
        </g>
      </svg>
</xsl:template>

<xsl:template match="objects">

  <xsl:for-each select="./object">
    <xsl:call-template name="createRectangle">
      <xsl:with-param name="count"
                      select="position()"/>
    </xsl:call-template>
  </xsl:for-each>
</xsl:template>

<xsl:template name="createRectangle">
  <xsl:param     name="count"/>
  <xsl:variable name="width"  select="./width"/>
  <xsl:variable name="height" select="./height"/>
  <xsl:variable name="style"  select="./style"/>

  <rect x="{$count*$width}"
        y="{$maxValue - $height}"
        width="{$width}" height="{$height}"
        style="{$style}"/>
</xsl:template>
</xsl:stylesheet>
```

## Remarks

The essence of Listing 17.16 involves a `for-each` loop that invokes the `createRectangle` template in order to generate a rectangle associated with each `object` element in the file *xsltGraph1.xml*. The actual SVG `rect` element is generated in the `createRectangle` template by the following code block:

```
<rect x="{$count*$width}"
      y="{$maxValue - $height}"
      width="{$width}" height="{$height}"
      style="{$style}"/>
```

Notice the fact that the y attribute of the rectangle requires the value of `maxValue` from the XML *xsltGraph1.xml* in order to render the rectangle with the correct height. The inclusion of the `maxValue` element made it possible to write an XSL stylesheet that leveraged the presence of this element; however, the likelier scenario is that your XML document does not contain such a value, which means that you need to add code to the XSL stylesheet in order to compute this maximum value. You can find an example of such a computation in one of the XSL stylesheets that accompany the XSL appendix that is at the end of this book.

## KEY CONSTRUCTS

There aren't any SVG-related constructs in this chapter because the examples are more closely tied to Unix shell scripts, Perl scripts, and XSLT. As such, you can use these examples and those in the relevant appendices as a starting point for writing your own scripts.

## CD-ROM LIBRARY

ON THE CD

The folder for this chapter on the book's companion CD-ROM contains the SVG documents that are required for viewing the following graphics images:

*simplePerl1.pl*

*simplerPerl1.svg*

*simplePerl2.pl*

*simplePerl2.svg*

*barSet1.txt*

*barSet1.pl*

*barSet1.svg*

*barSet1.sh*

*barSet2.pl*

*barSet2.svg*

*barSet2.txt*

*unixBarSet1.sh*

*unixBarSet1.svg*

*proprietary1.xyz*

*proprietary1.svg*

*convert1.pl*

*xsltToSVG1.xml*

*xsltToSVG1.xsl*

*xsltGraph1.xml*

*xsltGraph1.xsl*

## SUMMARY

This chapter focused on demonstrating how to write Perl and Unix shell scripts in order to generate SVG documents from text files. This chapter also contains an example of how you can write Perl scripts for generating SVG documents from text files that are based on a proprietary format. You saw examples of applying XSL stylesheets to XML files in order to generate SVG documents, one of which is an unadorned and basic bar chart. The XSLT appendix contains additional examples of bar charts, one of which renders horizontal and vertical axes and labels the elements of the bar chart.

# 18  Supplemental Patterns

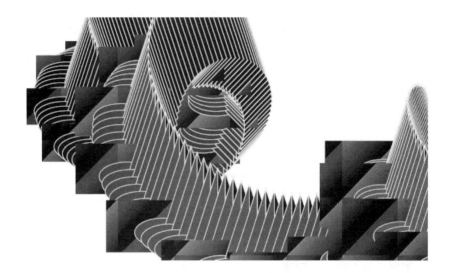

## OVERVIEW

This chapter presents some of the SVG documents that are available on the companion CD-ROM, but without a detailed discussion of the SVG code. Since the CD-ROM contains more than 20,000 SVG documents, only a small fraction of those samples can be included in this chapter. The selection process was based on several factors, such as color combinations, coding techniques, and aesthetic appeal. Some examples have an interesting visual effect, even though the underlying code is very simple; other examples might pique your interest in the technical details for creating specific effects. The documents were also selected based on several viewpoints. For instance, your viewpoint for evaluating the samples might be as a programmer/Web developer, as an artist, or perhaps as a technical neophyte who enjoys pleasant "eye candy." Some samples are interesting even though it is difficult to articulate the reason for their visceral appeal; to the extent that this is true, graphics resembles art. Nevertheless, determining the quality of a graphics image tends to be a subjective process, and this determination is ultimately based on your own tastes and needs.

The CD-ROM is organized in a systematic fashion whereby the files in each directory will illustrate a specific feature. In some cases, you will find similar variants of the same curve; that is, two examples might only differ by their color scheme. The rationale for including both samples is that either they illustrate a coding technique that will be useful and easy to enhance, or they produce vivid, interesting variations of each other. The other reason for their inclusion is that it's very convenient and advantageous to you in terms of time and effort; that is, viewing an SVG document requires no more than a double mouse click, whereas code changes (even simple ones) require significantly more time.

The directories with the string "shadow" contain samples with a shadow effect of the corresponding SVG documents in the associated directory. For example, the sub-folder `coreShadowPattern` contains samples with shadow effects, and these samples correspond to the samples in the sub-folder `corePattern`.

An additional important aspect of many of the SVG samples is that they contain "commented out" code. This feature is useful and convenient because you can see a different image simply be re-enabling one or two lines of code. For example, you might find multiple consecutive lines of "commented out" code, each of which contains variants on the `style` attribute for a particular geometric object. The inclusion of this code allows you to make code modifications quickly and easily.

## HOW TO VIEW THE FILES

Since you will not be able to view all the SVG documents on the entire CD-ROM in a single day, it's important to go through them in a systematic manner that will assist you in keeping track of the samples that you want to study in detail. One common approach for this type of task involves creating a single directory where you can place copies of your selected SVG documents. Unfortunately, this technique does not keep track of the location of the original file. A better approach involves creating a sub-directory under the directory containing the file of interest. For example, you could name the sub-directory something like LIST_0827, which records the date (in this case, it represents August 27th) that you browsed through the contents of its parent directory. This approach has another advantage: at any point in time (days, weeks, or months later) you can list all the files that you viewed on a given day. Choose a technique that you are comfortable with and that will help you keep track of the name and location of your selected files.

A good starting point is the set of files contained in the directory `corePatterns` under the `Supplemental\polarEquations` directory on the CD-ROM. The samples in this directory are based on polar equations that are used in many of the other sub-directories containing polar equations. After you have finished with this directory, you will probably have formulated an opinion regarding the type of images that are more appealing to you. For example, some people really like images that are based on Archimedean spirals and conchoids; other people prefer images that are based on Lituus curves and cochleoids.

Please remember that some of the samples are quite CPU-intensive and the rendering time can be affected by the available RAM. In general, the more complex the pattern, the longer the execution time. The vast majority of the samples are rendered in less than 10 seconds on a 2 gigahertz Pentium 4; the exceptions involve dynamically created Bezier curves and/or elliptic arcs, the Steiner-based examples, and most of the recursion-based examples that are in Chapter 16. SVG documents with the string CB contain checkerboard patterns that can also require longer execution times because they usually involve the dynamic creation of many SVG elements. If you decide that it takes too much time to render a particular SVG document, try viewing it on a faster machine.

Do you prefer rectilinear shapes with symmetric geometric patterns, or do you like curvilinear shapes co-mingled with sharp edges? In the former case, you will probably like the samples in the corePatterns folder; in the latter case, you will probably like samples in the sub-directories containing elliptic arcs. Given the variability of taste and preferences, it's impossible to create a single list of sample files that will appeal to everyone. However, after you've looked at all the samples in the corePatterns folder, you can check for similarly named files in other folders. This approach is systematic and enables you to make the most efficient use of your time. (Keep in mind, though, that you might be surprised by the other samples.)

Another consideration to keep in mind is that different patterns will appeal to you at different times. For instance, you might find that the Bezier-based samples involving Archimedean curves become the focus of your interest, and that you want to view only those samples in order to explore the possible ways that you can make your own enhancements. Follow your instincts and you will maximize your viewing pleasure!

## MAKING ENHANCEMENTS

There are some important non-technical aspects that are part of a mind-set that will assist you in learning how to create your own variations of the SVG code in this book. First, it is essential that you actively experiment with the code, which requires that you invest some of your time (and invariably necessitates a certain degree of trial and error). Note that the ability to visualize geometric patterns can be helpful, but it's not an absolute requirement. In the words of Darach Ennis, you benefit by being "curious and fearless"; in other words, don't be intimidated by the code or fearful of making "mistakes" as you dabble with the code. Although you might spend time struggling to achieve a specific effect, your experimentation can lead to inadvertently creating unexpected effects, some of which might be more interesting than your initial intent!

Another important aspect of creating your own variations is to start with simple changes. This is the philosophy that underlies an iterative approach whereby you progressively construct more interesting and visually rich graphics images. While it might be tempting to use complex techniques in order to create exotic-looking "knock-out" graphics as quickly as possible, this approach can quickly exhaust your supply of ideas.

In terms of technical details for writing your own enhancements, start with objects that you understand. For example, you can work with rectangles and triangles before you generalize them to polygons. Next, you can work with circles, ellipses, and Bezier curves. Since color is of paramount importance, experiment with combinations of different color gradients with these geometric objects. When you decide to incorporate conic sections or polar equations, you can also search the Web for equations that you can use in your code.

By now you ought to be convinced that many visual effects can be created very easily in SVG. Leverage these features in your code. For instance, it's almost effortless to specify the color, thickness, and "dash" pattern for stroke-related attributes of arbitrary geometric objects. (Imagine accomplishing the same thing in other programming languages!). Try using "extreme" values for these attributes; for example, small decimal values, negative values, or perhaps four-digit or five-digit values. In other words, experiment with boundary values as you try "pushing the envelope." Look for ways to combine rectilinear shapes (such as line segments and rectangles) with curved shapes such as elliptic arcs and Bezier curves in order to create sharp contrasts.

As you gain experience with writing SVG code, you can also try your hand at writing SVG code for common-place objects. Generally, it's better to avoid a connect-the-dots approach whereby you incorporate many of hard-coded values in your code. While this technique will help you create a specific image quickly, it's difficult to generalize the code or to make many variations of the image that can be easily transferred to other images that differ considerably from the original image. Again, it's important to learn how to master simple objects and add them to your repertoire so that you can later combine them in order to create more sophisticated graphics images.

Remember that there is a learning curve associated with acquiring any new skill, and this is definitely true vis-à-vis SVG. While it's difficult to quantify or predict the level of your creativity, you can influence your environment in ways that will make it easier to be creative. If you can, give yourself a block of unstructured time where you can experiment with SVG. Although it might initially seem unproductive, this type of activity can be very useful because it frees your mind from the stress of trying to achieve a specific goal and gives your mind time to absorb new information.

With all of the preceding in mind, here's a partial list of techniques (all of which are used in the sample code) that you can leverage in your code:

- vary the width and/or height of rectangles
- vary the major/minor axes of ellipses
- add perturbation factors such as randomly generated values
- multiply values by constant scale factors

- multiply values by trigonometric functions
- add rectilinear objects to conic sections and vice versa
- interchange x and y coordinate values
- use the modulus function
- use integer-valued numbers
- use very small or large periods for trigonometric functions
- overlay elements in pairs (reflected or parallel offset)
- add solid/dotted line segments from fixed locations
- use multiple stops in radial and linear gradients
- use patterns defined in SVG `defs` elements
- add shadow effects using constant offset values
- add striping effects with the modulus function
- add smoothly varying (R,G,B) color values

**ON THE CD**

The rest of the chapter displays a variety of graphics images that are available on the CD-ROM. Unless otherwise indicated, all the specified folders are sub-directories of the folder `Supplemental\polarEquations`.

## THE BARBEDRECTPATTERN FOLDER

This folder contains SVG documents that are based on polar equations combined with a rectangle appended with circular arcs. The example from this folder is the SVG document *cochleoidBarbedRectEllipsesLines5.svg*. Notice how the upper pair of arcs results in a spiny backbone that creates a quasi-reptilian effect.

**FIGURE 18.1**  A cochleoid-based set of rectangles and arcs.

## THE BEZIERCBPATTERN FOLDER

This folder contains SVG documents that are based on polar equations combined with checkerboard patterns. The examples in this folder often use an SVG pattern element that is defined in a statically defined SVG `defs` element that is located at the end of each SVG document. The example from this folder is the SVG document *archimedesCBQBezier2Ref4.svg*.

**FIGURE 18.2**   An Archimedean checkerboard pattern.

## THE BEZIERDOUBLESPINEPATTERN FOLDER

This folder contains SVG documents that are based on polar equations combined with a "double" set of Bezier curves. The second Bezier curve is rendered at slight offset to the first Bezier curve and uses a different `style` attribute in order to create complex interaction. The example from this folder is the SVG document *cardioid-ShrinkingDSpineEllipses2.svg*.

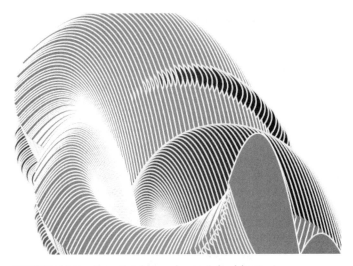

**FIGURE 18.3**  A cardioid-based set of double Bezier curves.

## THE BEZIERSPINEBLURPATTERN FOLDER

This folder contains SVG documents that are based on polar equations combined with Bezier curves that use SVG filter elements. The example from this folder is the SVG document *cissoidRectanglesDouble2.svg*, which contains a double cissoid curve as the tracing curve for a set of ellipses. The blur filter produces "smudged" ellipses, which helps to create a realistic visual effect.

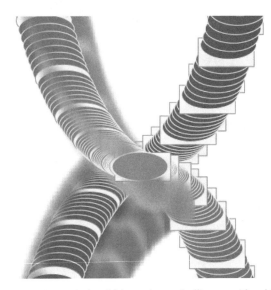

**FIGURE 18.4**  A cissoid-based set of ellipses with a blur filter.

## THE C3DEFFECTCOILPATTERN FOLDER

This folder contains SVG documents that are based on polar equations combined with a a set of ellipses that appear to coil around each of the rendered curves. The example from this folder is the SVG document *archimedesc3DEffectCoilEllipses4.svg*, which contains an Archimedean spiral with a coil-like pattern of ellipses that appear to wrap around the Archimedean curve. The ellipses in the coil are rendered with a multi-stop radial gradient that is defined in an SVG `defs` element (at the bottom of each document) that creates a three-dimensional effect.

**FIGURE 18.5** An Archimedean curve with an elliptic coil.

## THE CIRCLEFROSTEDEFFECT FOLDER

This folder contains SVG documents that are based on polar equations combined with a frosted shading effect. The ellipses are rendered with a multi-stop radial gradient that is defined in an SVG `defs` element (at the bottom of each document) that creates a frosted effect. The example from this folder is the SVG document *conchoid-FrostedEllipsesSVenetianMultiRectExpandingRectangles4.svg*.

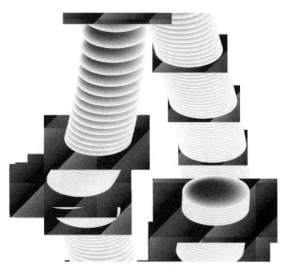

**FIGURE 18.6**    A conchoid curve with a frosted effect.

## THE CIRCLEFROSTEDEFFECTSHADOW FOLDER

This folder contains SVG documents that are based on polar equations combined with a shadow-enhanced frosted shading effect. The ellipses are rendered with a multi-stop radial gradient that is defined in an SVG `defs` element (at the bottom of each document) that creates a frosted effect. The files in this folder illustrate the fact that a simple code change (i.e., adding a shadow) can create a rich visual effect. The example from this folder is the SVG document *archimedesFrostedEllipsesShadow3Ref4.svg*.

**FIGURE 18.7**    An Archimedean curve with a frosted shadow effect.

## THE CIRCULARARCCOILPATTERN FOLDER

This folder contains SVG documents that are based on polar equations combined with elliptic arcs. The SVG documents in this folder render partial ellipses that create a "cut-away" view that creates a three-dimensional effect. The example from this folder is the SVG document *cosineLoop1CArcCoil1Ellipses1.svg*.

**FIGURE 18.8** A cosine-based loop with elliptic arcs.

## THE CIRCULARSPINARCCOILPATTERN FOLDER

This folder contains SVG documents that are based on polar equations combined with a circular arcs that are rotated as they are rendered. This enhancement to the code creates a highly asymmetric effect that highlights the contrast between smooth curvilinear shapes and the cut-away view that is generated from the rotated circular arcs. The example from this folder is the SVG document *cochleoidDup1Op1CSArcCoil1Ellipses2.svg*.

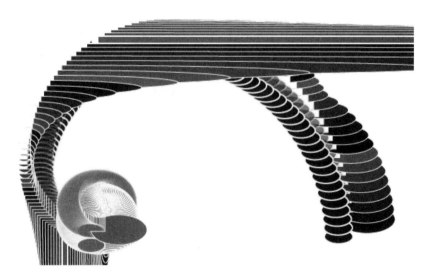

**FIGURE 18.9** A cochleoid-based curve with rotated circular arcs.

## THE COILLINKS FOLDER

This folder contains SVG documents that are based on polar equations that are rendered with a pattern that resembles an "exhaust pipe." This interesting effect is achieved very easily by means of the modulus function. The example from this folder is the SVG document *archimedesEllipsesLinksBlueRectanglesRef4.svg*.

**FIGURE 18.10**  An Archimedean curve with variable-sized ellipses.

## THE DIAMONDBOXPATTERN FOLDER

This folder contains SVG documents that are based on polar equations that are rendered with a diamond-like box, which is constructed by means of three quadrilaterals. The first example from this folder is *cochleoidM3CBPolyDiamondBoxEllipses2.svg* and the second SVG document is *sinePolyDiamondBoxPetal2WireFrame1VS3.svg*.

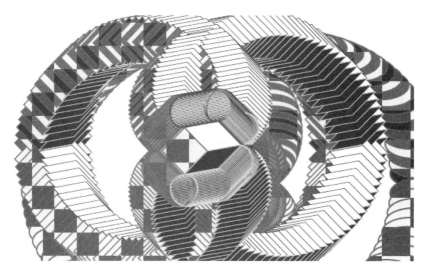

**FIGURE 18.11** A cochleoid curve with diamond-based boxes.

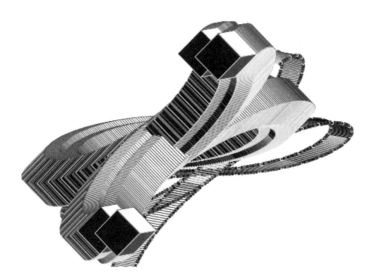

**FIGURE 18.12** A sine-based wireframe with diamond-based boxes.

## THE DOTTEDELLIPSESANDARCS FOLDER

This folder contains SVG documents that are based on polar equations and ellipses that manipulate the stroke-dasharray attribute. Observe how this attribute can create a highly textural look-and-feel that creates a slightly three-dimensional effect. The example from this folder is the SVG document *archimedesEADEllipticArc2Ref4.svg*.

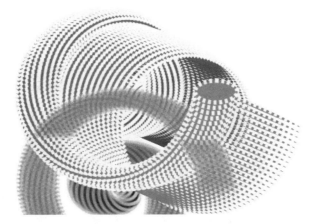

**FIGURE 18.13** An Archimedean curve with a perforated effect.

# THE DOTTEDTWISTINGPOLYGONPATTERN FOLDER

This folder contains SVG documents that are based on polar equations that are also combined with a `stroke-dasharray` attribute. This attribute is applied to rotating polygons that creates an effect resembling seashells. The example from this folder is the SVG document *archimedesDTPolyEllipses3Ref4.svg*.

**FIGURE 18.14** An Archimedean curve with a twisting dotted polygon.

## THE HALFELLIPSELAYERSPATTERN FOLDER

This folder contains SVG documents that are based on polar equations that are combined with a "layered" set of semi-ellipses. The example from this folder is the SVG document *lissajousLHCLayersEllipsesSV5.svg*.

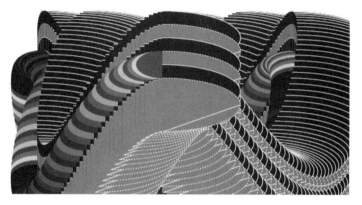

**FIGURE 18.15** A Lissajous curve with semi-ellipses.

## THE HALFELLIPSELAYERS2PATTERN FOLDER

This folder contains SVG documents that are based on polar equations that are also combined with a different "layered" set of semi-ellipses. The first example from this folder is the SVG document *archimedesHCLayers2EllipsesRef4.svg*, and the second example is the SVG document *cochleoidM3HCLayers2Ellipses2.svg*.

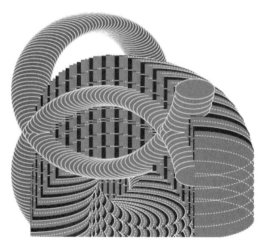

**FIGURE 18.16** An Archimedean curve with multiple semi-ellipses.

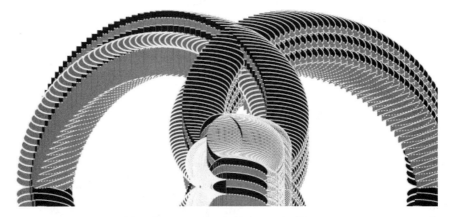

**FIGURE 18.17**   A cochleoid curve with multiple semi-ellipses.

## THE HALFELLIPSETWISTEDLAYERSPATTERN FOLDER

This folder contains SVG documents that are based on polar equations that are also combined with a "layered" set of semi-ellipses. The example from this folder is the SVG document *cochleoidDup1CB2TwHELayersEllipses2.svg*

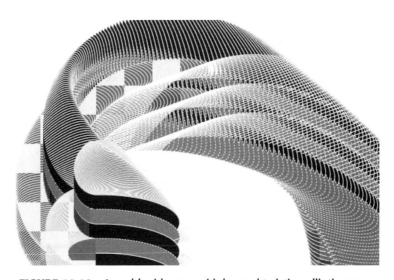

**FIGURE 18.18**   A cochleoid curve with layered twisting elliptic arcs.

## THE LUNEPATTERN FOLDER

This folder contains SVG documents that are based on polar equations that are combined with a "lune" that is based on a pair of elliptic arcs. The example from this folder is the SVG document *lituusCBEllipticLune4.svg*, which also contains a checkerboard pattern and a light dotted effect.

**FIGURE 18.19**   A Lituus curve with elliptic lunes.

## THE PARTIALPOLYGONPATTERN FOLDER

This folder contains SVG documents that are based on polar equations that are combined with trapezoids. The example from this folder is the SVG document *archimedesPPolyEllipsesExpanding2Rectangles4.svg*, which consists of a set of partial polygons that loop around each polar equation in a coil-like fashion.

**FIGURE 18.20** An Archimedean curve with partial polygons.

## THE PARTIALPOLYGONROTATEDPATTERN FOLDER

This folder contains SVG documents that are based on polar equations that are combined with trapezoids. The example from this folder is the SVG document *cochleoid-Dup1CBRotPPolyEllipses2.svg*, which consists of a set of rotated partial polygons that create a "cleaved" effect as they loop around each polar equation in a coil-like fashion.

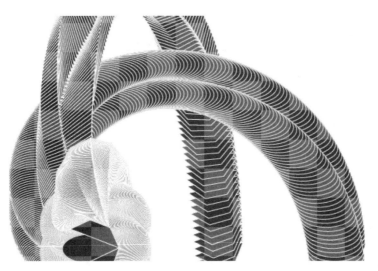

**FIGURE 18.21** A cochleoid with rotated partial polygons.

## THE ROTATEDTRIANGLES FOLDER

This folder contains SVG documents that are based on polar equations that are combined with rotated triangles. The example from this folder is the SVG document *archimedesDup1M1RTriangles2.svg*, which consists of an Archimedean curve and a set of richly colored rotated triangles.

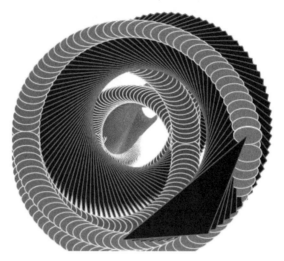

**FIGURE 18.22**   An Archimedean curve with rotated triangles.

## THE SINEWAVE1PATTERN FOLDER

This folder contains SVG documents that are based on polar equations that are combined with sine waves. The example from this folder is the SVG document *archimedesOp1M1SWLEllipses2.svg*, which is based on an Archimedean curve that combines several visual effects.

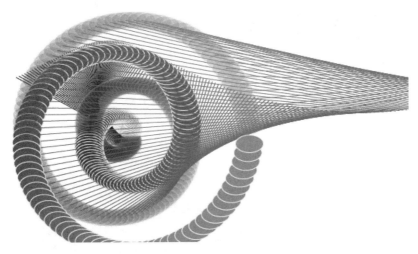

**FIGURE 18.23**    An Archimedean curve with line segment to a sine curve

# THE TETRAPATTERN FOLDER

This folder contains SVG documents that are based on polar equations that are combined with triangular pyramids. The example from this folder is the SVG document *twistingCosineLoop1EllipsesTetraExpandingSVenetianMultiRectangles2.svg*. also contains a Venetian shading effect checkerboard pattern and a light dotted effect.

**FIGURE 18.24**    A twisting cosine loop with triangular pyramids.

## THE TRAPEZOIDPATTERN FOLDER

This folder contains SVG documents that are based on polar equations that are combined with trapezoids. The example from this folder is the SVG document *sineTrC-CosineC2.svg*, which consists of a set of trapezoids that are bounded by a fixed rectangle in conjunction with a sine/cosine wave.

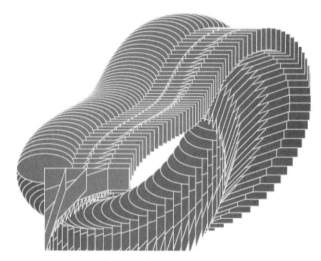

**FIGURE 18.25** A sine/cosine loop with trapezoids.

# THE TRIANGLELAYERSPATTERN FOLDER

This folder contains SVG documents that are based on polar equations that are combined with triangular pyramids. The example from this folder is the SVG document *cochleoidDup1CBTrLayersEllipses2.svg*.

**FIGURE 18.26**    A cochleoid curve with layered triangles.

# XSL Basics

## OVERVIEW

This appendix will give you an overview of XSL transformations so that you can write XSL stylesheets and apply them to XML documents in order to generate HTML files, SVG documents, or XML-based data. In most cases, an XSL stylesheet contains custom code in the sense that it is written for processing a particular XML document. As such, an XSL stylesheet contains custom templates that can also leverage built-in functions available in XSL in order to search, count, and manipulate some or all of the nodes in an associated XML document.

## WHAT IS XSL?

XSL (Extensible Stylesheet Language) is a recursion-based scripting language that allows you to transform XML-based data into another set of XML-based data, or to data in another format, such as HTML, SVG, or PDF. An XSL stylesheet is written with a specific set of XML tags in mind; that is, you need *a priori* knowledge of the format of the data source. You can write different XSL stylesheets that produce different outputs when they are applied to the same XML data. For example, you might have an XML document that contains sales-related data that specifies the date, amount, and salesperson of a particular sale. One XSL stylesheet might generate XML data that contains the sales summary for each employee; another XSL stylesheet might generate a bar graph depicting monthly sales. A third XSL stylesheet might generate a bar chart with quarterly sales data.

## WHAT SOFTWARE IS REQUIRED FOR XSL?

ON THE CD

You need an XSLT processor in order to apply an XSL stylesheet to an XML document. The CD-ROM that accompanies this book contains a copy of Instant Saxon (version 6.2.2) for a Windows PC. After installing Instant Saxon on your machine, include the installation directory in your path. For example, if you install Instant Saxon in the directory c:\InstantSaxon on your Windows PC, you need to modify PATH as follows:

```
set PATH=C:\InstantSaxon;%PATH%
```

Invoking Instant Saxon from the command line requires an XML document and an XSL document. For example, if you have the XML document *abc.xml* and the XSL stylesheet *abc.xsl*, and you want to save the generated output in the file *abc.txt*, type the following line at the command line:

```
saxon abc.xml abc.xsl >abc.txt
```

If you want to see the command line options, type the following:

```
saxon -?
```

You can also navigate to the following URL if you want to check for later versions: *http://sourceforge.net/projects/saxon.*

## WHAT ARE XSL STYLESHEETS?

In high-level terms, an XSL stylesheet consists of one or more directives, processing instructions, XSL variables, or templates (or "rules"). Templates can have names, and they can invoke (and pass required parameters to) other named templates. Every template is invoked based on the contents of the "match" pattern that is specified in each template; if a match occurs, then the "body" of the template will be executed. Since a template can invoke other templates, an XSL stylesheet can quickly become complex.

You will sometimes see multiple templates specifying overlapping conditions in their match attribute. Fortunately, every template is assigned a numeric priority, and the XSLT processor uses this priority in order to determine which template to invoke in the event of templates with overlapping conditions.

One obstacle you might experience involves the existence of "default" templates. You never see the default templates, but you will know when they've been executed because you'll see output (sometimes very copious) that you don't want. The only way to suppress that output is to override the default templates, which means that you must define a template for that purpose in your XSL stylesheet.

## THE XSL MINDSET

There are several factors that have a bearing on your learning curve for XSL (which obviously will vary from person to person) and your comfort level with recursion will probably be one of those factors. Unlike languages such as Java and C, which are imperative languages, XSL is a declarative language that vaguely resembles the processing style of LISP and Snobol (if you remember that far back!). Recursion is the natural style of coding in XSL (as is the case with LISP and Snobol), and you will often process "node sets" that contain a hierarchical set of nodes; this makes XSL well suited to processing tree-oriented data such as XML.

The features of XSL allow you to perform tree traversals and examine the contents of the elements that you find during a traversal of tree elements. When you're working in SQL, you often think in terms of "flat sets" (JDBC, which is a mechanism for database access, even has a ResultSet class); when you're working with XSL, think "hierarchical sets." Imagine yourself situated at (or on) a particular node of a tree of data—what would you ask yourself? Here's a list of some questions that might spring to mind:

1. who is my parent?
2. who are my siblings?
3. who are my descendants?
4. when I encounter a node, what are its attributes?

The first question is a set consisting of at most one element (zero if you're the root). The second and third questions involve sets with zero or more elements. The fourth question involves the attributes of the element (in a set of cardinality one). The answers to these questions (as well as much more complex ones) can be easily determined when you define the appropriate XSL templates in an XSL stylesheet.

## XSL NODES

An XML document contains a single root node that contains one or more children that are also nodes. Each node can contain a mixture of text data, attributes, and child nodes. XSL distinguishes among the following types of nodes:

- root node
- element nodes
- attribute nodes
- namespace nodes
- processing instruction nodes
- element nodes
- text nodes

You can distinguish between different types of nodes in an XSL stylesheet, which gives you fine-grained control of the manner in which you can manipulate the contents of an XML document.

## TRAVERSING TREES

Map directions for an address in a city that has a grid layout are simple: they consist of some combination of north, south, east, and west. You start from your location (the "context node") and move in one of four directions (although not always in a rectilinear fashion). Traversing an array is also simple: you search for predecessors or successors of the current element.

Tree traversal is more complex than traversing arrays, but it's facilitated by the features available in XSL. Instead of thinking in terms of successors and predecessors (as you would in an array or a linked list), think in terms of "ancestors" (such as your parent), and "descendants" (such as your children). When you are situated at a particular node in a tree, it's called the context node because the actions that you perform are relative to that node.

Observe that the set of all your descendants is a set of elements that is also a sub-tree of the XML document, with the current node as the root of the sub-tree. On the other hand, the set of all your ancestors is a set of elements is a sub-tree of the XML document whose root coincides with the root of the XML document, with the current node as a leaf node of the sub-tree. XPath gives you numerous ways (thirteen, in fact) of traversing an XML document, and they are discussed in the next section.

## WHAT IS XPATH?

XPath is the mechanism by which you select a node set that will be the focus of your attention in an XSL template. For example, if you want to list the names of the chapters of a book in an XML document, one conceivable scenario involves "navigating" to a <chapters> element, creating a node set with the <chapter> child nodes of the <chapters> element, and then displaying the contents of the <title> node of each <chapter> node. (This appendix will show you how to extract such information from an XML document.)

## WHAT IS A LOCATION PATH?

In XSL parlance, a *location path* consists of the "directions" to a node. A location path can consist of three components: an axis, a node test, and an optional predicate. In colloquial terms, think of an axis as the "direction" of travel; e.g., "downward" in the direction of the child nodes. A node test is a condition for testing whether a candidate node belongs to a set; e.g., is the candidate node a child node of the context node? Finally, the predicate might extract the value of an element node or an attribute; e.g., select the contents of the <name> node of a chapter node. Again, keep in mind that these are very informal descriptions that are intended to facilitate your understanding of a location path.

## XPATH AXES

You can think of XPath as a mechanism by which you can specify a node or a set of nodes ("node set") of an XML document that need to be processed in some fashion. Since an XML document consists of hierarchically related data, it makes sense that you need the ability to select the descendants, ancestors, and siblings of a given node (called the "context node"). XPath gives you this ability partly by providing thirteen "axes," each of which generates a (possibly empty) set of nodes relative to the context node. You've already seen the "ancestor" axis and the "descendant" axis in the previous section. In case you're interested, the complete list of axes is given below:

- `ancestor`
- `ancestor-or-self`
- `attribute`
- `child`
- `descendant`
- `descendant-or-self`
- `following`
- `following-sibling`
- `namespace`
- `parent`
- `preceding`
- `preceding-sibling`
- `self`

This appendix contains examples that will illustrate the use of some of these axes.

## XPATH FUNCTIONS

XPath contains the following set of Boolean-related functions that can be invoked in an XSL stylesheet:

- ▪ `boolean()`
- ▪ `not()`
- ▪ `false()`
- ▪ `lang()`
- ▪ `true()`

You can use Boolean-related functions where you need to test for the presence or absence of an attribute in an element and then execute different commands depending on the result of your test.

XPath contains the following set of numeric-related functions that can be invoked in an XSL stylesheet:

- ▪ `ceiling()`
- ▪ `floor()`
- ▪ `number()`
- ▪ `round()`
- ▪ `number()`

For example, you can use the numeric-related functions for currency manipulation where you can specify the number of decimal places. You can also use the `floor()` function when you are interested in integer-valued results.

XPath contains the following set of string-related functions that can be invoked in an XSL stylesheet:

- ▪ `concat()`
- ▪ `starts-width()`
- ▪ `contains()`
- ▪ `normalize-space()`
- ▪ `substring()`
- ▪ `substring-before()`
- ▪ `substring-after()`
- ▪ `string-length()`
- ▪ `translate()`

String functions are needed for manipulating text strings. For example, you can use the `substring()` function in order to capitalize the first letter of a string that represents a person's name.

## A SIMPLE STYLESHEET

Let's look at the following specific example of an XSL stylesheet:

**Listing A.1**  A simple stylesheet

```
<?xml version="1.0"?>
<xsl:stylesheet version="1.0" xmlns:xsl="http://www.w3.org/TR/WD-
xsl">

<xsl:template match="/">
  <xsl:apply-templates>
</xsl:template>
</xsl:stylesheet>

<!---
    There are no other templates here, so
    default rules will be applied instead
--->
```

There is nothing obvious about the meaning of the code in the preceding XSL stylesheet. In fact, if you've never seen XSL, it probably looks arcane and mysterious (and perhaps even useless). The first two lines are directives, and the rest of the XSL contains a single template that matches the root element of an XML document:

```
<xsl:template match="/">
  <xsl:apply-templates>
</xsl:template>
```

When you apply an XSL stylesheet to an XML document, the "/" means "match the root element of the XML document," which is required in every well-formed XML document. Think of this template as the "entry point" into the other templates defined in the XSL stylesheet. What happens after that? In our case, you see the following:

```
<xsl:apply-templates>
```

Since there is no other template in this XSL stylesheet, the "default rules" are invoked, one of which causes all the text in the XML file to be printed. If your XML document contains one megabyte of "pure data," then you will see that megabyte of data displayed on the screen. This is an example of an extremely compact XSL stylesheet that can generate copious amounts of output, depending on the amount of raw data in the XML document in question.

## THE XML FILE *BOOK.XML*

The file *book.xml* is an XML document that will be used in a number of examples involving XSL stylesheets, and its contents are shown in Listing A.2.

**Listing A.2**   book.xml

```
<book>
  <author>Oswald Campesato</author>
  <title>SVG Programming</title>
  <desc>A book about SVG and Java</desc>

  <chapters>
    <chapter>
     <number>1</number>
     <desc>sine waves and gradients</desc>
     <length>25</length>
    </chapter>

    <chapter>
     <number>2</number>
     <desc>sine-based SVG and animation</desc>
     <length>35</length>
    </chapter>

    <chapter>
     <number>3</number>
     <desc>polynomials and rational functions</desc>
     <length>40</length>
    </chapter>
  </chapters>

  <appendices>
    <appendix>
     <title>XSL Basics</title>
     <desc>An Overview of XSL</desc>
     <length>25</length>
    </appendix>
  </appendices>
</book>
```

Some of the questions you might ask about the information in this XML document are listed below:

1. What are the title and author of the book?
2. How many chapters are there? What are their titles?
3. What are the descriptions of the available appendices?
4. Which chapter is the shortest? The longest?

All of the preceding questions can be answered (in some cases with surprising ease) by applying an XSL stylesheet to the XML document. Before we look at some examples, notice that the <title> and <desc> tags appear in multiple locations, and hence their interpretation is context-dependent; that is, you need to differentiate between a `<title>` tag for the book and a `<title>` tag for a chapter (similarly for the `<desc>` tag).

## THE PATH TO AN ELEMENT

Every element in an XML document is determined by a unique path. For example, if you want to find the author element in the file *book.xml*, the complete path is /book/author. A match in an XSL template occurs when the condition specified in the match portion identifies a node, or when the concatenation of the match portion with a sub-path within the given template yield a full path that identifies a node. This point is illustrated in the following XSL stylesheet, which displays the name and author of the book in the file *book.xml*.

## FINDING ELEMENT CONTENTS

Listing A.3 displays the contents of the XSL stylesheet *titleAndAuthor.xsl* that extracts the title and author of the book in the file *book.xml*.

### Listing A.3    titleAndAuthor.xsl

```
<?xml version="1.0"?>
<xsl:stylesheet
    xmlns:xsl="http://www.w3.org/1999/XSL/Transform"
    version="1.0">

<xsl:template match="/">
  <xsl:value-of select="./book/title"/> by
  <xsl:value-of select="./book/author"/>
</xsl:template>
</xsl:stylesheet>
```

### Remarks

Listing A.3 matches the following two items in *book.xml*:

```
<book>
  <author>Oswald Campesato</author>
  <title>SVG Programming</title>
  ....
<book>
```

The full paths /book/author and /book/title specify the author and title, respectively, which match in the first template. Note that the concatenation of the root node "/" with the path "/.book/title" is "/./book/title," which resolves to the path "/book/title." Similarly, the concatenation of "/" and "./book/author" is "/./book/author," which resolves to the path "/book/author."

# A LEADING SLASH ("/") IS SIGNIFICANT

Listing A.4 displays the contents of the XSL stylesheet *titleAndAuthor2.xsl* that shows you another way to extract the title and author of the book in the file *book.xml*.

### Listing A.4   titleAndAuthor2.xsl

```
<?xml version="1.0"?>
<xsl:stylesheet
    xmlns:xsl="http://www.w3.org/1999/XSL/Transform"
    version="1.0">

<xsl:template match="/">
  <xsl:apply-templates/>
</xsl:template>

<xsl:template match="book/title">
  <xsl:value-of select="."/> by
<!-- make sure you include the leading "/" -->
  <xsl:value-of select="/book/author"/>
</xsl:template>

<xsl:template match="text()">
</xsl:template>

</xsl:stylesheet>
```

## Remarks

One crucial point about extracting data is the effect of including or excluding a leading "/" in your XSL code. Since both cases are legal, you won't see an error message; instead, you simply won't get the data that you expect. The distinction between the two is simple: including a "/" means an absolute path whereas its omission means a relative path. In Listing A.4 the highlighted "/" is necessary because you are in a template by virtue of having matched the path "book/title." You need to specify "/book/author" in order to extract the author of the book because the author element is a child of the root node; it is not a child of a node that matches the current template.

On the other hand, the following two lines achieve the same effect in the current XSL stylesheet:

```
<xsl:template match="book/title">
<xsl:template match="/book/title">
```

The first line specifies a relative path "`book/title`" in a template that can only be reached after the match that occurred with the template that matches the root element. The full path is the concatenation of "`/`" and "`book/title`," or "`/book/title`," which is the same as the full path specified in the second line. In other words, a relative path from the root node is the same as specifying the full path itself, which is why the preceding two lines have the same effect in this XSL stylesheet.

## COUNTING QUALIFIED ELEMENTS

Listing A.5 displays the contents of a stylesheet that counts and then displays the number of chapters in the file *book.xml*.

### Listing A.5   countChapters1.xml

```
<?xml version="1.0"?>
<xsl:stylesheet
    xmlns:xsl="http://www.w3.org/1999/XSL/Transform"
    version="1.0">

<xsl:template match="/">
  Chapters:  = <xsl:value-of select="count(//chapter)"/>
  All desc:  = <xsl:value-of select="count(//desc)"/>
  Book desc: = <xsl:value-of select="count(//chapter/desc)"/>
</xsl:template>

</xsl:stylesheet>
```

### Remarks

Listing A.5 demonstrates the use of the count function in XSL and the "`//`" in order to count the number of chapters in the book defined in *book.xml*. You already know that the desc element can refer to the description of the book as well as the description of each chapter in the book. Now you know how to distinguish these two types of elements; that is, "`//desc`" refers to any desc element whereas "`/chapter/desc`" refers to a desc element that is a child of a chapter element.

## INDEX VALUES OF ELEMENTS IN A LIST

If you want to display only the contents of the desc element of the first and the third chapters, you can use something like this:

```
<xsl:value-of select="//chapter[1]/desc"/>
<xsl:value-of select="//chapter[3]/desc"/>
```

Unlike other programming languages such as Java, C, and C++, indexes start from 1 instead of 0. If you apply an XSL stylesheet that processes individual elements in a list of elements and you notice that you are "off by one" (or nothing is displayed), verify that your index value is correct.

## DOCUMENT ORDER

The document order is the default order of the elements, which consists of a left-to-right traversal of the tree representing the XML document. You can change the default order by means of XSL built-in functions. Note that all the examples in this appendix and in this book will perform in-order node traversals.

## XSL VARIABLES

A simple example of assigning a value to a variable is given below:

```
<xsl:variable name="maxWidth" select="500"/>
```

This type of variable will be used for initializing variables that are used for rendering a bar chart or graph. In a subsequent example, you'll see how to assign the result of invoking a template as the value of a variable.

## XSL CONDITIONAL LOGIC

XSL allows you to define templates that contain the constructs "xsl:if," <xsl:choose>," and "for-each" that correspond to "if," "switch," and "for" loops, respectively. For example, the following fragment prints the string "red" if the position of the current node is even:

```
<xsl:if> test="position()mod 2=0">red</xsl:if>
```

Unfortunately, there is no "if-else" logic in XSL; instead, you need to use the <xsl:choose> construct. For example, the code fragment below displays the string "red" if the position of the current node is even, otherwise it displays the string "blue":

```
<xsl:variable name="color">
  <xsl:choose>
     <xsl:when test="position()mod 2=0">red</xsl:when>
     <xsl:otherwise>blue</xsl:otherwise>
  </xsl:choose>
</xsl:variable>
```

You can also assign the output of the previous fragment to a variable; the following example assigns the result of the <xsl:choose> logic to the variable "color":

```
<xsl:variable name="color">
  <xsl:choose>
     <xsl:when test="position()mod 2=0">red</xsl:when>
     <xsl:otherwise>blue</xsl:otherwise>
  </xsl:choose>
</xsl:variable>
```

The <xsl:for-each> construct is very handy for processing a set of nodes. For example, the following code fragment displays the contents of the chapter <desc> elements:

```
<xsl:for-each select="/book/chapters/chapter">
  <xsl:value-of select="./desc"/>
</xsl:for-each>
```

## GENERATING HTML DOCUMENTS

Listing A.6 displays the contents of the file *bookHTML1.xsl*, which demonstrates how to apply an XSL stylesheet to the XML data in *book.xml* in order to generate an HTML table.

### Listing A.6   bookHTML1.xsl

```
<?xml version="1.0"?>
<xsl:stylesheet
    xmlns:xsl="http://www.w3.org/1999/XSL/Transform"
    version="1.0">

<xsl:template match="/">
```

```
<html><body>
<table border="1">
  <tr>
    <th>Number</th>
    <th>Length</th>
    <th>Description</th>
  </tr>

  <xsl:apply-templates/>

  </table>
  </body></html>
</xsl:template>

<!-- IMPORTANT: don't include a leading "/" -->
<xsl:template match="chapters/chapter">
  <xsl:for-each select=".">
    <tr>
      <td><xsl:value-of select="./number"/></td>
      <td><xsl:value-of select="./length"/></td>
      <td><xsl:value-of select="./desc"/></td>
    </tr>
  </xsl:for-each>
</xsl:template>
<xsl:template match="author|title|desc|appendices">
</xsl:template>

</xsl:stylesheet>
```

# FINDING THE MAXIMUM VALUE OF A SET OF NUMBERS

Now we can determine which chapter in the book is the longest. The XSL stylesheet in *maxLength1.xsl* contains an example of how to compute the maximum value in a list of values.

### Listing A.7 maxLength1.xsl

```
<?xml version="1.0"?>
<xsl:stylesheet version="1.0"
     xmlns:xsl="http://www.w3.org/1999/XSL/Transform">

<!--- the 'max' template computes the maximum -->
 <xsl:variable name="maxLength">
   <xsl:call-template name="max">
     <xsl:with-param name="chapters"
```

```
                    select="/book/chapters/chapter"/>
    </xsl:call-template>
  </xsl:variable>

<xsl:template match="/">
Max length = <xsl:value-of select="$maxLength"/>
</xsl:template>

<xsl:template name="max">
  <xsl:param name="chapters"/>
    <xsl:choose>
      <xsl:when test="$chapters">
        <xsl:variable name="firstItem"
                      select="$chapters[1]/length"/>

        <xsl:variable name="rest-of-list">
          <xsl:call-template name="max">
            <xsl:with-param name="chapters"
                  select="$chapters[position()!=1]"/>
          </xsl:call-template>
        </xsl:variable>

        <xsl:choose>
          <xsl:when test="$firstItem &gt; $rest-of-list">
            <xsl:value-of select="$firstItem"/>
          </xsl:when>
          <xsl:otherwise>
            <xsl:value-of select="$rest-of-list"/>
          </xsl:otherwise>
        </xsl:choose>
      </xsl:when>

      <xsl:otherwise>0</xsl:otherwise>
    </xsl:choose>
  </xsl:template>

</xsl:stylesheet>
```

## Remarks

The first time you see this type of XSL code, you might feel slightly overwhelmed by its appearance. Unlike LISP and Snobol, this sort of calculation does not have a simple, compact syntax in XSL. The key idea involves recursively invoking the max template with the all-but-first list of chapters (in LISP it's called the CDR of the list) as shown below:

```
        <xsl:variable name="rest-of-list">
          <xsl:call-template name="max">
```

```
      <xsl:with-param name="chapters"
          select="$chapters[position()!=1]"/>
    </xsl:call-template>
  </xsl:variable>
```

The final invocation of the max template will (by necessity) contain an empty list of chapters, and the template returns the value 0 by means of this code fragment near the bottom of the stylesheet:

```
<xsl:otherwise>0</xsl:otherwise>
```

Notice how the code is executed: the "top" of the template will be executed until the end of the list of chapters is reached, then the "bottom" is executed (which returns 0), and finally the "middle" part of the template is executed, which contains the comparison that determines the maximum chapter length, as listed below:

```
<xsl:choose>
  <xsl:when test="$firstItem &gt; $rest-of-list">
    <xsl:value-of select="$firstItem"/>
  </xsl:when>
  <xsl:otherwise>
    <xsl:value-of select="$rest-of-list"/>
  </xsl:otherwise>
</xsl:choose>
```

You can easily modify the max template by using &lt; in order to create a min template that computes the minimum value of a set of numbers.

## GENERATING A BASIC BAR CHART IN SVG

Listing A.8 displays the contents of the XSL stylesheet *svgSalesGraph1.xsl* that generates an SVG document that contains a simple bar chart based on the data in the XML data in *sales.xml*. For simplicity, this example does not scale the data values or display labeled axes so that you can focus on the logic for generating the bar graph.

**Listing A.8**   svgSalesGraph1.xsl

```
<?xml version="1.0"?>
<xsl:stylesheet version="1.0"
    xmlns:xsl="http://www.w3.org/1999/XSL/Transform">

<xsl:variable name="barWidth"  select="20"/>
<xsl:variable name="maxHeight" select="400"/>
```

```
<xsl:template match="/">
 <xsl:call-template name="graph">
    <xsl:with-param name="sales"
         select="/sales/months/month"/>
 </xsl:call-template>
</xsl:template>

<xsl:template name="graph">
  <xsl:param name="sales"/>
  <xsl:variable name="bar" select="0"/>

  <svg width="100%" height="100%">

<!--
   For each sales item (i.e., month):
     1) set current bar color (either red or blue)
     2) invoke template to create SVG <rect> element
-->

    <xsl:for-each select="$sales">
       <xsl:variable name="revenue" select="./revenue"/>

       <xsl:variable name="color">
         <xsl:choose>
           <xsl:when test="position()mod 2=0">red</xsl:when>
           <xsl:otherwise>blue</xsl:otherwise>
         </xsl:choose>
       </xsl:variable>

      <xsl:call-template name="generateRect">
          <xsl:with-param name="."/>
          <xsl:with-param name="xPos"
                          select="position()*40"/>
          <xsl:with-param name="yPos"
                          select="$maxHeight - $revenue"/>
          <xsl:with-param name="revenue"
                          select="$revenue"/>
          <xsl:with-param name="color"
                          select="$color"/>
      </xsl:call-template>
    </xsl:for-each>
  </svg>
</xsl:template>

<!-- template generates SVG <rect> element -->
<xsl:template name="generateRect">
 <xsl:param     name="xPos"/>
```

```
<xsl:param    name="yPos"/>
<xsl:param    name="revenue"/>
<xsl:param    name="color"/>

<rect x="{$xPos}" y="{$yPos}"
      width="{$barWidth}" height="{$revenue}"
      style="fill:{$color}"/>
</xsl:template>

</xsl:stylesheet>
```

## Remarks

Listing A.8 initializes a set of variables and the main logic occurs in a "for-each" loop that sequentially processes the <month> elements contained in the file *sales.xml*. The revenue associated with each <month> element is passed as a parameter to the `gen-erateRect` template, which generates an SVG <rect> element whose altitude equals the revenue for the current month.

ON THE CD

After you are comfortable with the code in Listing A.8, you see how it forms the basis for the XSL stylesheet *svgSalesGraph2.xsl* on the CD-ROM which generates a more complete bar graph; that is, an x-axis labeled by the months of the year, a y-axis, and the revenue amount just above the top of each bar in the graph.

## KEY POINTS

- XSL stylesheets consist of one or more templates that are invoked when they match an element in an XML document.
- *Default templates* are invoked to process an element if no explicit template exists in the XSL stylesheet for processing the element in question.
- Every template has a priority used to determine which template to apply to an element when more than one template matches an element in a document.
- The higher the specificity of a template, the higher its priority. Templates defined in stylesheets that you import into your stylesheet have lower priority than the templates explicitly defined in your stylesheet.
- XSL allows you to specify 13 axes when searching for elements in an XML document.
- An index of a list of elements starts from 1 and not 0.
- XSL has built-in functions such as count that can be used for counting the number of nodes in an XML document (or a sub-tree of the document).
- XSL stylsheets consist of templates that can contain XML, HTML, or SVG elements, which means that you can apply an XSL stylesheet to an XML document in order to generate an HTML document, an SVG document, or another XML document.

- XPath enables you to examine each node in an XML document and determine whether it qualifies for inclusion in a node set.
- XSL contains five types of nodes and provides built-in functions that can determine which type of node is being processed.
- An XSL location path consists of an axis, a node test, and an optional predicate.
- XSL defines 13 axes that can be used in templates in order to generate node sets.

## SUMMARY

This appendix gave you an overview of some basic features of XSL, including nodes, axes, Xpaths, conditional logic, loop structures, and built-in functions. You saw examples of how to create XSL stylesheets and examples applying them to XML documents in order to generate HTML documents, SVG documents, and other XML-based data.

# Appendix

# B Introduction to XML[*]

XML is another example of a new computer language technology that has taken the industry by storm. The only language to match Java's buzz, and to acquire more instantaneous and ardent supporters, is XML.

Just what is this language, and what does it mean to business application developers? After reading the latest article extolling the virtues of XML, developers can easily get the impression that XML is the answer to all their problems, from uncommunicative business partners to the common cold. But what is the reality? What are the sorts of problems that XML can help the business application developer solve?

## THE BASICS

XML is an acronym for Extensible Markup Language. It is simply a language specification for documents that describe and contain data. XML's designers have attempted to combine the simplicity and the ubiquity of HTML with the rich descriptive capabilities of Standard Generalized Markup Language (SGML). HTML and XML are, in fact, both SGML document types.

An XML document is a text file that conforms to the XML language specification. It contains data in a structured format and descriptive information about the data. The primary role of an XML document is to present data generated by one application (or system) to another. Consequently, XML documents are well suited as general-purpose data repositories and data transport containers.

## XML VS. HTML

XML extends HTML primarily by allowing a document to describe its own tags (similar to a data type or, significantly, a record type). This capability allows a document to organize its data in a structured format. An XML document can also contain

---

[*]This article is adapted from one that appeared in *Java for COBOL Programmers, Second Edition* by John C. Byrne and Jim Cross, © 2002, Charles River Media, Inc. All rights reserved.

enough metadata (information about the data) so that any application can reliably parse the document and extract the data from the document.

In contrast, HTML is designed to describe documents in a format suitable for end-user viewing in a graphical browser. HTML documents do not contain information about the meaning of the data, nor are they structured in a way that makes it easy for a program to analyze. Therefore, an application may have a difficult time extracting relevant data from an HTML document.

A relatively simple example illustrates this point. Here is a portion of an HTML page that might be generated by an Internet book retailer. It informs an Internet browser how to represent the current contents of the shopping cart page to a potential purchaser.

```
<td bgcolor="#FFFFFF" width="51%">
<a href="../81332713233407">
<em>Debt of Honor</em></a>
<br>
Tom Clancy;
Paperback</b>
<font size=2 face="Verdana, Helvetica, Courier" color=#000000>

<NOBR>Price: <font color=#990>$6.99</font></b></NOBR><br>
</td>

<td bgcolor="#FFFFFF" width="51%">
<a href="../81332713233407">
<em>The Hunt for Red October</em></a>
<br>
Tom Clancy;
Hardcover</b>
<font size=2 face="Verdana, Helvetica, Courier" color=#000000>

<NOBR>Price: <font color=#990>$18.99</font></b></NOBR><br>
</td>
```

An Internet browser has no trouble understanding how to format and display this information to the end user. While viewing the page in a browser, the end user has no trouble understanding what the data means (the shopping cart contains two books, one for $6.99 and the other for $18.99).

How do we parse this document and to extract the item number and other information, including its price, from the HTML document? In theory, we could use a trial-and-error design approach to build a parser for this particular document. Perhaps we could fine-tune this algorithm so that it can process the shopping cart HTML page and extract the price of the book:

■   Look for the string NOBR>Price:
■   Skip past the font declaration (<font ..>).

- The characters before the next font declaration contain the price.
- Ignore the currency symbol in the price character string.
- Convert the price string into a numeric price variable.

Unfortunately, we cannot guarantee that our parser will work if the vendor makes even minor changes to the Web site, or that our parser wouldn't be confused by similar pages. More important, we have no guarantee that our parser would work with another vendor's HTML pages. Furthermore, important contextual information is hard to decipher. For example, what is the identifier (the order ID) for this shopping cart? Is it contained in the href identifier?

An XML document, on the other hand, contains information in a format that can be readily parsed by an application. An XML document might express a shopping cart using this type of syntax:

```
<Order orderNumber="81332713233407">

<LineItem>

<Title>Debt of Honor</Title>
<Author>Tom Clancy</Author>
<BookType>Paperback</BookType>
<Price>$6.99</Price>

</LineItem>

<LineItem>

<Title>The Hunt for Red October</Title>
<Author>Tom Clancy</Author>
<BookType>Hardcover</BookType>
<Price>$18.99</Price>

</LineItem>

</Order>
```

Clearly, this syntax is simpler to parse with a program and will produce more predictable results. An application can process and validate information from this document with confidence.

Notice that XML uses the begin tag . . . end tag construct in a manner similar to HTML. XML data is contained inside user-defined tags. For example, `<Title>` is the beginning of a tag, and `</Title>` is the end of the tag. Every XML document must conform to these and other requirements in order to be classified as well formed, or syntactically correct.

Tags can be nested as data elements inside other tags. Observe how the LineItem tag in our example contains each of these tags: Title, Author, BookType, and Price.

# DTDS

An XML document not only contains information in a predictable format, it can also describe the organization of the information it contains. The beginning of an XML document may contain a document type definition (DTD). This section of the XML document defines the structure of the document's contents. It identifies the tags that are allowed in this document and the relationships between the various tags in the document. An XML parser can use this information to make sure that the document is not only well formed (that is, it conforms to the generic XML syntax rules), but also valid (that is, conforms to the layout specified in its DTD).

For example, our XML shopping cart document could contain this partial DTD:

```
<!ELEMENT Order (LineItem)+>
<!ATTLIST Order orderNumber CDATA #REQUIRED>
<!ELEMENT LineItem (Title, Author+, BookType, Price)>
<!ELEMENT Title (#PCDATA)>
<!ELEMENT Author (#PCDATA)>
<!ELEMENT BookType (#PCDATA)>
<!ELEMENT Price (#PCDATA)>
<!ENTITY HARDCOVER "Hardcover">
<!ENTITY PAPERBACK "Paperback">
```

The first statement in this DTD describes an XML element whose name is Order. According to this DTD, an Order consists of one or more `LineItem` elements (represented by the `(LineItem)+` expression in our example). The Order must be further described using the attribute named `orderNumber`. An `orderNumber` attribute can contain any valid character sequence (CDATA). It is a required attribute, as specified by the `#REQUIRED` flag.

A `LineItem`, in turn, consists of a Title, one or more Authors (as indicated by the command Author+), a `BookType`, and a Price. These sub-elements are all user-defined data types, which can contain any character sequence (`#PCDATA`).

The last section of our DTD declares two variables named `HARDCOVER`, and `PAPERBACK`. These variables are assigned the String values "Hardcover" and "Paperback," respectively.

A DTD not only provides the structural information required to properly parse the document, it also allows the parser to examine the document for completeness and document integrity. If a DTD specifies that certain elements are required, then these elements must be present in the document. Conversely, only properly identified elements are allowed in an XML document.

An input parser application can quickly scan XML documents to validate that they match their required structure, independent of any data or content validation. An XML document can be independently checked to make sure it is both well formed (it conforms to proper generic XML syntax) and valid (it conforms to its DTD).

An XML document can either contain its DTD (that is, as the initial part of the document) or simply refer to it as a external file. Either a URL or a local file name can be referenced as the DTD repository.

# DTD COMPONENTS

A DTD describes these optional XML document components in any combination: elements, attributes, and entities.

## Elements

An element is the basic user-defined tag. An XML document is essentially a collection of elements. An element can contain text, other elements, or even a combination of the two. The syntax for an element in an XML document is <Name> content </Name>.

These are four of the elements from our XML sample:

```
<Title>Debt of Honor</Title>
<Author>Tom Clancy</Author>
<BookType>&PAPERBACK</BookType>
<Price>$6.99</Price>
```

Our sample also contained a LineItem element, which was comprised solely of other elements:

```
<LineItem>

<Title>Debt of Honor</Title>
<Author>Tom Clancy</Author>
<BookType>&PAPERBACK</BookType>
<Price>$6.99</Price>

</LineItem>
```

The LineItem element consists of other elements.

A document's DTD declares all the elements a document can contain, as well as other characteristics of each of the elements (that is, its attributes).

Once an element is defined, the main section of the document can contain one or more instances of this element

In our sample, an element named "Title" is defined in the DTD with the construct:

```
<!ELEMENT Title (#PCDATA)>
```

The `Title` element can now exist in the body of the sample document as follows:

```
<Title>Debt of Honor</Title>
```

## Attributes

An element can also be described in more detail with information that varies with each instance of the element in the document. For example, suppose we want our Order element to contain an attribute named `orderNumber`. In any particular Order element, this attribute would hold the unique ID that identified this Order.

Attributes are defined and used in much the same manner as elements. The DTD declares which attributes exist for an element. Particular elements in the document body can then be qualified with these attributes.

In our sample, an element named "Order" is declared in the DTD. It consists of one or more `LineItems`. An attribute for Order named "`orderNumber`" is defined as well. It can contain any valid string and is required for each instance of Order, as specified in this partial DTD:

```
<!ELEMENT Order (LineItem)+>
<!ATTLIST Order orderNumber CDATA #REQUIRED>
```

An Order element can now exist in the body of the sample document as follows:

```
<Order orderNumber="81332713233407">

<LineItem>

. . .

</LineItem>
</Order>
```

Notice that attributes are entered inside the initial element tag

```
(<Order . . >).
```

## Entities

An XML document can define its own constants or entities. These are named storage units (portions of valid XML content), defined and used by a document. An entity can contain character strings, markup commands, or even references to external documents. Here are two entities as declared in our sample DTD:

```
<!ENTITY HARDCOVER "Hardcover">
<!ENTITY PAPERBACK "Paperback">
```

After they are declared, entities can be used in any appropriate place in the XML document. In our sample document, we can use the entity (by name, with an ampersand as a prefix and a semicolon as a suffix) in place of the text represented by the entity. Consequently, both of these constructs are valid:

```
<BookType>&PAPERBACK;</BookType>
<BookType>"Paperback"</BookType>
```

Entities are often used for XML content that is frequently reproduced in the document, or that varies with each instance of the document type.

## DOCUMENT TYPE DECLARATION

An XML document begins by identifying itself as an XML document. The following represents a typical introduction to an XML document:

```
<?xml version="1.0" standalone="yes" encoding="UTF-8"?>
<!DOCTYPE Order [
. . . <! -- DTD specifications -->
]
```

The first expression declares the XML version to which the document conforms. Our document is a version 1.0 document.

Our document is also a standalone XML document, without references to other documents. Since it is a standalone document, it must contain its DTD, if one exists. It is possible for a simple standalone XML document to have no DTD.

Finally, the first line states that the document can contain only 8-bit ASCII characters. An XML document can contain 16-bit characters, similar to Unicode in Java. If this document were a 16-bit document, the required syntax would be encoding= "UTF-16."

The next line in the type declaration identifies the document type as Order. An Order comprises all the elements and attributes specified. These directives will be included inside the braces ([]).

The exclamation point is a tag that represents a comment. The text between <! and the closing > will be ignored by an XML parsing program.

## A COMPLETE XML DOCUMENT

The following sample XML document brings all these concepts together. It contains a document type declaration, an internal DTD specification, and then the actual data contents of the document:

```
<?xml version="1.0" standalone="yes" encoding="UTF-8"?>
<!  ---   A Book order in XML format  -- >
<!DOCTYPE Order [
<!ELEMENT Order (LineItem)+>
<!ATTLIST Order orderNumber CDATA #REQUIRED>
<!ELEMENT LineItem (Title, Author+, BookType, Price)>
<!ELEMENT Title (#PCDATA)>
<!ELEMENT Author (#PCDATA)>
<!ELEMENT BookType (#PCDATA)>
<!ELEMENT Price (#PCDATA)>
<!ENTITY HARDCOVER "Hardcover">
<!ENTITY PAPERBACK "Paperback">
]>


<Order orderNumber="81332713233407">

<LineItem>

<Title>Debt of Honor</Title>
<Author>Tom Clancy</Author>
<BookType>&PAPERBACK;</BookType>
<Price>$6.99</Price>

</LineItem>

<LineItem>

<Title>The Hunt for Red October</Title>
<Author>Tom Clancy</Author>
<BookType>&HARDCOVER;</BookType>
<Price>$18.99</Price>

</LineItem>

</Order>
```

# AUTHORING XML DOCUMENTS

In practice, you don't usually create XML documents by hand using only a text editor; instead, you can use an XML authoring tool or you will write an application that generates valid XML documents based on data from an existing system.

As of this writing, interactive XML authoring tools are in their beginning stages. However, there are several editing tools from a variety of sources, and some are freely available. XML Software (*www.xmlsoftware.com*) contains an excellent list of stand-alone XML editors, integrated DTD editors, and other very useful information concerning XML software.

## XML AND JAVA

Any programming language can create or process an XML document. Java is no exception. XML is not a specification of a programming language, nor is it a programming language interface. Rather, it describes how an application can represent data for the benefit of another application. As such, XML is very programming language neutral. For example, there are no predefined XML data types other than quoted character strings.

A number of XML parsers written in Java are available. Some are free, and others are commercial products. IBM, Sun, and a group called OpenXML have been very active in publishing useful XML products and tools. You can incorporate one of these tools into your Java project or write your own parser and XML document generator.

## XML AND HTML

Unlike HTML, XML does not define presentation attributes such as `</font>`. An XML document designer is free to define and use such tags, but they do not currently have a generally understood meaning.

Various initiatives have begun to define a standard for combining XML and HTML in the same document. Industry groups are working on a definition for an HTML DTD (that is, a standard DTD for the most commonly used HTML tags). The more modern browsers have some built-in ability to render XML documents in a suitable manner for end users, with some default formatting conventions.

Microsoft and others have proposed standards for combining HTML and XML in the same document. Two initiatives are the furthest along in their development: cascading style sheets (CSS), a simple syntax that allows style sheets to be associated with elements, and extensible style language (XSL), an XML document type with bits of formatting commands borrowed from HTML and other sources.

## WHERE TO USE XML

XML is important to the business application developer because it offers a standard language and syntax suitable for intersystem data transfer. Every business system needs to interact with at least one other system in some fashion. The other system can be an external system of a business partner or an internal system (perhaps a data warehouse) that needs information from another internal system (for example, the production order entry system).

Until now, the standard technique used to transfer information between two business systems has been to write a set of interface programs. System one would create an interface file with the required information. Or, system one might write the information to interface tables in a database. The target system will read that information, validate it, and update the target system database. In rare cases, the source or target system will access the other system's database directly, but this approach requires simultaneous access to both systems and developers who understand both systems.

Interface systems often require serious planning and attention. Carefully predefined and documented interface format specifications are necessary so that each system's developers can understand what is required. The normal process flows in both systems need to be accounted for. Most important, the data transformation requirements are embedded in the interface system logic.

As business requirements and the systems that support these requirements change, interface system requirements may change as well. Implementing these changes requires careful coordination and integrated testing plans, even if only two systems are involved. When multiple target systems or their interfaces need to be adjusted for a single-source system, modifications to the existing integration process can become unmanageable. If multiple business partners' systems are involved, one can only hope that their interface specifications are adaptable and up to date and that the original developers are still available.

XML promises to improve this process significantly. As general purpose, self-describing data repositories, XML files are readily accessible by multiple systems. Intricate coordination and data mapping designs are not as crucial since the XML files describe themselves. Systems need only to create XML documents based on an agreeable DTD or to input data from an XML file based on their own requirements. Modifications to the source or the target system do not need to be so closely coordinated. Often, new data tags (information) in an XML document can be ignored by a processing system if that system has no need for the data. The new data will not, by itself, obscure the data required by the processing system.

# EDI

EDI-based processes are prime candidates for improvements with XML. EDI is a standard definition (defined by ANSI or EDIFACT) of acceptable document structures for various types of business transactions. Document structures are defined for purchase orders, acknowledgments, invoices, and other transaction types.

Systems use EDI when they either generate a document in EDI format or receive and subsequently process an EDI document. EDI documents are intended to be transmitted from one business partner to another. In most cases, some data translation and reformatting is necessary so that EDI documents can be properly used by target systems.

Organizations called value-added networks (VANs) provide EDI-related services, such as secure and reliable document transmission services, business partner connections (that is, electronic access to your business partners), and document management (such as store and forward, translation, and logging). Examples of VANs are GE Information Systems (GEISCO), Sterling Commerce, and Harbinger.

To date, EDI standards have proved useful as well-defined data representation formats. However, their rigid structure (along with other issues, such as high implementation and transaction costs) has restricted the acceptance of EDI standards in many situations. Typically, EDI is employed as a data transfer mechanism between business partners only if the number of documents exchanged justifies the effort and the expense and both organizations have technically savvy IT organizations.

The XML language, combined with widely available Internet technologies, promises to radically change the way business documents are transferred between organizations. As you know, organizations are all interconnected today over the Internet. SSL (secure socket layer), encrypted digital signatures, and other technologies provide adequate transactional security for most situations. These technologies, coupled with XML's ability to combine flexible document content with well-understood document structure, enable organizations to confidently, effectively, and efficiently execute electronic business processes with a wide variety of business partners.

XML and EDI are not necessarily competitors of each other as potential solutions. An XML file can contain data that conforms to EDI content specifications, even if it does not conform to EDI's document structure specifications. All that is required is a suitable DTD. In fact, several initiatives are underway to do just that. EDI-based interface systems can easily wrap their documents in XML for external representation to business partners. The business partners can either process the documents directly or first convert the documents into a format suitable for a legacy EDI system.

# XML AND OAG

The Open Application Group (OAG) is an organization whose mission is to simplify integration processes between business systems. OAG frequently addresses integration issues as they apply to enterprise resource planning (ERP), accounting, and human resource packaged application systems.

OAG has defined a set of XML DTDs and is promoting these document definitions as standards for business documents such as purchase orders and invoices. They have also defined intersystem document types, such as journal transactions to a general ledger system. Business applications that support these document definitions can reliably integrate with other systems, even when the two systems come from distinct vendors.

For example, an accounts payable system from one vendor can generate an XML document that conforms to OAG's DTD specification for journals. An OAG-compliant general ledger from another system can accept that document as input, and post the transactions in an appropriate manner.

The following is a sample journal DTD from OAG. It has been simplified slightly from its complete representation.

Our sample begins with a pair of base DTDs named domains.dtd, and fields.dtd. These define the basic data type entity (STRDOM) and the field-level entity names that will be used in the OAG documents.

```
<!-- String Data: Generic Data Domains -->
<!ENTITY % STRDOM "(#PCDATA)">

<!ELEMENT ACCTPERIOD  %STRDOM;>
<!ELEMENT ACCTTYPE    %STRDOM;>
<!ELEMENT ACCTYEAR    %STRDOM;>
<!ELEMENT BUSNAREA    %STRDOM;>
<!ELEMENT COSTCENTER  %STRDOM;>
<!ELEMENT CURRENCY    %STRDOM;>
<!ELEMENT DRCR        %STRDOM;>
<!ELEMENT DEPARTMENT  %STRDOM;>
<!ELEMENT GLENTITYS   %STRDOM;>
<!ELEMENT GLNOMACCT   %STRDOM;>
<!ELEMENT NUMOFDEC    %STRDOM;>
<!ELEMENT ORIGREF     %STRDOM;>
<!ELEMENT SIGN        %STRDOM;>
<!ELEMENT USERID      %STRDOM;>
<!ELEMENT USERAREA    %STRDOM;>
<!ELEMENT VALUE       %STRDOM;>
<!ELEMENT VALUECLASS  %STRDOM;>
<!ELEMENT VERB        %STRDOM;>
```

Next, our sample contains a higher-level reusable DTD named segments.dtd. Of particular interest in the segment DTD are these elements:

**AMOUNT:** A general-purpose element that will contain an amount data item. An AMOUNT is a collection of the VALUE, NUMOFDEC, SIGN, CURRENCY, and DRCR elements. It has a required attribute named qualifier. This attribute can contain either of the types defined by the SEG_AMOUNT_QUALIFIERS entity or the type defined by a generic entity named SEG_AMOUNT_QUALIFIERS_EXTENSION. AMOUNT also has an attribute named type. This attribute can contain either of the values in the SEG_AMOUNT_TYPES entity or the value defined by a generic entity named SEG_AMOUNT_TYPES_EXTENSION.

**DATETIME:** A general-purpose element that contains a date-time data item. A DATETIME is a collection of the YEAR, MONTH, DAY, HOUR, MINUTE, SECOND, SUBSECOND, and TIMEZONE elements. It has a required attribute named qualifier.

This attribute can contain either of the types defined by the SEG_DATETIME_ QUALIFIERS entity or the type defined by a generic entity named SEG_DATE-TIME_QUALIFIERS_EXTENSION. DATETIME also has an attribute named type. This attribute can contain either of the values in the SEG_DATETIME_TYPES entity or the value defined by a generic entity named SEG_DATETIME_TYPES_EXTENSION.

```
<!-- -From oagis_segments.dtd -->

<!-- AMOUNT -->

<!ENTITY % SEG_AMOUNT_QUALIFIERS_EXTENSION "OTHER">
<!ENTITY % SEG_AMOUNT_QUALIFIERS
"(ACTUAL | APPRVORD | AVAILABLE | BUDGET | COMMISSION |
DISCNT | DOCUMENT | EXTENDED | ITEM | OPENITEM | ORDER |
ORDLIMIT | TAX | TAXBASE | TOTLIMIT |
%SEG_AMOUNT_QUALIFIERS_EXTENSION;)">
<!ENTITY % SEG_AMOUNT_TYPES_EXTENSION "OTHER">
<!ENTITY % SEG_AMOUNT_TYPES
"(T | F | %SEG_AMOUNT_TYPES_EXTENSION;)">
<!ELEMENT AMOUNT (VALUE, NUMOFDEC, SIGN, CURRENCY, DRCR)>
<!ATTLIST AMOUNT
qualifier %SEG_AMOUNT_QUALIFIERS; #REQUIRED
type %SEG_AMOUNT_TYPES; #REQUIRED
index CDATA #IMPLIED>

<!ENTITY % AMOUNT.ACTUAL.F  "AMOUNT">
<!ENTITY % AMOUNT.ACTUAL.T  "AMOUNT">
<!ENTITY % AMOUNT.DOCUMENT.T "AMOUNT">


<!-- DATETIME -->

<!ENTITY % SEG_DATETIME_QUALIFIERS_EXTENSION "OTHER">
<!ENTITY % SEG_DATETIME_QUALIFIERS
"(ACCOUNTING | AVAILABLE | CREATION | DELIVACT | DELIVSCHED |
DISCNT | DOCUMENT | DUE | EFFECTIVE | EXECFINISH | EXECSTART |
EXPIRATION | FORECASTF | FORECASTS | FROM | INVOICE | LABORFINSH |
LABORSTART | LASTUSED | LOADING | MATCHING | NEEDDELV | OPFINISH |
OPSTART | PAYEND | PROMDELV | PROMSHIP | PYMTTERM | REPORTNGFN |
REPORTNGST | REQUIRED | RESORCDWNF | RESORCDWNS | SETUPFINSH |
SETUPSTART | SHIP | TEARDOWNF | TEARDOWNS | TO |
%SEG_DATETIME_QUALIFIERS_EXTENSION;)">
<!ENTITY % SEG_DATETIME_TYPES_EXTENSION "OTHER">
<!ENTITY % SEG_DATETIME_TYPES
"(T | F | %SEG_DATETIME_TYPES_EXTENSION;)">
<!ELEMENT DATETIME (YEAR, MONTH, DAY, HOUR, MINUTE, SECOND,
    SUBSECOND,
```

```
TIMEZONE)>
<!ATTLIST DATETIME
qualifier %SEG_DATETIME_QUALIFIERS; #REQUIRED
type %SEG_DATETIME_TYPES; #IMPLIED
index CDATA #IMPLIED>

<!ENTITY % DATETIME.ACCOUNTING "DATETIME">
<!ENTITY % DATETIME.DOCUMENT  "DATETIME">
<!ENTITY % DATETIME.PAYEND    "DATETIME">


<!-- BSR -->
<!ELEMENT BSR (VERB, NOUN, REVISION)>

<!-- SENDER -->
<!ELEMENT SENDER (LOGICALID, COMPONENT, TASK, REFERENCEID,
   CONFIRMATION,
LANGUAGE, CODEPAGE, AUTHID)>

<!-- CNTROLAREA -->
<!ELEMENT CNTROLAREA (BSR, SENDER, DATETIME)>


<!--- From oagis_segments.dtd -->
```

After the base DTDs, we have a DTD for a specific document type. Our post journal DTD begins by describing the general structure of this document in a comment. According to the comment, a post_journal document consists of JOURNALs, which in turn, consists of one or more sets of JEHEADER and JELINEs.

```
<!--- From 001_post_journal_004.dtd -->

<!--
Structure Overview

POST_JOURNAL (JEHEADER, JELINE+)
JEHEADER ()
JELINE ()

Notes

-->

<!-- ====================================================== -->
```

The following syntax effectively copies the statements in the file named oagis_domains.dtd:

```
<!ENTITY % DOMAINS SYSTEM "oagis_domains.dtd">
%DOMAINS;

<!ENTITY % FIELDS SYSTEM "oagis_fields.dtd">
%FIELDS;

<!ENTITY % SEGMENTS SYSTEM "oagis_segments.dtd">
%SEGMENTS;

<!-- ====================================================== -->
```

Now, the DTD describes the valid content (that is, the elements and attributes) of POST_JOURNAL_004, a sort of container for journals:

```
<!ELEMENT POST_JOURNAL_004 (CNTROLAREA, DATAAREA+)>

<!ATTLIST VERB value CDATA #FIXED "POST">
<!ATTLIST NOUN value CDATA #FIXED "JOURNAL">
<!ATTLIST REVISION value CDATA #FIXED "004">


    <!ELEMENT DATAAREA (POST_JOURNAL)>
```

Next, the DTD describes the valid content (that is, the elements) of POST_JOURNAL (the actual journal information). A POST_JOURNAL consists of a JEHEADER (journal header), and one or more JELINE (journal line) elements:

```
        <!ELEMENT POST_JOURNAL (JEHEADER, JELINE+)>
```

This DTD segment describes the valid content (that is, the elements) of JE-HEADER (the journal header information). Some of the fields in JEHEADER are optional (as identified by a ?). Elements that are entity names, such as AMOUNT.DOCUMENT.T, are enclosed in parentheses.

```
                <!ELEMENT JEHEADER (
                (%AMOUNT.DOCUMENT.T;)?,
(%DATETIME.DOCUMENT;)?,
(%DATETIME.PAYEND;)?,
GLENTITYS, ORIGREF, DESCRIPTN?, DOCTYPE?, JEID?,
                LEDGER?, USERID?, USERAREA?)>
```

And finally, the DTD describes the valid content (that is, the elements) of JELINE (the journal line information):

```
                <!ELEMENT JELINE (
                (%AMOUNT.ACTUAL.T;),
```

```
(%AMOUNT.ACTUAL.F;)?,
GLNOMACCT, BUSNAREA?, COSTCENTER?, DEPARTMENT?,
DESCRIPTN?,
. . .

((%DATETIME.ACCOUNTING;) | (ACCTPERIOD, ACCTYEAR)),
USERAREA?)>
```

```
<!--- From 001_post_journal_004.dtd -->
```

A sample XML document based on the DTD we've defined would look like this:[*]

```
<?xml version="1.0" standalone="no"?>

<!--
$Revision: 6.0.1 $
$Date: 31 October 1998 $
Open Applications Group Sample XML Data
Copyright 1998, All Rights Reserved

$Name: 001_post_journal_004.xml $


-->

<!DOCTYPE POST_JOURNAL_004 SYSTEM "001_post_journal_004.dtd">

<POST_JOURNAL_004>
<CNTROLAREA>
<BSR>
<VERB>POST</VERB>
<NOUN>JOURNAL</NOUN>
<REVISION>004</REVISION>
</BSR>
<SENDER>
<LOGICALID>XX141HG09</LOGICALID>
<COMPONENT>INVENTORY</COMPONENT>
<TASK>RECEIPT</TASK>
<REFERENCEID>95129945823449</REFERENCEID>
<CONFIRMATION>1</CONFIRMATION>
<LANGUAGE>EN</LANGUAGE>
<CODEPAGE>test</CODEPAGE>
<AUTHID>JOE DOE</AUTHID>
```

---

[*]Portions of this XML document copyright © by Open Applications Group. All rights reserved.

```
</SENDER>
<DATETIME qualifier = "CREATION" >
<YEAR>1999</YEAR>
<MONTH>12</MONTH>
<DAY>31</DAY>
<HOUR>23</HOUR>
<MINUTE>59</MINUTE>
<SECOND>45</SECOND>
<SUBSECOND>0000</SUBSECOND>
<TIMEZONE>-0500</TIMEZONE>
</DATETIME>
</CNTROLAREA>
<DATAAREA>
<POST_JOURNAL>
<JEHEADER>
<AMOUNT qualifier = "DOCUMENT" type = "T">
<VALUE>2340500</VALUE>
<NUMOFDEC>2</NUMOFDEC>
<SIGN>+</SIGN>
<CURRENCY>USD</CURRENCY>
<DRCR>D</DRCR>
</AMOUNT>
<DATETIME qualifier = "DOCUMENT" type = "T">
<YEAR>1995</YEAR>
<MONTH>12</MONTH>
<DAY>31</DAY>
<HOUR>23</HOUR>
<MINUTE>59</MINUTE>
<SECOND>45</SECOND>
<SUBSECOND>0000</SUBSECOND>
<TIMEZONE>-0500</TIMEZONE>
</DATETIME>
<DATETIME qualifier = "PAYEND">
<YEAR>1998</YEAR>
<MONTH>01</MONTH>
<DAY>02</DAY>
<HOUR>12</HOUR>
<MINUTE>00</MINUTE>
<SECOND>00</SECOND>
<SUBSECOND>0000</SUBSECOND>
<TIMEZONE>-0500</TIMEZONE>
</DATETIME>
<GLENTITYS>CORPHEADQUARTER</GLENTITYS>
<ORIGREF>RCPT#12550699</ORIGREF>
<DESCRIPTN>INVENTORY RECEIVED FROM GLOBAL MANUFAC
TURING</DESCRIPTN>
<USERID>KURTC</USERID>
</JEHEADER>
```

```
<JELINE>
<AMOUNT qualifier = "ACTUAL" type = "T" >
<VALUE>2340500</VALUE>
<NUMOFDEC>2</NUMOFDEC>
<SIGN>+</SIGN>
<CURRENCY>USD</CURRENCY>
<DRCR>D</DRCR>
</AMOUNT>
<AMOUNT qualifier = "ACTUAL" type = "F" >
<VALUE>001001001</VALUE>
<NUMOFDEC>2</NUMOFDEC>
<SIGN>+</SIGN>
<CURRENCY>USD</CURRENCY>
<DRCR>D</DRCR>
</AMOUNT>
<GLNOMACCT>2310</GLNOMACCT>
<BUSNAREA>INVENTORY</BUSNAREA>
<COSTCENTER>CC123</COSTCENTER>
<DEPARTMENT>DEPT001ABC</DEPARTMENT>
<DESCRIPTN>INVENTORY</DESCRIPTN>
<DATETIME qualifier = "ACCOUNTING" >
<YEAR>1996</YEAR>
<MONTH>01</MONTH>
<DAY>02</DAY>
<HOUR>12</HOUR>
<MINUTE>09</MINUTE>
<SECOND>45</SECOND>
<SUBSECOND>0000</SUBSECOND>
<TIMEZONE>-0500</TIMEZONE>
</DATETIME>
</JELINE>
<JELINE>
<AMOUNT qualifier = "ACTUAL" type = "T" >
<VALUE>2340500</VALUE>
<NUMOFDEC>2</NUMOFDEC>
<SIGN>-</SIGN>
<CURRENCY>USD</CURRENCY>
<DRCR>C</DRCR>
</AMOUNT>
<GLNOMACCT>6940</GLNOMACCT>
<DESCRIPTN>ACCOUNTS PAYABLE</DESCRIPTN>
<ACCTPERIOD>03</ACCTPERIOD>
<ACCTYEAR>1999</ACCTYEAR>
</JELINE>
</POST_JOURNAL>
</DATAAREA>
</POST_JOURNAL_004>
```

## ONLINE XML

The use of XML is not restricted to batch operations. Real-time interfaces to systems necessarily define data structures. Often, these structures must be self-describing for a variety of reasons.

For example, suppose we have a real-time interface that performs some service on behalf of a client application. This service must support several client applications simultaneously. Suppose further that the interface specification needs to include additional data elements in order to support some new requirement. Not all client systems can be updated simultaneously; in fact, it is likely that at least some older client systems need to be supported for a year or more.

One traditional solution for this requirement is to include a version identifier in the interface structure. The real-time service module can examine the version of a particular message and respond to either the new or the old type of message. (In this situation, you are well advised to normalize either message type into some standard internal structure rather than actually leaving the original code as is. Otherwise, there will be two versions of the service module to maintain.)

An XML-based interface specification is a perfect choice for this situation. Each client service request that is based on XML will be self-describing. The service module can extract the data that is actually in a particular message, perhaps providing defaults for data that is not present in the message. The service module can respond with an XML-based return message containing either the new or the old data set. A client application can extract the information it requires from the response. An even more sophisticated solution would allow the client application to pass in an initial DTD at runtime. This DTD would define the structure of the request and response method that the client can accept.

These advantages work for the client application as well. Client applications that use XML-based messages when talking to services can talk to new and old services simultaneously. The structure of the messages is not tied to the various versions of the services, only the message content is. This greatly simplifies the coding required to support multiple versions of service modules talking to multiple versions of clients.

XML is also an excellent infrastructure for interactive messages between systems. For example, an online procurement system might send an XML-based catalog query to a supplier's system. The supplier's system could reply with catalog items described in XML, including prices. The procurement system could simply display the results in a browser or store the results in a database for later access.

## OTHER OPPORTUNITIES

Since XML data is so much more accessible than data stored in proprietary formats, entirely new application functions are possible. For example:

- **XML data repositories.** Information publishers can produce information in XML format. XML documents can be stored for later access by a variety of applications, not just by the applications that generated the information. Ideally, traditional reports will no longer exist, but will be replaced by XML documents. These documents will be presented to (and manipulated by) end users with XML-capable viewers. These viewers will provide many more analytical capabilities than are available with simple text searching of an ASCII file.

- **Information transfers that have not been cost effective until now.** Custom-built or EDI-based information transfer systems have traditionally been used for high-value or high-volume requirements. Other information transfers have not been addressed, although organizations would clearly benefit from the ability to transfer information between a wide variety of business partners.

  A classic example of information transfer is catalog content management. Buyers would like access to the most current catalog information, but the cost and complexity of accepting and processing catalog information from a variety of suppliers is generally too high. XML-based catalogs are a mechanism by which a supplier can publish a catalog, confident that buyers will be able to process it.

- **Intelligent searching.** XML-based searching guarantees better results. Not only can content be searched (as is the case today), but content can be cross-checked with meaning (structure). An XML search for "mark price" will not return lists of preprinted pricing labels when what you want is information about Mark Price, the basketball player. Not only can data and meaning be searched together, it is possible to search based on meaning only. An XML-enabled Web site can effectively publish which documents (or Web pages) contain information about certain data types.

- **Intelligent agents.** Applications can be built that will browse an environment (the Internet, your local systems, or perhaps just the hard drive on your PC) and detect items of interest. If you are interested in eventually buying at auction a 500-MHz PC when the price drops below $500, an agent can scan an auction site's XML-based auction status catalog for this information and create an e-mail for you when a system meets your target price.

# Appendix
# C  Perl Basics

## WHAT IS PERL?

Perl is a highly versatile scripting language that was released in the late 1980s, and has been available in versions 4, 5, and 6 (which is the current release). Perl has very strong roots in C, and each major version of Perl has been a significant rewrite of its predecessor. While Perl supports object-oriented features (e.g., objects and inheritance), it does not to the same extent as scripting languages such as Python and Ruby.

If you are new to Perl, you will quickly discover that it has very sophisticated text-processing capabilities. Perl can "overload" a variable in the sense that different prefix meta-characters for the same variable can represent different variable types. For example, $abc, @abc, and %abc represent a scalar, an array, and a hash, respectively. This mechanism has a dual effect: Perl scripts can be incredibly compact and powerful, yet difficult to understand for novices (and even more experienced Perl programmers). Therefore, while it is easy to become productive in Perl, you may find that true mastery of Perl requires a longer learning curve than some other scripting languages. One of the best ways to broaden your knowledge and deepen your understanding of Perl is through practice and reading code samples.

By necessity, this appendix can only cover a limited subset of the features of Perl, and it will focus on presenting basic yet useful constructs in Perl that you can use for automating standard text-related tasks and also for understanding the Perl scripts in this book. If you want to learn more about Perl, you can find a number of excellent books in bookstores or on the Web. A superb book for learning Perl is *Perl by Example* by David Medinets, after which you can read *Perl 5 How-To* by Mike Glover, Aidan Humphreys, and Ed Weiss, which contains very interesting combinations of Perl constructs.

## WHAT ARE PERL'S STRENGTHS?

The answer to this question depends partially on your needs. Perl is certainly known for its many built-in functions for text manipulation that give tremendous power to parse text. This capability made Perl attractive not only for text processing, but also for Web-based applications. Moreover, Perl provides many built-in functions that are system calls in C. For instance, you might be surprised to know that it's quite easy to write Perl scripts for creating pipes, queues, semaphores, shared memory, sockets, and interprocess communication. You can write a simple socket-based web server in Perl without much code (or difficulty) that runs on multiple platforms, and, because of Perl's portability, no code compilation is required. The powerful feature set of Perl will dispel the misconception that Perl is meant for CGI scripts. Indeed, it's the power of Perl that made it an early choice for CGI scripts.

## UPDATING THE path VARIABLE

After you have installed Perl on your machine, you need to modify your PATH variable so that it includes the directory that contains the Perl executable. If you installed Perl on a Windows NT machine, you need to do something like this,

```
SET PATH=C:\perl6\bin;%PATH%;
```

and if you are in a Unix environment you need to do the following:

```
PATH=/usr/local/bin/:$PATH; export PATH (for Bourne shell)
export PATH=/usr/local/perl6/bin:$PATH (for Korn shell)
```

Remember that you must replace the Windows NT directory C:\perl6\bin (or the Unix directory /usr/local/perl6/bin) with the directory where you installed Perl on your machine.

## LAUNCHING PERL FROM THE COMMAND LINE

You can use any legal filename for a Perl script, but by convention Perl scripts have the suffix ".pl." Suppose you want to run the Perl script called abc.pl. After you have updated your PATH variable in a shell on your machine, you can run script abc.pl as follows:

```
perl -w abc.pl
```

The "-w" switch is extremely useful and will provide valuable information, such as variables that have been invoked only once. This type of information often indicates that you mistyped a variable name. Perl has a number of command-line options, and you can see the entire list by typing the following at the command line:

```
perl -h
```

The preceding command will display something similar to the following output:

```
Usage: C:\bin\perl.exe [switches] [--] [programfile] [arguments]
  -0[octal]        specify record separator (\0, if no argument)
  -a               autosplit mode with -n or -p (splits $_ into @F)
  -C               enable native wide character system interfaces
  -c               check syntax only (runs BEGIN and CHECK blocks)
  -d[:debugger]    run program under debugger
  -D[number/list]  set debugging flags (argument is a bit mask or
      alphabets)
  -e 'command'     one line of program (several -e's allowed, omit
      programfile)
  -F/pattern/      split() pattern for -a switch (//'s are
      optional)
  -i[extension]    edit <> files in place (makes backup if
      extension supplied)
  -Idirectory      specify @INC/#include directory (several -I's
      allowed)
  -l[octal]        enable line ending processing, specifies line
      terminator
  -[mM][-]module   execute `use/no module...' before executing
      program
  -n               assume 'while (<>) { ... }' loop around program
  -p               assume loop like -n but print line also, like
      sed
  -P               run program through C preprocessor before
      compilation
  -s               enable rudimentary parsing for switches after
      programfile
  -S               look for programfile using PATH environment
      variable
  -T               enable tainting checks
  -u               dump core after parsing program
  -U               allow unsafe operations
  -v               print version, subversion (includes VERY
      IMPORTANT perl info)
  -V[:variable]    print configuration summary (or a single
      Config.pm variable)
  -w               enable many useful warnings (RECOMMENDED)
  -W               enable all warnings
  -X               disable all warnings
  -x[directory]    strip off text before #!perl line and perhaps cd
      to directory
```

## PERL BUILT-IN VARIABLES

Perl has a number of built-in variables that allow you to write very compact code. Scripts that use many built-in variables can be cryptic for people who are starting to learn about Perl. Other techniques will be used when it is possible to accomplish the same task. For instance, the built-in variable $_ refers to the current line, and you can use your own variable to store the value of the current line. On the other hand, the built-in variables $`, $' refer to the "prefix" match and the "post" match, respectively, and they do not have a simple counterpart. There are also a number of "Perlisms" that advanced Perl users incorporate in their scripts, and they will be used where deemed appropriate.

## PERL SCALAR VARIABLES

A *scalar variable* in Perl is a variable whose value can be an integer, a floating point number, or a string. Listing C.1 contains a simple example of printing the values of one integer-valued scalar variable and two string-valued scalar variables.

### Listing C.1   simple1.pl

```
my($age)    = 30;
my($weight) = 200;
my($name)   = "John Smith";

print "$name is $age old and weighs $weight\n";
```

### Remarks

After you include the path to the Perl executable in your PATH variable, you can launch the Perl script simple1.pl in Listing C.1 from the command line as follows,

```
perl -w simple1.pl
```

and the output is as follows:

```
John Smith is 30 years old and weighs 200
```

The "\n" in the print statement serves as a line feed in Unix (or line feed plus carriage return in Windows NT). You can also specify multiple line feeds such as:

```
print "abc\n\n\n";
```

You can also specify a "tab" character like this:

```
print "indented\t\t";
```

# PERL while LOOPS

The "while" loop in Perl is a very useful construct that is similar to its counterparts in C and many other programming languages. A "while" loop exits when a specified condition is no longer true, and the location of this condition can either be in the "while" statement itself or, by means of "if/then" logic, inside the loop. Listing C.2 contains an example of a "while" loop for printing the integers from 0 to 9 inclusive.

## Listing C.2    whileLoop1.pl

```
my($count) = 0;

while($count++ < 10 )

{

   print "count -> $count\n";

}
```

## Remarks

You can launch the Perl script in whileLoop1.pl in Listing C.2 from the command line as follows,

```
perl -w whileLoop1.pl
```

and the output is as follows

```
count -> 0
count -> 1
count -> 2
count -> 3
count -> 4
count -> 5
count -> 6
count -> 7
```

```
count -> 8
count -> 9
```

## PERL for LOOPS

The "for" loop is another useful construct and (just like "while" loops) it is also similar to its counterpart in C. As you can probably discern from the code fragment, Listing C.3 also prints the integers from 0 to 9 inclusive using a "for" loop.

### Listing C.3    forLoop1.pl

```
my($count) = 0;
for($count=0; $count<10; $count++)
{
  print "count -> $count\n";
}
```

### Remarks

You can launch the Perl script forLoop1.pl in Listing C.3 from the command line as follows,

```
perl -w forLoop1.pl
```

and the output is as follows:

```
count -> 0
count -> 1
count -> 2
count -> 3
count -> 4
count -> 5
count -> 6
count -> 7
count -> 8
count -> 9
```

## PERL ARRAYS

Arrays in Perl are actually much more flexible than arrays in other programming languages; in some respects, Perl arrays can be manipulated almost as though they were lists. Listing C.4 demonstrates how to create an empty array and append two scalar values to the array.

### Listing C.4    array1.pl

```
my($age)    = 30;
my($name)   = "Tom";
my($weight) = 200;
my(@attributes) = ();

push(@attributes, $age);
push(@attributes, $weight);

print "$name is $attributes[0] old and weighs $attributes[1]\n";
```

## Remarks

You can launch the Perl script `array1.pl` in Listing C.4 from the command line as follows,

```
perl -w array1.pl
```

and the output is as follows:

```
Tom is 30 old and weighs 200
```

Perl allows you to "splice" arrays; that is, you can delete, update, or insert a list of values at any position in an array. The pop function removes an item from the end of an array; the `shift` function does the same thing to the first element of an array. The `push` function appends an item to the end of an array.

# PERL HASHES

Hashes in Perl are similar to hashes in Java or "associative arrays" in awk (named after Aho, Weinberger, and Kernighan). One of the key strengths of hashes in Perl is the ease with which you can create multi-dimensional hashes and then sort and traverse the stored values. Listing C.5 demonstrates how to create a two-dimensional Perl hash that associates a integer-valued scalar with a set of people who are identified by their first name and last name.

### Listing C.5    simpleHash1.pl

```
my($lastName)    = "";
my($employeeId)  = "";

my(%Employees);
```

```
$Employees{"Jones"} = 2000;
$Employees{"Smith"} = 2000;
$Employees{"Smith"} = 3000;

foreach $lastName (keys %Employees)
{
   $employeeId = $Employees{$lastName};
   {
      print "$lastName has Id = $employeeId\n";
   }
}
```

## Remarks

You can launch the Perl script simpleHash1.pl in Listing C.5 from the command line as follows,

```
perl -w simpleHash1.pl
```

and the output is as follows

```
Jones has Id = 2000
Smith has Id = 3000
```

If you want to sort the elements of a hash, you can use something like the following,

```
foreach $lastName (sort (keys %Employees))
```

and if you want to list the elements of a hash in reverse sorted order, you can do so as follows:

```
foreach $lastName (reverse (sort (keys %Employees)))
```

As you've probably noticed, one drawback to one-dimensional hashes is obvious: you cannot distinguish between two people with the same last name. The next example shows how to create a two-dimensional hash to handle this situation.

## PERL MULTI-DIMENSIONAL ARRAYS

One of the key strengths of hashes in Perl is the ease with which you can create multi-dimensional hashes and then sort and traverse the stored values. Listing C.6 demonstrates how to create a two-dimensional Perl hash that associates an integer-valued scalar with a set of people who are identified by their first name and last name.

### Listing C.6    multiHash1.pl

```perl
my($firstName)    = "";
my($lastName)     = "";
my($lastNameHash) = "";
my($employeeId)   = "";

my(%Employees);
my(%AllLastNames);

$Employees{"Jones"}{"Tom"}  = 1000;
$Employees{"Smith"}{"Ann"}  = 2000;
$Employees{"Smith"}{"Bill"} = 3000;


while(($lastName, $lastNameHash) = each(%Employees))
{
   $AllLastNames{$lastName} = $lastName;
}

for $lastName (sort (keys %AllLastNames))
{
   $lastNameHash = $Employees{$lastName};

   while(($firstName, $employeeId) = each(%{$lastNameHash}))
   {
      print "$firstName $lastName has Id = $employeeId\n";
   }
}
```

## Remarks

You can launch the Perl script multiHash1.pl in Listing C.6 from the command line as follows,

```
perl -w multiHash1.pl
```

and the output is as follows:

```
Tom Jones has Id = 1000
Bill Smith has Id = 3000
Ann Smith has Id = 2000
```

# OPENING AND CLOSING FILES IN PERL

Perl makes it very easy to open and close files on the file system. Listing C.7 shows you how to open a file and display an error message if the file cannot be opened for any reason (e.g., the file does not exist).

### Listing C.7  openFile1.pl

```
my($fileName) = "somedata.txt";

# open the input file...
open(INPUT, "<$fileName") || die "cannot open $fileName: $!\n";

# some processing happens here...

# close the input file...
close(INPUT);
```

## Remarks

You can launch the Perl script multiHash1.pl in Listing C.7 from the command line as follows:

```
perl -w openFile1.pl
```

If the file does not exist, you will see the following message:

```
cannot open somedata.txt: No such file or directory
```

If the file was opened and closed successfully, then you will not see anything because we haven't done anything with the file. The next example shows you how to read the contents of a text file.

# READING FILES IN PERL

Listing C.8 displays the contents of the file somedata.txt that we will use for the purposes of illustrating how to read the contents of a file.

### Listing C.8  somedata.txt

```
# this is a comment line

Jones:Tom:1000
```

```
Smith:Ann:2000
Smith:Bill:3000
```

Listing C.9 displays the contents of readFile1.pl, which is a Perl script that reads the contents of the file *somedata.txt*.

### Listing C.9    readFile1.pl

```
my($count)       = 0;
my($currentLine) = "";
my($fileName)    = "somedata.txt";

open(INPUT, "<$fileName") || die "Cannot open $fileName: $!\n";

while($currentLine = <INPUT>)
{
   $count++;
}

print "File $fileName contains $count lines\n";
```

### Remarks

You can launch the Perl script readFile1.pl in Listing C.9 from the command line as follows:

```
perl -w readFile1.pl
```

If the file was opened successfully, you will see the following output:

```
File somedata.txt contains 5 lines
```

## READING FILE CONTENTS INTO PERL ARRAYS

Listing C.10 displays the contents of a Perl script that reads the contents of a file into a Perl array in a single line.

### Listing C.10    readFile2.pl

```
my($count)       = 0;
my($currentLine) = "";
my($fileName)    = "somedata.txt";
```

```
open(INPUT, "<$fileName") || die "Cannot open $fileName: $!\n";

(@fileContents) = <INPUT>;
$count = scalar(@fileContents);
print "File $fileName contains $count lines\n";
```

## Remarks

You can launch the Perl script readFile2.pl in Listing C.10 from the command line as follows,

```
perl -w readFile2.pl
```

and the output is as follows:

```
File somedata.txt contains 5 lines
```

## WRITING TO FILES IN PERL

You can open multiple files in Perl and also write to a file, either by appending to an existing file, creating a new file, or overwriting an existing file. Listing C.11 shows you how to read data from an existing file and then echo every line on the screen as well as writing each line to another file. Notice how the less-than symbol ("<") is for file input and the greater-than symbol (">") is for file output.

**Listing C.11**   writeFile1.pl

```
my($count)      = 0;
my($currentLine) = "";
my($fileName)    = "somedata.txt";
my($outputFile)  = "somedata.out";

open(INPUT, "<$fileName") ||
    die "Cannot open $fileName: $!\n";

open(OUTPUT, ">$outputFile") ||
    die "Cannot open $outputFile: $!\n";

while($currentLine = <INPUT>)
{
   print OUTPUT "LINE $.:  $currentLine";
   print "LINE $.:  $currentLine";
}
```

## Remarks

Listing C.11 shows you a command style in Perl: open all the necessary files at the beginning of the script and handle any possible errors. Note that the input file and the output file differ only by their suffix; you can probably guess what will happen if they specified the same file! Launch the Perl script writeFile1.pl in Listing C.11 from the command line as follows,

```
perl -w writeFile1.pl
```

and you will see the following output:

```
LINE 1:  # this is a comment line
LINE 2:
LINE 3:  Jones:Tom:1000
LINE 4:  Smith:Ann:2000
LINE 5:  Smith:Bill:3000
```

Notice the newly created file called *somedata.out* which contains the same data that is displayed in the shell.

The ability to open input streams is not limited to text files. For example, if you wanted to list all the Perl scripts in the current directory, you could do something like Listing C.12.

## Listing C.12   dir1.pl

```
my($count)      = 0;
my($currentLine) = "";

open(INPUT, "ls *pl|") || die "Cannot list files: $!\n";

while($currentLine = <INPUT>)
{
   $count++;
}

print "Found $count Perl scripts\n";
```

In a Windows NT environment, replace ls *pl with dir/b *pl. In actuality, there are portable commands available for perusing the contents of a directory; this example is intended to illustrate how you can use input streams that are unrelated to text files.

## SKIPPING COMMENT LINES IN TEXT FILES

Sometimes you need to selectively process lines in a text file. One approach involves reading the entire file into an array (which you will see later) and another approach involves processing the contents of a text file on a line-by-line basis. Listing C.13 displays the contents of a Perl script that uses the second approach.

### Listing C.13   skipComment1.pl

```
my($count)     = 0;
my($result)     = "";
my($currentLine) = "";
my($fileName)    = "somedata.txt";

open(INPUT, "<$fileName") || die "Cannot open $fileName: $!\n";

while($currentLine = <INPUT>)
{
   if( ($currentLine =~ /^#/) || ($currentLine =~ /^$/) )
   {
      next;
   }

   $count++;
}

print "File $fileName contains $count lines\n";
```

### Remarks

Listing C.13 contains a loop that uses the continue statement in order to skip blank lines and lines that start with a '#' character  The key construct in Listing 12 is the following line:

```
if( ($currentLine =~ /^#/) || ($currentLine =~ /^$/) )
```

The first part of the `if` statement checks if the current line starts with a '#' character and the second part of the `if` statement checks if the current line is blank. In both contexts, the "^" and "$" meta characters refer to the start-of-line position and end-of-line position, respectively. You may be familiar with the use of these meta characters in regular expressions or in `vi` commands. Incidentally, the while loop in Listing C.13 can be rewritten in the following Perlism:

```
while($_ = <INPUT>)
{
   if( ($_ =~ /^#/) || ($_ =~ /^$/) )
```

```
    {
      next;
    }

    $count++;
}
```

## REMOVING WHITE SPACE IN TEXT STRINGS

Listing C.14 contains an assortment of statements that remove white space from a text string.

**Listing C.14**   removeWhiteSpace1.pl

```
my($currentLine) = "\tline    with spaces    \n";

# remove all tabs
$currentLine =~ s/\t//g;

# remove all spaces
$currentLine =~ s/ //g;

# remove all white space
$currentLine =~ s/\s+//g;

# remove all leading white space
$currentLine =~ s/^\s+//;

# remove all trailing white space
$currentLine =~ s/\s+$//;

# remove trailing line feed
$currentLine =~ s/\n$//;

# remove all line feeds
$currentLine =~ s/\n//g;

# print the line
print "final line = $currentLine\n";
```

### Remarks

You can launch the Perl script removeWhiteSpace1.pl in Listing C.14 from the command line as follows:

```
perl -w removeWhiteSpace1.pl
```

and the output is as follows:

```
final line = linewithspaces
```

# EXTRACTING SUB-STRINGS FROM TEXT STRINGS

Text strings containing sets of numbers are easy to parse in Perl. Listing C.15 displays the contents of a Perl script that matches a line consisting of white space and two numbers.

**Listing C.15**   numberBoundary1.pl

```perl
my($currentLine) = " 123 456 ";

if( $currentLine =~ /^\s+(\d+)\s+(\d+)\s+$/ )
{
   print "number 1:  $1\n";
   print "number 2:  $2\n";
}
```

## Remarks

You can launch the Perl script numberBoundary1.pl in Listing C.15 from the command line as follows,

```
perl -w numberBoundary1.pl
```

and the output is as follows:

```
number 1: 123
number 2: 456
```

The entire logic in the Perl script is contained in the following line:

```perl
if( $currentLine =~ /^\s+(\d+)\s+(\d+)\s+$/ )
```

Although it may appear daunting, the components of the preceding code are as follows:

^ is the start-of-line meta character

^\s+ matches leading white spaces

\d+ matches the first number

\s+ matches the second set of white space characters

\d+ matches the second number

\s+ matches the third set of white space characters

$ is the end-of-line meta character

Note that the pattern \d+ matches any set of contiguous digits, whereas the pattern \d would only match a single digit; similar comments apply to \s+ and \s.

## SWITCHING WORD ORDER IN TEXT STRINGS

Perl has nine positional variables (similar to sed) that can be used for backward referencing matched sub-strings, as illustrated by the code in Listing C.16.

### Listing C.16 wordSwitch1.pl

```
my($currentLine) = "one two";

if( $currentLine =~ /(\w+)\s+(\w+)/ )
{
   print "original words: $1 $2\n";
   print "switched words: $2 $1\n";
}
```

### Remarks

You can launch the Perl script wordSwitch1.pl in Listing C.16 from the command line as follows,

```
perl -w wordSwitch1.pl
```

and the output is as follows:

```
original words: one two
switched words: two one
```

## THE PERL split FUNCTION AND TEXT STRINGS

The split function in Perl is a highly versatile function and is very useful when you want to parse a line containing multiple tokens or a variable number of tokens.

## Listing C.17   split1.pl

```perl
my($discard1)    = "";
my($discard2)    = "";
my($index)       = 0;

my(@numbersArray);
my($currentLine) = "mumbo jumbo 1 2 3";

($discard1, $discard2, @numbersArray) =
                            split(/\s+/, $currentLine);

foreach $index (0..$#numbersArray)
{
   print "Number $index equals $numbersArray[$index]\n";
}
```

## Remarks

You can launch the Perl script `split1.pl` in Listing C.17 from the command line as follows,

```
perl -w split1.pl
```

and the output is as follows:

```
Number 0 equals 1
Number 1 equals 2
Number 2 equals 3
```

If you do not know how many tokens there are in a line, or the number of tokens varies between different lines, you can do something like this:

```perl
(@lineArray) = split(/\s+/, $currentLine);
my($count) = scalar(@lineArray);
print "$currentLine has $count tokens\n";
```

If a line uses a colon (:) as a delimiter between tokens, you can use the following variant:

```perl
(@lineArray) = split(/:/, $currentLine);
```

## COMBINING split WITH OTHER FUNCTIONS

Listing C.18 displays the contents of the Perl script splitDate1.pl that demonstrates how to combine arrays, the split function, and the date function. The techniques in this example can be used in a variety of situations.

**Listing C.18**   splitDate1.pl

```perl
my($weekDay)  = "";
my($month)    = "";
my($monthDay) = "";
my($hrMinSec) = "";
my($timeZone) = "";
my($year)     = "";
my($hour)     = "";
my($minute)   = "";
my($second)   = "";

my($line)     = "";
my($length)   = 0;

my(@dateArray);

@dateArray = `date`;

$length = scalar(@dateArray);
$line   = join(' ', @dateArray);

if( $length == 6 )
{
   # Unix system
   ($weekDay,$month,$monthDay,$hrMinSec,$timeZone,$year) =
                                    split(/ /, $line);
}
else
{
   # non-Unix system (e.g., NT)
   ($weekDay,$month,$monthDay,$hrMinSec,$year) =
                                    split(/ /, $line);
}

($hour, $minute, $second) = split(/:/, $hrMinSec);

print "Today's date:    @dateArray\n";
print "Day of Week:     $weekDay\n";
print "Month:           $month\n";
print "Day of Month:    $monthDay\n";
```

```
print "Hour(s):        $hour\n";
print "Minute(s):      $minute\n";
print "Second(s):      $second\n";
print "Time Zone:      $timeZone\n";
print "Year:           $year\n";
```

## Remarks

You can launch the Perl script `splitDate1.pl` in Listing C.18 from the command line as follows,

```
perl -w splitDate1.pl
```

and the output is as follows:

```
Today's date:    Fri May 23 16:03:40  2003

Day of Week:     Fri
Month:           May
Day of Month:    23
Hour(s):         16
Minute(s):       03
Second(s):       40
Time Zone:
Year:
```

# THE PERL join FUNCTION

The Perl join function is useful when you need to concatenate a set of strings that are stored in an array.

### Listing C.19  join1.pl

```
my($discard1)    = "";
my($discard2)    = "";

my(@numbersArray);
my($currentLine) = "mumbo jumbo 1 2 3";

($discard1, $discard2, @numbersArray) =
                              split(/\s+/, $currentLine);

my($secondLine) = join(' ', @numbersArray);
print "second line $secondLine\n";
```

## Remarks

You can launch the Perl script `join1.pl` in Listing C.19 from the command line as follows,

```
perl -w join1.pl
```

and the output is as follows:

```
second line = 1 2 3
```

The combination of `split` and `join` is useful when you need to split a line containing one delimiter and then reconstitute the line with another delimiter. There are other ways to accomplish the same task; for example, if you need to replace a line with a colon (":") delimiter with a pipe symbol ("|"), you could also do something like the following, which does not require the use of either `split` or `join`:

```
$currentLine =~ s/:/\|/g;
```

Notice the use of a backslash ("\") in order to "escape" the pipe symbol.

## CREATING CUSTOM PERL FUNCTIONS

Listing c.20 displays a simple Perl script that invokes a custom function in order to calculate the sum of two numbers.

### Listing C.20  addTwo.pl

```
my($first) = 3;
my($second) = 4;

addTwoNumbers(3,4);

sub addTwoNumbers($$)
{
    my($sum) = 0;
    my($first, $second) = @_;

    $sum = $first + $second;
    print "The sum of $first and $second is $sum\n";
}
```

## Remarks

You can launch the Perl script `addTwo.pl` in Listing C.20 from the command line as follows,

```
perl -w addTwo.pl
```

and the output is as follows:

```
The sum of 3 and 4 is 7
```

For backward compatibility, functions written in pre-release 5 versions of Perl are invoked with an ampersand ("&") as given below:

```
&addTwoNumbers(3,4);
```

# PASSING ARRAYS TO PERL FUNCTIONS

Listing c.21 displays a Perl script that invokes a custom function in order to calculate the sum of the numbers in an array.

### Listing C.21   addArray.pl

```
my(@numArray)  = ();
push(@numArray,1);
push(@numArray,2);
push(@numArray,3);
push(@numArray,4);

addArray(@numArray);


sub addArray(@)
{
   my($index) = 0;

   my(@rest) = @_;

   foreach $index (0..$#rest)
   {
      $sum += $rest[$index];
   }

   print "The sum of all the numbers is $sum\n";
}
```

### Remarks

You can launch the Perl script `addArray1.pl` in Listing C.21 from the command line as follows,

```
perl -w addArray1.pl
```

and the output is as follows:

```
The sum of all the numbers is 10
```

## FINDING EXACT MATCHES IN TEXT STRINGS

Listing C.22 shows you how to perform various pattern matches which leverage the techniques and concepts that you've seen thus far.

### Listing C.22    multiMatch1.pl

```perl
my($line1) = "123";
my($line2) = "abcde";
my($line3) = "x = 3; # this is comment";
my($line4) = "123-45-6789";
my($left)  = "";
my($right) = "";

if( $line1 =~ /^\d+$/ )
{
   print "$line1 contains only digits\n";
}

if( $line2 =~ /^[a-zA-Z]$/ )
{
   print "$line2 contains only letters\n";
}

if( $line3 =~ /#/ )
{
   ($left, $right) = split(/#/, $line3);
   print "$line3 contains a comment:  $right\n";
}

$line3 =~ s/^\s+//;

if( $line3 =~ /^#/ )
{
```

```
      print "$line3 is a comment line\n";
   }

   if( $line4 =~ /^(\d\d\d)-(\d\d)-(\d\d\d\d)$/ )
   {
      print "$line4 has a SSN format\n";
   }
```

### Remarks

You can launch the Perl script `multiMatch1.pl` in Listing C.22 from the command line as follows,

```
perl -w multiMatch1.pl
```

and the output is as follows:

```
123 contains only digits
x = 3; # this is comment contains a comment:  this is comment
123-45-6789 has a SSN format
```

## VERIFYING DATE FORMATS IN PERL

The Perl script in Listing C.23 uses an array to store the number of days in each month (including leap years) and the Perl `split` function in order to validate a date string.

### Listing C.23   verifyDate1.pl.

```
my($date)  = "11/25/2003";
my($month) = 0;
my($day)   = 0;
my($year)  = 0;

my(@daysInMonth) = (0,31,28,31,30,31,30,31,31,30,31,30,31);

($month, $day, $year) = split(/\//, $date);

if( $year % 4 == 0 )
{
   if( ($year % 100 == 0) && ($year % 400 != 0) )
   {
      $daysInMonth[1] = 29;
   }
}
```

```
if( $year >= 1 )
{
   if( ($day <= $daysInMonth[$month]) && ($day >= 1) )
   {
      if( ($month > 0) && ($month <= 12) )
      {
         print "Date $date is valid\n";
      }
      else
      {
         print "Month $month is out of range\n";
      }
   }
   else
   {
      print "Day $day is out of range\n";
   }
}
else
{
   print "Year $year must be at least 1\n";
}
```

### Remarks

You can invoke the Perl script verifyDate1.pl from the command line as follows,

```
perl -w verifyDate1.pl
```

and the output will be as follows:

```
Date 11/25/2003 is valid
```

## READING FILE CONTENTS INTO AN ARRAY

Listing C.24 demonstrates how to read in ("slurp") an entire file into an array with a single Perl command.

### Listing C.24   arrayFile1.pl

```
my($fileName)    = "somedata.txt";
my($currentLine) = "";
my($index)       = 0;
```

```
my(@fileContents);


open(INPUT, "<$fileName") || die "Cannot open $fileName: $!\n";

(@fileContents) = <INPUT>;

foreach $index (0..$#fileContents)
{
   $currentLine = $fileContents[$index];
   print "$currentLine";
}
```

## Remarks

You can invoke the Perl script arrayFile1.pl from the command line as follows,

```
perl -w arrayFile1.pl
```

and the output will be as follows:

```
# this is a comment line

Jones:Tom:1000
Smith:Ann:2000
Smith:Bill:3000
```

This technique is useful when you want to minimize the amount of time that a file is open (for whatever reason). Since the array containing the file contents will be in main memory, you can process the array contents much faster than the line-by-line approach that was used in earlier examples.

## PRINT FILE CONTENTS IN REVERSE ORDER

### Listing C.25   reverseOrder1.pl

```
my($fileName)    = "somedata.txt";
my($currentLine) = "";
my($result)      = "";
my($index)       = 0;
my($lineCount)   = 0;

my(@fileContents);
```

```
open(INPUT, "<$fileName") || die "Cannot open $fileName: $!\n";

(@fileContents) = <INPUT>;

$lineCount = scalar(@fileContents);

for($index=$lineCount-1; $index>=0; $index--)
{
   $currentLine = $fileContents[$index];
   print "$currentLine";
}
```

You can invoke the Perl script `arrayFile1.pl` from the command line as follows,

```
perl -w arrayFile1.pl
```

and the output will be as follows:

```
Smith:Bill:3000
Smith:Ann:2000
Jones:Tom:1000

# this is a comment line
```

# SUMMARY

This appendix gave you an introduction to Perl and provided examples of scalar variables, arrays, and hashes. Perl can easily handle file input/output operations, and you can read the entire contents of a text file into a Perl array by means of a single command. You saw techniques for matching substrings and numbers in text string, as well as examples of removing multiple white spaces and switching word order.

# Appendix
# D
# About the CD-ROM

The CD-ROM included with this book contains complete source code for every example presented in the book. It also contains a supplemental folder with more than twenty thousand examples that are not covered in the book. The vast majority of these examples are located in various sub-folders of the SupplementalCode folder. Note that you must download an SVG viewer, as described on Chapter 1, to view the SVG documents. You need to use the Adobe SVG viewer for viewing the SVG documents that contain ECMAScript because the ECMAScript uses some Adobe-specific extensions.

## CD FOLDERS

### Software

This folder contains a copy of Perl and a copy of InstantSaxon that you can install on your machine. Chapter 17 contains examples of using Perl and XSL stylesheets in order to generate SVG documents. You need to update the PATH variable (as described in Chapter 17) in order to invoke Perl and InstantSaxon.

### Source Code

This folder contains all the files in the book, arranged by chapter. For example, the folder for Chapter 1 contains the sub-folder CDLibrary and figures that contain SVG documents and image files, respectively., that belong to Chapter 1.

#### CDLibrary

This folder contains SVG documents for each chapter in the book.

#### Figures

This folder contains PCX-formatted static files that correspond to the figures for each chapter of the book.

### Supplemental Code

This folder contains a number of sub-folders (some of which contain many additional sub-folders) with numerous examples that illustrate how to incorporate a particular type of geometric object.

## OVERALL SYSTEM REQUIREMENTS

The SVG documents in this book have been fully tested with the Adobe SVG viewer (version 3) on a 2 GHz Pentium 4 PC with Windows XP. Roughly 20% of the SVG code was developed on a 166 megahertz PC (and 64 megabytes of RAM) with the same version of the Adobe SVG viewer, and those documents were rendered with reasonable performance times. The minimum system requirements are:

- PC with a minimum Pentium III 500 MHz processor (2GHz is strongly recommended)
- minimum of 64 Mb RAM (128Mb recommended)
- CD-ROM drive
- hard disk with at least 200 Mbytes free space if you want to install the entire contents of the CD-ROM on your machine
- Windows 2000 or later
- Microsoft Internet Explorer 5.5 or higher

### Launching SVG Documents

The Adobe SVG viewer (version 3) is the recommended SVG viewer. After you have installed an SVG viewer, the SVG documents on the CD-ROM can be viewed in a browser simply by double-clicking on an SVG file. For example, if you want to view the SVG document *rectShadowEffect1.svg*, first navigate to the folder labeled "Source Code," then open the sub-folder "ch1," and then double-click on the file *rectShadowEffect1.svg*.

The primary factor that will affect the rendering time for the SVG documents is the processing power of your machine.

This book focuses on the nuts and bolts of creating graphics images, with performance a secondary consideration. In many cases, the rendering time for the graphics images can be improved, and the book contains suggestions for improving the performance. You will also find images that have a hard-coded width and height of 800 and 500, respectively, which means that some tweaking is required if you want to reduce them in order to incorporate them into HTML pages.

## LICENSE AGREEMENTS

The following license agreements pertain to the use of Perl and Saxon with the software in this book.

## Mozilla Public License Version 1.1

1. Definitions.

1.0.1.   "Commercial Use" means distribution or otherwise making the Covered Code available to a third party.

1.1.   "Contributor" means each entity that creates or contributes to the creation of Modifications.

1.2.   "Contributor Version" means the combination of the Original Code, prior Modifications used by a Contributor, and the Modifications made by that particular Contributor.

1.3.   "Covered Code" means the Original Code or Modifications or the combination of the Original Code and Modifications, in each case including portions thereof.

1.4.   "Electronic Distribution Mechanism" means a mechanism generally accepted in the software development community for the electronic transfer of data.

1.5.   "Executable" means Covered Code in any form other than Source Code.

1.6.   "Initial Developer" means the individual or entity identified as the Initial Developer in the Source Code notice required by Exhibit A.

1.7.   "Larger Work" means a work which combines Covered Code or portions thereof with code not governed by the terms of this License.

1.8.   "License" means this document.

1.8.1.   "Licensable" means having the right to grant, to the maximum extent possible, whether at the time of the initial grant or subsequently acquired, any and all of the rights conveyed herein.

1.9.   "Modifications" means any addition to or deletion from the substance or structure of either the Original Code or any previous Modifications. When Covered Code is released as a series of files, a Modification is:

A.   Any addition to or deletion from the contents of a file containing Original Code or previous Modifications.

B.   Any new file that contains any part of the Original Code or previous Modifications.

1.10.   "Original Code" means Source Code of computer software code which is described in the Source Code notice required by Exhibit A as Original Code, and which, at the time of its release under this License is not already Covered Code governed by this License.

1.10.1.   "Patent Claims" means any patent claim(s), now owned or hereafter acquired, including without limitation, method, process, and apparatus claims, in any patent Licensable by grantor.

1.11.   "Source Code" means the preferred form of the Covered Code for making modifications to it, including all modules it contains, plus any associated interface definition files, scripts used to control compilation and installation of an Executable, or source code differential comparisons against either the Original Code or another well known, available Covered Code of the Contributor's choice. The Source Code can be in a compressed or archival form, provided the appropriate decompression or de-archiving software is widely available for no charge.

1.12.   "You" (or "Your") means an individual or a legal entity exercising rights under, and complying with all of the terms of, this License or a future version of this License issued under Section 6.1. For legal entities, "You" includes any entity which controls, is controlled by, or is under common control with You. For purposes of this definition, "control" means (a) the power, direct or indirect, to cause the direction or management of such entity, whether by contract or otherwise, or (b) ownership of more than fifty percent (50%) of the outstanding shares or beneficial ownership of such entity.

2.  Source Code License.

2.1.   The Initial Developer Grant.

The Initial Developer hereby grants You a world-wide, royalty-free, non-exclusive license, subject to third party intellectual property claims:

(a)   under intellectual property rights (other than patent or trademark) Licensable by Initial Developer to use, reproduce, modify, display, perform, sublicense and distribute the Original Code (or portions thereof) with or without Modifications, and/or as part of a Larger Work; and

(b)   under Patents Claims infringed by the making, using or selling of Original Code, to make, have made, use, practice, sell, and offer for sale, and/or otherwise dispose of the Original Code (or portions thereof).

(c)   the licenses granted in this Section 2.1(a) and (b) are effective on the date Initial Developer first distributes Original Code under the terms of this License.

(d)   Notwithstanding Section 2.1(b) above, no patent license is granted: 1) for code that You delete from the Original Code; 2) separate from the Original Code; or 3) for infringements caused by: i) the modification of the Original Code or ii) the combination of the Original Code with other software or devices.

2.2.   Contributor Grant.

Subject to third party intellectual property claims, each Contributor hereby grants You a world-wide, royalty-free, non-exclusive license

(a)   under intellectual property rights (other than patent or trademark) Licensable by Contributor, to use, reproduce, modify, display, perform, sublicense and distribute the Modifications created by such Contributor (or portions thereof) either on an unmodified basis, with other Modifications, as Covered Code and/or as part of a Larger Work; and

(b)   under Patent Claims infringed by the making, using, or selling of Modifications made by that Contributor either alone and/or in combination with its Contributor Version (or portions of such combination), to make, use, sell, offer for sale, have made, and/or otherwise dispose of: 1) Modifications made by that Contributor (or portions thereof); and 2) the combination of Modifications made by that Contributor with its Contributor Version (or portions of such combination).

(c)   the licenses granted in Sections 2.2(a) and 2.2(b) are effective on the date Contributor first makes Commercial Use of the Covered Code.

(d)   Notwithstanding Section 2.2(b) above, no patent license is granted: 1) for any code that Contributor has deleted from the Contributor Version; 2) separate from the Contributor Version; 3) for infringements caused by: i) third party modifications of Contributor Version or ii) the combination of Modifications made by that Contributor with other software (except as part of the Contributor Version) or other devices; or 4) under Patent Claims infringed by Covered Code in the absence of Modifications made by that Contributor.

3. Distribution Obligations.

    3.1.    Application of License.

The Modifications which You create or to which You contribute are governed by the terms of this License, including without limitation Section 2.2. The Source Code version of Covered Code may be distributed only under the terms of this License or a future version of this License released under Section 6.1, and You must include a copy of this License with every copy of the Source Code You distribute. You may not offer or impose any terms on any Source Code version that alters or restricts the applicable version of this License or the recipients' rights hereunder. However, You may include an additional document offering the additional rights described in Section 3.5.

    3.2.    Availability of Source Code.

Any Modification which You create or to which You contribute must be made available in Source Code form under the terms of this License either on the same media as an Executable version or via an accepted Electronic Distribution Mechanism to anyone to whom you made an Executable version available; and if made available via Electronic Distribution Mechanism, must remain available for at least twelve (12) months after the date it initially became available, or at least six (6) months after a subsequent version of that particular Modification has been made available to such recipients. You are responsible for ensuring that the Source Code version remains available even if the Electronic Distribution Mechanism is maintained by a third party.

    3.3.    Description of Modifications.

You must cause all Covered Code to which You contribute to contain a file documenting the changes You made to create that Covered Code and the date of any change. You must include a prominent statement that the Modification is derived, directly or indirectly, from Original Code provided by the Initial Developer and including the name of the Initial Developer in (a) the Source Code, and (b) in any notice in an Executable version or related documentation in which You describe the origin or ownership of the Covered Code.

    3.4.    Intellectual Property Matters

        (a)    Third Party Claims.

If Contributor has knowledge that a license under a third party's intellectual property rights is required to exercise the rights granted by such Contributor under Sections 2.1 or 2.2, Contributor must include a text file with the Source Code distribution titled "LEGAL" which describes the claim and the party making the claim in sufficient detail that a recipient will know whom to contact. If Contributor obtains such knowledge after the Modification is made available as described in Section 3.2, Contributor shall promptly modify the LEGAL file in all copies Contributor makes available thereafter and shall take other steps (such as notifying appropriate mailing lists or newsgroups) reasonably calculated to inform those who received the Covered Code that new knowledge has been obtained.

(b)   Contributor APIs.

If Contributor's Modifications include an application programming interface and Contributor has knowledge of patent licenses which are reasonably necessary to implement that API, Contributor must also include this information in the LEGAL file.

(c)   Representations.

Contributor represents that, except as disclosed pursuant to Section 3.4(a) above, Contributor believes that Contributor's Modifications are Contributor's original creation(s) and/or Contributor has sufficient rights to grant the rights conveyed by this License.

3.5.    Required Notices.

You must duplicate the notice in Exhibit A in each file of the Source Code. If it is not possible to put such notice in a particular Source Code file due to its structure, then You must include such notice in a location (such as a relevant directory) where a user would be likely to look for such a notice. If You created one or more Modification(s) You may add your name as a Contributor to the notice described in Exhibit A. You must also duplicate this License in any documentation for the Source Code where You describe recipients' rights or ownership rights relating to Covered Code. You may choose to offer, and to charge a fee for, warranty, support, indemnity or liability obligations to one or more recipients of Covered Code. However, You may do so only on Your own behalf, and not on behalf of the Initial Developer or any Contributor. You must make it absolutely clear than any such warranty, support, indemnity or liability obligation is offered by You alone, and You hereby agree to indemnify the Initial Developer and every Contributor for any liability incurred by the Initial Developer or such Contributor as a result of warranty, support, indemnity or liability terms You offer.

3.6.    Distribution of Executable Versions.

You may distribute Covered Code in Executable form only if the requirements of Section 3.1-3.5 have been met for that Covered Code, and if You include a notice stating that the Source Code version of the Covered Code is available under the terms of this License, including a description of how and where You have fulfilled the obligations of Section 3.2. The notice must be conspicuously included in any notice in an Executable version, related documentation or collateral in which You describe recipients' rights relating to the Covered Code. You may distribute the Executable version of Covered Code or ownership rights under a license of Your choice, which may contain terms different from this License, provided that You are in compliance with the terms of this License and that the license for the Executable version does not attempt to limit or alter the recipient's rights in the Source Code version from the rights set forth in this License. If You distribute the Executable version under a different license You must make it absolutely clear that any terms which differ from this License are offered by You alone, not by the Initial Developer or any Contributor. You hereby agree to indemnify the Initial Developer and every Contributor for any liability incurred by the Initial Developer or such Contributor as a result of any such terms You offer.

3.7.    Larger Works.

You may create a Larger Work by combining Covered Code with other code not governed by the terms of this License and distribute the Larger Work as a single product. In such a case, You must make sure the requirements of this License are fulfilled for the Covered Code.

4.  Inability to Comply Due to Statute or Regulation.

If it is impossible for You to comply with any of the terms of this License with respect to some or all of the Covered Code due to statute, judicial order, or regulation then You must: (a) comply with the terms of this License to the maximum extent possible; and (b) describe the limitations and the code they affect. Such description must be included in the LEGAL file described in Section 3.4 and must be included with all distributions of the Source Code. Except to the extent prohibited by statute or regulation, such description must be sufficiently detailed for a recipient of ordinary skill to be able to understand it.

5.  Application of this License.

This License applies to code to which the Initial Developer has attached the notice in Exhibit A and to related Covered Code.

6.  Versions of the License.

6.1.    New Versions.

Netscape Communications Corporation ("Netscape") may publish revised and/or new versions of the License from time to time. Each version will be given a distinguishing version number.

6.2.    Effect of New Versions.

Once Covered Code has been published under a particular version of the License, You may always continue to use it under the terms of that version. You may also choose to use such Covered Code under the terms of any subsequent version of the License published by Netscape. No one other than Netscape has the right to modify the terms applicable to Covered Code created under this License.

6.3.    Derivative Works.

If You create or use a modified version of this License (which you may only do in order to apply it to code which is not already Covered Code governed by this License), You must (a) rename Your license so that the phrases "Mozilla", "MOZILLAPL", "MOZPL", "Netscape", "MPL", "NPL" or any confusingly similar phrase do not appear in your license (except to note that your license differs from this License) and (b) otherwise make it clear that Your version of the license contains terms which differ from the Mozilla Public License and Netscape Public License. (Filling in the name of the Initial Developer, Original Code or Contributor in the notice described in Exhibit A shall not of themselves be deemed to be modifications of this License.)

7.  DISCLAIMER OF WARRANTY.

COVERED CODE IS PROVIDED UNDER THIS LICENSE ON AN "AS IS" BASIS, WITHOUT WARRANTY OF ANY KIND, EITHER EXPRESSED OR IMPLIED, INCLUDING,

WITHOUT LIMITATION, WARRANTIES THAT THE COVERED CODE IS FREE OF DE-
FECTS, MERCHANTABLE, FIT FOR A PARTICULAR PURPOSE OR NON-INFRINGING.
THE ENTIRE RISK AS TO THE QUALITY AND PERFORMANCE OF THE COVERED
CODE IS WITH YOU. SHOULD ANY COVERED CODE PROVE DEFECTIVE IN ANY RE-
SPECT, YOU (NOT THE INITIAL DEVELOPER OR ANY OTHER CONTRIBUTOR) AS-
SUME THE COST OF ANY NECESSARY SERVICING, REPAIR OR CORRECTION. THIS
DISCLAIMER OF WARRANTY CONSTITUTES AN ESSENTIAL PART OF THIS LICENSE.
NO USE OF ANY COVERED CODE IS AUTHORIZED HEREUNDER EXCEPT UNDER
THIS DISCLAIMER.

8. TERMINATION.

8.1.   This License and the rights granted hereunder will terminate automatically if You fail
to comply with terms herein and fail to cure such breach within 30 days of becoming
aware of the breach. All sublicenses to the Covered Code which are properly granted
shall survive any termination of this License. Provisions which, by their nature, must
remain in effect beyond the termination of this License shall survive.

8.2.   If You initiate litigation by asserting a patent infringement claim (excluding declatory
judgment actions) against Initial Developer or a Contributor (the Initial Developer or
Contributor against whom You file such action is referred to as "Participant") alleging that:

(a)   such Participant's Contributor Version directly or indirectly infringes any
patent, then any and all rights granted by such Participant to You under Sections 2.1 and/or 2.2 of this License shall, upon 60 days notice from Participant
terminate prospectively, unless if within 60 days after receipt of notice You either: (i) agree in writing to pay Participant a mutually agreeable reasonable royalty for Your past and future use of Modifications made by such Participant, or
(ii) withdraw Your litigation claim with respect to the Contributor Version
against such Participant. If within 60 days of notice, a reasonable royalty and
payment arrangement are not mutually agreed upon in writing by the parties or
the litigation claim is not withdrawn, the rights granted by Participant to You
under Sections 2.1 and/or 2.2 automatically terminate at the expiration of the 60
day notice period specified above.

(b)   any software, hardware, or device, other than such Participant's Contributor
Version, directly or indirectly infringes any patent, then any rights granted to
You by such Participant under Sections 2.1(b) and 2.2(b) are revoked effective
as of the date You first made, used, sold, distributed, or had made, Modifications made by that Participant.

8.3.   If You assert a patent infringement claim against Participant alleging that such Participant's Contributor Version directly or indirectly infringes any patent where such
claim is resolved (such as by license or settlement) prior to the initiation of patent infringement litigation, then the reasonable value of the licenses granted by such Participant under Sections 2.1 or 2.2 shall be taken into account in determining the
amount or value of any payment or license.

8.4.    In the event of termination under Sections 8.1 or 8.2 above, all end user license agreements (excluding distributors and resellers) which have been validly granted by You or any distributor hereunder prior to termination shall survive termination.

9. LIMITATION OF LIABILITY.

UNDER NO CIRCUMSTANCES AND UNDER NO LEGAL THEORY, WHETHER TORT (INCLUDING NEGLIGENCE), CONTRACT, OR OTHERWISE, SHALL YOU, THE INITIAL DEVELOPER, ANY OTHER CONTRIBUTOR, OR ANY DISTRIBUTOR OF COVERED CODE, OR ANY SUPPLIER OF ANY OF SUCH PARTIES, BE LIABLE TO ANY PERSON FOR ANY INDIRECT, SPECIAL, INCIDENTAL, OR CONSEQUENTIAL DAMAGES OF ANY CHARACTER INCLUDING, WITHOUT LIMITATION, DAMAGES FOR LOSS OF GOOD-WILL, WORK STOPPAGE, COMPUTER FAILURE OR MALFUNCTION, OR ANY AND ALL OTHER COMMERCIAL DAMAGES OR LOSSES, EVEN IF SUCH PARTY SHALL HAVE BEEN INFORMED OF THE POSSIBILITY OF SUCH DAMAGES. THIS LIMITATION OF LIABILITY SHALL NOT APPLY TO LIABILITY FOR DEATH OR PERSONAL INJURY RESULTING FROM SUCH PARTY'S NEGLIGENCE TO THE EXTENT APPLICABLE LAW PROHIBITS SUCH LIMITATION. SOME JURISDICTIONS DO NOT ALLOW THE EXCLUSION OR LIMITATION OF INCIDENTAL OR CONSEQUENTIAL DAMAGES, SO THIS EXCLUSION AND LIMITATION MAY NOT APPLY TO YOU.

10. U.S. GOVERNMENT END USERS.

The Covered Code is a ''commercial item,'' as that term is defined in 48 C.F.R. 2.101 (Oct. 1995), consisting of ''commercial computer software'' and ''commercial computer software documentation,'' as such terms are used in 48 C.F.R. 12.212 (Sept. 1995). Consistent with 48 C.F.R. 12.212 and 48 C.F.R. 227.7202-1 through 227.7202-4 (June 1995), all U.S. Government End Users acquire Covered Code with only those rights set forth herein.

11. MISCELLANEOUS.

This License represents the complete agreement concerning subject matter hereof. If any provision of this License is held to be unenforceable, such provision shall be reformed only to the extent necessary to make it enforceable. This License shall be governed by California law provisions (except to the extent applicable law, if any, provides otherwise), excluding its conflict-of-law provisions. With respect to disputes in which at least one party is a citizen of, or an entity chartered or registered to do business in the United States of America, any litigation relating to this License shall be subject to the jurisdiction of the Federal Courts of the Northern District of California, with venue lying in Santa Clara County, California, with the losing party responsible for costs, including without limitation, court costs and reasonable attorneys' fees and expenses. The application of the United Nations Convention on Contracts for the International Sale of Goods is expressly excluded. Any law or regulation which provides that the language of a contract shall be construed against the drafter shall not apply to this License.

12. RESPONSIBILITY FOR CLAIMS.

As between Initial Developer and the Contributors, each party is responsible for claims and damages arising, directly or indirectly, out of its utilization of rights under this License and You agree to work with Initial Developer and Contributors to distribute such responsibility on an equitable basis. Nothing herein is intended or shall be deemed to constitute any admission of liability.

13. MULTIPLE-LICENSED CODE.

Initial Developer may designate portions of the Covered Code as "Multiple-Licensed". "Multiple-Licensed" means that the Initial Developer permits you to utilize portions of the Covered Code under Your choice of the MPL or the alternative licenses, if any, specified by the Initial Developer in the file described in Exhibit A.

## EXHIBIT A -Mozilla Public License.

``The contents of this file are subject to the Mozilla Public License Version 1.1 (the "License"); you may not use this file except in compliance with the License. You may obtain a copy of the License at http://www.mozilla.org/MPL/. Software distributed under the License is distributed on an "AS IS" basis, WITHOUT WARRANTY OF ANY KIND, either express or implied. See the License for the specific language governing rights and limitations under the License.

The Original Code is _____.

The Initial Developer of the Original Code is _____.

Portions created by _____ are Copyright (C) _____ _____. All Rights Reserved.

Contributor(s): _____.

Alternatively, the contents of this file may be used under the terms of the _____ license (the "[___] License"), in which case the provisions of [_____] License are applicable instead of those above. If you wish to allow use of your version of this file only under the terms of the [____] License and not to allow others to use your version of this file under the MPL, indicate your decision by deleting the provisions above and replace them with the notice and other provisions required by the [___] License. If you do not delete the provisions above, a recipient may use your version of this file under either the MPL or the [___] License."

[NOTE: The text of this Exhibit A may differ slightly from the text of the notices in the Source Code files of the Original Code. You should use the text of this Exhibit A rather than the text found in the Original Code Source Code for Your Modifications.]

## Perl License Agreement

### ActiveState Community License

Preamble:

The intent of this document is to state the conditions under which the Package may be copied and distributed, such that ActiveState maintains control over the development and distribution of the Package, while allowing the users of the Package to use the Package in a variety of ways. The Package may contain software covered by the Artistic License. The ActiveState Community License complies with Clause 5 of the Artistic License and does not limit your rights to software covered by the Artistic License.

Authorized electronic distributors of the Package are:

* Any ActiveState.com site

* Any complete, public CPAN mirror listed at www.perl.com

For more information on CPAN please see http://www.perl.com/.

Definitions:

"ActiveState" refers to ActiveState Tool Corp., the Copyright Holder of the Package.

"Package" refers to those files, including, but not limited to, source code, binary executables, images, and scripts, which are distributed by the Copyright Holder.

"You" is you, if you're thinking about copying or distributing this Package.

1. You may use this Package for commercial or non-commercial purposes without charge.

2. You may make and give away verbatim copies of this Package for personal use, or for use within your organization, provided that you duplicate all of the original copyright notices and associated disclaimers. You may not distribute copies of this Package, or copies of packages derived from this Package, to others outside your organization without specific prior written permission from ActiveState (although you are encouraged to direct them to sources from which they may obtain it for themselves).

3. You may apply bug fixes, portability fixes, and other modifications derived from ActiveState. A Package modified in such a way shall still be covered by the terms of this license.

4. ActiveState's name and trademarks may not be used to endorse or promote packages derived from this Package without specific prior written permission from ActiveState.

5. THIS PACKAGE IS PROVIDED "AS IS" AND WITHOUT ANY EXPRESS OR IMPLIED WARRANTIES, INCLUDING, WITHOUT LIMITATION, THE IMPLIED WARRANTIES OF MERCHANTIBILITY AND FITNESS FOR A PARTICULAR PURPOSE.

ActiveState Community License Copyright © 2000 ActiveState Tool Corp. All rights reserved.

# Index

\# symbol, 34, 474
$ symbol in Perl, 474
< symbol in Perl, 474
> symbol in Perl, 474
^ symbol in Perl, 474
/ symbol in XSL, 391, 427, 430–431

## A

AnimateTransform element
  attributes of, 186
  counter-rotating ellipses animation,
    191–193
  rectangle rotation with, 188–191
Animation
  animateColor element, 185–186
  animate element, 185–186
  animateTransform element, 186
  Bezier curves, modification of, 297–306
  chained animation effects, 196–199
  clip paths and, 186
  dur attribute and length of, 190
  dynamic creation of SVG elements and,
    292–297
  ECMAScript and, 252, 283–307
  ECMAScript requirements, 306
  HTML and graphics animations,
    238–247
  multiple animation effects, 193–196,
    201–203
  on-the-fly creation of new elements, 252
  oscillation of Bezier curves, 297–306
  rotating pie charts, 345–357
  scaling during, 201–203, 242–247

  text string, continuous rotation of,
    199–201
  "time-out periods" for, 306
  toggling effects, 287–292
Archimedean spirals, 324–331
Arcs
  asymmetric arc-based patterns, 65–67
  circular and elliptical arcs, 58–62
  coloring elliptical arcs, 61–62
  diamond patterns, 64–65
  major *vs.* minor arc types, 60
  petal-like patterns using, 62–63
  possible combinations for, 61
  rotation of, 60
Arrays
  multidimensional-arrays, 468–469
  passing to Perl functions, 482–483
  in Perl, 466–467, 471–472
  pie charts, defining arrays for, 340–341
  reading file contents into arrays in Perl,
    485–486
Asymmetry
  asymmetric arc-based patterns, 65–67
  asymmetric shadow effects, 96–98
Attributes, 5

## B

BarbedRectPattern folder, contents de-
    scribed, 403
Bar sets for graphs and charts
  homogeneous bar sets, 208–209,
    224–225
    code snippet for, 224–225

Bar sets for graphs and charts (*cont.*)
    Perl to generate, 379–382
    3D bar sets, 218–220
    UNIX scripts to generate, 382–386
    variable bar sets, 209–211
BezierCBPattern folder, contents
    described, 404
Bezier curves
    absolute *vs.* relative points, 96
    animation and modification of,
        297–306
    clip paths, code snippet for, 110
    code snippets for, 109–110
    cubic Bezier curves, 94, 102–107
        code snippet for, 109–110
        zipper effects, 124–126
    cubic Bezier curves and linear gradient
        shading, 102–104
    cubic quadratic Bezier Curves, 108–109
    defined and described, 94
    double cubic Bezier curves, 104–106
    double reflected cubic Bezier curves,
        106–107
    feGaussianBlur filter triangles and,
        157–158
    feTurbulence filter and, 155–156
    multi-quadratic Bezier clip paths, 96–98
    oscillation animation, 297–306
    patterns in folders, 404–405
    quadratic Bezier clip paths, 98–100
    quadratic Bezier curves, 94–96, 98–100,
        155–158
    text strings following, 179–180, 181–182
BezierDoubleSpinePattern folder, contents
    described, 404–405
BezierSpineBlurPattern folder, contents
    described, 405
Blurs
    BezierSpineBlurPattern folder, contents
        described, 405
    blur element applied to text, 172–173
    blur filters and text, 178–179
    Gaussian blurs, 138–144, 157–162
    text string blur, code snippet for, 181

Book.xml file, contents described, 427
"Buzzed" effects, 109

**C**
CDATA
    ECMAScript and, 240–241
    stylesheets and, 36–37
CD-ROM contents
    described, 489–499
    experimentation with code on, 401–402
    supplemental patterns described,
        399–419
    viewing files, 400–401
Charts and line graphs
    bar charts, drawing, 214–218
    bar charts, 3d effect, 218–220
    bar sets for, 208–211, 214–220, 224–225,
        379–386
    labeled grids for, 211–214
    line graphs, drawing, 221–224
    multiple line graphs, drawing, 222–224
    Perl to generate bar sets for, 379–382
    tips for preparing, 34, 116
    UNIX scripts for bar set generation,
        382–386
    XSLT for data separation, 207
    XSLT to generate bar charts, 393–396
    *see also* pie charts
Checkerboard patterns, 76–84
    in BeizerCBPattern folder, 404
    feGaussianBlur filter triangles and,
        159–161
    gradient checkerboards, 80–84
    quadratic Bezier clip paths and, 98–100
    rotate function and, 116–118
    3D checkerboard grids, 78–80
    Venetian checkerboards, 98–100
    Venetian gradient patterns, 89–91
CircleFrostedEffect folder, contents de-
    scribed, 406–407
CircleFrostedEffectShadow folder, contents
    described, 407
Circles
    circle element to render, 48–49

circular pie charts, drawing, 334–340

ECMAScript to update circle element, 257–260

ellipse element to render, 49–50

mouse-aware animations for HTML, 242–244

3D effects, 67–68

CircularArcCoil Pattern folder, contents described, 408

CircularSpinArcCoilPattern folder, contents described, 408

Classes, external stylesheets and, 38–39

ClipPath element

defining, 84–85

feTurbulence filter primitive combined with, 156

grid patterns and, 85–87

rect element and, 87–89

Clip paths

animation and, 186

Bezier clip paths, code snippet for, 110

clipPath element and, 84–85

described, 74

multi-quadratic Bezier clip paths, 96–98

quadratic Bezier clip paths and, 98–100

Code

on CD-ROM, commented out lines and modification of, 400

reusing and leveraging elements in, 311–312, 402–403

security and protection of, 228

source code on CD-ROM, 489–490

SVG code templates, 285–286, 310–313, 360–361

CoilLinks folder, contents described, 409

Color

elliptical arcs, coloring, 61–62

gradient color and mouse-click events, 237–238

hexadecimal specification, 20

linear color gradients, 24–26

opacity and composite colors, 16

radial color gradients, 24

resolution and, 284–285

RGB color specifications, 20–21

standard colors, 20–21

text with colored borders, 167–168

Cones

linear gradient shading and, 68–69

rotating cone effects, 69

Coordinate system, 7–8

y-axis, positive orientation of, 7

C3DEffectCoilPattern folder, contents described, 406

Curves. *See* Bezier curves

Cylinders

linear gradient shading, 70–71

scale function and, 130–132

**D**

Dashed line segments, 32–34

Debugging, 31, 240

Defs element, linear color gradient definition with, 24–25

Diagonal gradient patterns, 89–91

DiamondBoxPattern folder, contents described, 409–410

Diamond patterns, 64–65

DOCTYPE, 4

Document Object Model (DOM). *See* SVG DOM (Document Object Model)

Documents

order of in XSL, 432

Perl to generate simple documents, 376–379

text file to XML conversion, 376

Document Type Definition (DTD) in XML, 444–447

DOM. *See* SVG DOM (Document Object Model)

Dotted and dashed line segments, 32–34, 43

DottedEllipsesAndArcs folder, contents described, 410–411

DottedTwistingPolygonPattern folder, contents described, 411

Drawpath( ) function, 285

DTD (Document Type Definition) in
XML, 444–447
components of DTDs, 445–446
Dynamic elements, *vs.* hardcoding,
312–313

# E

ECMAScript
adding elements, 262–265, 269–278
animation and, 283–307
animation requirements, 306
Archimedean spirals combined with,
324–331
circle elements, updating, 257–260
circles, changing radius, code snippet
for, 247–248
code snippet examples, 278–280
code template example, 252–253
coding of, 240–241
dynamic addition of elements, 269–278
dynamic creation of elements, 292–297
dynamic removal of elements, 260–262
getAttribute/setAttribute, 242–247
if/else logic, 243–244, 256, 260, 269
interactivity and, 251–281, 269–273
leveraging elements in, 311–312
mouseClick1(), 245–246
mouse-controlled rotating circular pie
charts, 352–357
multi-fixed pointmesh patterns combined with, 324–331
multiple elements, managing, 265–278
ocsillating Bezier curve animation,
297–306
path elements
modifying for animation, 283–284
updating, 254–257
path elements and, 254–257, 278–279,
283–284
removing elements, 260–262
showAttributes(), 240
simple SVG path animation, 287–292
sine-based equations combined with,
313–324

SVG DOM (Document Object Model)
and, 228
"time-out periods" for animation, 306
toggling effects, 287–292
updating elements, 254–260, 265–269
Ellipses
code snippets to render, 71
counter-rotating ellipses animation,
191–193
ellipse element to render, 49–50
elliptical pie charts, drawing, 341–345
linear gradient to render, 50–52
radial gradient to render, 52–54
recursion-based ellipses, 369–372
URL enabled ellipses as hyperlinks,
232–234
Embedded stylesheets, 34–37
Encrypting code, 228
Error checking in SVG document, 285
Evt variable, 240
External stylesheets, 37–39
classes and, 38–39
code snippet for, 44

# F

FeFlood filter primitive, 144–146
code snippet to apply, 162
FeGaussianBlur filter primitive, 138–144
code snippet to apply, 161–162
quadratic Bezier curves and, 157–158
triangles and checkerboard patterns,
159–161
FeImage filter primitive, 147–149
FeMerge filter primitives, 149–151
FeTurbulence filter primitive, 151–157
code snippet to apply, 162–163
quadratic Bezier curves and, 155–156
Filter primitives
combining effects of, 149–151
feFlood filter primitive, 144–146
feGaussianBlur filter primitive,
138–144
feImage filter primitive, 147–149
feMerge filter primitives, 149–151

feTurbulence filter primitive, 151–157
listed, 161
Filters
blur filters, 178–179
filter element described, 137–138
*see also* filter primitives
For loops in Perl, 466
Freeze, as value for fill attribute, 190
Frosted effects, 406–407

**G**

Gaussian blurs, 138–144, 157–162
Global *vs.* local variables, 286–287
Gradients
diagonal gradient patterns, 89–91
gradient checkerboards, 80–84, 87–89
gradient grid patterns, 87–89
mouse-click events and gradient color,
237–238
multi-gradient checkerboards, 82–84
offset values and, 57–58
*see also* linear gradients; radial gradients
Graphs. *See* charts and line graphs
Grid patterns
clipPath element and, 85–87
feGaussianBlur filter primitive and,
142–144
generation of, 73–74
gradient grid patterns, 80–84, 87–89
labeled grids for charts, 211–214
pattern element definition and, 74–75
3D patterns, 78–80
*see also* checkerboard patterns

**H**

HalfEllipseLayersPattern folder, contents
described, 412
HalfEllipseLayers2Pattern folder, contents
described, 412–413
HalfEllipseTwistedLayersPattern folder,
contents described, 413
Hardware requirements, 490
Hashes in Perl, 467–469
Hexadecimal specification, 20

Hierarchical sets, in XSL, 423
Histograms, 34
Hourglass figures, 132–134
HTML
animated graphics, 238–247
embedding SVG code in, 228–232
hiding mouse-aware objects, 235–236
hyperlinks, URL enabled ellipses,
232–234
images embedded in SVG used with,
230–232
launching SVG documents in, code
snippet for, 247
mouse-aware specification, code snippet
for, 247–248
mouse-click events, 237–238
mouse-over events, 234–236
*vs.* XML, 441–443, 449
XSL document generation, 433–434
Hyperlinks, 232–234

**I**

Images
feImage filter primitive and, 147–149
HTML pages with images embedded in
SVG, 230–232
as URL-enabled HTML links, 230–232
Inheritance
in multiple SVG g element, 41–42
style attributes and, 40
Init() function, 285, 311
Instant Saxon (XSLT processor), download
information, 422
Intelligent agents and XML, 460
Interactivity
ECMAScript and, 251–281, 269–273
interactive addition of elements in EC-
MAScripts, 269–273
XML and, 459
Interface systems, 450
Internal stylesheets, code snippet for, 44

**J**

.js files, 228

## L

Languages, Unicode and representation of characters, 2

License agreements, 490–499

Lighting, lumination effects created with multi-stop radial gradients, 56–58

Linear gradients
 code snippet for, 43
 ellipses rendered with, 50–52
 radial gradients and, 53
 "start" and "end" color definition for, 24
 text display and, 175–176
 *see also* linear gradient shading

LinearGradients element, and feTurbulence filter primitive, 153–154

Linear gradient shading
 cones and, 68–69
 cubic Bezier curves and, 102–104
 cylinders, 70–71

Line attribute, rectangles rendered with, 14

Line graphs, 34
 drawing, 221–224
 labeled grids for, 211–214
 multiple line graphs, drawing, 222–224

Line segments
 animation, code snippet for, 203–204
 dotted and dashed line segments, 32–34
 rotation animation, 186–188, 203–204

Local *vs.* global variables, 286–287

Logic
 if/else logic in ECMAScript, 243–244, 256, 260, 269
 XSL conditional logic, 432–433

Lumination effects, multi-stop radial gradients and, 56–58

LunePattern folder, contents described, 414

Lune patterns, 414

## M

Marker element, 31–32
 code snippet for, 43

*Mastering XSLT,* 208

Matrix function, 114, 128–129
 code snippet for, 135–136

Measure, units of, 5

Memory consumption issues, 209–210, 284–285

Mesh patterns, multi-fixed point mesh patterns, 324–331

Mouse-aware and mouse-controlled graphics
 code for multiple mouse-aware rectangles, 268
 HTML and, 234–242, 247–248
 mouse-click events, 237–238
 mouse-over events, 234–236
 mouse-related events, list of possible, 253
 rotating circular pie charts, 352–357

Mouse-click events, 237–238

Mouse-over events, 234–236

Multiple elements, inheritance in, 41–42

Multi-stop radial gradients, 54–58

## N

Names and naming conventions
 for Perl scripts, 462
 used in book, 310

Navigation, URL-enabled ellipses and HTML navigation, 232–234

Nested shapes
 recursion to render, 361–364, 372–373
 rendering, 34–35

Nodes in XSL, 423–424

## O

OAG (Open Application Group), XML DTDs and, 451–458

Offset values, gradients and, 58

Opacity
 composite colors and, 16
 feFlood filter primitives and, 146
 feTurbulence filter and setting for, 155
 rectangles rendered with, 14–16
 text display and, 176–177

Open Application Group (OAG), XML
 DTDs and, 451–458
Oscillation animation, 197–306

## P

Parallelograms, as SVG polygons, 29–31
PartialPolygonPattern folder, contents
 described, 414–415
PartialPolygonRotatedPattern folder, contents described, 415
Path attribute, rectangles rendered with,
 12–14
Path element
 circles, ellipses, and Bezier curves rendered with, 47–48
 circular arcs drawn with, 59
 ECMAScript and, 278–279
 ECMAScript to modify, 283–284
 ECMAScript to update, 254–257
 rendering power of, 48
Paths
 absolute *vs.* relative in XSL, 430–431
 text strings following specified paths,
 179–180
 in XSL documents, 429
PATH variable, updating in Perl, 462
Pattern element
 code snippet for, 91
 defining, 74–75
 described, 73
 feTurbulence filter primitives and,
 153–155
 grid patterns and, 74–76
Performance issues, 490
 CD-ROM contents and, 401
 memory consumption issues, 209–210,
 284–285
 processing time issues, 360
 recursion and, 372–373
Perl
 ^ symbol, 474
 > symbol, 474
 < symbol, 474

$ symbol, 474
# symbol, 474
 advantages of, 461–462
 arrays in, 466–467, 468–469, 471–472,
 485–486
 bar set generation with, 379–382
 built-in variables, 464
 comment lines, skipping, 474–475
 concatenation of strings, 480–481
 custom functions, creating, 481–482
 date format verification, 484–485
 date function, 479–480
 described, 461
 document generation with, 376–379
 hashes in, 467–468
 join function, 480–481
 launching from command line, 462–463
 for loops, 466
 names for script files, 462
 opening and closing files, 470
 passing arrays to functions in, 482–483
 PATH variable, updating, 462
 pattern matching for text strings,
 483–484
 printing file contents in reverse order,
 486–487
 proprietary file conversion, 386–387
 reading files, 470–471
 scalar variables, 464–465
 split function, 477–480
 substrings, extracting, 476–477
 switching word order in text strings, 477
 text string manipulation, 475–478
 while loops, 465–466
 white space, removing from text strings,
 475–476
 writing to files, 472–473
 -w switch, 462
Petal patterns
 arc based, 62–63
 sine-based, 313–317
Pie charts, 34
 array definition for, 340–341

Pie charts (*cont.*)
circular pie charts, drawing, 334–340
data conversion for, 340–341
elliptical pie charts, drawing, 341–345
rotating pie charts, 345–357
separation effects between "slices," 339
Polar equations
in BeizerCBPattern folder, 404–405
Steiner equation, 309–311
Polygon attribute, 10–12
Polygons, parallelograms as SVG polygons, 29–31
Proprietary files, converting to SVG with Perl, 386–387

**Q**

Quadratic Bezier curves, code snippet for, 109

**R**

Radial gradients
code snippet for, 43
color gradients, 27–29, 43
ellipses rendered with, 52–54
linear gradients and, 53
multi-stop radial gradients, 54–58
Rectangles
bars sets for charts as, 208–211
code snippets for rendering, 21
linear grandients to render, 25–26
mouse events and HTML, 238–242
multiple animation effects and, 193–196
nested rectangles, rendering, 34–35
opacity to render, 14–16
parallelograms as SVG polygons, 29–31
path attribute to render, 12–14
polygon to render and specify, 10–12
radial gradients to render, 27–29
rect to render and specify, 8–9
rotation animation, 188–191
rotation animation, code snippets for, 204
"rounded," 9
shadow effects, rendering, 16–17
specifying and rendering, 8–9

Rect element, 8–9
clipPath element and, 87–89
Recursion
coding in XSL, 423
nested triangles rendered via, 361–364
performance issues, 372–273
recursion-based ellipses, 369–372
role with ECMAScripts, 359–360
Sierpinski curves, 364–369
Reflections, double reflected cubic Bezier curves, 106–107
Repeating patterns, 73–74
Result attribute, feImage filter primitive and, 149
RGB color specifications, 20
RotatedTriangles folder, contents described, 416
Rotate function, 113
checkerboard patterns, rotating, 116–118
code snippet for, 135
direction of rotation, 118
Rotation
of circular pie charts, 345–357
continuous rotation animation, 199–201
counter-rotating ellipses, animation, 191–193
line segment rotation, 186–188
code snippet for, 203–204
matrix function and, 128–129
rotate function, 113
rotating effects, 69, 71
text string rotation, 174–175, 199–201
code snippet for, 181

**S**

Scalable Vector Graphics. *See* SVG (Scalable Vector Graphics)
Scalar variables in Perl, 464–465
Scaling
checkerboard patterns, scaling, 118–120
code snippet for, 135
cubic Bezier curves and, 124–126
cylinders and, 130–131

horizontal scaling, specifications for, 120

mouse-aware animations for HTML, 242–244

mouse events and animations for HTML, 242–247

multiple scaled versions of an object, 130–131

multiple scale elements, 120–124

scale function, 113, 114, 130–133

skew function combined with, 132–133

text scaling animation, code snippet for, 204–205

vertical and horizontal scaling, 18–19, 120

vertical scaling, specifications for, 120

Scripting

   Unix scripts, bar set generation with, 382–386

   *see also* ECMAScript; Perl

Searching, XML and intelligent searching, 460

Security, code protection, 228

Shading

   cones and linear gradient shading, 68–69

   cylinders and linear gradient shading, 70–71

   3D effects, 67–68

   triangular wedges, rendering with shading, 17–18

Shadows and shadow effects

   Bezier curves and asymmetric shadow effects, 96–98

   feGaussianBlur filter primitive and, 140–142

   rectangles rendered with, 16–17

   text and, 171–173

   in 3D bar charts, 218–220

Shifting objects, translate function and, 114–116

Sierpinski curves, recursion to render, 364–369

SineWave1Pattern folder, 416–417

Size

   measure, units of, 5

*see also* scaling

Skew functions, 113, 114, 126–127

   axis orientation of, 127

   horizontal skew, code snippet for, 135

   scale function combined with, 132–133

   vertical skew, code snippet for, 135

Software, on CD-ROM, 489

Software requirements, *xix*, 421–422

Source code, access to, 228

Source code on CD-ROM, 489–490

Spinning effects, 69, 71

Split function in Perl, 477–480

SpreadMethod attribute, 104

StopAnimation function, 285

Stop-color values, 52

Stroke, stroke-width, and stroke-dasharray, 34, 54

Style attributes, 9–10

   inheritance of, 40

Stylesheets

   CDATA and, 36–37

   classes and, 38–39

   embedded stylesheets, 34–37

   external stylesheets, 37–39, 44

   text and, 169

   XSLT processor installation, 388

   *see also* XSL (Extensible Stylesheet Language)

Supplemental patterns, described, 399–419

SVG DOM (Document Object Model)

   adding elements, 262–265

   ECMAScript and, 228

   removing elements, 260–262

SVG (Scalable Vector Graphics)

   artists and, *xx–xxi*

   defined and described, *xvii*

   information web site, *xvii*

   specifications for, *xviii*

   viewers, 1, 3–4

   viewports, 18–19

   web development, 2–3

<svg> tag, 3–4

< symbol in Per, 474

> symbol in Perl, 474

Symbols

#, 34, 474

$ in Perl, 474

^ in Perl, 474

/ in XSL, 391, 427, 430–431

System requirements, 490

**T**

Templates

SVG code templates, 285–286, 310–313, 360–361

XSL stylesheets and, 422, 438

Tennison, Jeni, 208

TetraPattern folder, contents described, 417

Text

Bezier curve paths, code snippet for, 181–182

blur element and, 172–173

blur filter, code snippet for, 181

blur filters and, 178–179, 181

colored borders on, 167–168

continuous rotation of text string, animation, 199–201

drop-shadow effects, 171–172

in labeled grids for charts, 211–214

linear gradients and text display, 175–176

opacity and text display, 176–177

pattern matching in Perl, 483–484

rendering strings, code snippet for, 180–181

rotating text strings, 174–175, 181

rotation, code snippet for, 181

scaling and rotation of text string, animation, 201–203, 204–205

scaling animation, code snippet for, 204–205

split function in Perl and text strings, 477–478

strike through text, 168–169

style element and, 10

stylesheets and, 169

substrings, extracting in Perl, 476–477

text strings, rendering, 166

tspan element, 168–171

underlined text, 168–169

white space, removing from text strings in Perl, 475–476

word order, switching in Perl, 477

Text element, described, 165–166

Text files, converting to XML documents, 376

3D effects

in bar charts, 218–220

CircularArcCoil Pattern folder, contents described, 408

C3DEffectCoilPattern folder, contents described, 406

gradient shading, 67–68

Tic-tac-toe games, 269–273

Transformations, 6

animateTransform element, attributes of, 186

combining multiple functions, 129–134

described, 113–114

matrix function, 114, 128–129, 135–136

rotate function, 113, 116–118, 135

*see also* scaling; skew functions

Transform attribute, shifting g element with, 11–12

Translate function, 113, 114–116

code snippet for, 134–135

TrapezoidPattern folder, contents described, 418

Tree traversal in XSL, 424

TriangleLayersPattern folder, contents described, 419

Triangles

recursion to render nested triangles, 361–364

shading to render triangular wedges, 17–18

Troubleshooting

blank browser screen, 34

CPU and memory issues, 284–285

debugging tips, 31, 240

default templates, overriding, 422
error checking in SVG document, 285
hard-coded values as problematic, 93
rendering problems, 34
-w switch in Perl, 462
y-axis orientation and, 7
Tspan element, 168–171

**U**

Unicode, 2
Units of measure, 5
UNIX scripts, bar set generation with,
    382–386

**V**

Values, hard-coded values, 93, 402
Van Otegem, Michiel, 208
Variables
    built-in Perl variables, 464
    local *vs.* global, 286–287
    PATH variable in Perl, 462
    in XSL, 432
Venetian checkerboards, quadratic Bezier
    clip paths and, 98–100
Venetian gradient checkerboard patterns,
    89–91
Venetian shading effects, spreadMethod
    and, 104
Viewers, download information, 1, 3–4
Viewports, 18–19

**W**

Web development in SVG, 2–3
Web site addresses
    specifications for SVG, *xviii*
    SVG information, *xvii*
    World Wide Web (W3C) Consortium,
      *xvii*
    XML Software, 449
While loops in Perl, 465–466
White, Chuck, 208
Wire frame effects, sine-based, 317–324
World Wide Web (W3C) Consortium, *xvii*
-w switch in Perl, 462

**X**

XML (Extensible Markup Language)
    attributes in, 446
    authoring tools for, 448–449
    constants (entities), defining, 446–447
    data repositories, 460
    described, 441
    document type declaration in, 447
    DTD (Document Type Definition) in,
      444–447, 451–458
    EDI-based processes and, 450–451
    *vs.* HTML, 441–443, 449
    intelligent agents and, 460
    interactivity and, 459
    interface systems and, 450
    Java and, 449
    OAG and, 451–452
    online XML, 459
    real-time interfaces and, 459
    sample document, 447–448
    searching, intelligent searching, 460
    uses of, 449–450, 459–460
XML Software, 449
XPath, 208, 424–426, 439
XSL (Extensible Stylesheet Language), 208
    accessing contents of stylesheets,
      429–430
    bar charts, XSL stylesheet to generate,
      436–438
    book.xml file, contents described, 427
    Boolean operations in, 425–426
    computing maximum values, 434–436
    counting qualified elements, 431
    default rules for stylesheets, 422, 427
    described, 421
    document order, 432
    hierarchy in, 423–424
    HTML document generation, 433–434
    index values of listed elements, 432, 438
    location paths, 424–425
    logic, 391–392, 432–433
    nodes in, 423–424
    numeric-related functions in, 426
    paths, absolute *vs.* relative, 430–431

XSL (*cont.*)
  software requirements for, 421–422
  string-related functions in, 426
  stylesheet example, 426–427
  stylesheets described, 422
  "/" symbol in, 391, 427, 430–431
  templates and, 422, 438
  tree traversal, 424
  variables in, 432
  when logic in, 391–392
  XPath and, 424
  XPath axes and, 425
  XPath functions, 425–426

XSLT
  bar chart generation with, 393–396
  book recommendations, 208
  for-each loops, 393–396
  SVG generation with, 388–392
*XSLT and Xpath on the Edge,* 208
*XSLT in 21 Days,* 208

# Y

Y-axis, positive orientation of, 7

# Z

Zipper effects, 124–126